Passion for Peace

THOMAS MERTON

Passion for Peace

THE SOCIAL ESSAYS

EDITED AND
WITH AN INTRODUCTION BY
William H. Shannon

CROSSROAD · NEW YORK

1995
The Crossroad Publishing Company
370 Lexington Avenue, New York, NY 10017

Library of Congress Cataloging-in-Publication Data

Merton, Thomas, 1915–1968
    Passion for peace : the social essays / by Thomas Merton ; edited
and with an introduction by William H. Shannon.
        p.   cm.
    ISBN 0-8245-1494-7
    1. Peace—Religious aspects—Catholic Church.   2. Nonviolence—
Religious aspects—Catholic Church.   3. Race relations—Religious
aspects—Catholic Church.   4. United States—Race relations.
5. Merton, Thomas, 1915–1968—Views on war and peace.   6. Catholic
Church—Clergy—Biography.   I. Shannon, William Henry, 1917-   .
II. Title.
BX1795.P43M47   1995
261.8—dc20   94-48888
                                                                   CIP

CONTENTS

PART TWO

Following the Year of the *Cold War Letters*

1967

1968

INTRODUCTION

Life is a struggle; indeed it is often a series of struggles. People's true characters, in great measure, come to the fore in the way they handle the struggles unique to their lives. One way of coming to some understanding of Thomas Merton's character is by looking at the struggles his life brought him and seeing his character brought into clearer focus by the ways he dealt with them. In his earliest years he struggled to make sense out of life. This struggle, which took nearly half his life, found its initial resolution in his conversion to Christian Faith and just three years later, his entrance into the Abbey of Gethsemani. Once in the monastery, the ongoing quest for meaning took on new guises. He agonized for some years over his obvious talent as a writer and the threat it posed—or so he thought for some time—to his contemplative vocation. Another tension he had to face was the call he experienced— or seemed to be experiencing—to a deeper solitude. He felt drawn to transfer to a hermit order such as the Carthusians or the Camaldolese; and yet his sense of belonging to Gethsemani was strong. Later in his monastic life, he underwent a sense of estrangement from the structures of monasticism and the need to rethink what it meant to be a monk in the twentieth century and in the wake of the Second Vatican Council. On this issue of monastic reform, he was often at odds—and in substantive ways—with his more conservative abbot, Dom James Fox. It was an uncomfortable position to be in, first because Merton believed firmly in monastic obedience, and second because had a sincere affection for Dom James, despite the fact that they were often at cross-purposes on various matters of monastic life.

These and other struggles that help to make the Merton story an absorbing one have been detailed in the various biographical studies that have been published. There is one struggle that I think has not been given as much attention as it deserves. Merton faced it in 1961; I think it is safe to say he agonized over it throughout that year and the next and actually never set it aside. The struggle, simply stated, was this: Should I, a monk of Gethsemani vowed to silence and solitude, speak out against the terrible violence of war that threatens the very life of the planet, or should I keep a discreet silence as the appropriate stance for a monk?

It is not easy for us to grasp the anguish that this struggle posed for Merton. It was a new question for a monk, indeed a new question for almost any Christian of the day. We live at a time when it is not an uncommon thing for Roman Catholics to protest against war and to lobby for peace. Pax Christi USA has been in existence for more than twenty years. Many dioceses and parishes in the Roman Catholic Church have peace and justice committees that are alive and active. But in 1961, more than thirty years ago, things were much different. At that time no Catholic priest or bishop—at least none well known—had spoken out against war. Roman Catholics by and large were a patriotic lot. I remember a bishop of that time who in a public talk echoed the words of Stephen Decatur, the naval officer in the war of 1812 who said, "Our country . . . may she always be in the right. But our country, right or wrong." Thirty years ago a Roman Catholic bishop could get away with such a statement. Today such a crude nationalism on the part of a bishop would be intolerable, even scandalous.

Think of Thomas Merton living in that kind of religious and civic climate. Remember the reputation he had. A well-known Catholic priest and monk, he was looked to as an inspiring writer on spirituality. In Catholic circles no one rivaled him in prominence or influence. His earliest writings, especially his best-selling autobiography, *The Seven Storey Mountain,* had praised a spirituality of withdrawal from the world. Who of his thousands of readers could have anticipated that Merton, of all people, would ever start writing—and writing with deep passion—on such a worldly subject as war? Some of his many readers were scandalized and walked with him no more. Others shook their heads and asked themselves, "What in the world has happened to Thomas Merton? Why is he calling people to unite in a crusade to abolish all war? What does this have to do with his spirituality?"

Well, by 1961 quite a lot had happened to Thomas Merton and he was quite certain that what he had said about spirituality had a great deal to do with the social problems of the day and especially with the issue of war. What had happened to him was that his solitude had issued into what all true solitude must eventually become: compassion. Finding God in his solitude, he found God's people, who are inseparable from God and who, at the deepest level of their being (the level that only contemplation can reach), are at one with one another in God, the Hidden Ground of Love of all that is. This sense of compassion bred in solitude (something like the *karuna* of the Buddha born of his enlightenment) moved him to look once again at the world he thought he had left irrevocably twenty years earlier, in 1941, when he had entered the monastery. He now felt a duty, *precisely because he was a contemplative*, to speak out and to warn his fellow men and women about what he believed was the gravest possible danger threatening the civilized world. He confides his concern to Daniel Berrigan in a letter written on June 25, 1963: "What is the contemplative life if one does not listen to God in it? What is the contemplative life if one becomes oblivious to the rights of men [sic] and the truth of God in the world and in His Church?" (*HGL*, 79)

Merton felt that, however poorly equipped he might be for the role, he was called to be a prophet. He understood clearly the limitations of the prophet's vocation. A prophet is not necessarily one who has all the right answers; he or she *is* the one who knows at a given moment in history what the real problems are that humanity must face, what the proper goals are that need to be achieved, what the right questions are that must be asked. In a passage from *Conjectures of a Guilty Bystander* Merton offers a perceptive explanation for the popularity of his writings. "It seems to me that one of the reasons why my writings appeal to many people is precisely that I am not so sure of myself and do not claim to have all the answers." (p. 49) In his writings on war and peace, it is passion for the goals he sees rather than certitude about the way to achieve them that dominates. There were times that he felt lonely, diffident, distrustful of himself, even shocked by some of the things he heard himself saying. His concern lest he lead people in wrong directions shows up in his sensitivity to criticism, his apologies for over-hasty statements, his constant rewriting of articles to make his intent clearer and, he hoped, more palatable to his readers. Yet despite his misgivings about himself and his message, despite his concern about the abdication of responsibility on the part of so many of his fellow-citizens, he knew that he had to continue, with whatever means at his disposal, to combat war and to work for the creation of a stable and lasting peace. Commenting on the prison writings of Father Delp, he says:

> Christ our Lord did not come to bring peace as a kind of spiritual tranquilizer. He brought to his disciples a vocation

and a task: to struggle in the world of violence to establish
His peace not only in their own hearts but in society itself.

These were his marching orders. He had no choice but to obey.

Merton's contribution to this struggle to establish God's peace in a
world of violence was, I believe, threefold: (1) his passionate commitment, in article after article, to the position that war must be totally
outlawed; (2) his discernment of the way in which war must be opposed, namely, through nonviolence; and (3) his widening of the area
in which nonviolence must operate. Nonviolence is not just a stance
toward war; it is a way of life that affects everything we do. Merton
knew well the meaning of nonviolence. He had learned it from a master. One might expect that that master would have been Jesus Christ.
Actually, it was Mohandas Gandhi. If Merton eventually found the
nonviolence of Jesus in the Gospels (as I believe he did), he learned it
from this strange-looking, quaint little man, whose nonviolence and
effective civil disobedience won the world's somewhat bewildered respect as well as the independence of his native India. Merton read
Gandhi's writings carefully and was able to articulate clearly and firmly
what nonviolence involves. In the articles that make up this book,
there is much wisdom about nonviolence; it is a wisdom that we very
much need today as we strive to cope with the violence in our own
hearts as well as the violence that wracks our cities and paralyzes so
many countries in such diverse parts of the world.

This brings me back to a fundamental thesis of this introduction:
that Merton's writings on social issues flowed from a deep contemplative vision. I have the strong conviction that we shall only learn to
deal effectively with violence when we discover (or recover, for it is
really always there) in ourselves that contemplative awareness that enables us—as it had enabled Merton—to see the oneness we share with
all God's people—indeed with the whole of God's creation. Once a
person has achieved this contemplative insight, nonviolence ceases to
be a mere option and becomes a choice that brooks no rejection. But
let no one think that becoming nonviolent is an easy task. It calls for
painful, ongoing conversion, as slowly and almost imperceptibly we
begin to realize what it asks of us and to experience the wisdom it
imparts to us.

*****

This volume contains Merton's principal writings on war and peace.
In these essays he pleads the case against nuclear war. His task, he felt,

was to help people see that peace is indeed a viable possibility in our world. He had to expose for the terrible illusion that it is the Great Lie of history, which says that war is inevitable and permanent peace an unrealizable dream.

The historical context in which Merton wrote was that of the Cold War, a term coined by Walter Lippman to express the political and military standoff between the United States and the Union of Soviet Socialist Republics. It was a standoff that had reached an especially difficult point of tension in the early 1960s. For instance, it was the year 1962 that witnessed the confrontation between President John F. Kennedy and the Soviet premier, Nikita Khrushchev, over missile sites in Cuba.

With the breakup of the Soviet Union, it might seem, at first reflection, that the Cold War has come to an end. Would this mean, we cannot help but ask, that Merton's writings dealing with the Cold War are now of a purely historical interest and have nothing to say to us today? I think not. The Cold War, it seems clear, is still very much with us. The protagonists may have changed, but the reality is very much present. It is worth pointing out that the *American Heritage Dictionary*, in its 1992 edition, defines "cold war" in terms much more general than those originally used by Walter Lippman: "a state of political tension and military rivalry between nations that stops short of full-scale war." It even offers a meaning that involves groups smaller than nations: "a state of rivalry and tension between two factions, groups, or individuals that stops short of open, violent confrontation."

The violence that exists in so many places throughout the world— the murders that violate the safety of our city streets; the bloody wars that have taken thousands of lives; the ongoing tensions that continue to create a volatile instability in the Middle East; the genocide, the ethnic "cleansing" that goes on in Africa, the former Yugoslavia, and elsewhere—makes clear to us that "cold war" (and hot war, too) is very much with us today. The need to overcome war and the threat of war, the duty to work for peace in today's world remains a huge responsibility that we ignore at our own peril. And what is imperiled is not only the well-being of humankind but also our own authenticity.

Some of the things that Merton has to say on these issues are dated and probably only of historical and biographical interest. But I hasten to add that so much that he wrote speaks penetratingly to our own time. There is a certain perennial quality to his writing that gives it power to move us today. It is as if, in so many of these articles, he is actually writing in the 1990s. He is speaking to us.

This is true not only of his writing on war, but also on racial issues, which make up a substantial part of this book. In his writings about civil rights for both Afro-Americans and Native Americans, he addresses an issue that still remains largely unresolved today. Once again it is the contemplative who is able to point out to us the essential oneness that roots the equal dignity of all peoples. Merton, I believe, would have agreed with the sign I remember seeing scrawled on a wall in Andersonville, the Catholic section of Belfast, Ireland. It said: "If one of us is deprived of liberty, none of us is free."

*****

I have arranged the essays in this book in two unequal parts. The first part I am calling "The Year of the *Cold War Letters*." As I have explained in my biography of Merton, *Silent Lamp*, this is not a calendar year, but a period that extends from October 1961 to October 1962. I have so named it because Merton selected one hundred eleven letters he had written during this twelve-month period, had them mimeographed, and sent them to his friends under the title of *Cold War Letters*. It was during this period that Merton was obsessed with the need to speak out against nuclear war. The result was that, besides *The Cold War Letters*, there was a flurry of articles on war, peace, and nonviolence. How trying a year this was for him and how he agonized over the articles he wrote will come clear, I hope, in the introductions I have written to individual articles.

The second part is called, somewhat unimaginatively I suppose, "Following the Year of the *Cold War Letters*." During this period Merton continued to write on the war issue, but much less frequently. One of the reasons for the falling-off of such articles was the directive that came to him in April of 1962 from the Abbot General of the entire Cistercian Order forbidding him to write anything further on this issue. There was also another factor at work. Merton was not a one-issue person. Gradually he had broadened the spectrum of the social issues he felt obligated to discuss and had begun to talk about the "cold war" (sometimes breaking into hot war) that strained the relationship of nonwhites and whites in American society.

*****

Before closing this Introduction, I need to advise the reader that most of the articles that follow have been previously published, but in books that are now out of print. This book contains the substance of *Seeds of Destruction*, published by Farrar Straus and Giroux in 1964, and most of the articles compiled by Gordon Zahn in *The Non-Violent Alternative*, published by Farrar Straus and Giroux in 1980.

Those works were suitable for their time. They made easily accessible Merton's important articles on social issues, which many people did not even know he had written. While these books served the good purpose of unveiling another side of the monk who had spoken so eloquently on spirituality, they have one serious drawback. They fail to contextualize the many articles they include. Perhaps this was not necessary when they were first published, but, as we get to know more about Merton, we realize more and more clearly the interplay between his life and his writings. The writings shed light on his life story. His life story influenced the way the writings came into being.

In this book I have tried to supply the missing context. Properly situated historically, the articles in this book are a kind of autobiography of Merton the social critic. They portray his frequent run-ins with the censors, his concern not to be misunderstood, his ongoing fear that he had not expressed himself clearly and accurately, his compulsion to rewrite articles to make his meaning more intelligible. This background knowledge helps to make these articles come alive. They show us sides of Merton's character that simply do not come through in his other books. I hope that understanding these articles in their context will show readers a neglected side of Thomas Merton: his passion for peace and the ardor with which he pleaded for it, in a world that yearned for it so desperately.

Part One

THE YEAR OF THE
Cold War Letters

October 1961–October 1962

· 1 ·

THE ROOT OF WAR IS FEAR

Published in The Catholic Worker, *October 1961*

This article marked the initial and definitive entry of Thomas Merton into the struggle against war. Originally it was a chapter of a book Merton had been working on in early 1961, *New Seeds of Contemplation,* which would be published in January of 1962. In the late summer of 1961 Merton received approval of the censors for the publication of the book. Immediately on receiving that approval, he wrote to Dorothy Day (September 22, 1961), offering her Chapter 16 of the book for publication in *The Catholic Worker.* Chapter 16 carried the title, "The Root of War is Fear." In his letter to Day he mentioned, almost casually, that he had added a page of two "to situate these thoughts in the present crisis. (*HGL,* 140) This addition amounted to three long paragraphs into which Merton managed to pack a good deal of material, much of which was highly incendiary. And, of course, the addition had not been seen by the censors! **In the text that follows, the uncensored paragraphs are printed first and in bold type and are followed by Chapter 16 of *New Seeds of Contemplation.***

· · · · ·

The present war crisis is something we have made entirely for and by ourselves. There is in reality not the slightest logical reason for war, and yet the whole world is plunging headlong into frightful destruction, and doing so *with the purpose of avoiding war and preserving peace!* This is a true war-madness, an illness of the mind and the spirit that is spreading with a furious and subtle contagion all over the world. Of all the countries that are sick, America is perhaps the most grievously afflicted. On all sides we have people building bomb shelters where, in case of nuclear war, they will simply bake slowly instead of burning up quickly or being blown out of existence in a flash. And they are prepared to sit in these shelters

with machine guns with which to prevent their neighbor from entering. This is a nation that claims to be fighting for religious truth along with freedom and other values of the spirit. Truly we have entered the "post-Christian era" with a vengeance. Whether we are destroyed or whether we survive, the future is awful to contemplate.

The Christian

What is the place of the Christian in all this? Is he simply to fold his hands and resign himself to the worst, accepting it as the inescapable will of God and preparing himself to enter heaven with a sigh of relief? Should he open up the Apocalypse and run out into the street to give everyone his idea of what is happening? Or worse still, should he take a hard-headed and "practical" attitude about it and join in the madness of the warmakers, calculating how by a "first strike," the glorious Christian West can eliminate atheistic communism for all time and usher in the millennium? . . . I am no prophet and no seer but it seems to me that this last position may very well be the most diabolical of illusions, the great and not even subtle temptation of a Christianity that has grown rich and comfortable, and is satisfied with its riches.

What are we to do? The duty of the Christian in this crisis is to strive with all his power and intelligence, with his faith, hope in Christ, and love for God and man, to do the one task which God has imposed upon us in the world today. That task is to work for the total abolition of war. *There can be no question that unless war is abolished the world will remain constantly in a state of madness and desperation in which, because of the immense destructive power of modern weapons, the danger of catastrophe will be imminent and probably at every moment everywhere.* Unless we set ourselves immediately to this task, both as individuals and in our political and religious groups, we tend by our passivity and fatalism to cooperate with the destructive forces that are leading inexorably to war. It is a problem of terrifying complexity and magnitude, for which the Church herself is not fully able to see clear and decisive solutions. Yet she must lead the way on the road towards nonviolent settlement of difficulties and towards the gradual abolition of war as the way of settling international or civil disputes. Christians must become active in every possible way, mobilizing all their resources for the fight against war. First of all there is much to be studied, much to be learned. Peace is to be preached, nonviolence is to be explained as a practical method, and not left to be mocked as an outlet for crackpots who want to make a show of themselves. Prayer and sacrifice must be used as the most effective spiritual weapons in the war against war, and like all weapons they must be used with deliberate aim: not just with a vague aspiration for peace and security, but against violence and against war. This implies that we are also willing to sacrifice and restrain our own instinct for violence and aggressiveness in our relations with other people. We may never succeed in this campaign but whether we succeed or not the duty is evident. It is the great Christian task of our time. Everything else is secondary, for the survival of the human race itself depends on it. We must at least face this responsibility and do something about it. And the first job of all is to understand the psychological forces at work in ourselves and in society.

Chapter 16 (from *New Seeds of Contemplation*)

At the root of all war is fear, not so much the fear men have of one another as the fear they have of *everything*. It is not merely that they do not trust one another: they do not even trust themselves. If they are not sure when someone else may turn around and kill them, they are still less sure when they may turn around and kill themselves. They cannot trust anything, because they have ceased to believe in God.

It is not only our hatred of others that is dangerous but also and above all our hatred of ourselves: particularly that hatred of ourselves which is too deep and too powerful to be consciously faced. For it is this which makes us see our own evil in others and unable to see it in ourselves.

When we see crime in others, we try to correct it by destroying them or at least putting them out of sight. It is easy to identify the sin with the sinner when he is someone other than our own self. In ourselves, it is the other way around: we see the sin, but we have great difficulty in shouldering responsibility for it. We find it very hard to identify our sin with our own will and our own malice. On the contrary, we naturally tend to interpret our immoral act as an involuntary mistake, or as the malice of a spirit in us that is other than ourselves. Yet at the same time we are fully aware that others do not make this convenient distinction for us. The acts that have been done are, in their eyes, "our" acts and they hold us fully responsible.

What is more, we tend unconsciously to ease ourselves still more of the burden of guilt that is in us, by passing it on to somebody else. When I have done wrong, and have excused myself by attributing the wrong to "another" who is unaccountably "in me" my conscience is not yet satisfied. There is still too much left to be explained. The "other in myself" is too close to home. The temptation is, then, to account for my fault by seeing an equivalent amount of evil in someone else. Hence I minimize my own sins and compensate for doing so by exaggerating the faults of others.

As if this were not enough, we make the situation much worse by artificially intensifying our sense of evil, and by increasing our propensity to feel guilt even for things which are not in themselves wrong. In all these ways we build up such an obsession with evil, both in ourselves and in others, that we waste all our mental energy trying to account for this evil, to punish it, to exorcise it, or to get rid of it in any way we can.

We drive ourselves mad with our preoccupation and in the end there is no outlet left but violence. We have to destroy something or someone. By that time, we have created for ourselves a suitable enemy, a scapegoat in whom we have invested all the evil in the world. He is the cause of every wrong. He is the fomenter of all conflict. If he can only be destroyed, conflict will cease, evil will be done with, there will be no more war.

This kind of fictional thinking is especially dangerous when it is supported by a whole elaborate pseudo-scientific structure of myths, like those which Marxists have adopted as their ersatz for religion. But it is certainly no less dangerous when it operates in the vague, fluid, confused and unprincipled opportunism which substitutes in the West for religion, for philosophy and even for mature thought.

When the whole world is in moral confusion: when no one knows any longer what to think, and when, in fact, everybody is running away from the responsibility of thinking, when man makes rational thought about moral issues absurd by exiling himself entirely from realities into the realm of fictions, and when he expends all his efforts in constructing more fictions with which to account for his ethical failures, then it becomes clear that the world cannot be saved from global war and global destruction by the mere efforts and good intentions of peacemakers. In actual fact, everyone is becoming more and more aware of the widening gulf between efforts to make peace and the growing likelihood of war. It seems that no matter how elaborate and careful the planning, all attempts at international dialogue end in more and more ludicrous failures. In the end, no one has any more faith in those who even attempt the dialogue. On the contrary, the negotiators, with all their pathetic good will, become the objects of contempt and of hatred. It is the "men of good will," the men who have made their poor efforts to do something about peace, who will in the end be the most mercilessly reviled, crushed, and destroyed as victims of the universal self-hate of man which they have unfortunately only increased by the failure of their good intentions.

Perhaps we still have a basically superstitious tendency to associate failure with dishonesty and guilt—failure being interpreted as "punishment." Even if a man starts out with good intentions, if he fails we tend to think he was somehow "at fault." If he was not guilty, he was at least "wrong." And "being wrong" is something we have not yet learned to face with equanimity and understanding. We either condemn it with god-like disdain or forgive it with god-like condescension. We do not manage to accept it with human compassion, humility and identification. Thus we never see the one truth that would help us begin to solve our ethical and political problems: that we are *all* more or less wrong, and that we are *all* at fault, *all* limited and obstructed by our mixed motives, our self-deception, our greed, our self-righteousness and our tendency to aggressivity and hypocrisy.

In our refusal to accept the partially good intentions of others and work with them (of course prudently and with resignation to the inevitable imperfection of the result) we are unconsciously proclaiming our own malice, our own intolerance, our own lack of realism, our own ethical and political quackery.

Perhaps in the end the first real step toward peace would be a realistic acceptance of the fact that our political ideals are perhaps to a great extent illusions and fictions to which we cling out of motives that are not always perfectly honest: that because of this we prevent ourselves from seeing any good or any practicability in the political ideas of our enemies—which may of course be in many ways even more illusory and dishonest than our own. We will never get anywhere unless we can accept the fact that politics is an inextricable tangle of good and evil motives in which, perhaps, the evil predominate but where one must continue to hope doggedly in what little good can still be found.

But someone will say: "If we once recognize that we are all equally wrong, all political action will instantly be paralyzed. We can only act when we assume that we are in the right." On the contrary, I believe the basis for valid political action can only be the recognition that the true solution to our problems is *not* accessible to any one isolated party or nation but that all must arrive at it by working together.

I do not mean to encourage the guilt-ridden thinking that is always too glad to be "wrong" in everything. This too is an evasion of responsibility, because every form of oversimplification tends to make decisions ultimately meaningless. We must try to accept ourselves whether individually or collectively, not only as perfectly good or perfectly bad, but in our mysterious, unaccountable mixture of good and evil. We have to stand by the modicum of good that is in us without exaggerating it. We have to defend our real rights, because unless we respect our own rights we will certainly not respect the rights of others. But at the same time we have to recognize that we have willfully or otherwise trespassed on the rights of others. We must be able to admit this not only as the result of self-examination, but when it is pointed out unexpectedly, and perhaps not too gently, by somebody else.

These principles which govern personal moral conduct, which make harmony possible in small social units like the family, also apply in the wider area of the state and in the whole community of nations. It is however quite absurd, in our present situation or in any other, to expect these principles to be universally accepted as the result of moral exhortations. There is very little hope that the world will be run according to them all of a sudden, as a result of some hypothetical change of heart on the part of politicians. It is useless and even laughable to base political thought on the faint hope of a purely contingent and subjective moral illumination in the hearts of the world's leaders. But outside of political thought and action, in the religious sphere, it is not only permissible to hope for such a mysterious consummation, but it is necessary to pray for it. We can and must believe not so much that the mysterious light of God can "convert" the ones who are mostly responsible for the world's peace, but at least that they may, in spite of their obstinacy and their prejudices, be guarded against fatal error.

It would be sentimental folly to expect men to trust one another when they obviously cannot be trusted. But at least they can learn to trust God. They can bring themselves to see that the mysterious power of God can, quite independently of human malice and error, protect men unaccountably against themselves, and that He can always turn evil into good, though perhaps not always in a sense that would be understood by the preachers of sunshine and uplift. If they can trust and love God, Who is infinitely wise and Who rules the lives of men, permitting them to use their freedom even to the point of almost incredible abuse, they can love men who are evil. They can learn to love them even in their sin, as God has loved them. If we can love the men we cannot trust (without trusting them foolishly) and if we can to some extent share the burden of their sin by identifying ourselves with them, then perhaps there is some hope of a kind of peace on earth, based not on the wisdom and the manipulations of men but on the inscrutable mercy of God.

For only love—which means humility—can exorcise the fear which is at the root of all war.

What is the use of postmarking our mail with exhortations to "pray for peace" and then spending billions of dollars on atomic submarines, thermonuclear weapons, and ballistic missiles? This, I would think, would certainly be what the New Testament calls "mocking God"— and mocking Him far more effectively than the atheists do. The culminating horror of the joke is that we are piling up these weapons to protect ourselves against atheists who, quite frankly, believe there is no God and are convinced that one has to rely on bombs and missiles since nothing else offers any real security. Is it then because we have so much trust in the power of God that we are intent upon utterly destroying these people before they can destroy us? Even at the risk of destroying ourselves at the same time?

I do not mean to imply that prayer excludes the simultaneous use of ordinary human means to accomplish a naturally good and justifiable end. One can very well pray for a restoration of physical health and at the same time take medicine prescribed by a doctor. In fact a believer should normally do both. And there would seem to be a reasonable and right proportion between the use of these two means to the same end.

But consider the utterly fabulous amount of money, planning, energy, anxiety and care which go into the production of weapons which almost immediately become obsolete and have to be scrapped. Contrast all this with the pitiful little gesture: "pray for peace" piously canceling our four-cent stamps! Think, too, of the disproportion between our piety and the enormous act of murderous destruction which we at the same time countenance without compunction and without shame! It does not even seem to enter our minds that there might be some incongruity in praying to the God of peace, the God Who told us to love one another as He has loved us, who warned us that they who took the sword would perish by it, and at the same time planning to annihilate not thousands but millions of civilians and soldiers, men, women and children with discrimination, even with the almost infallible certainty of inviting the same annihilation for ourselves.

It may make sense for a sick man to pray for health and then take medicine, but I fail to see any sense at all in his praying for health and then drinking poison.

When I pray for peace I pray to pacify not only the Russians and the Chinese but above all my own nation and myself. When I pray for peace I pray to be protected not only from the Reds but also from the folly and blindness of my own country. When I pray for peace, I pray not only that the enemies of my country may cease to want war, but above all that my own country will cease to do the things that make war inevitable. In other words, when I pray for peace I am not just praying that the Russians will give up without a struggle and let us have our own way. I am praying that both we and the Russians may somehow be restored to sanity and learn how to work out our problems, as best we can, together instead of preparing for global suicide.

I am fully aware that this sounds utterly sentimental, archaic and out of tune with an age of science. But I would like to submit that pseudo-scientific thinking in politics and sociology have so far less than this to offer. One thing I would like to add in all fairness is that the atomic scientists themselves are quite often the ones most concerned about the ethics of the situation, and that they are among the few who dare to open their mouths from time to time and say something about it. But who on earth listens?

If men really wanted peace they would sincerely ask God for it and He would give it to them. But why should He give the world a peace which it does not really desire? The peace the world pretends to desire is really no peace at all.

To some men peace merely means the liberty to exploit other people without fear of retaliation or interference. To others peace means the freedom to rob brothers without interruption. To still others it means the leisure to devour the goods of the earth without being compelled to interrupt their pleasures to feed those whom their greed is starving. And to practically everybody peace simply means the absence of any physical violence that might cast a shadow over lives devoted to the satisfaction of their animal appetites for comfort and pleasure.

Many men like these have asked God for what they thought was "peace" and wondered why their prayer was not answered. They could not understand that it actually *was* answered. God left them with what they desired, for their idea of peace was only another form of war. The "cold war" is simply the normal consequence of our corruption of peace based on a policy of "every man for himself" in ethics, economics and political life. It is absurd to hope for a solid peace based on fictions and illusions!

So instead of loving what you think is peace, love other men and love God above all. And instead of hating the people you think are warmongers, hate the appetites and the disorder in your own soul, which are the causes of war. If you love peace, then hate injustice, hate tyranny, hate greed—but hate these things in *yourself*, not in another.

This article was reprinted in the January 1, 1962 issue of *Fellowship*, the journal of the Fellowship of Reconciliation.

THE SHELTER ETHIC

Published in The Catholic Worker, *November 1961*

The scenario about people sitting in their fallout shelters with machine guns to keep out their neighbors, which Merton fantasized about in the uncensored paragraphs of the previous article, was defended as a permissible ethical stance in the September 30, 1961 isssue of *America*. In an article entitled "Ethics at the Shelter Doorway," Father L. C. McHugh, S.J. cites Catholic moral teaching that the use of violence to defend life and its equivalent goods is justifiable in a case of just defense against an aggressor. He says, among other things:

> If a man builds a shelter for his family, then it is the family that has the first right to use it. The right becomes empty if a misguided charity prompts a pitying householder to crowd his haven to the hatch in the hour of peril; for this conduct makes sure that no one will survive.

America was inundated with letters to the editor. Eleven such letters were published in the issue of November 25, 1961. Some sided with Father McHugh; others did not. One writer wrote: "To me these speculations gave welcome reassurance that some people—theologians at least—are looking ahead." Another correspondent was not so kind: "No need for any further search to identify the priest in the parable of the Good Samaritan. It was Father McHugh." Fellow Jesuit Father John L. McKenzie, never a man to mince words, wrote: "In a crisis which demands heroic virtue, Father L. C. McHugh and others offer us the morality of the cornered rat . . . I can imagine Jesus Christ dying gracefully, which He did; I cannot imagine Him gunning down his neighbors to defend his rights to a hole in the ground."

> Thomas Merton entered into the controversy with an article
> entitled "The Machine Gun in the Fallout Shelter," published in
> *The Catholic Worker* as "Shelter Ethics." In October Merton sent
> it to James Forest, editor of the *Worker*. Then on November 5,
> 1961, he wrote to Forest: "Here is the revised article. I have
> beefed it up quite a bit." The article follows as it was actually
> published in the *Worker*. Other versions (for example, the one in
> *The Nonviolent Alternative*) are the "unbeefed-up" article.

· · · · ·

The October issue of *The Catholic Worker* carried an article by me
entitled "The Root of War," an excerpt from a book to be published
in December, *New Seeds of Contemplation*. This article did not intend
to enter directly in to the current controversy about the legitimacy of
defending one's safety in a fallout shelter by keeping others out at the
point of a gun. However, discussion of the article has involved me
implicitly in the controversy and therefore an explicit statement of my
position has become necessary. I feel this is something much more than
a simple "moral case." It is a symptom of the confusion and pervasive
madness of our society.

What precisely is the question? A great deal of discussion was
aroused in October by an article of an associate editor of *America*,
Father L. C. McHugh, S.J. Rather, to speak more accurately, a great
deal of discussion was raised by the confusing and one-sided presentation of that article in the national press. The article itself is perfectly
reasonable; it contains nothing with which a professor of ethics would
disagree. It states clearly that the natural law guarantees everyone a
right to defend his life and the safety of his dependents and that he
may even defend his life with violence, risking the death of the unjust
aggressor, if violence is clearly the last available recourse. It also makes
quite clear that the violence may only be used at the actual moment of
assault, and when the assault has been initiated with evident intent to
kill. Lethal violence may never be used merely to forestall the possibility of assault. Finally, the violence must be limited to what is strictly
necessary, and if possible the death of the unjust aggressor must be
avoided.

These are purely and simply the principles laid down by Catholic
moral philosophy, and it might be pertinent to observe, at this point,
that they are definitely applicable in the case of what our missile people
now refer to as "first strike" in nuclear war: by such principles as
these, one wonders how the idea of a surprise attack on an enemy who

is only feared as a potential aggressor could be accepted and blessed by a Christian moralist. Quite apart from the frightful injustice of the death and maiming of millions of innocent people, the mere fact of a surprise "first strike" on an all-out destructive scale, when no aggression has been initiated by the enemy, is clearly unjust and utterly unacceptable to a Christian moralist.

Most of the reports in the national press evidently failed to draw any attention to the most important paragraph in Father McHugh's article. I quote:

"To say that one has a right to employ violence in defense of life is not to say that one has the duty to do so. Indeed, in the Christian view, there is a great merit in turning the other cheek and bearing evils patiently out of the love of God." Father McHugh hastens to add that this is "heroism" and a "dedication to a full Christian ethic that is far above what God requires under pain of eternal loss."

He then points out that an "unattached individual" may well resign his place in the shelter in favor of someone else. This is excellent.

I have no intention whatever of criticizing Father McHugh, and I have absolutely no complaint about his principles. My intention is to speak about the whole situation that makes such discussion inevitable, and which dictated certain assumptions which to my mind completely falsify the Christian moral perspective in this problem. What is disturbing today is the widespread and unreserved acceptance of these assumptions.

What are they?

First of all that a shallow backyard shelter itself makes any sense. That one can surely save his life by taking refuge in one. That it is really worth the trouble having such a shelter, and that it is even so important to get into it that one can go to the lengths of killing another person in order to keep him out. This whole mentality is deeply disturbing. It seems to me to be equivalent to saying that if the only food left in the world were a single hamburger, it would be worth a fight to the death to get hold of it. A fallout shelter might be of some value in Colombia or Peru—or perhaps in Australia. In the event of an all-out atomic attack on the U.S. such a shelter recommends itself only to someone who wants to die in a small hole.

Secondly, a passive and uncritical acceptance of all the ambiguous political thought which is leading us step by step toward nuclear war. It implies a stoical resignation to the idea of such a war, and the conviction that nuclear war makes sense: that it may become "necessary" and even "Christian." Please do not misunderstand me: I am not trying to pin these opinions on the author of the article. I am just saying they are in the air that everybody breathes. They are disseminated like spiritual fallout by the irresponsible and immoral sensationalism of the mass-media.

Finally, in the moral thinking of many Catholics, there is a tacit assumption *that the fulfillment of the minimal obligation and nothing more, is normal for a Christian!* That anything beyond the very minimal becomes "heroic" and "cannot be demanded" of anyone. Perhaps we forget there are situations in which even the minimum demanded of a Christian can be "heroic." It is certainly true that one might be *obliged* to leave the supposed safety of a shelter at the risk of one's life in order to minister to the grave spiritual needs of the neighbor we so readily consider as a possible target for our rifle!

It seems to me that at this time, above all, instead of wasting our time in problematic ways of saving our own skin, we ought to be seeking with all our strength to act as better Christians, as men of peace, dedicated wholeheartedly to the law of love which is the law of Christ.

This grave problem has to be seen in the light of very extraordinary circumstances. We are in the midst of what is perhaps the most crucial moral and spiritual crisis the human race has ever faced during its history. We are all deeply involved in this crisis, and consequently the way each individual faces the crisis has a definite bearing on the survival of the whole race. This does not mean that individual rights are to be sacrificed without further discussion. But it does mean that the way in which each individual protects his own rights is a matter of great importance. Therefore, while each individual certainly retains the right to defend his life and protect his family, we run the risk of creating a very dangerous mentality and opening the way to moral chaos if we give the impression that from here on out it is just every man for himself, and the devil take the hindmost. This is not only fundamentally unchristian, but it is immoral on the purely natural level and is really disastrous even to the political interests of our nation.

It is tragic that the nonviolent resistance to evil which is of the very essence of the New Testament morality has come to be regarded as a specialty reserved for beatniks and eccentric cultists. What is the real purpose of the Sermon on the Mount? Certainly the injunction to "turn the other check" and to "give one's cloak also" is Oriental and hyperbolic. Certainly an absolutely literal fulfillment is not intended. But we cannot discard these inescapable injunctions of Christ our Lord. They give us the whole spirit and orientation with which even the natural law is to be fulfilled. Once the Law of Christ has been promulgated, it is no longer possible to isolate the natural law in a sphere of its own.

The natural law itself acquires a Christian perspective from the Sermon on the Mount. It has an aim higher than the mere avoidance of brutality, savagery and sin. It becomes obligatory for the Christian to orientate all his conduct according to the law of love and to make use of nonviolent means of persuasion whenever it is humanly possible. He must do this out of generous love both for his neighbor and for the truth.

Fallout does not dispense me from the basic obligation to love my neighbor as myself and even in a case where it might be obligatory to restrain him from violence by force, I am only allowed to use this force with love for truth, for justice, and for my neighbor. I can never cease to value him or his life, and I should be willing to learn to accept injustice and violence, even death, for the sake of love and truth. To regard this as mere sentimentality is to confess that one is blind to the real sense of Christian ethics.

Certainly a man owes protection to his family and dependents. No one questions that. Let it be quite clear that even nonviolent resistance not only recognizes but emphasizes this fundamental duty. There is no such thing as legitimate nonviolent passivity in this case. It is not ethically permissible for a man to stand by and let his helpless dependents be killed or overrun. Nonviolent resistance is active and positive. It takes very definite steps to protect rights, but these steps are nonviolent in the sense that self-sacrifice for the sake of truth and rights takes precedence over everything else, and especially over the use of physical force against the aggressor. The nonviolent resister has the duty to lay down his life if necessary to protect the rights of his family. He is also ready to lay down his life in defense of the truth. The emphasis is on the readiness to sacrifice one's own life, not on the promptitude with which one will kill another to save himself.

I admit that the practical question of how to resist nonviolently in the case we are discussing (the fallout shelter) presents very serious difficulties. Such a case would require mastery of the supremely difficult and heroic technique of nonviolent resistance. In practice, where nonviolent resistance is impossible, then force may and should be used, rather than passive acquiescence. I must emphasize this point very strongly, because it is generally unknown or misunderstood. Merely passive acquiescence in evil is in no sense to be dignified by the name of nonviolence. It is a travesty of Christian meekness. It is purely and simply the sin of cowardice. Those who imagine that this kind of apathy is nonviolent resistance are doing a great disservice to the cause of truth and confusing heroism with degenerate and apathetic passivity. Hence even the proponent of nonviolence will allow that in practice a man might use force to protect the life and safety of his family in a fallout shelter, assuming that he was not able to solve the problem in a legitimately nonviolent manner.

This does not alter the fact that it is both misleading and dangerous to place too much stress on the supposed value of hiding in a hole in the backyard. Let there be no nonsense about neighbor pitted against neighbor with revolvers and shotguns. Lives are not going to be saved by anarchy and arbitrary recourse to subjective fantasy. Above all let us get rid of this poisonous viewpoint that it is every man for himself, and one is being noble and dutiful if one is ready to shoot his neighbor. There are higher ideals we can keep in mind. Let us not forget that the supreme example of nonviolent resistance to evil is the crucifixion of Our Lord Jesus Christ, in which the Incarnate Son of God destroyed sin by taking the sins of the world upon Himself and dying on the Cross, while forgiving the men who were putting Him to death. Far from being an act of mere helpless passivity, as Nietzsche and other moderns claim, this was a free and willing acceptance of suffering in the most positive and active manner. The activity in this case was hidden and spiritual. It was an exercise of the supremely dynamic spiritual force of divine love.

A Christian is committed to the belief that Love and Mercy are the most powerful forces on earth. Hence every Christian is bound by his baptismal vocation to seek, as far as he can, with God's grace, to make those forces effective in his life, to the point where they dominate all his actions. Naturally no one is bound to attain to the full perfection of charity. But a Christian who forgets that this is his goal, ceases by that fact to live and act as a genuine Christian. We must strive, then, to imitate Christ and His sacrifice, in so far as we are able. We must keep in mind His teaching that supreme love consists in laying down one's life for one's friends.

This means that a Christian will never simply allow himself to develop a state of mind in which, forgetting his Christian ideal, he thinks in purely selfish and pragmatic terms. Our rights certainly remain, but they do not entitle us to develop a hard-boiled, callous, selfish outlook, a "me first" attitude. This is that rugged individualism which is so unchristian and which modern movements in Catholic spirituality have so justly deplored.

There is another and very grave aspect of the present problem. It is a purely practical and political aspect. What is going to happen to this country if it is suddenly attacked and all the citizens fly into a panic and start shooting each other up? Not only is this a very serious and actual danger, but it is undoubtedly an important part in the well-calculated policy of Communism. Why do you suppose Khrushchev has given world-wide publicity to his crescendo of nuclear tests? Do you suppose that this has been totally unrelated to the near panic in some quarters in the United States? Let us consider for a moment a statement made some years ago by one of our own missile experts, Dr. James B. Edson. He says: "It is of course more artful and sophisticated and sometimes more economical to use one of the agents (nuclear, biological or psychological) as a catalyst causing the target to destroy itself by its own energy. This can be done to ammunition dumps and people. It can also be done to enemies and nations, causing them to maneuver endlessly in response to threats they cannot foresee or cannot forestall."

In other words our moral theologians, in their innocence, do not take into account the almost infinitely subtle reasoning of the man of war. They do not reckon with the vast scope and probing calculations of power politicians and military technicians in the nuclear age. We are not just fighting with nuclear weapons. We are in a cold war that is total in the sense that it exploits every available resource and one of the most explosive forces in this warfare is the psychology of the helpless civilian. Let us for the love of heaven wake up to the fact that our own minds are just as filled with dangerous power today as the nuclear bombs themselves. And let us be very careful how we unleash the pent-up forces in the minds of others. The hour is extremely grave. The guarded statements of moral theologians are a small matter compared to the constant deluge of irresponsible opinions, criminal half-truths and murderous images disseminated by the mass media. The struggle for survival, freedom and truth is going to be won or lost in our thoughts, in our spirit. It is because the minds of men have become what they have become that the world is poised on the brink of total disaster.

Merton learned that Dorothy Day was not pleased with his article. True to form, he wrote a long letter, dated December 20, 1961, in which he attempted to clarify his position. (See *HGL,* 140–143) He concludes with an apology "for the totally insufficient tone of my last article in *CW* which seemed in so many ways to fall short of your editorial standards."

· 3 ·

TARGET EQUALS CITY

Not published during Merton's lifetime

This article was written by Merton some time near the beginning of the year 1962 and sent in mimeographed form to the circle of friends who regularly received copies of articles he was planning to publish. One of these friends, Herbert Mason, in a letter written on February 27, 1962, strongly urged him not to publish "Target Equals City." "Only your enemies," he said, "would publish that." Merton did not agree with Mason's comment. On March 9, 1962 he wrote: "I think the case is quite clear and needs to be stated. It would seem that this is the kind of evidence [namely, the material in the book he was using as his source, Robert C. Batchelder's, *The Irreversible Decision*] that needs to be stressed and is incontrovertible."

The censors were much stronger than Mason. One of them described the article as "fallacious" and "misleading." Moreover, it was, he said, against the mind of the General Chapter of the Order that a monk be "involved in public controversy" of this sort, *"especially on the side of pacifists"* [italics added].

The censor also complained: "The copy of the author's manuscript which I received was mimeographed." One cannot help but ask: Was this carelessness on Merton's part or naivete or just plain stupidity? After all, he did want the approval of the censor. And he must have realized that sending him a copy that obviously had been shared with others was not the best way of disposing the censor favorably toward his article.

It was this article, which never got published in Merton's lifetime, that more than any other brought the directive from the Abbot General, the highest authority in the Order, that Merton was to write nothing more on the issue of war and peace. This directive Merton received from his own Abbot in April of 1962.

. . . . .

There is one winner, only one winner in war. The winner is war itself. Not truth, not justice, not liberty, not morality. These are the vanquished. War wins, reducing them to complete submission. He makes truth serve violence and falsehood. He causes justice to declare not what is just but what is expedient as well as cruel. He reduces the liberty of the victorious side to a servitude equal to that of the tyranny which they attacked, in defense of liberty. Though moralists may intend and endeavor to lay down rules for war, in the end war lays down rules for them. He does not find it hard to make them change their minds. If he could, he would change God's own mind. War has power to transmute evil into good and good into evil. Do not fear that he will not exercise this power. Now more than ever he is omnipotent. He is the great force, the evil mystery, the demonic mover of our century, with his globe of sun-fire, and his pillar of cloud. Worship him.

It took five years for war to turn the Christian ethic of the "just war" inside out. The years 1940 to 1945 completely revolutionized the moral thinking of the allies who were fighting totalitarianism with a *just cause* if ever there was one.

Certainly no cause can be absolutely just and pure. You can always find something wrong with it. But for those who accepted the traditional doctrine on war, there was not much doubt that Hitler was the aggressor, and that we were the defenders.

When the Japanese bombed Pearl Harbor, there was no question about the morality of America's entering the war to defend its rights. Here was a very clear example of a "just cause" for war. Few doubted the fact. Those who did so were regarded as foolish because they were against all war on principle. They thought war was intrinsically evil. Twenty years later one is tempted to wonder if they were not more wise than men believed them to be.

At the end of World War II, many theologians openly began to discuss the question whether the old doctrine of the just war had any meaning. It seemed to them at that time that the obliteration bombing of cities on both sides, culminating in the total destruction of Hiroshima and Nagasaki by one plane with one bomb for each, had completely changed the nature of war. Traditional standards no long applied because, for one thing, there was no longer any distinction made between civilian and combatant. Where this distinction was obliterated, or tended to be obliterated, war could not be considered just.

Double effect could no longer be taken seriously when you "permitted" (without intending it) the slaughter of fifty thousand civilians in order to stop production in three or four factories. There was no proportion between the "permitted" evil and the "intended" good. (Investigation showed that even when there had been massive damage and countless deaths inflicted by obliteration bombing, the factories themselves were not always crippled for very long and soon resumed production.)

Double effect was completely out of the question when the slaughter of civilians was explicitly *intended* as a means to "breaking enemy morale" and thus breaking his "will to resist." This was pure terrorism, and the traditional doctrine of war excluded such immoral methods. Traditional morality also excluded torture of prisoners, murder of hostages chosen at random, extermination of racial groups for no reason other than race, etc. These methods were practiced by the enemy, and after the war ended *they were bequeathed to the Western nations.* France in Algeria, for instance.

How did precision bombing, (allowed by traditional standards of justice) turn into obliteration bombing? How did ethical theory gradually come to defend obliteration bombing, and even mass destruction by atomic weapons? How did we gradually reach our present position where the traditional doctrine of the just war has been so profoundly modified that it is almost unrecognizable? How is it that we are now almost ready to permit any outrage, any excess, any horror, on the grounds that it is a "lesser evil" and "necessary" to save our nation?

The deliberate terroristic annihilation of defenseless civilians for military and political purposes, is perhaps not completely new. In all ages there has been calculated terrorism, the slaughter of innocents in war. It was never seriously considered as either very necessary or very useful in the actual process of winning a war. It was more or less of a "bonus." (You remember perhaps the report on the raid that annihilated Dresden? The city was full of refugees fleeing from the Russians in the east. The death of several thousand extra victims was announced with sober joy as a "bonus" by those who commanded the raid.)

Traditional Christian teaching, which deplored war itself even under the best of conditions, never hesitated to condemn terrorism in war as a very grave crime. Now terrorism is no longer taken so seriously. It has become "necessary," the "only effective defense," and of course defense is a "duty." Hence we are seriously told that it is the "duty" of our government to arm to the teeth with nuclear weapons capable of wiping out whole cities, whole nations. A conservative estimate declares that the United States probably now stocks the equivalent in explosive power of *ten tons of TNT for every human being on the face of the earth*. We are generously going beyond the limits of strict duty, just in case.

Terror from the air, as a deliberately planned policy, was characteristic of the Nazi and Fascist Axis. As a matter of fact the honor of having initiated it in Europe belongs to Catholic nations: Franco's Spain and Fascist Italy. The place? Guernica, a Christian city in the Christian province of the Basque, in Christian Spain. Date: 1937. Also please remember Nanking, China. Same year. Not so many Christians. We protested.

Poland was the next victim. Reduced to nothing in a few days by Luftwaffe. 1939. England came next.

It is to the everlasting credit of the British that although the civilians of England suffered one crushing blow after another, and saw whole sections of their cities reduced to rubble, the government declared that the RAF would abide by traditional methods, and would confine itself to the strategic bombing of military targets only. But since daylight raids were very costly, most of the attacks had to be carried out at night. This made precision bombing very difficult, and in the end civilians suffered more than industry. So "area bombing," the destruction of the whole neighborhood that included a military target, was already British policy by the time America came into the war. America determined to stick to the traditional ethical code. Roosevelt at first announced that the AAF would confine itself to strategic bombing.

By 1942, however, England abandoned its quixotic attachment to standards which were simply preventing the RAF raids from being fully effective. At least that was what the RAF thought. It was Air Marshal Sir Arthur Harris who opened up with obliteration bombing against German cities in 1942. Not only was this aimed at the "sure" destruction of factories and military objectives that might otherwise be missed, but frankly and explicitly the intention was to "destroy enemy morale." "There are no lengths in violence to which we will not go" to achieve this end, declared Churchill. And another government spokesman, unidentified, said, "Our plans are to bomb, burn and ruthlessly destroy, in every way available to us, the people responsible for creating this war."

Here we have already one complete cycle. A country begins a defensive "just war." It starts by declaring its firm adherence to the ethical principles held by its Church, and by the majority of its civilian population. The nation accepts unjust suffering heroically. But then the military begins to grow impatient, seeing that its own methods of retaliation are not effective. It is *the military that changes the policy.* The new, more ruthless policy pays off. The civilian protest is silenced before it begins. Those who might otherwise have objected come to believe what they are told: "This will save lives. It is necessary to end the war sooner, and to punish the unjust aggressor."

The standards of justice are still in view—still *partially* in view. The injustice of the aggressor is very clearly seen. Justice in the use of means has been lost sight of, and what counts most is expediency.

We cannot lightly blame the courageous people who suffered so much and were so eager for the war to end. But . . . The allies had come around to adopting the same methods precisely, the same ruthless inhumanity which made the enemy unjust. Injustice was now common to both sides. Needless to say, both were now strenuously arguing and convincing themselves, in exactly the same terms, that their war effort was just, that their methods were just, and that it was necessary to do all that they did in order to win the victory, end the war quickly and "save lives."

Note also, on both sides there were sincere Catholics, encouraged by the clergy and by the Catholic press to accept and support these claims. There were therefore Catholics believing that each side was completely just. Catholics on both sides "served God" by killing each other . . . What had become of the meaning of the doctrine of the "just war"? What had become of Christian ethics in this situation? Did anyone stop to reflect on the total absurdity of this self-contradiction on the part of Christians? Not the least appalling contradiction lay in the fact that German Christians heroically sacrificed themselves to defend a government that cruelly persecuted the Church. In defense of Hitler's neopaganism which advocated a totally immoral policy they fought their fellow Christians of France, England and America.

Just war? Just cause? Just methods? Double effect?

Now America was in the war. America was obviously going to follow the tactics England had been forced to take over from the Nazis by the very logic of war. The USAF soon began obliteration bombing. A protest was published in *Fellowship*, the magazine of the Fellowship of Reconciliation, in 1944. Obliteration bombing was condemned by this magazine and by a group of Protestant ministers. The protest was taken seriously enough to get an official reply. Roosevelt said that these tactics were necessary to "shorten the war." There was a nationwide discussion of the issue. Americans were fifty to one against those who protested. They thought the moral scruples of these pacifists were ridiculous. To demand cessation of obliteration bombing was pure defeatism.

All distinction between precision bombing and obliteration bombing was forgotten in the general indignation. What mattered was to beat Hitler and right the wrong that had been done. Any methods that helped procure this end were justifiable.

One dissenting voice was that of a Catholic priest, Father John C. Ford, S.J., who argued that the obliteration bombing of cities was immoral and could not be defended by the principle of double effect.

Meanwhile the United States was working feverishly to develop the atomic bomb, believing that Hitler's scientists were on the point of perfecting this weapon that would multiply thousands of times the destructiveness of ordinary bombing.

However, before the atomic bomb was tested, the B29 bomber command in the Pacific had to come to realize the failure of precision bombing of Japanese military targets. It was not possible to seriously slow down production by this means.

Early in 1945, General Curtis LeMay decided, on his own responsibility, to initiate a devastating new tactic of massive low-flying fire raids delivered at night.

On the night of March 9–10 the whole of Tokyo was set afire with napalm bombs. The blaze was so furious that it boiled the water of the canals. Fire storms consumed all the oxygen, and many who were not burned to death suffocated. So frightful were the effects of this raid that it claimed as many casualties as the Atom bombing of Hiroshima.

Some apologists for all-out war point to this fact, saying that since there is in reality no difference between total war carried on by conventional weapons and total war carried on by nuclear weapons, there is no new moral issue involved. On the contrary, this calls for a clarification of the real moral issue. The issue is precisely this: not that atomic and nuclear weapons are immoral while conventional weapons are just, but that *any resort to terrorism and total annihilation is unjust, whatever be the weapons it employs.*

The Tokyo raid, followed by similar raids on more than fifty other Japanese cities, was justified on the grounds that much of the Japanese war effort depended on the "phantom industry," the detailed piece-work on small parts carried on by individuals in their homes. Hence residential areas came to be just as "legitimate" a target as factories themselves. This fact contributed to the loose generalization, now widely accepted, without further qualifications, that "in modern war everyone is to be considered a combatant." Hence even residential areas became "military targets." No more need for double effect!

Already in May and June of 1945 the American High Command was considering three choices of an appropriate target for the new bomb.

In discussing the choice of target, Truman and his advisers did not speak of this or that naval base, this or that fortress, this or that concentration of troops, this or that particular munitions plant. In Truman's own words: "Stimson's staff had *prepared a list of cities in* Japan that might serve as targets . . ." Later in the context Truman speaks of the entire city of Hiroshima as a "military target."

We must remember that in the list of cities originally considered was Kyoto, which is a religious and not a military center at all.

There were, of course, industries at Hiroshima, but its "military" importance was such that it had hardly been touched so far. It had even been neglected by LeMay's incendiaries.

In other words, the "targets" considered for the atomic bomb were purely and simply cities. Any city at all, by the mere fact of being a city, was now a "military target." The fact that Kyoto was among them indicates that moral and psychological effect, in other words terrorism, was the dominant consideration in the minds of the high command.

Hiroshima was chosen in order that an "untouched" target might show the power of the bomb. The idea was to unleash the maximum destructive power on a civilian center, to obliterate that center and destroy all further will to resist in the Japanese nation. The word "target" and the word "city" had become completely identified.

Once again, moral thinking had gone through a full cycle in the short space of two or three years. The United States had entered the war with the conviction of the justice of its cause and with the firm intention to abide by just means.

However, it is possible that the notion of "just means" was much more nebulous in the American mind than it had been in the English. Moral thinking guided by pragmatic principles tends to be very vague, very fluid. Moral decisions were now a series of more or less opportunistic choices based on short-term guesses of possible consequences, rather than on definite moral principles.

It is quite certain that though the American public conscience was characterized by a certain undefined sense of decency and fittingness in these matters, a sense more or less attributable to the vestiges of Christian tradition, this "moral sense" easily yielded to the more practical dictates of the situation.

The moral decision to use the bomb, without warning, on a Japanese city was dictated by the urgent desire to end the war promptly, without having to sacrifice thousands of American combatants in the planned invasion of the Japanese archipelago. Once again, the idea was "to punish the unjust aggressor" and to "save American lives." Certainly few Americans, before the bomb was dropped, would have questioned the validity of these considerations. The war had to be ended, and this was the way to do it.

It was not generally known that Japan was trying to establish diplomatic contacts with the allies through Russia in order to work out a negotiated peace instead of the unconditional surrender relentlessly demanded by the allies. Neither invasion of Japan nor use of the bomb was absolutely necessary for peace. However, the war mentality at this time made it impossible for policy-makers to see this. They were convinced the bomb was necessary and their conviction overwhelmed all other considerations.

Nevertheless the use of the bomb on two open cities was a dire injustice and an atrocity.

Even after the war ended, a questionnaire conducted by *Fortune* revealed that half the respondents felt the decision to use the bomb on Hiroshima and Nagasaki had been right, while nearly a quarter of them *regretted that more atomic bombs* had not been used on other Japanese cities! Such was, and is, the general moral climate in the U.S.A.

At the same time, the terrible effects of the bomb produced a moral shock and profound revulsions in certain quarters in America. Religious groups and publications protested more or less vehemently. Catholic voices, notably those of the *Commonweal,* the *Catholic World* and, of course, the *Catholic Worker* were raised against the "sin" of the bomb. But it is to be noted that *America* already took a much more "realistic" and complacent view of the event.

In general, articulate protest against the bomb on moral grounds has been confined to a minority. The majority of Americans have "sincerely regretted" the necessity to use it, they have, in a word, "felt bad" about it. But that is all. These decent sentiments have very easily yielded to other, more "practical" considerations, and the foreign policy of our country since Hiroshima, while occasionally making perfunctory gestures of respect in the direction of the Deity, has been a policy of direct reliance on the threat of atomic and nuclear annihilation.

There have of course been repeated statements of unwillingness to carry out these threats, on the vague grounds that the consequences would be too awful. The American mind in general has, however, not questioned the fundamental propriety of using the bomb. This is practically taken for granted.

As the pressures of the cold war become more intense, the fallout shelter scare has had a direct and intimate connection with the policy of nuclear deterrence. It has been clearly and explicitly part of a campaign to "engineer consent" and make nuclear war thoroughly acceptable, at least as a reasonable possibility, in the American public mind. This, in turn, is intended to convince our enemies that we "believe in" the bomb, and that, though we still utter pious hopes that it will never be necessary, we thoroughly intend to use it if we feel ourselves to be sufficiently threatened.

Here, then, is the moral situation:

1. There has been a complete breakdown in the old notion of the "just war" as accepted for centuries by Christian ethics and international law. As far as policy-makers are concerned, this concept has now become completely irrelevant. It has been supplanted by the concept of "limited war," which has no ethical connotations, but is simply "tactical" and is designed to avoid the more disastrous effects of an all-out war of annihilation. The "value" of a limited war, with or without tactical nuclear weapons, is that there is more of a chance that it may theoretically be "won" by one side or the other. At the same time, there seems to be every reason to believe that if one of the belligerents feels himself to be losing a limited war, he will resort to retaliation on the megatonic scale, and the war will become "total."

2. Moralists, while still clinging more or less resolutely to the idea that obliteration of civilian centers is evil (some show very little resolution in the attachment to this principle!) strive in general to patch up the traditional notion of just war and keep it functioning, by tying it up with the "limited" war of the tacticians. This ends by being a rather Pickwickian position, and in actual fact the moralists who still try to reconcile traditional notions with the new situation seek means of justifying massive nuclear retaliation as "self-defense."

Though no clear official pronouncement in this matter has been made by the Church, the repeated warnings of the Popes and their strong pleas for peace have insisted on the traditional principle that the rights of unarmed and noncombatant civilians must be respected and that failure to take these rights into account is a grave crime. Military policy, on the other hand, has completely discarded all consideration of these rights, except in perfunctory statements designed to assuage the scruples of the old-fashioned.

Theologians remain divided, but a strong and articulate group, especially in Europe, have taken their stand on the "relative pacifist" position which would outlaw all nuclear war and work for disarmament as the course of action most consistent with Christian morality.

It must be confessed that these issues are not as widely or as thoroughly discussed as they might be. The relative pacifist position does not get a very good hearing in the press, especially in the United States. The average Catholic is left with the impression that nuclear deterrence and the annihilation of Russian cities by H-bombs is *encouraged* by the Church, or at least left indifferently to the judgment of governments and military commands. The Church is by no means indifferent on this point. This fact is obscured because the moral thinking not only of the Christian laity but also of the clergy has been seriously confused by the mass media.

The Christian moral sense is being repeatedly eroded and worn down by the effect of the "cycles" we have described. A new policy is adopted on grounds that appear to be fully "just." Then, when the "ethical" means are found to be less expedient, more drastic measures are resorted to. Those violate justice, but the justification of them by publicists further weakens the moral sense. There are protests and questions. Soothing answers are provided by policy-makers and religious spokesmen are ready to support them with new adjustments. A new cycle is prepared. Once again there is a "just cause." Few stop to think that what is now regarded complacently as "justice" was clearly a crime twenty years ago.

How long can Christian morality go on taking this kind of beating?

There is only one winner in war. That winner is not justice, not liberty, not Christian truth.

The winner is war itself.

N.B. The facts in this article are taken mostly from a recent detailed study of the events which shaped the decision to use the A-bomb at the end of World War II. *The Irreversible Decision, 1939–1950* by Robert C. Batchelder (Houghton Mifflin) is a clear and persuasive plea for a clear and definite ethical stand in regard to nuclear war, in place of the vague and unprincipled pragmatism which guides decisions today. Our meditation can serve as a review and a recommendation of this book.

· 4 ·

NUCLEAR WAR AND
CHRISTIAN RESPONSIBILITY

Published in Commonweal, *February 9, 1962*

Commonweal invited Merton to write an article on peace in a nuclear age for their Christmas 1961 issue. In October he sent the article to the censors. Opposed by one censor, it was eventually approved, but not in time for Christmas. It was not published until February 9, 1962. Merton felt its publication that week was providential, since it coincided with the General Strike for Peace held in New York City.

Rather quickly he learned that it was one thing to publish in *The Catholic Worker*, whose readers would most likely be sympathetic to his views, quite another to reach a readership of much more divergent views. On March sixteen Merton wrote to Wilbur H. Ferry:

"The top brass in the American hierarchy is getting wind of my articles and is expressing displeasure. An editorial in the Washington *Catholic Standard* [March 9, 1962], evidently by a Bishop [Bishop Philip Hannan, auxiliary bishop of Washington, was then editor], takes very strong exception to the *Commonweal* article." [*HGL*, 210]

Merton did learn, however, that one member of the American hierarchy had apparently read his article with approval. Cardinal Albert Meyer, archbishop of Chicago, issued a Lenten pastoral letter in 1962 in which he clearly borrowed sentences and phrases from the *Commonweal* article.

Apart from this welcome support from Cardinal Meyer, Merton was distressed by what he considered a misreading of his article. Yet, typical of him, there were self-recriminations. On

February 4, 1962, with the *Commonweal* article about to be published, he wrote to John Tracy Ellis and expressed some misgivings about what he had written: "I may have given a wrong impression by some rather sweeping statements, and I have rewritten the article." [*HGL*, 176] As a matter of fact, he actually rewrote this article four different times. There is one version, fairly close to the original, but toned down a bit, which—as far as I have been able to ascertain—was never published in Merton's lifetime (though it is included in Zahn's *The Non-Violent Alternative* [pp. 12–19] under the title: "Peace: Christian Duties and Perspectives").

A second rewriting of the *Commonweal* article, much expanded, appeared in a safer place, *The Catholic Worker*. It was so lengthy that it had to be published in two parts (one in the May issue, the other in June). As a title for this two-part article, Merton chose a sentence that occurs near the very end of the *Commonweal* article: "We Have to Make Ourselves Heard." This long article eventually grew into a book, *Peace in a Post-Christian Era*, which Merton was forbidden to publish, but which he sent to many friends in mimeographed form. Finally, Merton chose parts of rewrites two and three, to make up yet a fourth alternate version of the original *Commonweal* article. Entitled "Peace: A Religious Responsibility," this version appeared as a chapter in the book *Breakthrough to Peace* and will be reproduced later in this volume.

I have taken the time to detail the various stages through which this *Commonweal* article went to show its central importance in Merton's peace writing. These various rewrites also indicate something of the anguish, anxiety, and loneliness Merton experienced in presenting the positions he felt obliged to take.

· · · · ·

It has been said so often that it has become a cliche, but it must be said again at the beginning of this article: the world and society of man now face destruction. *Possible* destruction; it is relatively easy, at the present time, to wipe out the entire human race either by nuclear, bacterial or chemical agents, separately or together. *Probable* destruction: the possibility of destruction becomes a probability in proportion as the world's leaders commit themselves more and more irrevocably to policies built on the threat to use these agents of extermination. At the present moment, the United States and the Soviet bloc are committed to a policy of genocide. Not only are they committed to the use of nuclear weapons for self-defense, but even to their use in first-strike attack if it should be expedient. This means that the policies of the United States and Russia are now frankly built on the presumption that each one is able, willing and *ready* to completely destroy the other at a moment's notice by a "first-strike"; that the one destroyed is capable of "post mortem retaliation" that would annihilate not only the attacker but all his allies and satellites, even though the defender were already wiped out himself.

There is no need to insist that in a world where another Hitler is very possible the mere existence of nuclear weapons constitutes the most tragic and serious problem that the human race has ever had to contend with. Indeed, the atmosphere of hatred, suspicion and tension in which we all live is precisely what is needed to produce Hitlers.

It is no exaggeration to say that our times are Apocalyptic, in the sense that we seem to have come to a point at which all the hidden, mysterious dynamism of the "history of salvation" revealed in the Bible has flowered into final and decisive crisis. The term "end of the world" may or may not be one that we are capable of understanding. But at any rate we seem to be assisting in the unwrapping of the mysteriously vivid symbols of the last book of the New Testament. In their nakedness, they reveal to us our own selves as the men whose lot it is to live in the time of a possible ultimate decision.

We know that Christ came into this world as the Prince of Peace. We know that Christ Himself is our peace (Eph. 2:14). We believe that God has chosen for Himself, in the Mystical Body of Christ, an elect people, regenerated by the Blood of the Savior, and committed by their baptismal promise to wage war with the great enemy of peace and salvation. As Pope John XXIII pointed out in his first encyclical letter, *Ad Petri Cathedram,* Christians are obliged to strive for peace "with all the means at their disposal" and yet, as he continues, this peace cannot compromise with error or make concessions to it. Therefore it is by no means a matter of passive acquiescence in injustice, since this does not produce peace. However, the Christian struggle for peace depends first of all upon a free response of man to "God's call to the service of His merciful designs." The lack of man's response to this call, says Pope John, is the "most terrible problem of human history." (Christmas message, 1958) Christ our Lord did not come to bring peace to the world as a kind of spiritual tranquilizer. He brought to His disciples a vocation and a task, to struggle in the world of violence to establish His peace not only in their own hearts but in society itself.

The Christian is and must be by his very adoption as a son of God, in Christ, a peacemaker (Matt. 5:9). He is bound to imitate the Savior who, instead of defending Himself with twelve legions of Angels (Matt. 25:55) allowed Himself to be nailed *to the cross* and died praying for His executioners. The Christian is one whose life has sprung from a particular spiritual seed: the blood of the martyrs who, without offering forcible resistance, laid down their lives rather than submit to the unjust laws that demanded an official religious cult of the Emperor as God. That is to say, the Christian is bound, like the martyrs, to obey God rather than the state whenever the state tries to usurp powers that do not and cannot belong to it. We have repeatedly seen Christians in our time fulfilling this obligation in a heroic manner by their resistance to dictatorships that strove to interfere with the rights of their conscience and of their religion.

We are no longer living in a Christian world. The ages which we are pleased to call the "ages of Faith" were certainly not ages of earthly paradise. But at least our forefathers officially recognized and favored the Christian ethic of love. They fought some very bloody and un-Christian wars, and in doing so they also committed great crimes which remain in history as a permanent scandal. However, certain definite limits were recognized. Today a non-Christian world still retains a few vestiges of Christian morality, a few formulas and cliches, which serve on appropriate occasions to adorn indignant editorials and speeches. But otherwise we witness deliberate campaigns to eliminate all education in Christian truth and morality. The Christian ethic of love tends to be discredited as phony and sentimental.

It is therefore a serious error to imagine that because the West was once largely Christian, the cause of the Western nations is now to be identified, without further qualification, with the cause of God. The incentive to wipe out Bolshevism may well be one of the apocalyptic temptations of twentieth-century Christendom. It may indeed be the most effective way of destroying Christendom, even though man may survive. For who imagines that the Asians and Africans will respect Christianity and embrace it after it has apparently triggered mass-murder and destruction of cosmic proportions? It is pure madness to think that Christianity can defend itself with nuclear weapons. The mere fact that we now seem to accept nuclear war as reasonable is universal scandal.

True, Christianity is not only opposed to Communism, but is in a very real sense at war with it. This warfare, however, is spiritual and ideological. "Devoid of material weapons," says Pope John, "the Church is the trustee of the highest spiritual power." If the Church has no military weapons of her own, it means that her wars are fought without any weapons at all and not that she intends to call upon the weapons of nations that were once Christian.

We must remember that the Church does not belong to any political power bloc. Christianity exists on both sides of the Iron Curtain and we should feel ourselves united by very special bonds with those Christians who, living under Communism, often suffer heroically for their principles.

Is it a valid defense of Christianity for us to wipe out these heroic Christians along with their oppressors, for the sake of "religious freedom?" It is pure sophistry to claim that physical annihilation in nuclear war is a *"lesser evil"* than the difficult conditions under which these Christians continue to live, perhaps with true heroism and sanctity preserving their faith and witnessing very effectively to Christ in the midst of atheism. Persecution is certainly a physical evil and a spiritual danger, but Christ has said that those who suffer persecution in His Name are blessed (Matt. 5:10–12).

At the same time, one of the most disturbing things about the Western world of our times is that it is beginning to have much more in common with the communist world than it has with the professedly Christian society of several centuries ago. On both sides of the Iron Curtain we find two profoundly disturbing varieties of the same moral sickness: both of them rooted in the same fundamentally materialist view of life. Both are basically opportunistic and pragmatic in their own way. And both have the following characteristics in common. On the level of *morality* they are blindly passive in their submission to a determinism which, in effect, leaves men completely irresponsible. Therefore moral obligations and decisions have become practically meaningless. At best they are only forms of words, rationalizations of pragmatic decisions that have already been dictated by the needs of the moment.

Naturally, since not everyone is an unprincipled materialist even in Russia, there is bound to be some moral sense at work, even if only as a guilt-feeling that produces uneasiness and hesitation, blocking the smooth efficiency of machine-like obedience to immoral commands. Yet the history of Nazi Germany shows us how appalling was the irresponsibility which would carry on even the most revolting of

crimes under cover of "obedience" for the sake of a "good cause."
This moral passivity is the most terrible danger of our time, as the
American Bishops have already pointed out in the joint letters of 1960
and 1961.

On the level of political, economic and military activity, this moral
passivity is balanced, or overbalanced, by a *demonic activism*, a frenzy
of the most varied, versatile, complete and even utterly brilliant technological improvisations, following one upon the other with an ever
more bewildering and controllable proliferation. Politics pretends to
use this force as its servant, to harness it for social purposes, for the
"good of man." The intention is good. The technological development
of power in our time is certainly a risk and challenge, but that does
not make it intrinsically evil. On the contrary, it can and should be a
very great good. In actual fact, however, the furious speed with which
our technological world is plunging toward disaster is evidence that
no one is any longer fully in control—and this includes the political
leaders.

A simple study of the steps which led to the dropping of the first
A-bomb at Hiroshima is devastating evidence of the way well-meaning
men, the scientists and leaders of a victorious nation, were guided step
by step, without realizing it, by the inscrutable yet simple "logic of
events" to fire the shot that was to make the cold war inevitable and
prepare the way perhaps inexorably for World War III. This they did
purely and simply because they thought in all sincerity that the bomb
was the simplest and most merciful way of ending World War II and
perhaps all wars, forever.

The tragedy of our time is then not so much the malice of the wicked
as the helpless futility even of the best intentions of "the good." There
are warmakers, war criminals, indeed. They are present and active on
both sides. But all of us, in our very best efforts for peace, find ourselves maneuvered unconsciously into positions where we too can act
as war criminals. For there can be no doubt that Hiroshima and Nagasaki were, though not fully deliberate crimes, nevertheless crimes. And
who was responsible? No one. Or "history." We cannot go on playing
with nuclear fire and shrugging off the results as "history." We are the
ones concerned. We are the ones responsible. History does not make
us, we make it—or end it.

In plain words, in order to save ourselves from destruction we have
to try to regain control of a world that is speeding downhill without
brakes, because of the combination of factors I have mentioned above:
almost total passivity and irresponsibility on the moral level, plus the

demonic activism in social, military and political life. The remedy would seem to be to slow down our activity, especially all activity concerned with the production and testing of weapons of destruction, and indeed to back-track by making every effort to negotiate for multilateral disarmament.

This may be of great help, but still only a palliative, not a solution. Yet *at least this* is perhaps feasible, and should at all costs be attempted, even at the cost of great sacrifice and greater risk. It is not morally licit for us as a nation to refuse the risk merely because our whole economy now depends on this war-effort. On the contrary, our national reliance on this substantial source of income and profit hardly qualifies as Christian.

Equally important, and perhaps even more difficult than disarmament, is the restoration of some moral sense and the resumption of genuine responsibility. Without this it is illusory for us to speak of freedom and "control." Unfortunately, even where moral principles are still regarded with some degree of respect, morality has lost touch with the realities of our situation. Moralists tend to discuss the problems of atomic war as if men still fought with bows and arrows. Modern warfare is fought as much by machines as by men. Even a great deal of the planning depends on the work of mechanical computers. An entirely new dimension is opened up by the fantastic process and techniques involved. An American President can speak of warfare in outer space and nobody bursts out laughing—he is perfectly serious. Science-fiction and the comic strips have all suddenly come true. When a missile armed with an H-bomb warhead is fired by the pressing of a button and its target is a whole city, the number of its victims is estimated in "megacorpses"—*millions* of dead human beings. A thousand or ten thousand more here and there are not even matter for comment. Under such conditions can there be serious meaning left in the fine decisions that were elaborated by scholastic theologians in the day of hand-to-hand combat? Can we assume that in atomic war the conditions which make double effect legitimate will be realized? Obviously not. And to make this perfectly clear, the explicit and formal declarations of governments leave no doubt that indiscriminate destruction is intended.

In atomic war, there is no longer the question of simply permitting an evil, the destruction of a few civilian dwellings, in order to attain a legitimate end: the destruction of a military target. It is well understood on both sides that atomic war is purely and simply massive and indiscriminate destruction of targets chosen not for their military significance alone, but for the importance in a calculated project of terror and annihilation. Often the selection of the target is determined by some quite secondary and accidental circumstance that has not the remotest reference to morality. Hiroshima was selected for atomic attack, among other reasons, because it had never undergone any noticeable air bombing and was suitable, as an intact target, to give a good idea of the effectiveness of the bomb.

It must be frankly admitted that some of the military commanders of both sides in World War II simply disregarded all traditional standards that were still effective. The Germans threw those standards overboard with the bombs they unloaded on Warsaw, Rotterdam, Coventry and London. The allies replied in kind with the saturation bombing of Hamburg, Cologne, Dresden and Berlin. Spokesmen were not wanting on either side, to justify these crimes against humanity. And today, while "experts" calmly discuss the possibility of the United States being able to survive a war if "only fifty millions" (!) of the population were killed; when the Chinese speak of being able to "spare" three hundred million and "still get along," it is obvious that we are no longer in the realm where moral truth is conceivable.

The only sane course that remains is to work frankly and without compromise for the total abolition of war. The pronouncements of the Holy See all point to this as the only ultimate solution. The first duty of the Christian is to help clarify thought on this point by taking the stand that all-out nuclear, bacterial or chemical warfare is unacceptable as a practical solution to international problems because it would mean the destruction of the world. There is simply no "good end" that renders such a risk permissible or even thinkable on the level of ordinary common sense.

At this point someone will say, "The Church has not condemned nuclear war." First of all there is no need to condemn something that already quite obviously stands condemned by its very nature. Total war is murder. The fact that the Church tolerates limited war and even theoretically tolerates the limited use of "tactical" nuclear weapons for defensive purposes does not mean that she either advocates or tolerates indiscriminate killing of civilians and military. Pope Pius XII, in 1954, made this perfectly clear. He said: "Should the evil consequences of adopting this method of warfare ever become so extensive as to pass entirely beyond the control of man, then indeed its use must be rejected as immoral." Uncontrolled annihilation of human life is "not lawful under any title." There is much debate over the term "entirely beyond control." If a missile with a nuclear warhead can be aimed so as to destroy Leningrad rather than Helsinki, is this sufficient to be termed control? One doubts this was the mind of Pius XII.

It might be possible to get people to admit this in theory, but it is going to be very difficult in practice. They will admit the theory because they will say that they "certainly do not want a war" in which nuclear agents will be used on an all-out scale. Obviously no one wants the destruction of the human race or of his own nation, although he will not admit it in practice because foreign policy entirely depends on wielding the threat of nuclear destruction. But it is an issue of such desperate seriousness, we have to face the fact that the calculated use of nuclear weapons as a political threat is almost certain to lead eventually to a hot war. Every time another hydrogen bomb is exploded in a test, every time a political leader boasts his readiness to use the same bomb on the cities of his enemy, we get closer to the day when the missiles armed with nuclear warheads will start winging their way across the seas and the polar ice cap.

The danger must be faced. Whoever finds convenient excuses for this adventurous kind of policy, who rationalizes every decision dictated by political opportunism and justifies it, must stop to consider that he may be himself cooperating in the evil. On the contrary, our duty is to help emphasize with all the force at our disposal that the Church earnestly seeks the abolition of war; we must underscore declarations like those of Pope John XXIII pleading with world leaders to renounce force in the settlement of international disputes and confine themselves to negotiation.

Let us suppose that the political leaders of the world, supported by the mass media in their various countries, and carried onward by a tidal wave of even greater and greater war preparations, see themselves swept inexorably into a war of disastrous proportions. Let us suppose that it becomes morally certain that these leaders are helpless to arrest the blind force of the process that has been irresponsibly set in motion. What then? Are the masses of the world, including you and me, to resign themselves to their fate and march on to global suicide without resistance, simply bowing their heads and obeying their leaders as showing them the "will of God"? I think it should be evident to everyone that this can no longer, in the present situation, be accepted unequivocally as Christian obedience and civic duty.

On the contrary, this brings us face to face with the greatest and most agonizing moral issue of our time. This issue is not merely nuclear war, not merely the possible destruction of the human race by a sudden explosion of violence. It is something more subtle and more demonic.

If we continue to yield to theoretically irresponsible determinism and to vague "historic forces" without striving to resist and to control them, if we let these forces drive us to demonic activism in the realm of politics and technology, we face something more than the material evil of universal destruction. We face *the moral responsibility of global suicide*. Much more than that, we are going to find ourselves gradually moving into a situation in which we are practically compelled by the "logic of circumstances" deliberately *to choose the course that leads to destruction*.

We all know the logic of temptation. We all know the vague, hesitant irresponsibility which leads us into the situation where it is no longer possible to turn back and how, arrived in that situation, we have a moment of clear-sighted desperation in which we freely commit ourselves to the course that we recognize to be evil. That may well be what is happening now to the whole world. The actual destruction of the human race is an enormous evil, but it is still, in itself, only a physical evil. Yet the free choice of global suicide, made in desperation by the world's leaders and ratified by the consent and cooperation of all their citizens, would be a moral evil second only to the crucifixion. The fact that such a choice might be made with the highest motives and the most urgent purpose would do nothing whatever to mitigate it. The fact that it might be made as a gamble, in the hope that some might escape, would never excuse it. After all, the purposes of Caiphas were, in his own eyes, perfectly noble. He thought it was necessary to let "one man die for the people."

The most urgent necessity of our time is therefore not merely to prevent the destruction of the human race by nuclear war. Even if it should happen to be no longer possible to prevent the disaster (which God forbid), there is still a greater evil that can and must be prevented. It must be possible for every free man to refuse his consent and deny his cooperation to this greatest of crimes.

In what does this effective and manifest refusal of consent consist? How does one "resist" the sin of genocide? How are the conscientious objectors to mass suicide going to register their objection and their refusal to cooperate? Ideally speaking, in the imaginary case where all-out nuclear war seemed inevitable and the world's leaders seemed morally incapable of preventing it, it would become legitimate and even obligatory for all sane and conscientious men everywhere in the world to lay down their weapons and their tools and starve and be shot rather than cooperate in the war effort. If such a mass movement should spontaneously arise in all parts of the world, in Russia and America, in China and France, in Africa and Germany, the human race could be saved from extinction. This is indeed an engaging hypothesis—but it is no more than that. It would be folly to suppose that men hitherto passive, inert, morally indifferent and irresponsible might suddenly recover their sense of obligation and their awareness of their own power when the world was on the very brink of war. Indeed we have already reached that point. Who says "No!" except for a few isolated individuals regarded almost generally as crackpots by everybody else?

It is vitally necessary that we form our conscience in regard to our own participation in the effort that threatens to lead us to universal destruction. We have to be convinced that there are certain things already clearly forbidden to all men, such as the use of torture, the killing of hostages, genocide (or the mass extermination of racial, national or other groups for no reason than that they belong to an "undesirable" category). The destruction of civilian centers by nuclear annihilation bombing is genocide. We have to become aware of the poisonous effect of the mass media that keep violence, cruelty and sadism constantly present in the minds of uninformed and irresponsible people. We have to recognize the danger to the whole world in the fact that today the economic life of the more highly-developed nations is centered largely on the production of weapons, missiles and other engines of destruction. We have to consider that hate propaganda, and the consistent nagging and baiting of one government by another, has always inevitably led to violent conflict. We have to recognize the implications of voting for politicians who promote policies of hate.

These are activities which, in view of their possible consequences, are so dangerous and absurd as to be morally intolerable. If we cooperate in these activities we share in the guilt they incur before God. It is no longer reasonable or right to leave all decisions to a largely anonymous power elite that is driving us all, in our passivity, towards ruin. We have to make ourselves heard. Christians have a grave responsibility to protest clearly and forcibly against trends that lead inevitably to crimes which the Church deplores and condemns. Ambiguity, hesitation and compromise are no longer permissible. War must be abolished. A world government must be established. We have still time to do something about it, but the time is rapidly running out.

· 5 ·

RED OR DEAD:
The Anatomy of a Cliche

Published in Fellowship, *March 1962*

Sweating out the adverse criticisms of his *Commonweal* article and doing several rewrites of it put no damper on Merton's compulsion to publish on war-peace issues. In March 1962, Merton saw the appearance of "Red or Dead: The Anatomy of a Cliche" in *Fellowship*, "Testament to Peace: Father Max Metzger's Thoughts about the Duty of a Christian" in *Jubilee*, and "Christian Ethics and Nuclear War" in *The Catholic Worker*.

"Red or Dead" was published without being submitted to the censors. Merton wrote to John Heidbrink, editor of *Fellowship*, that Father Abbot had decided (with a bit of help, perhaps?) that the statutes of the Order did not require censorship for the publication of articles appearing in a small magazine with a "restricted influence." *Fellowship*, Merton felt, fit this category.

In a footnote to the article he explains the meaning of the title: "In the current use of this phrase it would seem that Red means 'under Communist rule' and not 'converted to Communism,' though those who use the phrase with conviction seem to believe that if one is under Communist rule one is likely to be easily converted, hence 'better dead than red.'"

* * * * *

When an issue of credible gravity can be made to depend on an insane half truth, it becomes important to analyze the so-called "thinking" that is involved.

The whole world is in the grip of pathological war preparations—all initiated in order to "preserve peace"—and we find men who are considered sane, seriously resolving the whole problem into the alternative: "red or dead." Either you survive and become a Communist, or else risk annihilation in the act of destroying communism. For the latter, the destruction of communism has become the one all-important aim of life, more important than the survival of civilization, crucial enough to risk the annihilation of the entire human race.

To put it coldly and bluntly, the policy of nuclear deterrence which the majority of Americans, Christian and non-Christian alike, seem to have implicitly accepted, at least in a general, tacit way by not protesting against it, depends on a readiness to annihilate completely without warning, the great civilian population centers of the enemy country, together with their military installations. It is for this end that we are paying taxes. It is from the preparations for nuclear war that a very significant percentage of the population is deriving its income either directly or indirectly. It is on these preparations that the whole economy of the country rests.

In these circumstances I wonder if the cliche about being Red or dead does not acquire a sinister hidden meaning. I wonder if, after all, without quite realizing the fact, we are beginning to feel that our own inner contradictions are beyond solution, and are beginning to sense the climax of despair which they have prepared for us.

From the moment you take the "red or dead" cliche as the expression of a realistic alternative, from the moment you pretend to base serious discussion upon this alternative, you are implicitly admitting the following propositions, which I for one find completely untenable.

1—You are saying that the very survival of democracy is bound up with total nuclear war. That without recourse to the threat of total nuclear war, without the readiness to wage such a war, without the ability to annihilate the enemy by a "first strike," the survival of democracy, freedom and western civilization are no longer conceivable.

2—In other words, you are saying that it is not possible for democracy, for western civilization, to survive by peaceful means. That we have exhausted the resources of humanity and reasonableness which would make negotiation thinkable except on a basis of terror.

3—You are saying that if we of the West survive at all, we can only survive as Communists. That is a choice between surviving and becoming a Communist, or dying in defense of the ideals of democracy, the capitalist economy, freedom, the American Way of Life. If you push this far enough you are simply implying that the American Way of Life cannot survive except by war, but that communism can survive without recourse to total nuclear war.

4—You are also saying that since for the Communists survival automatically means victory, they must be prevented at all cost from surviving. That since for the West survival without nuclear war practically means defeat, then to reject nuclear war in order to survive is purely and simply to admit defeat.

5—The last assumption is at once the most horrible, the most absurd and the most revealing. It is purely and simply that if we are reduced to a choice between the survival of the Communists and the destruction of the entire human race, then the brave, noble, heroic and even *Christian* course is to choose the destruction of the human race. This is of course not frankly admitted, because their reasoning always leaves a kind of irrational loophole for "survival." There is always a *chance* that some "fifty million on our side" might be left standing after everyone else had been blown up. No one seems to consider the possibility that such survival might be at once culpable, subhuman and infernally awful.

Insane Reasoning

To my mind this whole line of "reasoning" is purely and simply insane, if not actually demonic. For all its gestures of conquest it is a mentality of defeat. It is nothing but appeasement in reverse—it does not grovel, but it destroys itself, assuming there is no alternative between groveling and destruction. Such an assumption is a pure surrender to irrationality and to hysteria. Nothing could be more directly contrary to the spirit of liberty, and of reasonable initiative characteristic of the American tradition.

1—This kind of thinking represents a *mentality of defeat.* All down the line it presumes that democratic values are not strong enough to prevail by peaceful means. All down the line it accepts the very arguments which Marx long ago drew up against the capitalist system: *that it could not survive except by recourse to war,* and that *it would resort to any extreme* in order to crush opposition. To admit this Marxian analysis as the last word on western civilization is, it seems to me, a complete moral and intellectual capitulation. It means the complete justification of all the self-righteous arguments on which the Communists base their hostility to us.

2—It represents a mentality of *despair.* While claiming to believe in democratic ideals, in freedom, in the creativity supposedly inherent in our way of life, it admits in reality a *radical doubt of all these values.* It has no practical faith in them because it cannot believe they have retained enough power to overcome the opposition raised by communism. Only nuclear weapons can do the trick. This attitude is the result of the secularist, irreligious pragmatic spirit which has actually undermined the whole moral structure of the West. It springs from the emptiness, the resentment, the sense of futility and meaninglessness which gnaw secretly at the heart of western man.

3—It is finally nothing else than a *mentality of suicide*. It is the self-destructive, self-hating resentment that follows from accumulated petty humiliations, repeated errors, reiterated blunders and stupidities with which we have continually lost face before those whom we secretly despised. In order to release the pent-up and desperate pressures of our self-hate we are now ready to destroy ourselves and the whole world with us in one grand explosion. And we justify ourselves by claiming that we prefer death (for ourselves and everyone else) to tyranny. What right have we to choose death for everyone else? Is not that an act of supreme tyranny and injustice?

The Nazi Mentality

Where have we seen this kind of thinking before? We do not have to look far. Have we already forgotten Hitler? Have we already forgotten his paranoid hatreds, his love for "definitive solutions," for "finalizing" such problems as the existence of races he did not happen to like? Have we forgotten his ultimate determination to bring all Germany down with himself to destruction? Have we forgotten that for the Nazis the greatest virtue, the greatest reasonableness, was to be found in blind obedience to the destructive mania of the Fuehrer?

Those in this country who are now seriously thinking that it would be worthwhile to risk the destruction of the whole world rather than allow it to become Communist are not only defeatists who have lost their grasp of the democratic ideal, they are thinking like Hitler. They have a Nazi mentality. And unfortunately they have much more powerful weapons of destruction than the Nazis ever knew. Their so-called "thought," their puerile aberrations are no small matter. In so far as they are prepared seriously to implement their thinking by destructive action, these men are already war criminals. And those who follow them in their line of thought are in danger of becoming criminals themselves.

Total War Is Mass Murder

Summary and conclusion: We are rational and responsible beings. *No form of defeatism is permitted to us, neither appeasement nor bullying.*

We have no right to solve our problems by blowing ourselves up. Even if it were possible to destroy Russia and survive ourselves, this would not be permitted. It would be a crime greater than any of Hitler's acts of genocide and such crimes never go unpunished. We have no right to abandon the Christian moral values on which our society was built and adopt the moral opportunism and irresponsibility of atheistic materialism. If we live and act like atheists we will turn our world into a living hell, and that is precisely what we are doing—for the Russians are not the only men in the world who are Godless! We who still try to be Christians must be warned. Even for the best of ends it is not permitted to do evil. Total war is nothing but mass murder.

We have got to find a human and reasonable way of solving our problems. And above all we must refuse to believe in any form of propaganda which tell us that nuclear war is necessary and right. We must say *no* to all such propaganda and demand that our government continue to seek a sane and prudent way to disarmament. If we give up hope of the only rational solution our blood and the blood of all mankind will be upon our own heads.

· 6 ·

TESTAMENT TO PEACE:
Father Metzger's Thoughts
About the Duty of the Christian

Published in Jubilee, *March, 1962*

In a letter of November 13, 1961, Merton accepted from John Heidbrink, executive secretary of the Fellowship of Reconciliation, the offer of the loan of a life of Father Max Metzger, a Roman Catholic priest who was martyred by the Nazis in 1943. Merton wrote an article on Father Metzger together with a selection of some of his sayings. He apparently sent mimeographed copies to friends. On February 15, 1962 he wrote Heidbrink: "I have had a lot of good reactions from the piece on Father Metzger." He speaks of Karl Stern, who knew Metzger in Germany and who told Merton that he "prayed to" Father Metzger every day. Merton suggested that his name not be attached to the article. "I regard it," Merton said, "as his material rather than mine."

It got published—anonymously—not in *Fellowship* but in *Jubilee*. The article was set up in two columns: the larger with Father Metzger's words, and a kind of sidebar with Merton's words. Here only Merton's reflections will be given, though I will offer two brief samples from Father Metzger's writings:

a. "I HAVE OFFERED MY LIFE FOR THE PEACE OF THE WORLD AND THE UNITY OF CHRIST'S CHURCH. GOD HAS ACCEPTED IT AND I AM GLAD."

b. "THE NEED OF OUR DAY—AND THROUGH IT GOD IS SPEAKING TO US—IMPERATIVELY DEMANDS THE UTMOST EFFORT TO HEAL THE DISMEMBERMENT OF THE CHRISTIAN CHURCH, TO MAKE CHRIST'S KINGDOM OF PEACE EFFECTUAL THROUGHOUT THE WORLD."

. . . . .

When Hitler finally plunged the Western World into war by his attack on Poland, the German Catholics, and especially the German Catholic press, feeling that their duty was first of all to support Reich und Volk, followed Hitler into battle without complaint. The Catholic who might perhaps have suffered from some pangs of conscience was officially reassured that this was a perfectly "just war." We who are far removed from the scene can judge the situation with critical and perhaps severe detachment. We can see, for instance, for what understandable reasons the German Catholic press at that time wanted to continue in existence, and supported Hitler's war effort in order to avoid immediate suppression. We forget that here and there in the columns of Catholic papers and magazines were items which said much to those who knew how to read between the lines, and which could hardly be published without heroism on the part of those who knew how closely their proofs were scrutinized by the Gestapo.

The example of Father Max Josef Metzger, a Catholic priest executed by Hitler's Gestapo in the Brandenburg Prison, Berlin, on April 17, 1944, should make us realize that not everyone needs to be a passive utensil of the militarist. Father Metzger was a true patriot. He never failed his country, even though in Hitler's eyes he was a "traitor to Reich and Fuehrer." He died for Germany just as heroically and just as wholeheartedly as any soldier who fell on the battlefield. And he died for peace. It was indeed his attempt to work out a plan for peace in conjunction with bishops in other countries, that was regarded by Hitler as "treason."

Father Metzger had been a chaplain in World War I. He had revolted against the senseless horrors of a war that achieved nothing, that only brought about moral and physical destruction and prepared the way for a still greater cataclysm.

Right after the war he became a devoted worker in the cause of peace. He was in contact with the International Fellowship of Reconciliation. He attended many peace conferences and congresses, and founded a secular institute, the Society of Christ the King, devoted to the lay apostolate and works of mercy, particularly to work in the cause of international peace. He was also ardently devoted to the cause of Christian unity. He was, with Abbe Couturier in France, one of the most original and far-sighted precursors of the present flourishing Catholic ecumenical movement. His best-known work is the UNA SANCTA movement which began in 1939 with the retreat of a group of Catholic and Protestant clergymen, together, in search of a basis for agreement and fraternal union that would remotely prepare the way for Christian unity. UNA SANCTA is today one of the most lively and flourishing of Catholic ecumenical endeavors.

Father Metzger was arrested three times before his last imprisonment which ended with his execution. He was jailed by the Gestapo in 1934, 1938, 1939 and finally in 1943. The first three prison terms involved sedulous examination of Father Metzger, in an effort to pin some kind of charge on him, and especially to implicate him in a conspiracy against the Fuhrer. He was not engaged in any such conspiracy.

What finally emerged as "treason" sufficient to warrant a death sentence was his sincere, almost naive effort to get a peace plan going which he thought would end the war. Through the intermediary of a Swedish woman, who was interested in UNA SANCTA, Father Metzger wanted to get letters out of Germany to bishops in various warring and neutral countries. He thought that the bishops would be able to influence their governments to seek a negotiated peace instead of the "unconditional surrender" that was to cost Germany so many burned and gutted cities, so many thousands of civilian dead. The Swedish lady turned out to be a Gestapo agent. The Metzger letters, suggesting as they did that Germany needed to be "spared" and that the Reich would not come back to destroy all her enemies, was of course regarded as treason by Hitler.

Let us remember this formula: in the madness of modern war, when every crime is justified, the nation is always right, power is always right, the military is always right. To question those who wield power, to differ from them in any way, is to confess oneself subversive, rebellious, traitorous. Father Metzger did not believe in power, in bombs. He believed in Christ, in unity, in peace. He died as a martyr for his belief.

· 7 ·

CHRISTIAN ETHICS AND NUCLEAR WAR

Published in The Catholic Worker, *March 1962*

"Christian Ethics and Nuclear War" was published while the censors were still debating about it. On February 5, 1962 Merton wrote to James Forest, editor of *The Catholic Worker* to hold up the printing of the article. Through some misunderstanding it was published. A footnote by Merton in the April issue of the *Worker* attempted to explain the misunderstanding.

· · · · ·

When the preparations for the Second Vatican Council began to be discussed, a writer in *Réalités* produced an article which was not lacking in astute intuitions. It was called "The Last Chance Council." Doubtless this provoking title was dismissed by most of us Catholics as the flippancy of an irreligious mind. One feels nevertheless that the present cold war crisis has brought home, at least obscurely, to many Christians, whether Catholic or Protestant, a sense that the Church is now facing a test that may prove to be decisive and perhaps in some sense "final." Christianity may be on the point of being driven back into the catacombs and losing, in the process, millions of faithful.

Worse still, the possibility of the complete destruction of human society and even extinction of life on the planet might, if Christians themselves were deeply involved in responsibility for it, be in some sense on their part a disastrous failure and betrayal. Though these fears have generated a climate of wide-spread uneasiness and even of implicit desperation, they are not without certain correlative hopes. We believe that the Church could not be brought face to face with any desperate situation which did not at the same time contain a challenge and a promise. For Christians to come "under judgment" in a historical crisis implies not mere blind doom, but rather a difficult choice, a "temptation" if you like, and one in which the future of Christianity and of the whole world may hinge on the heroism and integrity of the faithful. In other words, we find ourselves confronting the possibility of nuclear war with more than the common and universal urgency because we Christians are at least dimly aware that this is a matter of choice for us and that the future of Christianity on earth may depend on the moral quality of the decisions we are making.

This is the climate in which all Christians are facing (or refusing to face) the most crucial moral and religious problem in twenty centuries of history.

It is doubtful whether for most Christians the real underlying religious issue is clearly visible. On the contrary, at least in America, the average priest and minister seems to react in much the same way as the average agnostic or atheist. The interests of the west, the NATO, and the Church are all confused with one another, and the possibility of defending the west with a nuclear first strike on Russia is accepted without too much hesitation as "necessary" and a "lesser evil." We assume without question that western society equals Christendom and Communism equals Antichrist. And we are ready to declare without hesitation that "no price is too high" to pay for our religious liberty. The cliches sound noble, perhaps, to those who are not shocked by its all too evident meaninglessness. The fact is that genocide is too high a price and no one, not even Christians, not even for the highest ideals, has the right to take measures that may destroy millions of innocent noncombatants and even whole defenseless populations of neutral nations or unwilling allies. Note that some of these nations might be Christian, at least in principle. The bland assumption is always, of course that nuclear warheads, ICMB's and polaris submarines are dictated by "prudence." There seems to be very little awareness that this position is not only psychologically irresponsible, but plainly immoral according to all Christian standards and by that very fact supremely imprudent. Such thinking, or rather thoughtlessness, is due to the slow corruption of the Christian ethical sense by theorizing in a vacuum, juggling with moral cliches devoid of serious content, and the weakening of genuine human compassion. The scandalous consequences of this has been not only confusion, inertia, indecision and even culpable silence on the part of many Christian spokesmen, but worse still some Christian leaders have actively joined in the Cold War and call on God Himself to justify the moral blindness and hubris of generals and industrialists, and to bless nuclear war as a holy and apocalyptic crusade. As C. Wright Mills has said, "Priests and Ministers have fallen over one another to enlist in 'the Swiss Guard' of the poor elite."

While this blindness and confusion are common to great numbers of Christians, nominal or otherwise, there are also strong and articulate movements against war. At this moment of crisis they are gaining in strength, in spite of the increasing pressure of suspicion and disapproval. For the unpleasant fact is that the Russians have succeeded in getting the cause of peace identified in the popular mind with the cause of the Soviet Bloc. Hence anyone who dared to stand up for peace and disarmament in the West, by that very fact runs the risk of being called a fellow traveler. This is one of the most disturbing aspects of the thoughtless passivity, the crude opportunism and astonishing lack of discernment which have become characteristic of western political thought in the cold war. But the fact that our politicians have let themselves be out-maneuvered by more subtle and better organized adversaries does not dispense us from promoting reasonable and persistent peace negotiations whether the position happens to be popular or not. It should be immediately clear to any objective observer that the western defender of peace and of disarmament, even if he has no special ideology at all, is plainly concerned with the survival of western freedom and democracy. This is especially true of Christian movements like Fellowship of Reconciliation. In Europe the FOR unites Catholics and Protestants. In America it is exclusively Protestant, not by choice but due to unfortunate circumstances in this country. A Pax group, an offshoot of the English Pax movement, is now being formed to concentrate Catholic opposition to nuclear war in the U.S. and to articulate Christian policies for peace. Those who have joined fully expect to receive harsh criticism and opposition from their co-religionists but they feel that the crisis is too serious for them to remain silent and inactive without incurring moral guilt. The members of Pax are not necessarily pure pacifists. They are opposed however to all nuclear war.

The popular image of the Catholic Church, particularly of American Catholicism, does not readily admit such a possibility as this. Catholics are regarded as a monolithic mass, directed passively from above, without thoughts or feelings of their own. The outspoken hostility with which right-wing Catholics have reacted to the Encyclical *Mater et Magistra* as socialistic ought to warn the rest of men that the phenomenon of Catholic "passivity" is more complex than they realize.

Recent official statements of the American Catholic Bishops deplore the irresponsibility and secularism which affects Catholics as much as everybody else. This would suggest that the American Catholic tends to be a passive unit in the affluent mass society of the U.S.A. and that he consecrates the values of this secular society with a few authoritative formulas he has heard in the pulpit.

This is especially true in the matter of war. It is commonly said, even by Catholics, that "the Church has never condemned nuclear war," which is completely false. Of course the Pope has never pronounced as an **ex cathedra** definition which would formally outlaw nuclear war. Why should he? Does every **infima species** of mortal sin need to be defined and denounced by the extraordinary magisterium? Do we now need an **ex cathedra** fulmination against adultery before Catholics will believe themselves bound in conscience to keep the 6th commandment? There is no need for nuclear war to be solemnly outlawed by an extraordinary definition. It should not even need to be condemned by the ordinary papal teaching. In fact, however, it has been so condemned.

The Christmas messages of Pope Pius XII during and after World War II became stronger and stronger in their denunciation of total war and all those policies by which the allies, with a "good conscience," forced the unconditional surrender of their enemies. Already in 1944, before Hiroshima, Pope Pius asserted that "the theory of war as an apt and proportionate means of solving international conflicts is now out of date" and declared that the duty of banning all wars of aggression was binding on all. This duty "brooks no delay, no procrastination, no hesitation, no subterfuge." Few, it seems, were listening. The saturation bombing of open cities was purely and simply mass murder by Christian moral standards and it is sophistry to argue that because this was "tolerated" the H-bomb automatically becomes legitimate. Pope Pius XII denounced nuclear annihilation bombing very clearly and without any possibility of being mistaken. He declared that from the moment a weapon was so large and so destructive that it wiped out everything and everyone indiscriminately, it could not be tolerated by Christian morality. Here are his words:

> Should the evil consequences of adopting this method of warfare ever become so extensive as to pass utterly beyond the control of man, then indeed its use must be rejected as immoral. In that event it would no longer be a question of defense against injustice and necessary protection of legitimate possessions but of the annihilation pure and simple of all human

life within the affected area. That is not lawful on any title. (Address to the World Medical Association, Sept., 1954)

We must note that this applies equally to offensive and defensive war. While it is obligatory to defend one's nation against unjust aggression, only legitimate means can be taken for this. And if the destructive effect of war is far greater than the political injustice suffered, war is not legitimate. "If the damage caused by war is disproportionate to the injustice suffered, it may well be a matter of obligation to suffer the injustice," said Pope Pius XII to army doctors on October 19, 1953.

These are of course general statements of principle which are meant to be clarified by the Bishops, theologians and clergy. The Pope does not make individual moral decisions for all the members of the Church, but enunciates and defines the norms according to which they should make their personal decisions for themselves. Unfortunately, statements like this one on nuclear war, though dutifully reported in the press and respectfully noted by the faithful, are seldom really assimilated by them. That is why the serious moral implications of the measured-Papal denunciations of nuclear war seem to have been overlooked.

The Popes have not merely been trying to say that nuclear war is not nice, but that it upsets traditional Catholic norms of the morality of war. In plain language this is an essentially new kind of war and one in which the old concept of the "just war" is irrelevant because the necessary conditions for such a war no longer exist. A war of total annihilation simply cannot be considered a "just war," no matter how good the cause for which it is undertaken.

Such is the view taken by no less authoritative a theologian than Cardinal Ottaviani, Secretary of the Holy Office. Writing before the development of the H-bomb, Cardinal (then Monsignor) Ottaviani says this without ambiguity:

> The war of their treatises is not the war of our experience . . . Principles derive from the very nature of things: the difference between war as it was and war as we know it is precisely one of nature . . . Modern wars can never fulfill the conditions which govern, theoretically, a just and lawful war. Moreover no conceivable cause could ever be sufficient justification for the evils, the slaughter, the moral and religious upheavals which war today entails.

Such is the thesis in an article entitled "War Is To Be Forbidden Entirely," published in Latin in his **Public Laws of the Church** (Rome 1947). Unfortunately such opinions have not been widely disseminated, although Bishop Fulton J. Sheen has publicly taken the same standpoint in this country.

It must be said also that statements like this do not exclude the use of nuclear weapons in tactical warfare, assuming that such warfare can be "kept within limits," a possibility which hardly interests the military mind of 1962.

Perhaps the most cogent and articulate statements of Catholic opinion on nuclear war are now coming from Europe. A German Dominican, Father Franziskus Strattmann, has courageously broken through the conventional thought barriers to discover how, in the Middle Ages, the Gospel ethic was "supplemented—perhaps we must say stifled—by religiously neutral natural law," and from this developed the theory of just wars, whose elastic principles were to be stretched indefinitely by later casuistry until they have now reached the breaking point. He admits nevertheless that even the natural law clearly repudiates modern war. A recent collection of essays, *Nuclear Weapons and Christian Conscience* (Merlin Press, London 1961), frankly takes the stand that the immoral hypotheses of "realists" who seek to justify nuclear war are "doing more from within to undermine western civilization than the enemy can do from the outside." These Catholic writers protest with all their strength against the "habitual moral squalor" of the prevailing opportunism, and remind the Christian who may have forgotten the Cross that in a situation like ours we may be forced to choose "the ultimate weapon of meaningful suffering" or deny the Christian faith itself. It is absurd and immoral to pretend that Christendom can be defended by the H-bomb.

As St. Augustine would say, the weapon with which we would attempt to destroy the enemy would pass through our own heart to reach him. He would be annihilated morally and no doubt physically as well. The H-bomb may possibly wipe out western society if it is used by Communists, but it will destroy Christendom spiritually if it is used as a weapon of aggression by Christians.

It must be noted that those Catholic writers are not formal pacifists. They admit the traditional theory of the "just war" but feel that this concept is no longer viable. At the same time they attack the extreme argument that Christianity must be by its very nature pacifistic. One of the writers blames this idealistic view for encouraging the opposite cynical extreme, "double think about double effect." The book questions the moral honesty of manufacturing and stockpiling nuclear weapons while "suspending the decision to use them." It questions the morality of using nuclear weapons even as a threat.

Another question: to what extent can the individual claim to remain uncommitted when his government pursues a policy that leads directly to nuclear war? One of the writers answers: "In modern warfare, responsibility for all that is not antecedently, clearly and publicly ruled out must be accepted by anyone who in any way participates in waging the war." This means that if you go to work for Boeing with the impression that you will not have to build bombers, or for Chrysler missiles with a mental reservation that you won't manufacture anything with a warhead, you remain partly responsible for the nuclear war which you have helped to prepare, even though you may have had good intentions and desired nothing but to make an "honest living."

Problems facing the individual conscience are doubtless crucially important, but it would be of little use for individuals to fold their arms with a sweet smile and a pure heart and refuse to take part in political life. The moral and political problems are inextricable from one another, and it is only by sane political action that we can fully satisfy the moral requirements that face us today as Christians. The clarification of the basic moral issue of nuclear war is an all important first step, but there is much to be done after that. What faces us all, Christians and non-Christians alike, is the titanic labor of trying to change the world from a camp of warring barbarians into a peaceful international community from which war has been perpetually banned. Chances of success in this task seem almost ludicrously impossible. Yet if we fail to face this responsibility we will certainly lose everything.

The immediate responsibility of Christians is to contribute whatever they can to an atmosphere of sanity and trust in which negotiations and disarmament may eventually become feasible. But if they continue in ignorance, suspicion, resentment and hatred of Communism, forgetting that the Communist, whatever his failing, is also a human being who might conceivably want peace, they may do more than anyone else to foment the blind, unchristian, murderous rage which makes war inevitable.

A Footnote by Thomas Merton

Published in The Catholic Worker, *April 1962*

The article "Christian Ethics and Nuclear War" which appeared in the last issue of the *Catholic Worker* was unfortunately an uncorrected and unrevised first draft not intended for publication, but which got into print due to a misunderstanding. While I by no means disclaim responsibility for this article, I would like to say that in the form in which it was published it contained errors of perspective which I would have wished to correct, and which might, as they stand, lend themselves to misinterpretation.

In the first place it had never been my intention to say that the Popes have formally outlawed nuclear war. They have certainly deplored every form of unlimited and indiscriminate destruction in war, whether by nuclear or by conventional weapons. They have repeatedly pleaded with world leaders to refrain from nuclear war and from actions leading up to it. But they have also affirmed the traditional teaching on self-defense in such a way that it still remains licit for a theologian to defend "limited war" and the use of "tactical nuclear weapons" which most theologians in the United States seem to do. Though I cannot agree with their arguments I certainly do not deny their right to defend this position.

I must add, however, that I can find nothing in any Papal document that clearly allows a nuclear first strike on the enemy heartland and cities as compatible with Christian morals. Nor do I find anything there that legitimates a first strike even on the military installations of the enemy. And we know today that in practice, a massive attack on military installations would inevitably involve nearby cities.

Heated protest and criticism have been aroused in some quarters by recent articles of mine, in which I suggested that the United States was gradually moving towards a policy that favored a first nuclear strike, if it were deemed expedient. President Kennedy might have seemed to settle this issue in the past by declaring that we would "never strike first." At the same time, it is no secret that Presidents change their minds under pressure of circumstances. Quite recently President Kennedy has formally declared, "In some circumstances we might have to take the initiative" in the use of nuclear weapons. In other words we might very well launch a pre-emptive first strike. At the same time this year sees an increase of nine billion dollars in defense spending, one third of which has been allotted to nuclear weapons. In the matter of first strike: while European theologians in general either declare nuclear weapons to be immoral or allow them only under strictly limited conditions, American theologians have started from the position that "limited war and tactical nuclear weapons" were permissible and moved on to a more hazardous position. Some are now prepared to claim that a nuclear first strike (even megatonic?) might in some circumstances be considered a form of "defense" and hence might be reconciled with the "just war theory." Such reasoning cannot help but give the impression that there are no longer any serious moral restraints in war provided one thinks he has a "just cause." And the Lord knows, we are convinced of that!

In view of this danger which is certainly serious, in spite of the desperately "good intentions" of those who imagine they can keep peace by nuclear threats, my thoughts have been directed to the moods and attitudes which prevail in the American public, especially the Catholic public. I find these moods and attitudes tending more and more to be one-sided, morally insensitive, obtuse, bellicose and even fanatical. Christians will not only accept war, but some actually seem to want it.

It is true that we have a duty to resist all forms of materialistic and totalitarian encroachments on our religious liberty. But our desperation in the face of an ever growing world-Communism has made it more and more difficult for religious Americans to seriously consider disarmament and negotiations as practical possibilities. Yet there can be no question that the Popes want us to proceed by peaceful means and to avoid war. This does not mean "peace at any price" but it certainly means bolder and more constructive attitudes towards disarmament. If we dismiss all hope of settling our tremendous problems peacefully, we are necessarily going to embark on a course of warlike opportunism in which the Christian conscience will be falsified or even forcibly silenced. As long as we allow ourselves to be convinced that we alone are honest and peace-loving and that the Russians are purely and simply devils in human form, we will fail to see the small opportunities for agreement and we will also tend to give provocation in subtle ways, encouraging them in their own desperate moves. Only a climate of sanity and Christian prudence can avert war. But if Christians themselves become obsessed with prejudice and hatred, a peaceful atmosphere will be impossible to maintain. There is no question this process has long since begun. In a word, we are faced with a choice between trusting in Christ and His Law, or trusting in bombs and missiles. Which way are we going?

8

RELIGION AND THE BOMB

Published in Jubilee, *May 1962*

Upset that "Christian Ethics and Nuclear War" had been published before the censors had given their approval, Merton not only wrote the "Footnote" that appeared in the April issue of *The Catholic Worker*, but also, in a letter of April 28, 1962, apologized to the Abbot General, Gabriel Sortais, for the mistake. He told him that the article would appear in corrected form in *Jubilee*. He even gave the article a new title. In a letter of May 16, 1962, Merton wrote to Ernesto Cardenal: "'Christian Ethics and Nuclear War' was revised and appears in *Jubilee* as 'Religion and the Bomb.'" (*CFT,* 131) Sister Therese Lentfoehr in her catalogue of Merton materials in her possession wrote that the original article was "*heavily reworked* with numerous corrections and inserts in blue ink and red pencil." [The catalogue is at Columbia University, with a copy at the Thomas Merton Study Center, Louisville, Kentucky.]

Yet despite the "heavy reworking," Merton was not happy with this article. On May 8, 1962 he wrote to Wilbur H. Ferry: "I do not realize how strident I have been until I get into print. The one in this month's *Jubilee* will set a whole lot of people on their ear, and I guess it is my fault. I could after all have been more circumspect and moderate, and there are smoother ways of saying the same thing. I lash out with a baseball bat. Some professor of non-violence I am." (*HGL,* 211)

· · · · ·

The developments of the last year have brought home to everyone that war will never be prevented by the sheer menace of nuclear weapons. The H-bomb is too powerful to make war a practical, let alone ethical solution to international problems. An all out nuclear war is something that simply cannot be "won." And yet even though we must agree with the coy statement of Herman Kahn, "Almost nobody wants to be the first man to kill one hundred million people," it turns out that quite a few men, on both sides of the Iron Curtain, are willing to commit themselves to policies and objectives which may make a nuclear war inevitable.

Since the fifth century, Christian theologians and statesmen have accepted the doctrine of the "just war." Theoretically the just war is a *defensive* war in which force is strictly limited and the greatest care is taken to protect the rights and the lives of non-combatants and even of combatants. History teaches us that these requirements were seldom met in practice. Nevertheless, before the invention of gunpowder, the overwhelming advantage in a contest before equally matched forces belonged to the defender in the walled city or castle.

But today the traditional idea of the "just war" is fraught with ambiguities if not outright absurdities, since nuclear weapons are *purely offensive* weapons. Not only that, they are weapons which cannot help but annihilate non-combatants, open cities and even neutrals, due to their enormous and uncontrollable destructive power. Finally, these are weapons against which *there is no really effective defense*. Furthermore, it seems that nuclear weapons are very likely to be used in a massive all out first strike if they are to be used at all. If tactical nuclear weapons are used in a so-called "limited war" there is no guarantee whatever that the loser will not resort to massive and megatonic retaliation. For a belligerent to control himself in this matter he would have to be far more heroically virtuous than if he were to disarm completely and trust in divine providence.

Hence the theologian is faced with a problem of great complexity if he wants to justify nuclear war by traditional Christian methods.

Meanwhile, in the prevailing climate of uneasiness with the growing realization that huge stockpiles of nuclear weapons and new missiles not only do not deter a nuclear strike but may well invite one, Christians are beginning to see that the first strike does not necessarily have to come from the Communist side. Though it is true that President Kennedy has declared that the United States would "never strike first," it has been known for presidents to change their minds under pressure and in any case there are many possibilities of accident, miscalculation, misinterpretation and plain confusion which might lead to a first strike in the name of Democracy, Liberty and—Christianity!

The mere suggestion of such a possibility still raises furious protest. One is asked immediately to "prove" it. Well, the United States has been doing a great job preparing for nuclear war, and has given special attention to making our nuclear strike capacity fully *credible*.

Our government clearly wants everyone to know that we have the biggest and best supply of nuclear weapons in the world and that we intend to use them whenever we feel sufficiently provoked to do so. The whole concept of deterrence, on which hopes of peace are still being based by "realists," depends on the *credibility* of this threat. The Russians on their own side are uttering even greater threats. When the full force of two huge mass societies and all their propaganda are devoted to putting this idea across, who am I to disbelieve? I find all that they say about their readiness and willingness to wage a nuclear war as entirely credible.

In this grave crisis the future of Christianity and of the whole world may hinge on the heroism and integrity of the faithful. In other words, we find ourselves confronting the possibility of nuclear war with more than common and universal urgency, because we Christians are at least dimly aware that this may still be a matter of *choice* for us and that the future of Christianity on earth may depend on the moral quality of the decision we are making.

It is doubtless confusing to say that the "future of Christianity" is now at stake. What is Christianity? Is it the Church? Is it Christian civilization? The mere clarification of terms would require an article to itself. Let us briefly note three points:

1. The future of the Church, the Body of Christ, is not subject to the vagaries of political history. There is and there can be no ambiguity and no uncertainty about the Church's fulfillment of her appointed task on earth. For the Church is Christ Himself, present in the world He has redeemed, present in mystery, in poverty, in ways that are a scandal to human wisdom and to the ruthless leaders of men. Just as "the world" defeated itself in condemning to death the Lord of glory, so now also worldly power works for its own confusion and for the establishment of the Kingdom of God even when it attacks that Kingdom most savagely and, it would seem, with the greatest chance of final success.

2. But taking "Christianity" in a wider sense, we are confronted with a far different situation. Christianity can be taken to signify the whole complex of Judaeo-Christian attitudes, beliefs and culture. It signifies all the basic and vital assumptions which have formed the world-view of the West, and on which western civilization has been built. More than that, it can even be taken to include implicitly all that

is rich and spiritual in all cultures in so far as these riches can be understood to be "naturally Christian."

"Christianity," in this sense, has been the mother and protector of all that is good in Western humanism, in culture, in free society. Without Christianity the virtues, the tolerance, the humaneness, the philanthropy which have been taken to justify the liberal agnosticism of the nineteenth century, would hardly have been able to exist. Even the vestiges of humanism in Marxist society can be traced to a Judaeo-Christian origin.

Without a broad, humane climate of Christian culture, the Christian faith and the full life of a member of the Church would be practically inaccessible to the average person.

In other words, if "Christianity" is destroyed, life in Christ will become a matter of extraordinary heroism, an austere venture and an unconditional commitment of which very few will be capable, particularly if it means going against the formidable, tyrannic compulsions of mass-society.

3) Whether we like it or not, we have to admit we are already living in a post-Christian world, that is to say a world in which Christian ideas and attitudes are relegated more and more to the minority.

It is frightening to realize that the facade of Christianity which still generally survives has perhaps little or nothing behind it, and that what was once called "Christian society" is little more than a materialistic neo-paganism with a Christian veneer. And where the Christian veneer has been stripped off we see laid bare the awful vacuity of the mass-mind, without morality, without identity, without compassion, without sense, rapidly reverting to tribalism and superstition. Here spiritual religion has yielded to the tribal-totalitarian war dance and to the idolatrous cult of the machine.

Christianity, in a word, is everywhere yielding to the hegemony of naked power.

Although since Hiroshima there has been a semblance of religious and spiritual renewal in the West, and even in some of the Iron Curtain countries, the reality and depth of the renewal can certainly be questioned. It is true that statistics show quantitative growth, but this does not necessarily imply a development in quality. On the contrary, it is often apparent that the religious aspirations of very many are confused, superficial and pathetically insecure.

The Cold War has been playing on these inadequate religious sensibilities. It has aroused the dread of imminent disaster. It has at the same time awakened deep hatreds and indeed it has revealed the profoundest tendencies to destructiveness and to suicidal despair.

Precisely the greatest danger of "Cold War religion" is that it provides these destructive tendencies with an apparent ethical and religious justification. It makes nuclear war look like spiritual heroism. It justifies global suicide as sacrifice and martyrdom. If we had not almost completely lost our innate Christian and religious sense we would be utterly aghast at the perversion of the deepest and most sacred of realities. We would be able to see the awful truth that in many ways the Cold War is *systematically perverting and eroding the Christian conscience.*

This is the climate in which all Christians are facing (or refusing to face) the most crucial moral and religious problem in twenty centuries of history.

It is doubtful whether for most Christians the real underlying religious issue is clearly visible. On the contrary, at least in America, the average priest and minister seems to react in much the same way as the average agnostic or atheist. The interests of the West, the NATO, and the Church are all confused with one another, and the possibility of defending the West with a nuclear first strike on Russia is sometimes accepted without too much hesitation as "necessary" and a "lesser evil." We assume that Western society and Christendom are still identical and that communism equals Antichrist. And we are ready to declare without hesitation that "no price is too high" to pay for our religious liberty. The cliche sounds noble to those who are not shocked by its sinister ambiguities.

"Paying the price" used to be equated with Christian sacrifice, or at least with some form of suffering or hardship in which one's own interests were set aside in view of a higher good. But now when we say "no price is too high" we are, it turns out, counting not only our own megacorpses (hopefully excluding our own sacrificial selves from the ghastly score) but also twenty, fifty, a hundred, two hundred million dead on the enemy side. No price is too high to pay! In an orgy of sacrificial ardor we will not hesitate to sacrifice *their* children. We will not hesitate to contaminate future generations. No price is too high! We will even annihilate neutrals. We will douse the whole hemisphere with lethal fallout. We will go the limit. We will let Europe and the Near East be immolated. We will sacrifice India (whose inhabitants have not, meanwhile, been consulted). We will allow the underdeveloped countries to make the supreme gift of themselves for our religious and political freedoms.

Should it really be necessary to spell out the fact that this slogan—
"No price is too high"—somehow lacks nobility?

Even if it were established beyond doubt that we were really defending religious freedom, this claim (at such cost) would still be absurd and immoral. But are we so sure that when we speak of defending
our liberty, our rights, our personal integrity, we are not purely and
simply talking about irresponsibility, good times, a comfortable life,
the freedom to make the hard sell and the fast buck?

What are we defending? Our religion or our affluence?

Or have we so identified the two that the distinction is no longer
clear?

Cold war and theology

There can be no question that we have to defend in every way possible
the true religious, political and cultural values without which our lives
would lack meaning. But these values cannot be defended by capitulation to a war policy that leads inevitably to the defeat and destruction
of both sides. The arguments of those who are now trying to prove
that an all-out nuclear war can be "won" lack even the semblance of
plausibility. Their own most optimistic figures, based on extremely
bland assumptions which they have fed into their computers, show
that even if America "survived" a victory over Russia she could easily
become a victim of a determined aggressor like Red China, which in
any case will soon have its own nuclear weapons.

While there can be no religious justification for a policy of all-out
nuclear aggression, there is a strong and articulate body of theological
opinion in favor of nuclear deterrence and an "adequate posture of
defense." Father John Courtney Murray, who holds this view, hastens
to qualify it by saying the following:

1) The uninhibited violence of nuclear war "disqualifies it as an apt
and proportionate means for the resolution of international conflicts
and even for the redress of just grievances."

2) Appeal to the *jus belli* "seriously blocks progress of the international community toward that mode of political organization which
Pius XII regarded as the single means for the outlawry of all war,
even of defensive war." (In both these statements Father Murray is
practically paraphrasing words of Pius XII.)

3) While he quotes Pius XII to support his contention that the
stockpiling of atomic weapons for defense is legitimate, he adds "this

does not morally validate everything that goes on at Cape Canaveral
or "Los Alamos."

However, Father Murray does not offer a pacifist solution. Taking
his stand on the natural law and on the traditional just war theory, he
believes that defensive wars may be necessary and that they ought to
be fought with conventional weapons or with small nuclear bombs.
This is all very well on paper, but when we realize that the twenty
kiloton bomb that was dropped on Hiroshima is now regarded as
small and is included among the tactical weapons which Father Murray
would licit, we see that his position is not so simple. Also, footnotes
and other interpolations seem to suggest that he is not only considering
the illicitness of megatonic nuclear weapons but also that he is apparently working toward the idea that even a preemptive strike could be
in some sense regarded as "defense." One wonders if this does not
after all tend to validate morally "everything that goes on at Cape
Canaveral or Los Alamos."

An eminent Catholic theologian in England, Canon L. L. McReavy,
declares with equivocation that this policy of nuclear deterrence, in so
far as it relies on *serious threat of massive nuclear retaliation* against
the cities of the enemy is *morally unacceptable*. In an article published
in the *Clergy Review* two years ago Cannon McReavy states, "A positive intention to commit an immoral act in certain circumstances, however much one may hope they will never arise, *is itself here and now
immoral.*" However, he adds that nuclear weapons may be stockpiled
for possible use against "legitimate (military) targets." Here again we
fall back into the same practical difficulty, for there is no indication
whatever that military strategists are going to make the fine distinction
of the moral theologian. Bombs are bombs, and it is utterly laughable
to suppose that even a five megaton H-bomb would have been constructed for use against "fleet at sea." And what about the fifty megaton bomb?

So Canon McReavy himself admits (in a letter to the *Catholic Herald*) it is probable that nuclear weapons "will not in fact be used with
the discrimination required by the moral law, and I *regard it as morally
certain that if megaton weapons are used at all, even as a last resort
and in self-defense, they will be used immorally.*"

Because of these practical ambiguities there is a strong argument in
favor of "relative" or "nuclear" pacifism.

Perhaps one of the most popular and interesting manifestations of
the growing religious resistance to nuclear war is the collection, *God*

and the H-Bomb (Bellmeadow Press–Bernard Geis Associates, $3.50). This is an anthology of statements, declarations, articles and sermons which have been put together by Steve Allen, who is well known as a fighter for peace. Protestant, Catholic and Jewish leaders in Europe and America are represented here, all stating their conviction that total nuclear war is immoral, and demanding that positive action be taken to prevent it. These statements of philosophers and theologians are supported by official declarations of church groups and by a quotation from Pope Pius XII. Bishop Sheen here goes on record with the statement: "Large scale nuclear warfare which denies all distinction between soldiers and civilians, and which makes nurses, doctors, lepers, infants, the aged and the dying objects of direct attack, is certainly immoral."

The Protestant view of Christian nuclear pacifism is forcefully stated by Dr. Norman K. Gottwald of Andover Newton Theological College: "To call nuclear war Christian sacrifice is to reject all that Jesus stood for: it is surely to transfer orthodox terminology to the cult of the deified state. This is nothing more than western Shintoism." Dr. Gottwald shows quite correctly that the theologian who stretches his theology so far that he supports so-called "nuclear realism" is, in fact, taking the next to last step before a final and complete justification of totalitarian autocracy.

Perhaps the most moving religious analysis of the situation, in this book, is the essay by Rabbi Samuel Dresner on "Man: God and Atomic War." There is no question that the crisis of our time does not reveal its inner significance until it is examined in the light of Biblical revelation. Rabbi Dresner, speaking as one who is saturated with the Old Testament prophets, declares simply that the survival of man depends, now as always, decisively and without equivocation, on an inner revolution of man's spirit, and a full return to that God Who, in the modern world, is singularly and terrifyingly "absent."

A veteran Catholic pacifist, the German Dominican, Father Franziskus Strattmann, who, even in the days of the Weimar Republic and later under Hitler, continued to write, speak and work for peace, is also represented in *God and the H-Bomb*. He shows that in the Middle Ages, the Gospel ethic was "supplemented—perhaps we may say stifled—by religiously neutral law." and from this developed the theory of just wars, whose elastic principles were to be stretched indefinitely by later casuistry until they have now reached the breaking point. He admits nevertheless that even the natural law clearly repudiates modern war.

A recent collection of essays by Catholics, *Nuclear Weapons and Christian Conscience* (Merlin Press, London, 1961), frankly takes the stand that the hypotheses of "realists" who seek to justify nuclear war are "doing more from within to undermine Western civilization than the enemy can do from the outside." These Catholic intellectuals protest with all their strength against the "habitual moral squalor" now prevailing, and remind the Christian who may have forgotten the Cross that in a situation like ours we may be forced to choose "the ultimate weapon of meaningful suffering" or deny the Christian faith itself. It is absurd and immoral to pretend that Christendom can be defended by the H-bomb.

As St. Augustine would say, the weapon with which we would attempt to destroy the enemy would pass through our own heart to reach him. We would be annihilated morally and no doubt physically as well. The H-bomb may possibly wipe out Western society if it is used by the Communists, but it will destroy Christendom spiritually if it is used as a weapon of aggression by Christians.

It must be noted that these Catholic writers are not formal pacifists. They admit the traditional theory of the "just war" but feel that this concept is no longer viable. At the same time they attack the extreme argument that Christianity must be by its very nature pacifistic. One of the writers blames this idealistic view for encouraging the opposite cynical extreme, "doublethink about double effect." The book questions the moral honesty of manufacturing and stockpiling nuclear weapons while "suspending the decision to use them."

Another problem raised by this book: to what extent can the individual claim to remain uncommitted when his government pursues a policy that leads directly to all out nuclear war? One of the writers answers: "In modern warfare, responsibility for all that is not antecedently, clearly and publicly ruled out must be accepted by anyone who in any way participates in waging war."

The fight for peace

This brief sampling of recent articulate religious opposition to nuclear war should encourage us. There is still hope. Religious spokesmen have not all abandoned themselves to silence or equivocation. Yet it remains true that there is still a general apathy and passivity among the faithful and the clergy. Perhaps it is exact to say that they are afflicted with a kind of moral paralysis. Hypnotized by the mass media, which tend to be bellicose, baffled and intimidated by the general atmosphere of suspicion, bewildered by the silence or by the ambiguity of their pastors and religious leaders, and remembering the failure of the peace movements that preceded World War II, people tend to withdraw into a state of passive and fatalistic desperation. There they have been literally run to earth by the shelter salesmen, and have set themselves despondently to digging holes in their backyards against the day when the missiles begin to fly.

What are the chances of a religious peace movement in such a grim situation? They would seem to be very slight. On one hand, the astute and tireless propaganda of the Soviets has succeeded without too much difficulty in giving disarmament a bad name by associating it entirely with Communist cold war pressures. Anyone in the West who speaks up for disarmament, by that very fact automatically runs the risk of being called a Communist agent or a fellow traveler.

Pacifism has a noxious reputation. It is not properly understood. Distinctions between nuclear pacifism and absolute pacifism are not made. The pacifist is automatically categorized as a kind of pathetic idiot, a coward trying to salvage his self-respect by an appeal to confused and sentimental ideals. He can do no good. He only plays into the hands of the enemy.

It is true that pacifist movements tend to attract a certain number of professional oddballs. It is also perfectly true that peace movements in democratic countries run the risk of being exploited by Communist elements, whether secret or overt. But it should not be necessary to state that one can favor a policy of nuclear disarmament, even unilateral, without being a Red, a beatnik or a "pacifist."

It may flatter the self-esteem and serve the material interests of the war-minded politicians to treat pacifism as an esoteric bohemian cult. And this is what keeps the stereotyped image of the long-haired pacifist continually alive. Nevertheless reputable peace movements, like the Fellowship of Reconciliation (F.O.R.), have proved by their long record of integrity and service that they represent the Christian and democratic traditions of the Western world, and mean to defend them by means that have more affinity with the Gospel than with Machiavelli, Hobbes, Hegel, Lenin or Hitler

Far from advocating blind submission to the Red army, such movements believe in firm resistance and they believe that their form of resistance, which is non-violent, stands a far better chance of eventual success than uncontrolled nuclear terror. In short, the reputable peace movements stake their hopes on the power of spiritual weapons rather than on political and military violence.

In so doing, they have managed to earn the derision even of Christians. The fact remains that they have something positive to offer.

The F.O.R. goes back to the time of the first World War. It originated in Europe, where it has long united both Catholics and Protestants in a common front against war and against all forms of social injustice and violence. In America the F.O.R. remains almost exclusively Protestant, not by choice but because of the peculiar Protestant-Catholic tensions that still generally exist here, in spite of our incipient ecumenism.

A Catholic peace movement, *Pax*, an offshoot of the English *Pax*, is now being formed in the U.S. to concentrate and express Catholic opposition to nuclear war in this country. The members of *Pax* are not necessarily pure pacifists. They do however tend to be interested in non-violent methods, and Dom Bede Griffiths, a member of the English group and a Benedictine Prior, has written a stimulating article on non-violence which appears in *God and the H-Bomb*. Considerable interest has been shown also in French Catholic non-violent action. The Dominican, Pie-Raymond Regamey, has written an important book called *Non-Violence and the Christian Conscience*, which is not yet available in English.

Someone will ask: is it after all permissible for a Catholic to be a limited pacifist? Is not even relative pacifism an expression of radicalism and disobedience, which would be unthinkable in a true Catholic? If the Church has not formally and expressly condemned nuclear war, is not the Catholic who claims to be a nuclear pacifist, by that fact pretending to be "more Catholic than the Church?"

Here we must quite frankly face the ambiguous statement that the Church has "never condemned nuclear weapons." Is this really exact?

Certainly the pope has never uttered a formal *ex cathedra* condemnation that would outlaw nuclear war. But is it necessary for him to do this? Is it not sufficient that the principles be clarified by the teaching authority of the Church and left to the faithful to apply for themselves?

There exist more than a score of clear statements by Pius XII and John XXIII which deplore, in the strongest terms, all recourse to war and violence in the settlement of international disputes. These statements are not something new. They were not made necessary by the atomic bomb. Even before World War II, Pope Pius XII warned that war with conventional methods could be criminal. In 1939, after the blitzkreig in Poland, Pope Pius declared that the unlawful use of *conventional* weapons against civilians and refugees "cried out to heaven for vengeance."

He also said, in October, 1953, that "all glorification of war is to be condemned as a deviation of the mind and heart." In his 1944 Christmas Message, before Hiroshima, he had asserted that "the theory of war was as an apt and proportionate means of solving international conflicts is now out of date," and he declared that the duty of banning all wars of aggression was *binding on all.*" This duty, he said, *"brooks no delay, no procrastination, no hesitation, no subterfuge.*" Pope Pius XII denounced nuclear annihilation bombing very clearly and without any possibility of being mistaken. In an address to the World Medical Association in 1954, he declared that from the moment a weapon was so destructive that its effects could not be controlled and limited to military objectives, it became immoral. Here are his words:

> "Should the evil consequences of adopting this method of warfare ever become so extensive as to pass utterly beyond the control of man, then indeed its use must be rejected as immoral. In that event it would no longer be a question of defense against injustice and necessary protection of legitimate possessions, but of the annihilation pure and simple of all human life within the affected area. This is not lawful on any title."

We must note that this applies equally to offensive and defensive war. While it is obligatory to defend one's nation against unjust aggression, only legitimate means can be used. And if the destructive effect of war is far greater than the political injustice suffered, war is not legitimate. "If the damage caused by the war is disproportionate to the injustice suffered, it may well be a matter of obligation to suffer the injustice," Pope Pius XII said to army doctors on October 19, 1953.

Unfortunately, statements like this one, though dutifully reported in the press and respectfully noted by the faithful, are seldom really assimilated by them. That is why the serious moral implications of the measured papal denunciations of nuclear war appear overlooked.

The popes have not merely been trying to say that nuclear war is not nice, but that it radically affects traditional Catholic norms of the morality of war. This is an essentially new kind of war and one in which the old concept of the "just war" ceases to be relevant because the necessary conditions for such a war are extremely difficult to maintain. A war of total annihilation simply cannot be considered a "just war," no matter how good the cause for which it is undertaken.

Such is the view taken by no less authoritative a theologian than Cardinal Ottaviani, Secretary of the Holy Office. Writing before the development of the H-bomb, the Cardinal (then Monsignor) said without ambiguity:

"The war of their treatises is not the war of our experience. Principles derive from the very nature of things: the difference between war as it was and as we know it is *precisely one of nature*. . . . Modern wars can never fulfill the conditions which govern, theoretically, a just and lawful war. Moreover, no conceivable cause could ever be sufficient justification for the evils, the slaughter, the moral and religious upheavals which war today entails."

Such is the thesis in an article by Cardinal Ottaviani entitled "War is to be forbidden entirely," published in Latin in his *Public Laws of the Church* (Rome, 947). Unfortunately such opinions have not been widely disseminated. It may be said also that statements like this do not exclude the defensive use of nuclear weapons in tactical warfare, assuming that such warfare can be "kept within limits."

Let us add one more authoritative statement. The French bishops, when questioned about the lawfulness of nuclear weapons, replied in June, 1950, that such a question *did not even need to be asked* since nuclear war was already condemned by the "*elementary sense of humanity*." The bishops nevertheless spelled out the answer quite clearly for those who no longer knew how to listen to the law of God implanted in their hearts. They said, "We condemn (nuclear weapons) with all our strength."

After so many statements, made so clearly and with such authority, can we still assume that a Catholic who protests against nuclear war is "trying to be more Catholic than the Church?" Is it not evident that this glib dismissal of a grave question provides an all too convenient escape for the Catholic layman, or even the priest, who does not want to face up to his full responsibility?

How can we go on deceiving ourselves that it is somehow a Christian duty, prescribed by the Church, for us to collaborate in nuclear mass murder just because Pope Pius XII also affirmed that the state still retained its legitimate right of self-defense?

Certainly the moral risks of nuclear war do not deprive any nation of the basic natural right to defend itself by ordinary means. Nor do they dispense the citizen from helping the nation to defend itself. The point at issue is not self-defense, but the *means used* in self-defense. It is pure sophistry and absurd logic to contend that because Pius XII said that self-defense by legitimate means was still mandatory, therefore self-defense by *any* means has now become legitimate.

If the nation prepared to defend itself by methods that will almost certainly be immoral and illicit, then the Christian has *not only the right but also the duty to* question the validity of these methods, and to protest against them, even to the point of refusing his cooperation in their unjust and immoral use.

Conclusions

Throughout this article we have addressed ourselves in a general way to all those who still cling to the Judaeo-Christian traditions of the Western world. In conclusion let us consider our obligation as Catholics. Certainly this obligation cannot and must not be reduced to the choice of one particular political and military policy. But we must recognize the basic moral principle that the *unlimited* and *terroristic* use of nuclear weapons, or for that matter of conventional weapons, is always immoral, always criminal, and therefore always totally unacceptable to the Christian conscience.

This principle having been clarified, we can go on to examine other methods of defending ourselves against the enemies of our nation and of our Christian heritage.

The real problem is not so much the choice of particular means, the selection of a more or less acceptable policy. The malady lies deeper than that. The present confusion and irresponsibility which lead so many "good Catholics" to accept, instinctively and without question, a strategy which has been repeatedly criticized by the popes, must be symptomatic of that "deviation of the mind and heart" deplored by Pius XII. And the fact that Catholics can point to theologians and publicists who encourage them in their aberration makes the problem all the more serious. The truth is, that when the popes warn against our grave and imminent danger of being involved in war crimes, we do not hear them, and their message does not register. At best, if we are paying attention at all, we are hunting for the escape clause that enables us to continue in maintaining the more precarious moral position.

If we are going to defend Christianity and save it from the disastrous inroads of materialism and totalitarian autocracy, we must begin by realizing that the struggle necessarily begins within ourselves, both personally and as a group. The problem affects both the individual and the collective conscience of Christians.

If we spontaneously approve of nuclear terrorism, if we become apologists for the uninhibited use of naked power, we are thinking like Communists, we are behaving like Nazis, and we are well on the way to becoming either one or the other. In that event we had better face the fact that we are destroying our own Christian heritage.

9

CHRISTIAN ACTION
IN WORLD CRISIS

Published in Blackfriars *(Oxford, England), June 1962*

On March 17, 1962 Merton wrote to Charles Thompson, editor of the bulletin of the Pax Society of Britain, telling him: "An essay on 'Christian Action in World Crisis' has been passed by the censors and will be shortly in *Blackfriars*. You may want to run a digest of it or parts of it. I mention that it got through the censors for this is always something of an achievement these days." He goes on to say that he has been accused of rebelling against papal authority, because he quotes statements of the popes against war. Orthodoxy seems to consist, he says somewhat wearily, in quoting *only* the papal statements which assert that nations have a right to defend themselves.

. . . . .

A death struggle can also be a struggle for life, a new birth. Perhaps the present crisis is the birth agony of a new world. Let us hope that it is. No one can dare to predict what is about to be born of our confusion, our frenzy, our apocalyptic madness. Certainly the old order is changing, but we do not know what is to come. All we know is that we see the many-crowned and many-headed monsters rising on all sides out of the deep, from the ocean of our own hidden and collective self. We do not understand them, and we cannot. We panic at the very sight of their iridescent scales, just jaws that flame with nuclear fire. But they pursue us relentlessly even into absurd little caves fitted out with battery radios and hand-held blowers. We find no security even in the spiritual cave of forgetfulness, the anaesthesia of the human mind that finally shuts out an unbearable truth, and goes about the business of life in torpor and stoical indifference.

And yet the monsters do not have to come to life. They are not yet fully objective like the world around us. They do not have the substance which is given to things by the creative power of God: they are the spiritual emanations of our sick and sinful being. They exist in and by us. They are from us. They cannot exist without us. They are our illusion. They are nightmares which our incredible technological skill can all too easily actualize. But they are also dreams from which we can awaken before it is too late. They are dreams which we can still, perhaps, choose not to dream.

The awful problem of our time is not so much the dreams, the monsters, which may take shape and consume us, but the moral paralysis in our own souls which leaves us immobile, inert, passive, tongue tied, ready and even willing to succumb. The real tragedy is in the cold, silent waters of moral death which climb imperceptibly within us, blinding conscience, drowning compassion, suffocating faith and extinguishing the Spirit. A progressive deadening of conscience, of judgment and of compassion is the inexorable work of the cold war.

One thing is getting to be more and more certain. The balance of terror, which dictates all the policies of the two great armed power blocs, cannot stay "balanced" much longer. It will crash. It may crash very soon. Napoleon said you cannot sit on bayonets. You have to use them, if you have them. This is a thousand times more true of the monstrous weapons which offer an overwhelming advantage to the one who strikes first and who strikes hardest, who smashes everything the enemy has before the enemy can wake up to his danger.

The slightest false move, the most innocent miscalculation, an ill chosen word, a misprint, a trivial failure in the mechanism of a computer, and one hundred million people evaporate, burn to death, go up in radioactive dust, or crawl about the face of the earth waiting for death to release them from agony.

We are not good at resisting sin, even under the best conditions. But under the most violent provocation, under the most diabolical pressures, when we have abdicated from reason and morality, when we have frankly gone back to the law of the jungle, how much chance is there, humanly speaking, that we can live without disaster?

Two things are clear, first, the enemy is not just one side or the other. The enemy is not just Russia, or China, or Communism, or Castro, or Krushchev, or capitalism, or imperialism. The enemy is both sides. The enemy is in all of us. The enemy is war itself, and the root of war is hatred, fear, selfishness, lust. Pope Pius XII said in 1944, "If ever a generation has known in the depths of its being the cry of 'War on war' it is our own." As long as we arm only against Russia, we are fighting for the real enemy and against ourselves. We are fighting to release the monster in our own soul, which will destroy the world. We are fighting for the demon who strives to reassert his power over mankind. We have got to arm not against Russia but against war. Not only against war, but against hatred. Against lies. Against injustice. Against greed. Against every manifestation of those things, wherever they may be found, and above all in ourselves.

Yet at the same time we must not ignore the spiritual border line that separates the nations of the west, with their Christian background, from the officially atheistic Communist bloc. We must avoid two extremes: seeing all good on our side and all evil on their side, or, on the contrary, dismissing both sides as totally evil. The fact remains that although the Communists have explicitly rejected the Christian ethical tradition, there may still remain in Communist dominated countries strong surviving elements of that tradition. And although we of the west appeal to the Christian tradition in favor of our own cause, and do this quite legitimately, yet nevertheless there are materialistic and atheistic elements at work among us just as powerful and just as destructive of our tradition as the materialism and atheism of the official Communist ideology.

On both sides there are powerful and fanatical pressure groups dominated by their political obsessions, who drive towards nuclear war. On both sides the vast majority desire nothing but peace. The extremists on both sides are very much alike, though they regard one another as opposites. The moderates on both sides also have very much in common. One sometimes wonders if the real dividing line is not to be drawn between the fanatics (whether Russian or American) and the moderate, ordinary people of both sides.

In any case the policy makers and propagandists are tending more and more in the direction of what they call "realism": that is to say an all-out nuclear strike involving the mass destruction of civilians. In effect, the extreme bellicosity which leads each of the great power blocs to depend more and more on the threat of a pre-emptive attack, with no limit to the megatonic impact of the nuclear weapons and no discrimination between civil and military objectives, *is equally immoral on both sides, equally inhuman and incompatible with Christian ethics.*

In this restricted sense it may indeed be possible to find the same demonic evil at work, perhaps in different degrees, on both sides. Once one adopts the policy of nuclear "realism" which is purely and simply a policy of annihilation, then one abandons the moral advantage of fighting for freedom, justice and democracy. None of these values is likely to survive an all-out nuclear war. Even if one nation manages to win such a war, the conditions will be such that social, moral and spiritual values with which we are familiar, and which we should certainly be prepared to defend with our lives, will no longer be recognizable in the moral debacle. Such at least is the belief of Pope Pius XII and of John XXIII.

The conclusion is, then, that we must defend freedom and sanity against the bellicose fanaticism of all warmakers, whether "ours" or "theirs" and that we must strive to do so not with force but with the spiritual weapons of Christian prayer and action. But this action must be at once non-violent and decisive. Good intentions and fond hopes are not enough.

The present world crisis is not merely a political and economic conflict. It goes deeper than ideologies. It is a crisis of man's spirit. It is a great religious and moral upheaval of the human race, and we do not really know half the causes of this upheaval. We cannot pretend to have a full understanding of what is going on in ourselves and in our society. That is why our desperate hunger for clear and definite solutions sometimes leads us into temptation. We oversimplify. We seek the cause of evil and find it here or there in a particular nation, class, race, ideology, system. And we discharge upon this scapegoat all the virulent force of our hatred, compounded with fear and anguish, striving to rid ourselves of our fear by destroying the object we have arbitrarily singled out as the embodiment of all evil. Far from curing us, this is only another paroxysm which aggravates our sickness.

The moral evil in the world is due to man's alienation from the deepest truth, from the springs of spiritual life within himself, to his alienation from God. Those who realize this, try desperately to persuade and enlighten their brothers. But we are in a radically different position from the first Christians, who revolutionized an essentially religious world of paganism with the message of a new religion that had never been heard of.

We on the contrary live in an irreligious world in which the Christian message has been repeated over and over until it has come to seem empty of all intelligible content to those whose ears close to the word of God even before it is uttered. In their minds Christianity is no longer identified with newness and change, but only with the static preservation of outworn structures. Doubtless Christians themselves have helped to create this unfortunate impression.

This should teach us that though the words of the Gospel still objectively retain all the force and freshness of their original life, it is not enough now for us to make them known and clarify them. It is not enough to announce the familiar message that no longer seems to be news. Not enough to teach, to explain, convince. Now, above all, it is the time to embody Christian truth in action even more than in words. No matter how lucid, how persuasive, how logical, how profound our theological and spiritual statements may be, they are often wasted on anyone who does not already think as we do. That is why the serene and almost classic sanity of moralists exposing the traditional teaching of Christian theologians on the "just war" is almost a total loss in the general clamor and confusion of half truths, propaganda slogans, and pernicious cliches. Who will listen and agree, except another professional theologian? What influence can such statements have in preserving sanity, clear and logical though they may be?

What is needed now is the Christian who manifests the truth of the Gospel in social action, with or without explanation. The more clearly his life manifests the teaching of Christ, the more salutary will it be. Clear and decisive Christian action explains itself, and teaches in a way that words never can.

What is wanted now is therefore not simply the Christian who takes an inner complacency in the words and example of Christ, but who seeks to follow Christ perfectly, not only in his own personal life, not only in prayer and penance, but also in his political commitments and in all his social responsibilities. The Christian conscience can hardly be at peace with a minimalist ethic which justifies and permits as much as possible force and terror, in international politics and in war, instead of struggling in every way to restrain force and bring into being a positive international authority which can effectively prevent war and promote peace.

We are at a point of momentous choice. Either our frenzy of desperation will lead to destruction, or our patient loyalty to truth, to God and to our fellow man will enable us to perform the patient, heroic task of building a world that will thrive in unity and peace. At this point, Christian action will be decisive. That is why it is supremely important for us to keep our heads and refuse to be carried away by the wild projects of fanatics who seek an oversimplified and immediate solution by means of inhuman violence.

Christians have got to speak by their actions. Their political action must not be confined to the privacy of the polling booth. It must be clear and manifest to everybody. It must speak loudly and plainly the Christian truth, and it must be prepared to defend that truth with sacrifice, accepting misunderstanding, injustice, calumny, and even imprisonment or death. It is crucially important for Christians today to adopt a genuinely Christian position and support it with everything they have got. This means an unremitting fight for justice in every sphere—in labor, in race relations, in the "third world" and above all in international affairs.

This means (to adopt a current military cliche) closing the gap between our interior intentions and our exterior acts. Our social actions must conform to our deepest religious principles. Beliefs and politics can no longer be kept isolated from one another. It is no longer possible for us to be content with abstract and hidden acts of "purity of intention" which do nothing to make our outward actions different from those of atheists or agnostics.

Nor can we be content to make our highest ideal the preservation of a minimum of ethical rectitude prescribed by natural law. Too often the nobility and grandeur of natural law have been debased and deformed by the manipulations of theorists until natural law has become indistinguishable from the law of the jungle, which is no law at all. Hence those who complacently prescribe the duty of national defense on the basis of "natural law" often forget entirely the norms of justice and humanity without which no war can be permitted. Without those norms, natural law becomes mere jungle law, that is to say crime.

The Popes have repeatedly pleaded with Christian people to show themselves in all things disciples of Christ the Prince of Peace, and to embody in their lives their faith in His teaching. "All His teaching is an invitation to peace," says Pope John XXIII in the 1961 Christmas Message. Deploring the ever increasing selfishness, hardness of heart, cynicism and callousness of mankind, as war becomes once again more and more imminent, Pope John says that Christian goodness and charity must permeate all the activity, whether personal or social, of every Christian. The Pontiff quotes St. Leo the Great in a passage which contrasts natural ethics with the non-violent ethic of the Gospel: "To commit injustice and to make reparation—this is the prudence of the world. On the contrary, *not to render evil for evil, is the virtuous expression of Christian forgiveness.*" These words, embodying the wisdom of the Church and the heart of her moral teaching, are heard without attention and complacently dismissed even by Catholics.

Too often, in practice, we tend to assume that the teaching of Christian forgiveness and meekness applies only to the individual, not to nations or collectivities. The state can go to war and exert every form of violent force, while the individual expresses his Christian meekness by shouldering his gun without resistance and obeying the command to go out and kill. This is not Pope John's idea at all. He utters a solemn warning to rulers of nations: "With the authority we have received from Jesus Christ we say: *Shun all thought of force; think of the tragedy of imitating a chain reaction of acts, decisions and resentments which could erupt into rash and irreparable deeds.* You have received great powers not to destroy but to build, not to divide but to unite, not to cause tears to be shed but to provide employment and security."

Christian action is based on the Christian conscience, and conscience has to be informed by moral truth. What are the moral options open to the Catholic in regard to nuclear war? This has seldom been made clear, and it is tragic to observe that many Catholics are in a state of ignorance and confusion on some very important points. The vague statement that "a Catholic cannot be a pacifist" is taken in much too sweeping and absolute a sense. Actually it is true that in the Christmas Message of 1956 Pope Pius XII reminded the faithful of their duty to face the "unpleasant reality. . . . of an enemy determined to impose on all peoples, in one way or another, a special and intolerable way of life." Referring to violent tactics used by Communism, including atomic blackmail and the ruthless suppression of resistance in weaker nations, the Pope said that these tactics would have to be resisted. Pius XII clearly had the recent Hungarian uprising in mind when he declared that Christians might have the right and the duty to resist oppression by force if no other means were available or effective.

Hence he said that in the case of extreme danger a legitimately constituted government, after every effort to avoid war has been expended in vain, might lawfully wage a war of self-defense against unjust attack. The Pope laid down many clear conditions for the legitimacy of such a war. It would have to be strictly a war of defense, against evidently unjust attack. All efforts at keeping peace must have been unavailing. Legitimate means of defense must be used. There must be hope of effective self-defense and of favorable outcome. In view of such a situation, if the nation takes defensive precautions with legitimate instruments of internal and external policy, then the citizen would have an obligation to serve the nation in its defense effort. He could not appeal to his conscience to refuse military service imposed by law. At the same time the Pope deplored the necessity of such laws and pointed to "general disarmament as an effective remedy."

Without commenting in detail on this statement of Pius XII, two things must be stressed: first that the Pope is not setting aside the Christian conscience in matters of war. The Christian remains obligated in conscience to weigh the matter seriously and to consider whether or not the conditions laid down are in fact fulfilled. In the case of all-out nuclear war, there exists a serious problem as to whether or not the "means" may be considered legitimate, either in themselves or in the manner in which they are obviously to be used.

Far from dismissing or slighting the individual conscience in this matter, the Pope says immediately that "there are occasions in the lives of nations *when only recourse to higher principles* can establish clearly the boundaries between right and wrong." He adds: "It is therefore consoling that in some countries, amid today's debates, men are talking about conscience and its demands."

It must therefore clearly be stated that the measured and clearly qualified terms in which Pius XII admitted that there could still be a just war, at least (so the context seems to suggest) with conventional weapons, this did not mean that the government purely and simply had the last word and that Christian conscience was no longer to be consulted. He was not prescribing blind obedience to any government in any situation in which the power struggle might dictate war by any methods as the expedient thing.

Note also that the obligation is not strictly *to fight and to kill* but to *serve the country* in some capacity, according to its laws. Hence the Catholic who feels that in conscience he ought to choose the more perfect way of avoiding bloodshed and serving in the ambulance corps or in some other non-combatant capacity retains the right to follow his conscience in this matter, and indeed ought to follow it. And his requests ought to be respected.

But do these distinctions apply in an all-out nuclear war?

One other remark made by Pius XII in the same address is very important. He devotes several paragraphs to the problem of discerning accurately when peace is and is not really threatened, when there is and is not a serious emergency, and how the calculated threats and recriminations of power politicians are really to be interpreted. This gravely affects the whole question of that "extreme danger" which makes defensive measures urgent and obligatory.

In conclusion, we must not forget that Pope Pius XII's affirmation that a just war could still be possible and that the Christian might be bound to serve in it, must always be seen against the background of his insistence upon general disarmament and the policy of peace. He explicitly states in this message that it is not "abandoning that mission of peace which flows from our apostolic office," still less "calling Christendom to a crusade."

Clearly we cannot assert that a Catholic is bound in conscience to accept passively every form of war and military force that his government may decide to use against an enemy. According to this view, a good Christian is one who shrinks from no work of violent destruction commanded by the state in war. How far that would be from the primitive idea that the good Christian normally refused military service and suffered violence in himself rather than inflicting it on others. Such a misconception could lead to the awful conclusion that a Catholic commanded by a new Hitler to operate the furnaces of another Dachau would be only "doing his duty" if he obeyed. The noble Christian concept of duty and sacrifice must not be debased to the point where the Christian becomes the passive and servile instrument of inhuman governments.

In brief: A Catholic is permitted to hold the following views of nuclear war:

(a) Many sound theologians have taught that the traditional conditions of a just war cannot be fully realized today and that, as Pope Pius XII himself said, "the theory of war as an apt and proportionate means of solving international conflicts is now out of date." In practice, what has been called "relative pacifism" can very certainly be held and is held by many Catholics. Without rejecting the traditional teaching that a "just war" can theoretically be possible under certain well-defined conditions, this view holds that nuclear war is by its very nature beyond the limits of the traditional doctrine. This is supported by very clear statements of Cardinal Ottaviani and Pope Pius XII. Hence, though it is not the definitive "teaching of the Church" it is certainly not only a tenable doctrine but seems to be the soundest and most traditional opinion.

(b) Though absolute pacifism in a completely unqualified form has been reproved, nevertheless today the pacifist standpoint pure and simple tends in practice to rejoin the above view, since a Catholic can be a pacifist in a particular case where there are very serious reasons for believing that even a limited war may be unjust, or may "escalate" to proportions which violate justice. It is to be noted that *when a war is evidently unjust* a Catholic not only *may* refuse to serve but he is *morally obliged to refuse to participate* in it.

(c) Catholic tradition has always admitted the legality of a defensive war where there is a just cause, right intention and use of the right means. It is argued that a limited nuclear war for defensive purposes can fulfill the requirements of a just war, and that therefore it is right and just to possess stockpiles of nuclear weapons and to threaten retaliation for a nuclear attack. This may be and is held by many Catholics, and it is probably the majority opinion among Catholics in the United States. But it can be said that this position, while specious and reasonable in theory, becomes very dangerous when we consider the actual facts. All theologians agree that the unrestricted use of nuclear weapons for the simple purpose of annihilation of civilian centers is completely immoral. It is nothing but murder and is never permitted, any more than a nuclear pre-emptive strike on civilian centers would be permitted by Christian ethics.

Could a pre-emptive attack on the military installations of the enemy be admitted as a "just" defensive measure? To do so would seem very rash in view of the disastrous consequences of the retaliatory war that would inevitably be unleashed, and would inevitably entail the total mass-destruction of great centers of population. The statement quoted above from Pope John XXIII, while not formally declaring such an action intrinsically evil, is a solemn warning not to initiate, by any form of aggression, a chain of acts of war and violence. While it may be all very well for theologians to theorize about a limited nuclear war, it is all too clear that the game of nuclear deterrence uses the cities of the enemy as hostages, and that the policies of the two great power blocs are frankly built on the threat of an all-out war of annihilation.

In such a situation our Christian duty is clear. Though no Catholic is formally obliged to adhere to a policy of immediate nuclear disarmament, whether multi-lateral or unilateral, he is certainly obliged to do everything he can, in his own situation, to work for peace. It is difficult to see how one can work for peace without ultimately seeking disarmament. If he holds one of the above opinions which are tenable he becomes obliged to a course of action which will promote peace according to his views.

It would, however, be a serious mistake to limit Christian obligations in the present crisis to a course of action that does not conflict with sound moral principles. The problem is deeper. What is needed is a deeply Christian social action that will have the power to renew society because it springs from the *inner renewal of the Christian and of his Church*.

The real problem of our time is basically spiritual. One important aspect of this problem is the fact that in so many Christians, the Christian conscience seems to function only as a rudimentary vestigial faculty, robbed of its vigor and incapable of attaining its full purpose: a life transformed in the charity of Christ.

The mature moral conscience is one that derives its strength and its light not from external directives alone but above all from an inner spiritual connaturality with the deepest values of nature and of grace. Such a conscience is rooted and grounded in human compassion and in the charity of Christ. The most important thing for us all to do (and this is a spiritual task which is essential to Christian renewal) is to recover this hidden "ground" in which sound spiritual judgment and fruitful action can grow abundantly.

But the great danger of our cold war obsessions is their dreadful capacity to sterilize that inner "ground" and make it utterly fruitless. When this happens we tend to judge by a connaturality with violence, and not with love. Constantly exposed to dread, to anguish, to a strange force which menaces our security and our attachment to an affluent society with its privileges and all its soothing irresponsibilities and comforts, we come to feel that menace as a *spiritual* fact. In so far as our existence is at stake, and the structure of our religious beliefs and practices is at stake along with it, we experience the threat of Communism and of war as a kind of ultimate spiritual test. We have to face it with a radical decision, with a self-commitment analogous in some respects to martyrdom. Indeed there is no question that we may have to be, in actual fact, martyrs.

True, there is a fateful element of ambiguity even in the promise that our death at the hands of a persecutor can rate as martyrdom. Are we to die because we are Christians or because we are bourgeois? It does make a difference. But at any rate, the possibility of destruction or at least of persecution by a ruthless and clever enemy, whose power and success we are never allowed to forget, begets intolerable anguish. This anguish, shared with others like ourselves, mounting into indignation and resentment, produces a kind of spurious exaltation. The will to resist by any available means, and without concern even for the most disastrous possible miscarriage of our hopes, then appears to us as bravery. We allow our desperation and our hatred to swallow up our moral judgment, because we feel like crusaders. The enthusiasm we are able to feel, from time to time, when we reflect on the frightful power of our weapons, may also assume a decidedly noxious pseudo-religious quality.

Yet all this proceeds from an inner ground of false spirituality, of debased and brain-washed enthusiasm. Like the disciples who wanted to call down fire upon the city of the Samaritans, we do not realize by what spirit we are inspired. Unfortunately this cold war mentality not only blinds us to true Christian values but makes all our judgments spring from this ground of sterility and frustration in which the best seed can only die and in which the weeds of hatred and incipient fascism (or Communism for that matter) very easily flourish.

It is therefore above all vitally necessary to cultivate an inner ground of deep faith and purity of conscience, which cannot exist without true sacrifice. Genuine Christian action has, in fact, to be based on a complete sacrificial offering of our self and our life, in the service of truth. Short of this, we cannot attain sufficient detachment from our own selfish interests and from the peripheral concerns of a wealthy, spiritual indolent society. Without this detachment we cannot possibly see nuclear war as it really is, and we will consequently betray Christ and His Church, in the mistaken conviction that in defending our wealth we are defending Christian truth.

The Catholic, who believes, as the Popes themselves seem quite clearly to believe, that a nuclear war will most probably be a completely unjust war because its destructive effects cannot be controlled, and that it is in any case unreasonable and totally undesirable, will be obliged to base his political activity on the conviction that war must be prevented here and now, and that we must try as best we can to work for its eventual abolition. This does not mean necessarily an all-out campaign to "ban the bomb" immediately. But it certainly does mean an insistence on peaceful means of settling international disputes. If a Catholic feels himself obliged in conscience to oppose all nuclear armaments and to demand even immediate unilateral disarmament as the best way to peace, though his director of conscience may not agree with his politics he cannot forbid him to hold his view.

There are many reasons to believe that the social action of someone like Dorothy Day, who is willing to refuse co-operation even in civil defense drills and ready to go to jail for her belief in peace, is far more significantly Christian than the rather subtle and comfy positions of certain casuists. When I consider that Dorothy Day was confined to a jail cell in nothing but a light wrap (her clothes having been taken from her) and that she could only get to Mass and Communion in the prison by dressing in clothes borrowed from prostitutes and thieves in the neighboring cells, then I lose all inclination to take seriously the self-complacent nonsense of those who consider her kind of pacifism sentimental.

10

BREAKTHROUGH TO PEACE I:
Introduction

On November 10, 1961 Merton wrote to Daniel Berrigan: "With New Directions [a publishing house; James Laughlin was its publisher], I am trying to get up a little paperback anthology of good strong articles by all kinds of people about peace." Called *Breakthrough to Peace: Twelve Views on the Threat of Thermonuclear Extermination*, the book included articles by such well-known authors as Herbert Butterfield, Norman Cousins, Allan Forbes, Jr., Jerome D. Frank, Erich Fromm, Lewis Mumford, Gordon Zahn, and others. The book was finally published in September of 1962. Since this was after the "ban" that prohibited Merton from writing any further on war and peace, it was thought best not to name him as editor. Writing to James Forest on September 22, 1962, Merton says: "As for *Breakthrough*, it was (as far as my contribution is concerned) approved before the ax fell. I have not gone around publicizing the fact that I edited the book. Officially there is no one named as editor." (*HGL*, 271) He did, however, write an introduction to the book and one of the articles. I have no indication that the introduction was sent to the censors.

Merton was pleased with the reception the book received, and especially delighted at the publicity that came from *The Los Angeles Times*. He wrote to Madame Camille Drevet in Paris on January 17, 1963: "The introduction to *Breakthrough to Peace* has had some rather good fortune in this country. It was printed in its entirety in a prominent place in one of the largest newspapers in the country, *The Los Angeles Times*." (*WTF*, 97)

· · · · ·

The nineteenth century can be called an age of peace and comfort, though if we reflect a little we will remember the war in Crimea, the Indian Mutiny, the Opium War in China, the Franco-Prussian War and the bloody and utterly savage war between the northern and southern

United States. In spite of these conflicts our grandfathers believed that war was gradually getting to be a thing of the past. They did not know that these were all preludes to the gigantic struggle which has continued to rend and batter the world of the twentieth century. But now in 1962 we are beginning to realize that our age has been practically nothing but one big fire of war dying down only to flame up in greater fury, growing in its appetite for violent destruction, and gradually threatening the very survival of civilized man.

The First World War, we are told, was not fully intended by anyone; but political and military strategists moved one step too far and could not turn back. The war was confidently and savagely fought with the expectation that it would end all wars and make the world finally and imperturbably safe for the free and comfortable life.

The very treaty which attempted to restore order to Europe and to guarantee that there would be no further conflict made another and greater war inevitable. And yet during the twenties and thirties, there was a succession of peace conferences, a procession of peace movements, not to mention the nonviolent revolution in India. Men studied, talked, agitated, prayed and suffered to bring about a permanent peace. Never had so much been said about peace, never had war been so thoroughly and universally execrated. Militarists remained, of course, but it cannot be denied that serious efforts at disarmament were made. So serious were these efforts that, when the Second World War broke out, the western nations, particularly America, were not ready. Before Pearl Harbor the majority of Americans strenuously and articulately opposed entrance into the war. France, meanwhile, relied with blind faith on the Maginot Line, a complex and expensive system which proved completely useless against deadly new weapons of attack. The allies cannot be said to have "wanted" war. But they wanted a political and economic situation that made war inevitable.

In the unexampled and criminal frightfulness of World War II, massive attacks on defenseless civilian centers came to be accepted as perfectly normal in spite of protests of the Pope and other spokesmen for traditional ethics. It was believed that systematic terrorism was essential to beat down all resistance of the "Fascist war criminals" and bring them to an unconditional surrender that would definitely end all war. Finally the atomic bomb was dropped on Hiroshima and Nagasaki—the climax of this ruthless policy.

Yet at the very moment when the bomb fell, the cold war between America and Russia was already on. The threat of this bomb, which ended the hot war with Japan, was to be the chief weapon of the cold war. Instead of producing peace, the atom bomb started the most fantastic arms race in history.

Nuclear deterrence has proved to be an illusion, for the bomb deters no one. It did not prevent war in Korea, Indochina, Laos, the Congo. It did not prevent the Russian suppression of the Hungarian revolt. And now those who once relied on deterrence, on the threat of massive retaliation, are insensibly moving toward a policy that assumes a *first strike capacity*. This policy is dictated by the very weapons themselves. The missile armed with a nuclear warhead is the perfect weapon of offense, so perfect that no defense against it has yet been devised. An H-bomb is the cheapest of all mass engines of destruction. It costs only two hundred and fifty thousand dollars to make, and one can go all the way up the megaton scale without prohibitively increasing either the expense or the engineering difficulty. It has been said that the H-bomb "gives more destructive power for the dollar" than any other weapon in existence. Knowing man's love for a good bargain, this atrocious estimate should certainly give us food for thought.

There has been relatively little agitation for peace since World War II. One feels that public opinion has been embittered and disillusioned by the futility of the peace movements after the First World War. This disillusionment is of course compounded by the fact that the biggest "peace movement" in the world today is simply part of the Soviet propaganda front, and is another powerful psychological weapon in the cold war, cynically exploiting the deepest desires of modern man and his most pathetic need in what is frankly a war effort, leading inevitably to hot war or to revolution. In this grim situation, with the U.N. too weak and unsubstantial to offer any hope of a higher authority to restrain the lawless and truculent aspirations of national powers, we seem to be drifting helplessly toward another disaster which will make all previous wars look like rumbles in a back alley. As long as each nation remains the sole judge of its own case, and decides for itself what is right and wrong without further appeal except to the power of the bomb, it would seem that war must be inevitable. The question that now seems to preoccupy leaders and policy-makers is not whether war can be avoided, but whether war can be kept with "safe" limits.

In this situation, where issues are too enormous for the mind of the average man to grasp, when the threat is too appalling for his political habits and instincts to instruct him adequately, the tendency is to take refuge in fanaticism or in passive desperation.

Fanatics yield to the pressures of inner resentment and frustration, and seek a show-down because they cannot bear the intolerable burden of waiting and uncertainty. The passive and the despairing accept the absurdity of life with a shrug and seek forgetfulness in an automatic, drugged existence which renounces all effort and all hope. In both cases people become more and more resigned to their destruction and to the destruction of the civilized world. Indeed, one gets the feeling that they are almost eager to see the whole thing blow up, and get it over with.

This precisely is the great danger. This is what the open mind, the humanist and Christian mind, the mind which desires the survival of reason and of life, must now confront most decisively. No one of us can say for sure what the future will bring, but we are not responsible for what is beyond our control. We are responsible for the present and for those present actions and attitudes of ours from which future events will develop. It is therefore supremely important that we get a grip on ourselves and determine that we will not relinquish either our reason or our humanity; that we will not despair of ourselves, or of man, or of our capacity to solve our problems; that we will make use of the faculties and resources we still have in abundance, and use them for positive and constructive action in so far as we can. We will resist the fatal inclination to passivity and despair as well as the fatuous temptation to false optimism and insouciance which condition us equally well to accept disaster. In a word we will behave as men, and if Christians, then as members of Christ.

Our problem is a moral and spiritual problem. It is a problem of enormous and frightful complexity. We have no alternative but to face it, in all its ramifications, and do what we can about it. This is the duty which history itself has imposed on us, which our forefathers, in their mixture of wisdom and folly, have bequeathed to us. It will not do us any good to wish we were other than we actually are, or that we were in some other century, some other planet. We cannot escape present reality. We cannot all offer ourselves to be frozen up and comfortably hibernate through the critical years that are to come, in order to wake up painlessly in a new world.

But if we are to face the problem as it is, we must first of all admit its true nature. If it is a *moral* problem, then it implies the appropriate response of reason and of freedom. It implies choice, based on knowledge. It implies willingness to study, to reason, to communicate. It implies the capacity to judge. It implies not only that judgment which the individual makes in the secrecy of his conscience, but also political expression and action.

We must judge and decide not only as individuals, preserving for ourselves the luxury of a clean conscience, but also as members of society taking up a common burden and responsibility. It is all too easy to retire into the ivory tower of private spirituality and let the world blow itself to pieces. Such a decision would be immoral, an admission of defeat. It would imply a secret complicity with the overt destructive fury of fanatics.

Moral decisions have to be based on adequate knowledge. The scientist must tell us something reliable about the behavior of bombs and missiles. The political commentator must keep us in touch with the developments of strategy and with the plans that are being made for our defense or for our destruction. He must tell us what underlies the fair assurances we read in the mass media or hear in the speeches of the statesman and publicist. We must be informed of what goes on in the rest of the world, what is hoped and feared by our opposite numbers in the land of "the enemy." We must try to remember that the enemy is as human as we are, and not an animal or a devil.

Finally, we must be reminded of the way we ourselves tend to operate, the significance of the secret forces that rise up within us and dictate fatal decisions. We must learn to distinguish the free voice of conscience from the irrational compulsions of prejudice and hate. We must be reminded of objective moral standards, and of the wisdom which goes into every judgment, every choice, every political act that deserves to be called civilized. We cannot think this way unless we shake off our passive irresponsibility, renounce our fatalistic submission to economic and social forces, and give up the unquestioning belief in machines and process which characterizes the mass mind. History is ours to make: now above all we must try to recover our freedom, our moral autonomy, our capacity to control the forces that make life and death in our society.

It is necessary to discuss the fateful problems of our time, and independent minds have not hesitated to do so, even though the trend of the masses is toward an ever more submissive and inert acceptance of meaningless slogans. No such slogans will be found in this book. Nor do these writers offer easy solutions. Indeed, they do not pretend to an infallibility which can promise anything beyond the austerity of a task that may turn out to be fruitless. But they seek to offer sincere and unprejudiced judgments of our predicament and their analysis is not without very significant hopes, if only we can be faithful to the reason and wisdom which we have not yet irrevocably lost.

The fact remains that we may lose both, through our own fault, and forfeit our heritage of civilization and of humanity to enter a post-historic world of technological animals. There is no guarantee even now that reason can still prevail. But we must do what we can, relying on the grace of God for the rest.

The essays in this book attempt to break through thought barriers and open up rational perspectives. Hence each one of the writers assumes, in his own way, that the questions he raises are not already closed forever by prejudice or by the informal dictatorship of "thought control." If we assume that the basic questions have already been answered, our doom is sealed. On the contrary, if we recognize that we still have the obligation and, we hope, the time to re-examine certain fundamental assumptions, we may perhaps be able to open the way for developments in policy that will help future generations work out a fully constructive and peaceful solution.

The moral or political principles on which our most critical decisions are to be made may, in themselves, be relatively simple, but the assumptions on which they are based are immensely complicated. It is not difficult to appeal to traditional norms of justice and law, and apply them to our present situation in such a way as to come up with logical and plausible conclusions. But the very plausibility of the conclusions tends to be the most dangerous thing about them, if we forget that they may be based on premises which we take to be axiomatic and which, in fact, have been invalidated by recent developments of weapons technology. Indeed, the technological data on which we are basing our moral or political decision may be profoundly influenced by certain assumptions which have been fed into the computers in the first place. There is a very serious danger that our most crucial decisions may turn out to be no decisions at all, but only the end of a vicious circle of conjectures and gratuitous assumptions in which we unconsciously make the argument come out in favor of our own theory, our own favorite policy.

The written and spoken statements of nuclear "realists" seem to give grounds for very grave concern in this regard. It would be a disaster if ethical and political thought were to take too seriously the claims of men who dismiss the noxious effects of fallout as altogether negligible, and who minimize the destructive power of the bomb whenever they consider the possible destruction of our own cities. Yet on the basis of such conjectures as these, a moralist or a publicist, exercising a really decisive effect on a huge segment of public opinion, might issue a declaration in favor of nuclear war, and this judgment might itself be the deciding factor in swinging the whole policy of the United States in the direction of preemptive attack. Even more serious than this, is the fact that the moral, or amoral preconceptions of the military mind, and particularly the oversimplified assessment of a political threat, implemented by a dogmatic and fanatical political creed, will certainly have grave influence upon military decisions at a high level.

It is therefore vitally important to create a general climate of rationality, and to preserve a broad tolerant, watchful and humanist outlook on the whole of life, precisely in order that rash and absurd assumptions may not have too free a circulation in our society.

That is what these essays attempt to do. All of them, in their own way, approach the problems related to nuclear war with a freely questioning mind, in search of facts and principles which tend to upset the crude assumptions already too widely accepted by the majority, particularly in America. Hence these essays all share a common note of urgency and protest, and by that very fact alone they manifest their intention to continue fighting in defense of genuine democracy, freedom of thought, and freedom of political action.

One of the most absurd and dangerous of all prejudices is the popular assumption that anyone who doubts the bomb is the only ultimate solution, proves himself by that very fact to be subversive. For those who believe this, these essays will prove disturbing. The present writers prescribe austere remedies. They demand thought, patience, the willingness to face risks, in order to enter new and unexplored territory of the mind. They refuse to be satisfied with negativism and destruction, or with the despair that masks as heroism and prepares for the apocalyptic explosion in which all the humanized, social and spiritual values that we know will go up in radioactive smoke.

The perspectives in this book are, then, humanistic in the deepest and most spiritual sense of the word. They look beyond the interests of any restricted group toward the deepest and most critical needs of man himself. In so doing, they are, at least implicitly, faithful to the Judaeo-Christian tradition on which our civilization was built. There is no hope for us if we lose sight of these perspectives. There is no other human way out.

11

BREAKTHROUGH TO PEACE II:
Peace: A Religious Responsibility

As I mentioned earlier, this essay, published in *Breakthrough to Peace*, was actually a fourth revision of the Commonweal article of February 9, 1962. On December 17, 1962, Merton wrote to Hildegard Goss-Mayr who, together with Dorothy Day and a group of women peace activists, was in Rome lobbying the bishops at the Second Vatican Council with the hope that they would make a strong statement against war. Merton tells her that he is sending her "three envelopes full of materials more or less related to the question of nuclear war." He adds: "In one is the book *Breakthrough to Peace* in which I have an essay on 'Peace: A Religious Responsibility,' which is pretty much a summary of what I have had to say on the subject. The introduction to that book, which I also wrote, is useful perhaps as a summary of the *status quaestionis*." Among other articles included, he specifically mentions "Target Equals City." He invites her to share these materials with anyone who might be interested. Whether Merton's materials influenced the statement eventually made by the bishops is an interesting but thus far unanswered question. We do know that some of the bishops (for example, John J. Wright of Pittsburgh and Cardinal George Bernard Flahiff of Winnepeg, Manitoba) had copies of some of Merton's materials.

* * * * *

Preamble

Between 1918 and 1939 religious opposition to war was articulate and widespread, all over Europe and America. Peace movements of significant proportions were active in Germany, Britain, and the United States. Yet they were crushed without difficulty and almost without protest by totalitarian regimes on the one hand, and silenced by the outbreak of a clearly defensive war on the other. Since 1945 there has been nothing to compare with the earlier movements of protest. Instead we have witnessed the enormous and crudely contrived fiction of the Communist Peace Movement which has been accepted with disillusioned resignation on one side of the Iron Curtain while, on the other, it has managed to make almost all efforts of independent civilian or religious groups to oppose nuclear war seem dishonest or subversive.

Yet never was opposition to war more urgent and more necessary than now. Never was religious protest so badly needed. Silence, passivity, or outright belligerence seem to be characteristic official and unofficial Christian reactions to the H-bomb. True, there has been some theological and ethical debate. This debate has been marked above all by a seemingly inordinate hesitation to characterize the uninhibited use of nuclear weapons as immoral. Of course the bomb has been condemned without equivocation by the "peace Churches" (Quakers, Mennonites, etc.). But the general tendency of Protestant and Catholic theologians has been to consider how far nuclear war could be reconciled with the traditional "just war" theory. In other words the discussion has been not so much a protest against nuclear war, still less a positive search for peaceful solutions to the problem of nuclear deterrence and ever increasing Cold War obsessions, but rather an attempt to justify, under some limited form, a new type of war which is tacitly recognized as an imminent possibility. This theological thought has tended more and more to accept the evil of nuclear war, considering it a lesser evil than Communist domination, and looking for some practicable way to make use of the lesser evil in order to avoid the greater.

This does not imply a purely pacifist rejection of war as such. Assuming that a "just war" is at least a theoretical possibility and granting that in a "just war" Christians may be bound to defend their country, the question we want to examine here is whether or not the massive and unlimited use of nuclear weapons, or the use of them in a limited first strike which is foreseen as likely to set off a global cataclysm, can be considered under any circumstances just.

The great problem is in fact that both in the East and in the West nuclear weapons are taken for granted. Nuclear war is now assumed to be a rational option or at least nuclear deterrence is accepted as a reasonable and workable way of "preserving peace." The moral issue is generally set aside as irrelevant. But if in all these cases, a use of nuclear weapons even to threaten total or quasi-total destruction of an enemy is immoral, then we are living in a completely noxious situation where most of our political, economic, and even religious thinking is inseparably bound up with assumptions that may ultimately prove criminal. And if this is so we must be prepared to face terrible consequences. For moral truth is not a sentimental luxury. It is as much a necessity to man and his society as air, water, fire, food and shelter.

This essay takes the stand that the *massive and uninhibited use of nuclear weapons,* either in attack or in retaliation, is contrary to Christian morality. And the arguments will be drawn particularly from Catholic sources. Recent Popes had declared ABC warfare (that is, atomic, biological and chemical warfare) to be a "sin, an offense and an outrage" (Pius XII). It may be quite true that these Popes have also affirmed a nation's right to defend itself by *just means,* in a *just war.* It may also be true that a theological argument for the use of "tactical nuclear weapons" may be constructed on the basis of some of the Popes' statements. But when we remember that the twenty kiloton A-bomb that was dropped on Hiroshima is now regarded as "small" and a "tactical device" and when we keep in mind that there is every probability that a force that is being beaten with small nuclear weapons will resort to big ones, we can easily see how little moral value can be found in these theorizings.

"Tactical nuclear weapons" and "limited war" with conventional forces are of course proposed with the best intentions: as a "realistic" way to avoid the horror of total nuclear warfare. Since it is claimed that men cannot get along without some kind of war, the least we can do is to insure that they will only destroy one another in thousands instead of in millions. Yet curiously enough, the restraint that would be required to keep within these limits (a restraint that was unknown on either side after the early phases of World War II), would seem to demand as much heroism and as much control as disarmament itself. It would therefore appear more realistic as well as more Christian and more humane to strive to think of total peace rather than of partial war. Why can we not do this? If disarmament were taken seriously, instead of being used as a pawn in the game of power politics, we could arrive at a workable agreement. It might not be ideal, but it would certainly be at once safer, saner and more realistic than war, whether limited or total. But we make ourselves incapable of taking either disarmament or peace with total seriousness, because we are completely obsessed with the fury and the fantasies of the Cold War. The task of the Christian is to make the thought of peace once again seriously possible. A step towards this would be the rejection of nuclear deterrence as a basis for international policy. Nuclear war is totally unacceptable. It is immoral, inhuman, and absurd. It can lead nowhere but to the suicide of nations and of cultures, indeed to the destruction of human society itself.

We must now face the fact that we are moving closer and closer to war, not only as a result of blind social forces but also as the result of our own decisions and our own choice. The brutal reality is that, when all is said and done, we seem to *prefer* war; not that we want war itself, but we are blindly and hopelessly attached to all that makes war inevitable.

I The Dance of Death

No one seriously doubts that it is now possible for man and his society to be completely destroyed in a nuclear war. This possibility must be soberly faced, even though it is so momentous in all its implications that we can hardly adjust ourselves to it in a fully rational manner. Indeed, this awful threat is the chief psychological weapon of the cold war. America and Russia are playing the paranoid game of nuclear deterrence, each one desperately hoping to preserve peace by threatening the other with bigger bombs and total annihilation.

Every step in this political dance of death brings us inexorably closer to hot war. The closer we get to hot war, the more the theoretical possibility of our total destruction turns into a real possibility.

There is no control over the arbitrary and belligerent self-determination of the great nations ruled by managerial power elites concerned chiefly with their own self-interest. The UN is proving itself unable to fulfill the role of international arbiter and powerless to control the pugnacity of the nuclear club. Indeed, the big powers have been content to use the UN as a forum for political and propagandist wrestling matches and have not hesitated to take independent action that led to the discrediting of the UN whenever this has been profitable to them. Hence the danger that the uncontrolled power of nuclear weapons may break loose whenever one of the belligerents feels himself sufficiently strong and sufficiently provoked to risk an all-out war. Repeated threats to use the bomb have doubtless been mostly bluff, but one day somebody's bluff is going to be called, perhaps in a very drastic fashion.

Meanwhile the United States alone possesses a stockpile of nuclear weapons estimated at 60,000 megatons. This is enough to wipe out the present civilized world and to permanently affect all life on the planet earth. These nuclear bombs can be delivered by some 2,500 planes. It is no secret that such planes are constantly in the air, ready to strike. There are 200 missiles available to U.S. forces, mostly of intermediate range, and this does not suggest the immediate likelihood of a purely push-button war. But it is estimated that by 1963 there will be two thousand more of them, of which a large proportion will be intercontinental missiles based in "hard" installations. Attack on hard installations means ground bursts and therefore more fallout as well as more bombs. Hence even an attack concentrated on our missile bases is bound to have a destructive effect on many population centers.

An ICBM can carry an H-bomb warhead to a destination five thousand miles away, twenty times faster than the speed of sound. Intermediate range missiles can be fired from submarines and deliver H-bombs which could reduce the eastern United States to a radioactive wasteland. H-bombs will soon be fitted to satellites and will be able to reach a target within a few minutes, without hope of interception.

It must be remembered that H-bombs are relatively cheap to produce, and it is not difficult to build and deliver big ones. Poison gas can also be delivered by long-range missiles. One such gas is manufactured in quantity by the U.S. Army Chemical Corps and it can exterminate whole populations of men as if they were insects. A similar nerve gas, originally developed by the Nazis, is manufactured in Soviet Russia. This gas is considered to be more effective against civilian populations than any nuclear agent. It leaves industry and property intact and there is no fallout! Shelters offer no protection against chemical agents.

In a word, the logic of deterrence has proved to be singularly illogical, because of the fact that nuclear war is almost exclusively offensive. So far there is no indication that there can be any really effective defense against guided missiles. All the advantage goes to the force that strikes first, without warning. Hence the multiplication of "hard" weapons sites, and of "deep shelters" becomes provocative and instead of convincing the enemy of our invulnerability, it only invites a heavier preemptive attack by bigger bombs and more of them. The cost of moving a significant portion of industry, business and the population underground is prohibitive and the whole idea is in itself nonsensical, at least as a guarantee of "peace."

Far from producing the promised "nuclear stalemate" and the "balance of terror" on which we are trying to construct an improbable peace, these policies simply generate tension, confusion, suspicion, and paranoid hate. This is the climate most suited to the growth of totalitarianism. Indeed, the Cold War itself promises by itself to erode the last vestiges of true democratic freedom and responsibility even in the countries which claim to be defending these values. Those who think that they can preserve their independence, their civic and religious rights by ultimate recourse to the H-bomb do not seem to realize that the mere shadow of the bomb may end by reducing their religious and democratic beliefs to the level of mere words without meaning, veiling a state of rigid and totalitarian belligerency that will tolerate no opposition.

In a world where another Hitler and another Stalin are almost certain to appear on the scene, the existence of such destructive weapons and the moral paralysis of leaders and policy makers combined with the passivity and confusion of mass societies which exist on both sides of the Iron Curtain, constitute the gravest problem in the whole history of man. Our times can be called apocalyptic, in the sense that we seem to have come to a point at which all the hidden, mysterious dynamism of the "history of salvation" revealed in the Bible has flowered into final and decisive crisis. The term "end of the world" may or may not be one that we are capable of understanding. But at any rate we seem to be assisting at the unwrapping of the mysteriously vivid symbols in the last book of the New Testament. In their nakedness they reveal to us our own selves as the men whose lot it is to live in a time of possible ultimate decision. In a word, the end of our civilized society is quite literally up to us and to our immediate descendants, if any. It is for us to decide whether we are going to give in to hatred, terror, and blind love of power for its own sake, and thus plunge our world into the abyss, or whether, restraining our savagery, we can patiently and humanely work together for interests which transcend the limits of any national or ideological community. We are challenged to prove we are rational, spiritual and humane enough to deserve survival, by acting according to the highest ethical and spiritual norms we know. As Christians, we believe that these norms have been given to us in the Gospel and in the traditional theology of the Church.

II The Christian as Peacemaker

We know that Christ came into this world as the Prince of Peace. We know that Christ Himself is our peace (Eph. 2:14). We believe that God has chosen for Himself, in the Mystical Body of Christ, an elect people, regenerated by the Blood of the Savior, and committed by their baptismal promise to wage war upon the evil and hatred that are in man, and help to establish the Kingdom of God and of peace.

This means a recognition that human nature, identical in all men, was assumed by the Logos in the Incarnation, and that Christ died out of love for all men, in order to live in all men. Consequently we have the obligation to treat every other man as Christ Himself, respecting his life as if it were the life of Christ, his rights as if they were the rights of Christ. Even if the other shows himself to be unjust, wicked and odious to us, we cannot take upon ourselves a final and definitive judgment in his case. We still have an obligation to be patient, and to seek his highest spiritual interests. In other words, we are formally commanded to love our enemies, and this obligation cannot be met by a formula of words. It is not enough to press the button that will incinerate a city of five million people, saying in one's heart "this hurts me more than it hurts you," or declaring that it is all for love.

As Pope John XXIII pointed out in his first encyclical letter *Ad Petri Cathedram*, Christians are obliged to strive for peace "with all the means at their disposal" and yet, as he continues, this peace cannot compromise with error or make concessions to it. "Therefore it is by no means a matter of passive acquiescence in injustice, since this does not produce peace. However, the Christian struggle for peace depends first of all upon a free response of man to "God's call to the service of His Merciful designs." (Christmas message, 1958) Christ Our Lord did not come to bring peace to the world as a kind of spiritual tranquilizer. He brought to His disciples a vocation and a task, to struggle in the world of violence to establish His peace not only in their own hearts but in society itself. This was to be done not by wishing and fair words but by a total interior revolution in which we abandoned the human prudence that is subordinated to the quest for power, and followed the higher wisdom of love and of the Cross.

The Christian is and must be by his very adoption as a son of God, in Christ, a peacemaker (Matt. 5:9). He is bound to imitate the Savior who, instead of defending Himself with twelve legions of angels (Matt. 26:55), allowed Himself to be nailed to the Cross and died praying for His executioners. The Christian is one whose life has sprung from a particular spiritual seed: the blood of the martyrs who, without offering forcible resistance, laid down their lives rather than submit to the unjust laws that demanded an official religious cult of the emperor as God. That is to say, the Christian is bound, like the martyrs, to obey God rather than the state whenever the state tries to usurp powers that do not and cannot belong to it. We have repeatedly seen Christians in our time fulfilling this obligation in a heroic manner by resistance to dictatorships that strove to interfere with the rights of their conscience and their religion.

Hence it must be stated quite clearly and without any compromise that the duty of the Christian as a peacemaker is not to be confused with a kind of quietistic inertia which is indifferent to injustice, accepts any kind of disorder, compromises with error and with evil, and gives in to every pressure in order to maintain "peace at any price." The Christian knows well, or should know well, that peace is not possible on such terms. Peace demands the most heroic labor and the most difficult sacrifice. It demands greater heroism than war. It demands greater fidelity to the truth and a much more perfect purity of conscience. The Christian fight for peace is not to be confused with defeatism. This has to be made clear because there is a certain complacent sophistry, given free currency by the theologians who want to justify war too easily, and who like to treat anyone who disagrees with them as if he were a practical apostate from the faith who had already surrendered implicitly to communism by refusing to accept the morality of an all-out nuclear war. This, as any one can easily see, is simply begging the question. And one feels that those who yield to this temptation are perhaps a little too much influenced by the pragmatism and opportunism of our affluent society.

There is a lot of talk, among some of the clergy, about the relative danger of nuclear war and a "Communist takeover." It is assumed, quite gratuitously, that the Communist is at the gates, and is just about to take over the United States, close all the churches, and brainwash all the good Catholics. Once this spectral assessment of the situation is accepted, then one is urged to agree that there is only one solution: to let the Reds have it before they get our government and our universities thoroughly infiltrated. This means a preemptive strike, based not on the fact that we ourselves are actually under military attack, but that we are so "provoked" and so "threatened" that even the most drastic measures are justified.

If it is argued that there can be no proportion between the awful destruction wrought by nuclear war and the good achieved by exorcising this specter of Communist domination, the argument comes back: "better dead than red." And this, in turn, is justified by the contention that the destruction of cities, nations, populations, is "only a physical evil" while Communist domination would be a "moral evil."

It must be said at once that this has no basis in logic, ethics, politics or sound moral theology. Two quotations from Pope Pius XII will suffice to establish the true Catholic perspective on these points.

The destruction of cities and nations by nuclear war is *"only a physical evil?"* Pope Pius XII calls aggressive ABC warfare a "sin, an offense and an outrage against the majesty of God." And he adds: "It constitutes a crime worthy of the most severe national and international sanctions." (Address to the World Medical Congress, 1954) Father John Courtney Murray, S.J., whom no one can accuse of being a "pacifist" (he favors the liceity of "limited nuclear war" and also believes that such a war would have practical value) has stated, "The extreme position of forcing a war . . . simply to kill off all communists, cannot be a legitimate Catholic opinion."

The real issue here is not actually a moral principle so much as a state of mind. This state of mind is the one which we find in the American mass media. It is made up of a large number of very superficial assumptions about what is going on in the world and about what is likely to happen. We are in a sorry state, indeed, if our survival and indeed our Christian faith itself are left entirely at the mercy of such assumptions!

III Beyond East and West

We are no longer living in a Christian world. The ages which we are pleased to call the "ages of faith" were certainly not ages of earthly paradise. But at least our forefathers officially recognized and favored the Christian ethic of love. They fought some very bloody and unchristian wars, and in doing so, they also committed great crimes which remain in history as a permanent scandal. However, certain definite limits were recognized. Today a non-Christian world still retains a few vestiges of Christian morality, a few formulas and cliches, which serve on appropriate occasions to adorn indignant editorials and speeches. But otherwise we witness deliberate campaigns to oppose and eliminate all education in Christian truth and morality. Not only non-Christians but even Christians themselves tend to dismiss the Gospel ethic of non-violence and love as "sentimental." As a matter of fact, the mere suggestion that Christ counseled non-violent resistance to evil is enough to invite scathing ridicule.

It is therefore a serious error to imagine that because the West was once largely Christian, the cause of the Western nations is now to be identified, without further qualification, with the cause of God. The incentive to wipe out Bolshevism with H-bombs may well be one of the apocalyptic temptations of twentieth century Christendom. It may indeed be the most effective way of destroying Christendom, even though man survive. For who imagines that the Asians and Africans will respect Christianity and receive it after it has apparently triggered mass-murder and destruction of cosmic proportions? It is pure madness to think that Christianity can defend itself by nuclear preemption. The mere fact that we now seem to accept nuclear war as reasonable and Christian is a universal scandal.

True, Christianity is not only opposed to Communism, but in a very real sense, at war with it. However this warfare is spiritual and ideological. "Devoid of material weapons," says Pope John, "the Church is the trustee of the highest spiritual power." If the Church has no military weapons of her own, it means that her wars are fought without violence, not that she intends to call upon the weapons of nations that were once Christian, in defense of the Gospel. Whatever we may think of the ethics of nuclear war, it is clear that the message of the H-bomb is neither salvation nor "good news."

But we believe, precisely, that an essential part of the "good news" is that spiritual weapons are stronger than material ones. Indeed, by spiritual arms, the early Church conquered the entire Roman world. Have we lost our faith in this "sword of the Spirit?" Have we perhaps lost all realization of its very existence?

Of course we must repudiate a tactic of inert passivity that purely and simply leaves man defenseless, without any recourse whatever to any means of protecting himself, his rights, or Christian truth. We repeat again and again that the right, and truth, are to be defended by the most efficacious possible means, and that the most efficacious of all are precisely the spiritual ones, which have always been the only ones that have effected a really lasting moral change in society and in man. The Church tolerates defensive use of weapons only in so far as men are unable to measure up to the stricter and more heroic demands of spiritual warfare. It is absolutely unchristian to adopt, in practice, a standard of judgment which practically rejects or ignores all recourse to the spiritual weapons, and relegates them entirely to the background as if they had no efficacy whatever, and as if material weapons (the bigger the better) were the ones that really counted.

It seems that a great deal of the moral discussion about nuclear war is based, in fact, on the assumption that spiritual weapons are quixotic and worthless and that material weapons alone are worthy of serious consideration. But this attitude is precisely what leads to a fundamental vitiation of the Church's traditionally accepted doctrine on the use of violence in war: it seeks in every possible way to evade the obligation to use war only as a last resort, purely in *defense*, and with the use of *just means only.*

Inevitably, as soon as the obsession with bigger and bigger weapons takes hold of us, we make it impossible for ourselves to consider the just rights of non-combatants. We twist and deform the truth in every possible way in order to convince ourselves that non-combatants are really combatants after all, and that our "attack" is in reality "defense," while the enemy's "defense" really constitutes an "attack." By such tactics we disqualify ourselves from receiving the guidance of light and grace which will enable us to judge as spiritual men and as members of Christ. Obviously, without this special gift of light, we remain utterly incapable of seeing or appreciating the superiority of spiritual weapons, prayer, sacrifice, negotiation, and non-violent means in general.

This results in the unhappy situation that non-Christians with rather dubious doctrinal support in irreligious philosophies have been able to take over characteristically Christian spiritual methods, appropriating them to themselves and thus further discrediting them in the eyes of the orthodox believer who is already confused by the now instinctive justification of war and weapons as the "normal" Christian way of solving international problems.

We must remember that the Church does not belong to any political bloc. Christianity exists on both sides of the Iron Curtain and we should feel ourselves united by very special bonds with those Christians who, living under Communism, often suffer heroically for their principles.

Is it a valid defense of Christianity for us to wipe out those heroic Christians along with their oppressors, for the sake of "religious freedom?"

Let us stop and consider where the policy of massive retaliation and worse still of preemptive strike may lead us. Are we to annihilate huge population centers, at the same time showering vast areas around them with lethal fallout? Do we believe it is necessary to do this in order to protect ourselves against the menace of world communism?

In these countries which we may perhaps be ready to annihilate, the vast majority is not Communist. On the contrary, while the people have resigned themselves passively to Communist domination, and have become quite convinced that there is no hope to be looked for from us because we are their declared enemies, and intend to wipe them out, they are by no means Communists. They do not want war. They have, in many cases, lived through the horrors and sacrifices of total war and experienced things which we are barely able to imagine. They do not want to go through this again.

We, in the name of liberty, of justice, of humanity, are pursuing a policy which promises to crush them with even greater horror, except that it may be perhaps "merciful" that millions of them will simply be blown out of existence in the twinkling of an eye. Merciful? When many of them have a Christian background, many are faithful Christians?

What good will our belligerent policy do us in those countries? None at all. It will only serve to reinforce the fatalistic conviction of the necessity of armament and of war that has been dinned into these populations by the Communist minority which dominates them.

How do we justify our readiness to wage a war of this kind? Let us face the fact that we feel ourselves terribly menaced by Communism. Certainly we believe we have to defend ourselves. Why are we menaced? Because, as time goes on, the Communists have gained a greater and greater advantage over us in the Cold War. Why have they been able to do this? This is a question of historic fact, which however is not absolutely clear, but anyone will admit that our very reliance on the massive power of the bomb has to a great extent crippled us and restricted our freedom to maneuver, and the Communists have been operating under the *protection* of this massive threat that is too enormous to let loose for any but the most serious causes. Hence, instead of the serious provocation, the massive attack, we are confronted with a multiplicity of little threats all over the world, little advances, little gains. They all add up, but even the total of all of them does not constitute a sufficient reason for nuclear war.

But we are getting mad, and we are beginning to be thoroughly impatient with the humiliation of constant defeat. The more humiliated we become, the worse we compromise our chances, the greater errors we make.

We used to have an unrivaled reputation among the backward people of the world. We were considered the true defenders of liberty, justice and peace, the hope of the future. Our anger, our ignorance and our frustration have made us forfeit this tremendous advantage.

IV Moral Passivity and Demonic Activism

One of the most disturbing things about the Western World of our time is that it is beginning to have much more in common with the

Communist world than it has with the professedly Christian society of several years ago. On both sides of the Iron Curtain we find two pathological varieties of the same moral sickness: both of them rooted in the same basically materialistic view of life. Both are basically opportunistic and pragmatic in their own way. And both have the following characteristics in common. On the level of *morality* they are blindly passive in their submission to a determination which, in effect, leaves men completely irresponsible. Therefore moral obligations and decisions tend to become practically meaningless. At best they are only forms of words, rationalizations of pragmatic decisions that have already been dictated by the needs of the moment.

Naturally, since not everyone is an unprincipled materialist even in Russia, there is bound to be some moral sense at work, even if only as a guilt-feeling that produces uneasiness and hesitation, blocking the smooth efficiency of machine-like obedience to immoral commands. Yet the history of Nazi Germany shows us how appalling was the irresponsibility which would carry out even the most revolting of crimes under cover of "obedience" to "legitimately constituted authority" for the sake of a "good cause." This moral passivity is the most terrible danger of our time, as the American bishops have already pointed out in their joint letters of 1960 and 1961.

On the level of political, economic and military activity, this moral passivity is balanced, or over-balanced by a *demonic activism*, a frenzy of the most varied, versatile, complex and even utterly brilliant technological improvisation, following one upon the other with an ever more bewildering and uncontrollable proliferation. Politics pretends to use this force as its servant, to harness it for social purpose, for the "good of man." The intention is good. The technological development of power in our time is certainly a risk and challenge, but it is by no means intrinsically evil. On the contrary, it can and should be a very great good. In actual fact, however, the furious speed with which our technological world is plunging toward disaster is evidence that no one is any longer fully in control—least of all, perhaps, the political leaders.

A simple study of the steps which led to the dropping of the first A-bomb on Hiroshima is devastating evidence of the way well-meaning men, the scientists, generals and statesmen of a victorious nation, were guided step by step, without realizing it, by the inscrutable yet simple "logic of events" to fire the shot that was to make the Cold War inevitable and prepare the way inexorably for World War III. This they did purely and simply because they thought in all sincerity that the bomb was the simplest and most merciful way of ending World War II and perhaps all wars, forever.

The tragedy of our time is then not so much the malice of the wicked as the helpless futility of the best intentions of "the good." There are warmakers, war criminals, indeed. They are present and active on *both sides.* But all of us, in our very best efforts for peace, find ourselves maneuvered unconsciously into positions where we too can act as war criminals. For there can be no doubt that Hiroshima and Nagasaki were, though not fully deliberate crimes, nevertheless crimes. And who was responsible? No one. Or "history." We cannot go on playing with nuclear fire and shrugging off the results as "history." We are the ones concerned.

In plain words, in order to save ourselves from destruction we have to try to regain control of a world that is speeding downhill without brakes because of the combination of factors I have just mentioned: almost total passivity and irresponsibility on the moral level, plus demonic activism in social, political and military life.

First of all we must seek some remedy in the technological sphere. We must try to achieve some control over the production and stockpiling of weapons. It is intolerable that such massive engines of destruction should be allowed to proliferate in all directions without any semblance of a long-range plan for anything, even for what is cynically called "defense." To allow governments to pour more and more billions into weapons that almost immediately become obsolete, there by necessitating more billions for newer and bigger weapons, is one of the most colossal injustices in the long history of man. While we are doing this, two thirds of the world are starving, or living in conditions of subhuman destitution.

Far from demanding that the lunatic race for destruction be stepped up, it seems to me that Christian morality imposes on every single one of us the obligation to protest against it and to work for the creation of an international authority with power and sanctions that will be able to control technology, and divert our amazing virtuosity into the service of man instead of against him.

It is not enough to say that we ought to try to work for a negotiated disarmament, or that one power bloc or the other ought to take the lead and disarm unilaterally. Methods and policies can and should be fairly considered. But what matters most is the obligation to travel in every feasible way in the direction of peace, using all the traditional and legitimate methods, while at the same time seeking to improvise new and original measures to achieve our end.

Long ago, even before the A-bomb, Pope Pius XII declared it was our supreme obligation to make "war on war" (1944). At that time he stressed our moral obligation to ban all wars of aggression, stating this duty was binding on *all* and that it "brooks no delay, no procrastination, no hesitation, no subterfuge." And what have we seen since then? The A-bomb, the H-bomb, the ICBM, the development of chemical and bacteriological weapons, and every possible evasion and subterfuge to justify their use without limitation as soon as one or the other nation decides that it may be expedient!

Therefore a Christian who is not willing to envisage the creation of an effective international authority to control the destinies of man for peace is not acting and thinking as a mature member of the Church. He does not have fully Christian perspectives. Such perspectives must by their very nature, be "Catholic," that is to say world-wide. They must consider the needs of mankind and not the temporary expediency and shortsighted policy of a particular nation.

To reject a "world-wide" outlook, to refuse to consider the good of mankind, and to remain satisfied with the affluence that flows from our war economy, is hardly a Christian attitude. Nor will our attachment to the current payoff accruing to us from weapons make it any easier for us to see and understand the need to take the hard road of sacrifice which alone leads to peace!

Equally important, and perhaps even more difficult than technological control, is the restoration of some moral sense and the resumption of genuine responsibility. Without this it is illusory for us to speak of freedom and "control." Unfortunately, even where moral principles are still regarded with some degree of respect, morality has lost touch with the realities of our situation. Modern warfare is fought as much by machines as by men. Even a great deal of the planning depends on the work of mechanical computers.

Hence it becomes more and more difficult to estimate the morality of an act leading to war because it is more and more difficult to know precisely what is going on. Not only is war increasingly a matter for pure specialists operating with fantastically complex machinery, but above all there is the question of absolute secrecy regarding everything that seriously affects defense policy. We may amuse ourselves by reading the reports in mass media and imagine that these "facts" provide sufficient basis for moral judgments for and against war. But in reality, we are simply elaborating moral fantasies in a vacuum. Whatever we may decide, we remain completely at the mercy of the governmental power, or rather the anonymous power of managers and generals who stand behind the facade of government. We have no way of directly influencing the decisions and policies taken by these people. In practice, we must fall back on a blinder and blinder faith which more and more resigns itself to trusting the "legitimately constituted authority" without having the vaguest notion what that authority is liable to do next. This condition of irresponsibility and passivity is extremely dangerous. It is hardly conducive to genuine morality.

An entirely new dimension is opened up by the fantastic processes and techniques involved in modern war. An American President can speak of warfare in outer space and nobody bursts out laughing—he is perfectly serious. Science fiction and the comic strip have all suddenly come true. When a missile armed with an H-bomb warhead is fired by the pressing of a button and its target is a whole city, the number of its victims is estimated in "megacorpses"—millions of dead human beings. A thousand or ten thousand more here and there are not even matter for comment. To what extent can we assume that the soldiers who exercise this terrible power are worthy of our confidence and actually realize what they are doing? To what extent can we assume that impassively following their lead and concurring in their decision— at least by default—we are acting as Christians?

V The Moral Problem

In all-out nuclear war, there is no longer question of simply permitting an evil, the destruction of a few civilian dwellings, in order to attain a legitimate end: the destruction of a military target. It is well understood on both sides that all-out nuclear war is purely and simply massive and indiscriminate destruction of targets chosen not for their military significance alone, but for their importance in a calculated project of terror and annihilation. Often the selection of the target is determined by some quite secondary and accidental circumstance that has not the remotest reference to morality. Hiroshima was selected for atomic attack, among other reasons, because it had never undergone any notable air bombing and was suitable as an intact target to give a good idea of the effectiveness of the bomb.

It must be frankly admitted that some of the military commanders on both sides in World War II simply disregarded all the traditional standards that were still effective. The Germans threw those standards overboard with the bombs they unloaded on Warsaw, Rotterdam, Coventry and London. The allies replied in kind with saturation bombing of Hamburg, Cologne, Dresden and Berlin. Spokesmen were not wanting on either side to justify these crimes against humanity. And today, while "experts" calmly discuss the possibility of the United States being able to survive a war if *only fifty million* (!) of the population are killed, when the Chinese speak of being able to *spare* "three hundred million" and "still get along," it is obvious that we are no longer in the realm where moral truth is conceivable.

The only sane course that remains is to work frankly and without compromise for a supra-national authority and for the total abolition of war. The pronouncements of the Holy See all seem to point to this as the best ultimate solution.

The moral duty of the Christian is by no means simple. It is far from being a neat matter of ethical principle, clear cut, well defined, and backed by a lucid authoritative decision of the Church. To make the issue seem too simple is actually to do a great disservice to truth, to morality and to man. And yet now more than ever we crave the simple and the clear solution. This very craving is dangerous, because the most tempting of all "simple" solutions are the ones which prescribe annihilation or submit to it without resistance. There is a grim joke underlying all this talk about "red or dead." The inherent destructiveness of the frustrated mind is able to creep in here and distort the whole Christian view of life and of civilization by evading the difficult and complex way of negotiation and sacrifice, in order to resort, in frustrated desperation, to "magic" power and nuclear destruction. Let us not ignore this temptation; it is one of the deepest and most radical in man. It is the first of all temptations, and the root of all the others. "You shall be as gods . . ." (Genesis 3:5).

On the contrary, our Christian obligation consists in being and remaining men, believing in the Word Who emptied Himself and became man for our sakes. We have to look at the problem of nuclear war from the viewpoint of humanity and of God made man, from the viewpoint of the Mystical Body of Christ, and not merely from the viewpoint of abstract formulas. Here above all we need a reasoning that is informed with compassion and takes some account of flesh and blood, not a legalistic juggling with principles and precedents.

In the light of these deep Christian truths we will better understand the danger of fallacious justifications of every recourse to violence, as well as the peril of indifference, inertia and passivity.

It is not a question of stating absolutely and infallibly that every Christian must renounce, under pain of mortal sin, any opinion that the use of the bomb might be legitimate. The H-bomb has not been formally and officially condemned, and doubtless it does not need to be condemned. There is no special point in condemning one weapon in order to give casuistical minds an opportunity to prove their skill in evasion by coming up with another, "licit" way of attaining the same destructive end. It is not just a matter of seeing how much destruction and murder we can justify without incurring the condemnation of the Church.

But I submit that at this time above all it is vitally important to avoid the "minimalist" approach. The issue of nuclear war is too grave and too general. It threatens everybody. It may affect the very survival of the human race. In such a case one is not allowed to take any but unavoidable risks. We are obliged to take the morally more secure alternative in guiding our choice. Let us remember too that while a doubt of the existence of an obligation leaves us with a certain freedom of choice, the doubt of an evil fact does not permit such freedom.

We may well dispute the legitimacy of nuclear war on principle: but when we face the *actual fact* that recourse to nuclear weapons may quite probably result in the quasi-total destruction of civilization, even possible suicide of the entire human race, we *are absolutely obliged to take this fact into account and to avoid this terrible danger.*

It is certainly legitimate for a Catholic moralist to hold in theory that a limited nuclear war, in defense, is permitted by traditional Christian moral principles. He may even hold the opinion that the strategic use of nuclear, bacteriological and chemical weapons is theoretically permissible for defense, provided that there is a possibility that what we are defending will continue to exist after it has been "defended."

But when we come face to face with the terrible doubt of fact, *dubium facti,* the absolutely real and imminent probability of massive and uncontrolled destruction with the annihilation of civilization and of life, then there is no such latitude of choice. We are most gravely and seriously bound by all norms of Christian morality, however minimal, to choose the safer course and try at all costs to avoid so general a disaster.

Let us remember that even if one were to admit the theoretical legitimacy of nuclear weapons for purposes of defense, that use would become gravely unjust, without a shadow of doubt, as soon as the effects of nuclear destruction overflowed upon neutral or friendly nations. Even though we may feel justified in risking the destruction of our own cities and those of the enemy, we have no right whatever to bring destruction upon helpless small nations which have no interest whatever in the war and ask only to survive in peace. It is not up to us to choose that *they* should be dead rather than red.

Pope Pius XII said in 1954 (concerning ABC warfare, described above as a sin, an offense and an outrage against God): "Should the evil consequences of adopting this method of warfare *ever become so extensive as to pass entirely beyond the control of man, then indeed its use must be rejected as immoral.*" He adds that uncontrolled annihilation of life within a given area "IS NOT LAWFUL UNDER ANY TITLE."

Nor is it moral to overindulge in speculation on this dangerous point of "control." A lax interpretation of this principle would lead us to decide that a twenty megaton H-bomb dropped on Leningrad is "fully under control" because all its effects are susceptible to measurement, and we know that the blast will annihilate Leningrad while the fallout will probably wipe out the population of Helsinki and Riga, depending on the wind. Obviously what the Pope meant was much more strict than that. He meant that if there was uncontrolled annihilation of everybody in Leningrad, without any discrimination between combatants and non-combatants, enemies, friends, women, children, infants and old people, then the use of the bomb would be "not lawful under any title," especially in view of the "bonus" effects of fallout drifting over neutral territory, certainly without control. And I do not think "clean" bombs are going to get around this moral difficulty either.

Hence though nuclear warfare as such has not been entirely and formally condemned, the mind of the Church is obviously that every possible means should be taken to avoid it; and John XXIII made this abundantly clear in his Christmas message of 1961 where he pleaded in most solemn terms with the rulers of all nations to "shun all thought of force" and remain at peace. The words of Pope John in this connection imply grave reservations even with regard to limited war which might possibly "escalate" and reach all-out proportions.

There can be no doubt whatever that the absence of formal condemnation cannot be twisted into a tacit official approval of all-out nuclear war. Yet it seems that this is what some of our theologians are trying to do.

On the contrary, our duty is to help emphasize with all the force at our disposal that the Church earnestly seeks the abolition of war; we must underscore declarations like those of Pope John XXIII pleading with world leaders to renounce force in the settlement of international disputes and confine themselves to negotiations.

Now let us suppose that the political leaders of the world, supported by the mass media in their various countries, and carried on by a tidal wave of greater and greater war preparations, see themselves swept inexorably into a war of cataclysmic proportions. Let us suppose that it becomes morally certain that these leaders are helpless to arrest the blind force of the process that has irresponsibly been set in motion. What then? Are the masses of the world, including you and me, to resign themselves to our fate and march to global suicide without resistance, simply bowing our heads and obeying our leaders as showing us the "will of God"? I think it should be evident to everyone that this can no longer, in the present situation be accepted unequivocally as obedience and civic duty.

It is true that Pope Pius XII in his Christmas message of 1956 declared that a Catholic was bound in duty to help his country in a just war of defense. But to extend this to all-out nuclear war is begging the question because papal pronouncements on nuclear war cast doubts upon its justice. No theologian, however broad, however lax, would insist that one was bound in conscience to participate in a war that was *evidently* leading to global suicide. Those who favor nuclear war can only do so by making all kinds of suppositions concerning the political and military facts: that it will be only a limited war or that the destructive effects of H-bombs are not as terrible as we have been told. However much they limit the score sheet of megacorpses, it is difficult for us to admit the morality of all-out nuclear war.

This brings us face to face with the greatest and most agonizing moral issue of our time. This issue is not merely nuclear war, not merely the possible destruction of the human race by a sudden explosion of violence. It is something more subtle and more demonic. If we continue to yield to theoretically irresistible determinism and to vague "historic forces" without striving to resist and control them, if we let these forces drive us to demonic activism in the realm of politics and technology, we face something more than the material evil of universal destruction; we face *moral responsibility for global suicide*. Much more than that, we are going to find ourselves gradually moving into a situation in which we are practically compelled by the "logic of circumstances" deliberately *to choose the course that leads to destruction*.

The great danger is then the savage and self-destructive commitment to a policy of nationalism and blind hate, and the refusal of all other policies more constructive and more in accordance with Christian ethical tradition. Let us realize that this is a matter of *choice*, not of pure blind determinism.

We all know the logic of temptation. We all know the confused, vague, hesitant irresponsibility which leads us into the situation where it is no longer possible to turn back and how, arrived in that situation, we have a moment of clear-sighted desperation in which we freely commit ourselves to the course we recognize as evil. That may well be what is happening now to the whole world.

The free choice of global suicide, made in desperation by the world's leaders and ratified by the consent and cooperation of their citizens, would be a moral evil second only to the crucifixion. The fact that such a choice might be made with the highest motives and the most urgent purpose would do nothing whatever to mitigate it. The fact that it might be made as a gamble, in the hope that some might escape, would never excuse it. After all, the purpose of Caiphas was, in his own eyes, perfectly noble. He thought it was necessary to let "one man die for the people."

The most urgent necessity of our time is therefore not merely to prevent the destruction of the human race by nuclear war. Even if it should happen to be no longer possible to prevent the disaster (which God forbid), there is still a greater evil that can and must be prevented. It must be possible for every free man to refuse his consent and deny his cooperation to this greatest of crimes.

VI The Christian Choice

In what does this effective and manifest refusal of consent consist? How does one "resist" the sin of genocide? Ideally speaking, in the imaginary case where all-out nuclear war seemed inevitable and the world's leaders were evidently incapable of preventing it, it would be legitimate and even obligatory for all sane and conscientious men everywhere in the world to lay down their weapons and their tools and starve and be shot rather than cooperate in the war effort. If such a mass movement should spontaneously arise in all parts of the world, in Russia and America, in China and France, in Africa and Germany, the human race could be saved from extinction. This is indeed an engaging hypothesis—but it is no more than that. It would be folly to suppose that men hitherto passive, inert, morally indifferent and irresponsible might suddenly recover their sense of obligation and their awareness of their own power when the world was on the very brink of war.

In any case, as has been said above, the ordinary man has no access to vital information. Indeed, even the politicians may know relatively little about what is really going on. How would it be possible to know when and how it was necessary to refuse cooperation? Can we draw a line clearly, and say precisely when nuclear war becomes so dangerous that it is suicidal? If a war of missiles breaks out, we will have at the most thirty minutes to come to our momentous conclusions—if we ever know what is happening at all. It seems to me that the time to form our conscience and to decide upon our course of action is NOW.

It is one thing to form one's conscience and another to adopt a specific policy or course of action. It is highly regrettable that this important distinction is overlooked and indeed deliberately obfuscated. To decide, in the forum of conscience, that one is obligated in every way, as a Christian, to avoid actions that would contribute to a worldwide disaster, does not mean that one is necessarily committed to absolute and unqualified pacifism. One may start from this moral principle, which is repeatedly set before us by the Popes and which cannot be seriously challenged, and one may then go on to seek various means to preserve peace. About these different means, there may be considerable debate.

Yet it seems clear to me that the enormous danger represented by nuclear weapons and the near impossibility of controlling them and limiting them to a scale that would fit the traditional ethical theory of a just war, makes it both logical and licit for a Catholic to proceed, from motives of conscience, to at least a relative pacifism, and to a policy of nuclear disarmament.

In so doing, however, he has a strict obligation to see that he does not take a naive and oversimplified position which would permit him to be ruthlessly exploited by the politicians of another nuclear power. The logic of all serious efforts to preserve peace demand that our very endeavors themselves do not help the war effort of the "enemy," and thus precipitate war. There is sometimes a danger that our pacifism may be somewhat shortsighted and immature. It may consequently be more an expression of rebellion against the status quo in our own country than an effective opposition to war itself.

In a word, there are three things to be considered: (1) Christian moral principles, which by their very nature favor peace, and according to which nuclear war remains, if not absolutely forbidden, at least of exceedingly dubious morality; (2) The facts about weapons systems and defense policies. Our moral decision, and the morality of our participation in the economic and political life of a society geared for nuclear war, demand imperatively that we realize the real nature of the military policies to which we contribute by taxation and perhaps also by our work in industry. So much in our national life is today centered on the most intense and most overwhelming arms race in the history of man. Everything points to the fact that these frightful weapons of destruction may soon be used, most probably on the highest and most expanded scale; (3) We must finally consider factors by which these military policies are dictated.

The Christian moral principles are relatively clear. While there is still intense debate over details, no Christian moralist worthy of the name can seriously defend outright a nuclear war of unqualified aggression.

The facts about ABC warfare are also clear enough. There is no question of the immense destructiveness of the weapons available to us. There is no question that the destruction of civilization and even global suicide are both possible. There is no question that the policies of the nuclear powers are geared for an all-out war of incredible savagery and destructive force.

What remains to be explored by the Christian is the area that is least considered, which also happens to be the area that most needs to be examined and is perhaps the one place where something can be done.

By what are our policies of hatred and destructiveness dictated? What seems to drive us inexorably on to the fate which we all dread and seek to avoid? This question is not hard to answer. What started the First World War? What started the Second World War? The answer is, simply, the rabid, shortsighted, irrational and stubborn forces which tend to come to a head in nationalism.

Christopher Dawson has said:

> The defeat of Hitlerism does not mean that we have seen the end of such movements. In our modern democratic world, irrational forces lie very near the surface, and *their sudden eruption under the impulse of nationalist or revolutionary ideologies is the greatest of all the dangers that threaten the modern world* . . . It is at this point that the need for a reassertion of Christian principles becomes evident. In so far as nationalism denies the principle (of higher order and divine justice for all men) and sets up the nation and the national state as the final object of man's allegiance, *it represents the most retrograde movement the world has ever seen,* since it means a denial of the great central truth on which civilization was founded, and the return to the pagan idolatries of tribal barbarism.

Dawson then goes on to quote Pope Pius XII who distinguishes between "national life" and "nationalistic politics." National life is a combination of all the values which characterize a social group and enable it to contribute fruitfully to the whole policy of nations. Nationalistic politics on the other hand are divisive, destructive, and a perversion of genuine national values. They are "a principle of dissolution within the community of peoples."

This then is the conclusion: The Christian is bound to work for peace by working against global dissolution and anarchy. Due to nationalist and revolutionary ideologies (for Communism is in fact exploiting the intense nationalism of backward peoples), a world-wide spirit of confusion and disorder is breaking up the unity and the order of civilized society.

It is true that we live in an epoch of revolution, and that the breakup and re-formation of society is inevitable. But the Christian must see that his mission is not to contribute to the blind forces of annihilation which tend to destroy civilization and mankind together. He must seek to build rather than to destroy. He must orient his efforts towards world unity and not towards world division. Anyone who promotes policies of hatred and of war is working for the division and the destruction of civilized mankind.

We have to be convinced that there are certain things already clearly forbidden to all men, such as the use of torture, the killing of hostages, genocide (or the mass extermination of racial, national or other groups for no reason that they belong to an "undesirable" category). The destruction of civilized centers by nuclear annihilation bombing is genocide.

We have to become aware of the poisonous effect of the mass media that keep violence, cruelty and sadism constantly present to the minds of unformed and irresponsible people. We have to recognize the danger to the whole world in the fact that today the economic life of the more highly-developed nations is in large part centered on the production of weapons, missiles, and other engines of destruction.

We have to consider that hate propaganda, and the consistent heckling of one government by another, has always inevitably led to violent conflict. We have to recognize the implications of voting for politicians who promote policies of hate. We must never forget that our most ordinary decisions may have terrible consequences.

It is no longer reasonable or right to leave all decisions to a largely anonymous power elite that is driving us all, in our passivity, towards ruin. We have to make ourselves heard.

Every individual Christian has a grave responsibility to protest clearly and forcibly against trends that lead inevitably to crimes which the Church deplores and condemns. Ambiguity, hesitation and compromise are no longer permissible. We must find some new and constructive way of settling international disputes. This may be extraordinarily difficult. Obviously war cannot be abolished by mere wishing. Severe sacrifices may be demanded and the results will hardly be visible in our day. We have still time to do something about it, but the time is rapidly running out.

Part Two

FOLLOWING THE YEAR OF THE
Cold War Letters

· 12 ·

THE CHRISTIAN FAILURE:
A Review

This review of the book by Rev. Ignace Lepp (Newman Press, 1962), was written by Thomas Merton under the pseudonym of Benedict Monk. It appeared in *The Catholic Worker*, January 1963. It was also published in *Continuum* (Autumn 1963) under the title of "Passivity and Abuse of Authority."

・ ・ ・ ・ ・

Father Lepp's diary provides these very interesting texts, written during the Nazi occupation of France, when many of the French clergy and the well-to-do laity collaborated with the puppet Vichy Government, anticipating the Nazi domination of Europe. They had no special love for the Nazis, but they passively accepted the totalitarian power of Hitler and preferred it to Communism. They were convinced that Europe had to be Nazi or Communist, and they chose Nazism as a "lesser" evil because they had hopes for the continued existence of the Church in France if they "played ball" with the conquerors.

Father Lepp attributed this mentality of the clergy in part to their seminary training which, he thought, made them unable to cope with the issue properly. They were not fully in touch with reality. They dealt only with abstract dilemmas which could not be really resolved in practice, and which as a result left French Catholics more or less passive and submissive to an evil which they should have been able to resist.

One of the grave problems of religion in our time is posed by the almost total lack of protest on the part of religious people and clergy, in the face of enormous social evils. It is not that these people are wicked or perverse (as the Communists would sometimes have us believe) but simply that they are no longer fully capable of seeing and evaluating certain evils as they truly are: as crimes against God and as betrayals of the Christian ethic of love. A case in point is the social injustice in the nominally "Catholic" countries of Latin America, against which the hierarchy has recently protested. Another case is that of nuclear war, which the Popes have repeatedly denounced but which the majority of Catholics in America and other Western nations tend to accept passively and without question simply because it is "better than being a Communist." It is a "lesser evil." This however is not a serious moral judgment and is in no sense an answer. It represents nothing but a psychology of evasion, irresponsibility and negativism, hiding behind such grandiose concepts as "defense of freedom and religion," "obedience to civil authority," "self-sacrifice" and so on.

It seems that a psychology of evasion and helplessness, glorified and encouraged by persons in authority who are able to take advantage of it, has gradually come to replace the true virtue of Christian obedience. This is a psychology of subservient opportunism which, in reality, has nothing Christian about it, but on the contrary, gives ample scope for the irresponsibility of the mass mind and in the end threatens to destroy both Christian and democratic liberty.

True Christian obedience should liberate man from servitude to the "elements of this world" (cf. Galatians 4: 1–11) so that we may be able freely to obey civil authority when it is legal and just, and that in the presence of injustice and falsity we may "obey God rather than men" (cf. Acts 5: 17–32). But a pseudo-Christian obedience is nothing more than the mechanical and irrational submission of beings who have renounced freedom and responsibility in order to become cogs in an official machine. It is not the obedience of sons of God but the compliance of functionaries in a military bureaucracy. Here the supreme virtue is to agree with authority no matter whether it is right or wrong, to maintain one's position by flattery, compliance and mechanical efficiency. It is the obedience of an Eichmann who will commit any crime in order to retain his position in organized falsity and infamy.

The first text shows that typical members of the French clergy in 1942 thought Father Lepp was a rebel, a trouble maker and a madman because instead of passively obeying an illegal government, he was aiding the publication of an underground Christian paper for the Resistance. For him to do this, they felt, was defying the manifest will of God by refusing to submit. For them, obedience was really opportunism and servility.

Father Lepp: "Last night I had a heated discussion with a few fellow priests on the subject of the publication of the underground paper *Temoinage Chretien*. They cannot understand why Catholics in public life and priests should edit this paper and it was no use my trying to point out that the Vichy government is not a divine institution. In the eyes of these well-meaning priests it is only Communists, enemies both of God and France, who are interested in sabotaging the efforts of the 'national revolution' which this government claims as its own. At this moment, when the Allied landing in North Africa gives us more reason to doubt the final victory of the Nazis these good priests are still utterly convinced of it.

"It is not that they want German victory, because not one of them upholds Nazi-ism, but the training they received at the seminaries has formed their intellect on such exclusively abstract lines that they are unable to cope with practical life and they battle against dilemmas that exist only in their minds. Listening to them, one would imagine that France and the world must choose either Hitler or Stalin—or, in other words, a 'New Europe' under Nazi leadership or the occupation of Europe under the 'Red hordes.' Whatever the Nazi crimes, to these priests they seem less terrifying than the horrors for which the Communists are responsible. It is quite impossible to convince them that there is a possibility of avoiding the domination of both Hitler and Stalin. And if one maintains the possible return of a French parliamentary democracy they repeat all the Vichy banalities about the decadence and corruption of the 'people's republic' with a fervor worthy of a better cause." (p. 34–35)

Note that a characteristic of this psychology is in fact a latent despair of freedom and of democratic government. The either/or complex, which resigns itself fatalistically to the supposed "choice" between Nazism and Communism is, in fact, a flight from the difficulties and responsibilities without which democratic life and freedom are impossible.

But this evasion is really not a fully free and deliberate choice. It is rather a regression and irresponsible capitulation to power: for since the Christian cannot, by definition, become an atheist Communist, he falls back on the other brand of Totalitarianism which may still pretend to tolerate religions. In reality, this is a surrender of the Christian conscience to demonic forces at work for the destruction of society and of the Church.

The chief criterion of moral values comes to be "survival." Of course it is presented not just as the survival of the individual, but as the "freedom of religion" etc. Yet this implies that the individual Catholic will retain his comfortable and privileged position . . . or so he thinks. For this, then, he will shut his eyes to monstrous evils, acquiesce in an unjust and tyrannical system, and prove himself obedient by never doing anything to rock the boat.

The next text shows the pitiful servility of this psychology, which goes to considerable trouble to invest good reasons, religious reasons, for its defection.

"It shocks me to think of all the Catholics who made no protest when some of their preachers had no scruples in flattering Petain and acclaiming him as a sort of Joan of Arc. Even Peguy, the typical individualist, finds he is called upon to comply with the worst kinds of pseudo-Christian principles. Petain is known to be more religious minded than Paul Reynaud and yet all kinds of legends are invented to make him out some kind of saint. His entourage is shrewd enough to encourage these legends because they realize that numerically the Catholics are the only class on which the regime could stand. It seems as if the nostalgia for a theocratic regime is still prevalent among some Catholics—how otherwise can one explain why the confusion between religious and political views is so welcome to them. Not only have the subsidies for denominational schools been welcomed with real gratitude but many people hope and trust that Petain will restore the establishment of the Church in France.

"The authoritarian character of the Church has developed in many Catholics a tendency to evade all spiritual responsibility; they assert that the Church is the steward of eternal truth and then content with themselves with repeating mechanically the liturgical and dogmatic formulas without making an intellectual effort to understand them and bring them to life. They seem to have lost the determination to obey moral laws; all they are concerned with is to be told by authority what to do and what not to do. I find it hard to believe that this is what Christ came for, but as far as the subconscious mind of many Catholics is concerned, a long time has elapsed since evangelical liberty was replaced by pharisaical observance of the law. So it is not surprising that these Catholics also tend to evade personal responsibility in the sphere of temporal organizations. If a democracy is not to deteriorate into a mere demagogy, each person must be prepared to look after his own affairs and to contribute to the affairs of the community. It is so much easier to leave it all trustingly to the leader—Franco in Spain, Petain in France; even the atheists Mussolini and Hitler know how to make the most of this inertia. Our Lord has good reason to speak of 'sheep' when he charged Peter to take care of his Church." (p. 35–36)

Father Lepp points out that this mentality may have in it something of a "nostalgia for theocracy." Hence a wrong idea of obedience and a false supernaturalism ought to be regarded as sources of dangerous confusion, when they destroy the distinction between the sacred and the secular: in other words when the authority of a secularist power is purely and simply identified with the divine authority and even usurps the functions which rightly belong only to the conscience.

Note that Father Lepp attributes the distortion of the right notion of Christian obedience to defects with the Church itself. Abuses of authority by ministers of the Church lead to a weakening of the moral sense of the Christians, instead of strengthening it. The result of this is that in very grave social issues, where the conscience of the Catholic layman should play a positive and decisive part, the layman wants to be instructed by the priest who, in turn, being out of touch with the reality of the problem, hands down an abstract decision devoid of genuine moral seriousness. This results in an abdication of responsibility and passive submission to an evil that ought to be identified, denounced and resisted, not "obeyed." Thus by defection of the Christian conscience democracy degenerates into demagogy and Fascism—or Communism.

The last text shows to what extremes this philosophy can lead. Emmanuel Mounier, protesting by a hunger strike against unjust imprisonment and being in danger of death, was refused absolution by a priest who could not conceive this resistance as anything other than rebellion against God. Yet in fact, the resistance offered by Mounier was not only politically right, but was the answer demanded by Christian morality to injustice and untruth. It was Mounier who was obedient in all truth. The priest, misled by a defective formation, was betraying truth and justice. He was false to Christ.

Hence the ultimate danger of this thoroughly un-Christian psychology is that it perverts the Christian conscience and punishes the Christian who, led by his moral sense and his Christian faith, seeks to offer heroic obedience to the will of God, and who therefore deserves all the support and comfort that the Church can give him.

"A friend of mine told me of the long hunger strike which Mounier has imposed upon himself in prison. A few days ago he felt his strength fading and fearing to die almost at once, he asked for a priest so that he could receive absolution and Holy Communion. But the priest (I shouldn't be surprised to hear that he was a 'holy man') refused him absolution on the grounds that he had disobeyed legitimate authority and was not prepared to repent his disobedience. There seems no limit to the stupidity of men, even of priests. One sometimes needs great strength and pure faith not to be discouraged and to remain loyal to the Church almost, as it were, in spite of herself." (p. 34)

In conclusion, we must remark that this dangerous psychology is not always merely passive. It can become not only active but extremely aggressive and violent in support of a totalitarian myth. Once again, the ostensible motives may be "religious" but the fruits of cruelty, inhumanity and fanaticism identify these motives as anti-Christian.

· 13 ·

THE PRISON MEDITATIONS
OF FATHER DELP:
Introduction

Published by Herder and Herder, New York City, in 1963

Merton wrote his introduction to this book in October 1962. What follows is the complete introduction taken from the book. Abridged versions of it were published as "A Martyr to the Nazis" in *Jubilee*, March 1963; as "Spirituality for an Age of Overkill" in *Continuum*, Spring 1963; and as "The Church in a Disillusioned World" in *The Way* (London) May 1963.

Father Alfred Delp, a south German Jesuit, was arrested on July 28, 1944—just fifty years ago, as I write this brief introduction in July of 1994—accused of complicity in the plot to murder Hitler. Father Delp was a philosopher who had studied with Martin Heidegger. Prisoner number 1442, he was hanged for the crime of "defeatism"—his belief that Germany would not win the war, a belief that was considered treason—on February 2, 1945. In his cell he left only his glasses, his rosary, and *The Imitation of Christ*. His last recorded words were: "If I have to die, at least I know why. How many people can say that today?"

· · · · ·

T hose who are used to the normal run of spiritual books and meditations will have to adjust themselves, here, to a new and perhaps disturbing outlook. Written by a man literally in chains, condemned to be executed as a traitor to his country in time of war, these pages are completely free from the myopic platitudes, and the insensitive complacencies of routine piety. Set in the familiar framework of seasonal meditations on the Church year, these are new and often shocking insights into realities which we sometimes discuss academically but which here are experienced in their naked, uncompromising truth. These are the thoughts of a man who, caught in a well-laid trap of political lies, clung desperately to a truth that was revealed to him in solitude, helplessness, emptiness and desperation. Face to face with inescapable physical death, he reached out in anguish for the truth without which his spirit could not breathe and survive. The truth was granted him, and we share it in this book, awed by the realization that it was given him not for himself alone, but for us, who need it just as desperately, perhaps more desperately, than he did.

One of the most sobering aspects of this book is the conviction it imparts that we may one day be in the same desperate situation as the writer. Though we may perhaps still seem to be living in a world where, in spite of wars and rumors of wars, business goes on as usual, and Christianity is what it has always been, Father Delp reminds us that somewhere in the last fifty years we have crossed a mysterious limit set by Providence and have entered a new era. We have, in some sense, passed a point of no return, and it is both useless and tragic to continue to live as if we were still in the nineteenth century. Whatever we may think of the new era, whether we imagine it as the millennium, the noosphere, or as the beginning of the end, there has been a violent disruption of society and a radical overthrow of that modern world which goes back to Charlemagne.

In this new era the social structures into which Christianity had fitted so comfortably and naturally have all but collapsed. The secularist thought patterns which began to assert themselves in the Renaissance, and which assumed control at the French Revolution, have now so deeply affected and corrupted modern man that even where he preserves certain traditional beliefs, they tend to be emptied of their sacred inner reality, and to mask instead the common pseudo-spirituality or the outright nihilism of mass-man. The meditations of Father Delp were written not only in the face of his own death, but in the terrifying presence of this specter of a faceless being that was once the image of God, and toward which the Church nevertheless retains an unchanging responsibility.

The first pages were written in Advent of 1944, when the armies of the Third Reich launched their last hope, hopeless offensive in the Ardennes. Defeat was already certain. The Nazis alone refused to see it. Hitler was still receiving lucky answers from the stars. Father Delp had long since refused to accept the collective delusion. In 1943, at the request of Count Von Moltke and with the permission of his religious

Superiors, he had joined in the secret discussions of the 'Kreisau Circle,' an anti-Nazi group that was planning a new social order to be built on Christian lines after the war. That was all. But since it implied a complete repudiation of the compulsive myths and preposterous fictions of Nazism, it constituted high treason. Since it implied that Germany might not win it was 'defeatism'—a crime worthy of death.

The trial itself was a show, staged by a specialist in such matters. It was handled with ruthless expertise and melodramatic arrogance before an obedient jury and public of SS men and Gestapo agents. The scenario did not provide for a serious defense of the prisoners. Such efforts as they made to protest their innocence were turned against them and only made matters worse. Count Von Moltke and Father Delp were singled out as the chief villains, and in Delp's case the prosecution smeared not only the prisoner but the Jesuit Order and the Catholic Church as well. Moltke came under special censure because he had the temerity to consult bishops and theologians with sinister 're-Christianizing intentions.' The prosecution also tried to incriminate Moltke and Delp in the attempted assassination of Hitler the previous July, but this was obviously out of the question and the charge was dropped. This was plainly a religious trial. The crime was heresy against Nazism. As Father Delp summed in up in his last letter: 'The actual reason for my condemnation was that I happened to be and chose to remain a Jesuit.'

Nearly twenty years have passed since Father Delp was executed in the Plotzensee prison on February 2, 1945. During these twenty years the world has been supposedly 'at peace.' But in actual fact, the same chaotic, inexhaustible struggle of armed nations has continued in a different form. A new weaponry, unknown to Father Delp, now guarantees that the next total war will be one of titanic destructiveness, when a single nuclear weapon contains more explosive force than all the bombs in World War II put together. In the atmosphere of violent tension that now prevails, there is no less cynicism, no less desperation, no less confusion than Father Delp saw around him. Totalitarian fanaticisms have not disappeared from the face of the earth: on the contrary, armed with nuclear weapons, they threaten to possess it entirely. Fascism has not vanished: the state socialism of the Communist countries can justly be rated as a variety of fascism. In the democratic countries of the west, armed to the teeth in defense of freedom, fascism is not unknown. In France, a secret terrorist organization seeks power by intimidation, violence, torture, blackmail, murder. The principles of this organization of military men are explicitly fascist principles. Curiously enough, neo-Nazism recognizes its affinities with the French terrorists and proclaims its solidarity with them. Yet among the French crypto-fascists are many who appeal paradoxically to Christian principles, in justification of their ends!

What in fact is the position of Christians? It is ambiguous and confused. Though the Holy See has repeatedly affirmed the traditional classical ethic of social and international justice, and though these pronouncements are greeted with a certain amount of respectful interest, it is increasingly clear that their actual influence is often negligible. Christians themselves are confused and passive, looking this way and that for indications of what to do or think next. The dominating factor in the political life of the average Christian today is fear of Communism. But, as Father Delp shows, the domination of fear completely distorts the true perspectives of Christianity and it may well happen that those whose religious activity reduces itself in the long run to a mere negation, will find that their faith has lost all content.

In effect, the temptation to negativism and irrationality, the urge to succumb to pure pragmatism and massive use of power, is almost overwhelming in our day. Two huge blocs, each armed with a quasi-absolute, irresistible offensive force capable of totally annihilating the other, stand face to face. Each one insists that it is armed in defense of a better world, and for the salvation of mankind. But each tends more and more explicitly to assert that this end cannot be achieved until the enemy is wiped out.

A book like this forces us to stand back and reexamine these oversimplified claims. We are compelled to recall that in the Germany of Father Delp's time, Christians were confronted with more or less the same kind of temptation. First there must be a war. After that a new and better world. This was nothing new. It was by now a familiar pattern, not only in Germany but in Russia, England, France, America and Japan.

Was there another choice? Is there another choice today? The western tradition of liberalism has always hoped to attain a more equable world order by peaceful collaboration among nations. This is also the doctrine of the Church. Father Delp and Count Von Moltke hoped to build a new Germany on Christian principles. Pope John XXIII in his encyclical *Mater et Magistra* clarified and exposed these principles. If there remains a choice confronting man today, it is the crucial one between global destruction or global order. Those who imagine that in the nuclear age it may be possible to clear the way for a new order with nuclear weapons are even more deluded than the people who followed Hitler, and their error will be a thousand times more tragic, above all if they commit it in the hope of defending their religion.

Father Delp had no hesitation in evaluating the choice of those who, in the name of religion, followed the Nazi government in its policy of conquest first and a new world later. He said:

'The most pious prayer can become a blasphemy if he who offers it tolerates or helps to further conditions which are fatal to mankind, which render him unacceptable to God, or weaken his spiritual, moral or religious sense.'

This certainly applies to cooperation with militant atheism first of all, but it applies equally well to any current equivalent of Nazism or militaristic Fascism.

ii

What did Father Delp mean by 'conditions fatal to mankind'?

His prison meditations are a penetrating diagnosis of a devastated, gutted, faithless society in which man is rapidly losing his humanity because he has become practically incapable of belief. Man's only hope, in this wilderness which he has become, is to respond to his inner need for truth, with a struggle to recover his spiritual freedom. But this he is unable to do unless he first recovers his ability to hear the voice that cries to him in the wilderness: in other words, he must become aware of his devastated and desperate condition before it is too late. There is no question of the supreme urgency of this revival. For Father Delp it seems clear that the time is running out.

In these pages we meet a stern, recurrent foreboding that the 'voice in the wilderness' is growing fainter and fainter, and that it will soon no longer be heard at all. The world may then sink into godless despair.

Yet the 'wilderness' of man's spirit is not yet totally hostile to all spiritual life. On the contrary, its silence is still a healing silence. He who tries to evade solitude and confrontation with the unknown God may eventually be destroyed in the meaningless chaotic atomized solitariness of mass society. But meanwhile it is still possible to face one's inner solitude and to recover mysterious sources of hope and strength. This is still possible. But fewer and fewer men are aware of the possibility. On the contrary: 'Our lives today have become godless to the point of complete vacuity.'

This is not a cliche of pulpit rhetoric. It is not a comforting slogan to remind the believer that he is right and that the unbeliever is wrong. It is a far more radical assertion, which questions even the faith of the faithful and the piety of the pious. Far from being comforting, this is an alarming declaration of almost Nietzschean scandalousness. 'Of all messages this is the most difficult to accept—*we find it hard to believe that the man of active faith no longer exists.*' An extreme statement, but he follows it with another: 'Modern man is not even *capable* of knowing God.' In order to understand these harsh assertions by Father Delp we must remember they were written by a man in prison, surrounded by Nazi guards. When he speaks of 'modern man,' he is in fact speaking of the Nazis or of their accomplices and counterparts. Fortunately not all modern men are Nazis. And even in reference to Nazis, when stated thus bluntly and out of context, these statements are still too extreme to be true. They are not meant to be taken absolutely, for if they were simply true, there would be no hope left for anyone, and Father Delp's message is in fact a message of hope. He believes that 'the great task in the education of present and future generations is to *restore man to a state of fitness for God.*' The Church's mission in the world today is a desperate one of helping create conditions in which man can return to himself, recover something of his lost humanity, as a necessary preparation for his ultimate return to God. But as he now is, alienated, void, internally dead, modern man has in effect no capacity for God.

Father Delp is not saying that human nature is vitiated in its essence, but we have been abandoned by God or become radically incapable of grace. But the dishonesty and injustice of our world are such, Father Delp believes, that we are blind to spiritual things even when we think we are seeing them: and indeed perhaps most blind when we are convinced that we see. 'Today's bondage,' he says, speaking of Germany in 1944, 'is the sign of our untruth and deception.'

The untruth of man, from which comes his faithlessness, is basically a matter of arrogance, or of fear. These two are only the two sides of one coin—attachment to material things for their own sake, love of wealth and power. Alienation results in arrogance of those who have power or in the servility of the functionary who, unable to have wealth and power himself, participates in a power structure which employs him as a utensil. Modern man has surrendered himself to be used more and more as an instrument, as a means, and in consequence his spiritual creativity had dried up at it source. No longer alive with passionate convictions, but centered on his own empty and alienated self, man becomes destructive, negative, violent. He loses all insight, all compassion, and his instinctual life is cruelly perverse. Or else his soul, shocked into insensitivity by suffering and alienation, remains simply numb, inert and hopeless. In such varying conditions, man continues in 'blind conflict with reality' and hence his life is a repeated perpetration of a basic untruth. Either he still hopes in matters and in the power he acquires by its manipulation, and then his heart is one to which 'God himself cannot find access, it is so hedged around with insurance.' Or else, in abject self-contempt, alienated man 'believes more in his own unworthiness than in the creative power of God.'

Both these conditions are characteristic of materialist man, but they also appear in a pseudo-Christian guise. This is particularly true of the negative, lachrymose and 'resigned' Christianity of those who manage to blend the cult of the status quo with a habit of verbalizing on suffering and submission. For such as these, indifference to real evil has become a virtue, and preoccupation with petty or imaginary problems of piety substitute for the creative unrest of the truly spiritual man. A few phrases about the Cross and a few formal practices of piety concord, in such religion, with a profound apathy, a bloodless lassitude, and perhaps an almost total incapacity to love. It is the indifference of a man who, having surrendered his humanity, imagines that he is therefore pleasing to God. Unfortunately Father Delp suggests that such a one is already faithless, already prepared for any one of the modern pseudo religions, the worship of the Class, Race or State.

What can be done to save such resigned and negative Christians from becoming crypto-fascist? Certainly no amount of 'baroque glamorizing' of the mysteries of faith, no dramatic banalities, no false glitter of new apologetic techniques. Seen from the silence of Father Delp's prison cell, the much publicized movements dedicated to so many worthy ends take on a pitiable air of insignificance. Too often, he says, these efforts represent a failure to meet the genuine needs of man. Sometimes they do not imply even an elementary awareness of man's real desperation. Instead of being aimed at those whom the Church most needs to seek, these movements seem to him in many cases to concern themselves with the hunger of pious souls for their own satisfaction; they produce an illusion of holiness and a gratifying sense that one is accomplishing something.

Instead of the difficult exploratory and diagnostic work of seeking modern man in his spiritual wilderness with all its baffling problems, these movements are scarcely aware of anything new in the world—except new means of communication. For them, *our problems are still the same ones* the Church has been confronting and solving for two thousand years. It is assumed that we know what is wrong, and that all we lack is zeal and opportunity to fix it: then everything will be all right. It is not a question of truth or insight but of power and will, we imagine: all we need is the capacity to do what we already know. Hence we concentrate on ways and means of gaining influence so that we can obtain a hearing for our familiar answers and solutions. But in actual fact we are, with everybody else, in a new world, unexplored. It is as though we were already on the moon or on Saturn. The walking is not the same as it was on earth.

Too much religious action today, says Father Delp, concentrates on the relatively minor problems of the religious minded minority and ignores the great issues which compromise the very survival of the human race. Man has gradually had the life of the spirit and the capacity for God crushed out of him by an inhuman way of life of which he is both the 'product and the slave.' Instead of striving to change these conditions, and to build an order in which man can gradually return to himself, regain his natural and supernatural health, and find room to grow and respond to God, we are rather busying ourselves with relatively insignificant details of ritual, organization, ecclesiastical bureaucracy, the niceties of law and ascetical psychology. Those who teach religion and preach the truths of faith to an unbelieving world are perhaps more concerned with proving themselves right than with really discovering and satisfying the spiritual hunger of those to whom they speak. Again, we are too ready to assume that we know, better than the unbeliever, what ails him. We take it for granted that the only answer he needs is contained in formulas so familiar to us that we utter them without thinking. We do not realize that he is listening not for words but for the evidence of thought and love behind the words. Yet if he is not instantly converted by our sermons we console ourselves with the thought that this is due to his fundamental perversity.

Father Delp says, 'None of the contemporary religious movements take for their starting point the position of mankind as human beings . . . they do not help man in the depths of his need but merely skim the surface . . . They concentrate on the difficulties of the religious minded man who still has religious leanings. They do not succeed in coordinating the forms of religion with a state of existence that no longer accepts its values.' Before we can interest non-Christians in the problems of cult and of conduct that seem important and absorbing to us, we must first try to find out what they need, and perhaps also we might devote a little more thought to the question whether it is not possible that, in a dialogue with them, *they* might have something to give *us*. Indeed, if we do not approach the dialogue with a genuine dialogue, if it is simply a benign monologue in which they listen to us in abashed and grateful awe, we cannot give them the one thing they most need: the love which is our own deepest need also. 'Man,' says Father Delp, 'must be educated to resume his proper status of manhood, and religion must be taught intensively by truly religious teachers. The profession has fallen into disrepute and it will have to be reestablished.' What is needed, he says, is not simply good will and piety, but 'truly religious men *ready to cooperate in all efforts for the betterment of mankind and human order.*'

However, these efforts must not be a matter of an interested and manipulative religious politic. The world has become disillusioned with religious politics devoid of genuine human and spiritual concern, interested only in preparing the way for peremptory doctrinal and moral demands. Father Delp makes it clear that we are in no position to make such demands on modern man in his confusion and despair. The following paragraph is one of the most sobering and perhaps shocking in the book, but it contains profound truths for those who know how to listen:

> 'A Church that makes demands in the name of a peremptory God no longer carries weight in a world of changing values. The new generation is separated from the clear conclusions of traditional theology by a great mountain of boredom and disillusion thrown up by past experience. We have destroyed man's confidence in us by the way we live. We cannot expect two thousand years of history to be an unmixed blessing and recommendation. History can be a handicap too. But recently a man turning to the Church for enlightenment has all too often found only a tired man to receive him—a man who then had the dishonesty to hide his fatigue under pious words and fervent gestures. At some future date the honest historian will have some bitter things to say about the contribution of the Churches to the creation of the mass mind, of collectivism, dictatorships and so on.'

More than this, Father Delp realizes the profound responsibility of the Christian to his persecutors themselves 'lest those who are our executioners today may at some future time be our accusers for the suppression of truth.'

In such statements as these, Father Delp makes no attempt to gloss over what he believes to be the truth, and he speaks with all the authority of a confessor of the faith who knows that he must not waste words. He himself adds, in all frankness: 'Whoever has fulfilled his duty of obedience has a right to cast a critical eye over the realities of the Church and where the Church fails the shortcomings should not be glossed over.' It is impossible to dismiss these criticisms as the words of an embittered rebel, disloyal to the Church. Father Delp *died* for the Church. The words of one who has been obedient unto death cannot be dismissed or gainsaid. These meditations 'in face of death' have a sustained, formidable seriousness unequaled in any spiritual book of our time. This imposes upon us the duty to listen to what he has said with something of the same seriousness, the same humility and the same courage.

Nevertheless it must be recognized that since 1945 other voices have joined themselves to Father Delp's and have reiterated the same criticisms. Perhaps they have done so in milder or more general terms, but there is a widespread recognition of the fact that the Church is seriously out of contact with modern man, and can in some sense be said to have failed in her duty to him. This awareness, though stated in general terms, can be discerned in statements of certain bishops, even of the Pope himself. Certainly the convocation of the Second Vatican Council was intended, in the mind of John XXIII, to meet precisely the situation which Father Delp described with an almost brutal forthrightness.

Archbishop Hurley of Durban has recommended a radical reform in seminary education to enable priests to meet the new needs that confront the Church. Though stated with less urgency than the strictures of Father Delp, these recommendations of the South African Archbishop reflect something of the same sense of crisis.

> Unless the change of methods is systematically pursued a first class crisis will result, for there is no better way of promoting a crisis than by allowing a situation to drift into change without adjusting the approach of those most directly involved in the situation. Priests engaged in the pastoral ministry are the persons most directly involved in the Church's day to day life and activity. There is therefore no more urgent task confronting us than a reconsideration of the methods by which our priests are trained for their ministry. If we fail to face up to it the developing crisis may strain to a breaking point the relations between a laity in desperate need of a new approach and to some extent led to expect it, and a clergy incapable of supplying the need. (Pastoral Emphasis in Seminary Studies, Maynooth, 1962)

iii

The diagnosis of our modern sickness has been given to us by Father Delp in the most serious unambiguous terms. What of the prognosis?

First of all, he asks us to face the situation squarely, but warns that it is not enough to take a perverse pleasure in contemplating our own ruin. 'Pious horror at the state of the world will not help us in any way. An apocalyptic mood of general disgust and contempt for the hopes of our struggling fellow-Christians would only further aggravate the negativism and despair which he has so lucidly pointed out to us. Yet at the same time there can be no question that we must start from where we are: we must begin with the fact that in the midst of a twisted and shattered humanity we too are leading an 'existence that has become a reproach.' Yet here he lays open to us the paradox on which our salvation depends: the truth that even in our blindness and apparent incapacity for God, God is still with us, and that an encounter with him is still possible. Indeed, it is our only hope.

Impatience, willfulness, self-assertion, and arrogance will not help us. There is no use in Promethean self-dramatization. Things have gone too far for that. The encounter with God is not something we can conjure up by some magic effort of psychological and spiritual force. Indeed, these are the temptations of the secular false prophets: the masters of autonomy, for whom 'untrammeled subjectivity is the ultimate secret of being,' the artists of Faustian self-assertion whose efforts 'have silenced the messengers of God' and reduced the world to a spiritual waste land.

The Advent discovery which Father Delp made, pacing up and down his cell in chains, was that in the very midst of his desolation the messengers of God were present. This discovery was in no way due to his own spiritual efforts, his own will to believe, his own purity of heart. The 'blessed messages' were pure gifts from God, which could never have been anticipated, never foreseen, never planned by a human consciousness. Unaccountably, while he saw with a terrible and naked clarity the horror of his world gutted by bombs, he saw at the same time the meaning and the possibilities of man's condition. In the darkness of defeat and degradation, the seeds of light were being sown.

> What use are all the lessons learned through our suffering and misery if no bridge can be thrown from one side to the other shore? What is the point of our revulsion from effort and fear if it brings no enlightenment and does not penetrate the darkness and dispel it? What use is it shuddering at the

world's coldness which all the time grows more intense, if
we cannot discover the grace to conjure up better conditions?

In his Advent meditations, with all the simplicity of traditional
Christian faith, and in images that are seldom remarkable for any special originality, Father Delp proceeds to describe the ruin of Germany
and of the Western world as an 'advent' in which the messengers of God
are preparing for the future. But this golden future is not a foregone
conclusion. It is not a certainty. It is an object of hope. But it is
contingent upon the spiritual alertness of man. And man, as Father
Delp has already repeated so often, is totally sunk in darkness.

Man must begin by recognizing and accepting his desolation, in all
its bitterness.

'Unless a man has been shocked to his depths at himself and the
things he is capable of, as well as the failings of humanity as a whole,
he cannot understand the full import of Advent.'

The tragedy of the concentration camps, of Eichmann and of countless others like him, is not only that such crimes were possible, but
that the men involved could do what they did *without being in the
least shocked and surprised at themselves.* Eichmann to the very last
considered himself an obedient and God fearing man! It was the dehu-
manized bureaucratic conscientiousness that especially appalled Father
Delp: the absurd and monumental deception that practices the greatest
evil with ritual solemnity as if it were somehow noble, intelligent and
important. The inhuman complacency that is *totally incapable* of seeing
in itself either sin, or falsity, or absurdity, or even the slightest
impropriety.

Two things then are necessary to man. Everything depends on these.

First he must accept without reserve the truth 'that life. . . . by itself
has neither purpose nor fulfillment. It is both powerless and futile
within its own range of existence and also as a consequence of sin. To
this must be added the rider that life demands both purpose and
fulfillment.'

'Secondly it must be recognized that it is God's alliance with man,
his being on our side, ranging himself with us, that corrects this state
of meaningless futility. *It is necessary to be conscious of God's decision
to enlarge the boundaries of his own supreme existence by condescend-
ing to share ours, for the overcoming of sin.'*

In other words, Father Delp is reiterating the basic truth of Christian
faith and Christian experience, St. Paul's realization of the paradox of
man's helplessness and God's grace, not as somehow opposed, fighting

for primacy in man's life, but as a single existential unity—sinful man redeemed in Christ.

Acceptance does not guarantee a sudden illumination which dispels all darkness forever. On the contrary it means seeing life as a long journey into the wilderness, but a journey with an invisible Companion, toward a secure and promised fulfillment not for the individual believer alone but for the community of man to whom salvation has been promised in Jesus Christ. But as soon as these familiar words are uttered, we imagine that it is now once again a question of lulling ourselves to sleep in devout psychological peace. 'Everything will be all right. Reality is not as terrible as it seems.'

On the contrary, Father Delp will have us turn back to the real contemporary world in all its shocking and inhuman destructiveness. We have no other option. This is the prime necessity. The urgent need for courage to face the truth of untruth, the cataclysmic presence of an apocalyptic lie that is at work not only in this or that nation, this or that class and party, this or that race, but in all of us, everywhere. 'These are not matters that can be postponed to suit our convenience. They call for immediate action because untruth is both dangerous and destructive. It has already rent our souls, destroyed our people, laid waste our land and our cities; it has already caused our generation to bleed to death.'

Yet at the same time, truth is hidden in the very heart of untruth. 'Our fate no matter how much it may be entwined with the inescapable logic of circumstance, is still nothing more than the way to God, the way the Lord has chosen for the ultimate consummation of his purpose.'

The light and truth which are hidden in the suffocating cloud of evil are not to be found only in a stoical and isolated individual here and there who has surmounted the horror of his fate. They must appear somehow in a renewal of our entire social order. 'Moments of grace both historical and personal are inevitably linked with an awakening and restoration of genuine order and truth.' This is most important. It situates the profound and mystical intuitions of Father Delp in a securely objective frame of reference. His vision has meaning not for himself alone but for our society, our Church and for the human race.

In other words, Father Delp prescribes not only acceptance of our 'fate' but much more, acceptance of a divinely appointed task in history. It is, note clearly, not simply the decisions to accept one's personal salvation from the hands of God, in suffering and tribulation, but the decision to become *totally engaged in the historical task of the Mystical Body of Christ* for the redemption of man and his world.

It is then not only a question of accepting suffering, but much more, of accepting *happiness*. This in its turn implies much more than a stoical willingness to put up with the blows of fortune, even though they may be conceived as 'sent by God.' It means a total and complete *openness to God*. Such openness is impossible without a full reorientation of man's existence according to exact and objective order which God has placed in his creation and to which the Church bears infallible witness.

If we surrender completely to God, considered not only as an inscrutable and mysterious Guest within ourselves, but as the Creator and Ruler of the world, the Lord of history and the Conqueror of evil and of death, then we can recover the meaning of existence, we rediscover our sense of direction. 'We regain faith in our own dignity, our mission and our purpose of life precisely to the extent that we grasp the idea of our life flowing forth within us from the mystery of God.'

Perfect openness, total receptivity, born of complete self-surrender, bring us into uninhibited contact with God. In finding him we find our true selves. We return to the true order he has willed for us.

Such texts show that Father Delp was at the same time profoundly mystical and wide open to the broadest ideals of Christian humanism. It was by the gift of mystical intuition that he not only found himself in God but also situated himself perfectly in God's order and man's society, even though paradoxically his place was to be a condemned man in the prison of an unjust and absurd government. Yet it was here that he could write, without exaggeration, 'To restore divine order and to proclaim God's presence—these have been my vocation.'

Father Delp's exact obedience to God, his perfect acceptance of God's order in the midst of disorder, was what gave him a sublime authority in denouncing the cowardice of Christians who seek refuge from the reality in trifling concerns, petty sectarian opinions, futile ritualism or religious technicalities which they alone can understand. Christians must not be afraid to be people, and to enter into a genuine dialogue with other men, precisely perhaps with those men they most fear or stand most ready to condemn.

'The genuine dialogue no longer exists,' says Father Delp, 'because there are no genuine partners to engage in it. People are frightened. They are scared to stride out firmly and honestly to the boundaries of their potential powers because they are afraid of what they will find at the borderline.'

In his impassioned plea for Christian liberty and personal dignity, Father Delp stands out as an advocate of true Christian humanism. This is exactly the opposite of the Promethean pseudo-humanism of anti-Christian culture since the Renaissance.

The supposed 'creativity' claimed by the untrammeled subjectivism of men who seek complete autonomy defeats itself, because man centered on himself inevitably becomes destructive.

The humanism of Father Delp, which is also the humanism of the Church, recognizes that man has to be rescued precisely from this spurious autonomy which can only ruin him. He must be liberated from fixation upon his own subjective needs and compulsions, and recognize that he cannot fully become himself until he knows his need for the world and his duty of serving it.

In bare outline, man's service of the world consists not in brandishing weapons to destroy other men and hostile societies, but in creating an order based on God's plan for his creation, beginning with a minimum standard for a truly human existence for all men. Living space, law and order, nourishment for *all*, are basic needs without which there can be no peace and no stability on earth. No faith, no education, no government, no science, no art, no wisdom will help mankind if the unfailing certainty of the minimum is lacking.

There is also an ethical minimum: honesty in every field, self respect and mutual respect for all men, human solidarity among all races and nations. There must finally be a 'minimum of transcendence,' in other words the cultural and spiritual needs of man must be met. In the words of Pope John XXIII, in *Mater et Magistra:* 'Today the Church is confronted with *the immense task of giving a human and Christian note to modern civilization:* a note that is almost asked by that civilization itself for its further development *and even for its continued existence.*' It is no easy task to meet these minimal standards. At the present moment the fury and compulsions of the Cold War seem to be the chief obstacle to our progress. Yet we too are in the same 'advent' as Father Delp, and its laws are the same for us. If we pay attention, rouse ourselves from the despairing sleep, open our hearts without reserve to the God who speaks to us in the very wilderness where we now are, we can begin the work he asks of us: the work of restoring order to society, and bringing peace to the world, so that eventually man may begin to be healed of his mortal sickness, and that one day a sane society may emerge from our present confusion.

Is this impossible? When Father Delp died, he surrendered his life into the hands of God with the full conviction that it was not only possible, but that the work would one day be done.

But he also believed that the only hope for the world was this return to order and the emergence of the 'new man,' who knows that 'adoration of God is the road that leads man to himself.'

Unless man is made new, in the new order for which Father Delp laid down his life, there is no hope for our society, there is no hope for the human race. For man, in his present condition, has been reduced to helplessness. All his efforts to save himself by his own ingenuity are futile. They bring him closer and closer to his own destruction.

Such then is the deeply disturbing yet hopeful message of these pages. It is the message not of a politician, but of a mystic. Yet this mystic recognized his inescapable responsibility to be involved in politics. And because he followed messengers of God into the midst of a fanatical and absurd political crisis, he was put to death for his pains.

What remains now is to understand this final most important lesson. The place of the mystic and the prophet in the twentieth century is not totally outside of society, not utterly remote from the world. Spirituality, religion, mysticism are not an unequivocal rejection of the human race in order to seek one's own individual salvation without concern for the rest of men. Nor is true worship a matter of standing aside and praying for the world, without any concept of its problems and its desperation.

Thy mystic and the spiritual man who in our day remain indifferent to the problems of their fellow men, who are not fully capable of facing those problems, will find themselves inevitably involved in the same ruin. They will suffer the same deceptions, be implicated in the same crimes. They will go down to ruin with the same blindness and the same insensitivity to the presence of evil. They will be deaf to the voice crying in the wilderness, for they will have listened to some other, more comforting voice, of their own making. This is the penalty of evasion and complacency.

Even contemplative and cloistered religious, perhaps especially these, need to be attuned to the deepest problems of the contemporary world. This does not mean that they must leave their solitude and engage in the struggle and confusion in which they can only be less useful than they would be in their cloister. They must preserve their unique perspective, which solitude alone can give them, and from their vantage point they must understand the world's anguish and share it in their own way, which may, in fact, be very like the experience of Father Delp.

No one has a more solemn obligation to understand the true nature of man's predicament than he who is called to a life of special holiness and dedication. The priest, the religious, the lay-leader must, whether he likes it or not, fulfill in the world the role of a prophet. If he does not face the anguish of being a true prophet, he must enjoy the carrion comfort of acceptance in the society of the deluded by becoming a false prophet and participating in their delusions.

· 14 ·

DANISH NON-VIOLENT RESISTANCE TO HITLER

Published in The Catholic Worker, *July-August 1963*

| Thomas Merton wrote this article under the pseudonym of Bene-
dict Moore. |

· · · · ·

One of the rare glimmers of humanity in Eichmann's patient labors to exterminate the Jews, as recorded by Hannah Arendt's recent series of articles in the *New Yorker,* was the non-violent resistance offered by the entire nation of Denmark against Nazi power mobilized for genocide.

Denmark was not the only European nation that disagreed with Hitler on this point. But it was one of the only nations which offered explicit, formal and successful non-violent resistance to Nazi power. The adjectives are important. The resistance was successful because it was explicit and formal, and because it was practically speaking unanimous. The entire Danish nation simply refused to cooperate with the Nazis, and resisted every move of the Nazis against the Jews with non-violent protest of the highest and most effective caliber, yet without any need for organization, training, or specialized activism: simply by unanimously and effectively expressing in word and action the force of their deeply held moral convictions. These moral convictions were nothing heroic or sublime. They were merely ordinary.

There had of course been subtle and covert refusals on the part of other nations. Italians in particular, while outwardly complying with Hitler's policy, often arranged to help the Jews evade capture or escape from unlocked freight cars. The Danish nation, from the King on down, formally and publicly rejected the policy and opposed it with an open, calm, convinced resistance which shook the morale of the German troops and SS men occupying the country and changed their whole outlook on the Jewish question.

When the Germans first approached the Danes about the segregation of Jews, proposing the introduction of the yellow badge, the government officials replied that the King of Denmark would be the first to wear the badge, and that the introduction of any anti-Jewish measures would lead immediately to their own resignation.

At the same time, the Danes refused to make any distinction between Danish and non-Danish Jews. That is to say, they took the German Jewish refugees under their protection and refused to deport them back to Germany—an act which considerably disrupted the efficiency of Eichmann's organization in Denmark until 1943 when Hitler personally ordered that the "final solution" go into effect without further postponement.

The Danes replied by strikes, by refusals to repair German ships in their shipyards, and by demonstrations of protest. The Germans then imposed martial law. But now it was realized that the German officials in Denmark were changed men. They could "no longer be trusted." They refused to cooperate in the liquidation of the Jews, not of course by open protest, but by delays, evasions, covert refusals and the raising of bureaucratic obstacles. Hence Eichmann was forced to send a "specialist" to Denmark, at the same time making a concession of monumental proportions: all the Jews from Denmark would go only to Theresienstadt, a "soft" camp for privileged Jews. Finally, the special police sent direct from Germany to round up the Jews, were warned by the SS officers in Denmark that Danish police would probably forcibly resist attempts to take the Jews away by force, and that there was to be no fighting between Germans and Danes. Meanwhile the Jews themselves had been warned and most of them had gone into hiding, helped of course by friendly Danes: then wealthy Danes put up money to pay for transportation of nearly six thousand Jews to Sweden which offered them asylum, protection and the right to work. Hundreds of Danes cooperated in ferrying Jews to Sweden in small boats. Half the Danish Jews remained safely in hiding in Denmark, during the rest of the war. About five hundred Jews who were actually arrested in Denmark went to Theresienstadt and lived under comparatively good conditions: only forty-eight of them died, mostly of natural causes.

Denmark was certainly not the only European nation that disapproved more or less of the "solution" which Hitler had devised for the Judenfrage. But it was the only nation which, as a whole, expressed moral objection to this policy. Other nations kept their disapproval to themselves. They felt it was enough to offer the Jews "heartfelt sympa-

thy," and, in many cases, tangible aid. But let us not forget that generally speaking the practice was to help the Jew at considerable profit to
oneself. How many Jews in France, Holland, Hungary, etc., paid for-
tunes for official permits, bribes, transportation, protection, and still
did not escape!

The whole Eichmann story, as told by Hannah Arendt (indeed as
told by anybody) acquires a quality of hallucinatory awfulness from
the way in which we see how people in many ways exactly like ourselves, claiming as we do to be Christians or at least to live by humanistic standards which approximate, in theory, to the Christian ethic,
were able to rationalize a conscious, uninterrupted and complete cooperation in activities which we now see to have been not only criminal
but diabolical. Most of the rationalizing probably boiled down to the
usual half-truths: "What can we do? There is no other way out, it is
a necessary evil. True, we recognize this kind of action to be in many
ways 'unpleasant.' We hate to have to take measures like these: but
then those at the top know best. It is for the common good. The
individual conscience has to be overruled when the common good is
at stake. Our duty is to obey. The responsibility for those measures
rests on others . . . etc."

Curiously, the Danish exception, while relieving the otherwise unmitigated horror of the story, actually adds to the nightmarish and
hallucinated effect of incredulousness one gets while reading it. After
all, the Danes were not even running a special kind of non-violent
movement. They were simply acting according to the ordinary beliefs
which everybody in Europe theoretically possessed, but which, for
some reason, nobody acted on. Quite the contrary! Why did a course
of action which worked so simply and so well in Denmark, not occur
to all the other so-called Christian nations of the West just as simply
and just as spontaneously?

Obviously there is no simple answer. It does not even necessarily
follow that the Danes are men of greater faith or deeper piety than
other Western Europeans. But perhaps it is true that these people had
been less perverted and secularized by the emptiness and cynicism, the
thoughtlessness, the crude egoism and the rank amorality which have
become characteristic of our world, even where we still see an apparent
surface of Christianity. It is not so much that the Danes were Christians, as that they were human. How many others were even that?

The Danes were able to do what they did because they were able to
make decisions that were based on clear convictions about which they
all agreed and which were in accord with the inner truth of man's own

rational nature, as well as in accordance with the fundamental law of God in the Old Testament as well as in the Gospel: thou shalt love thy neighbor as thyself. The Danes were able to resist the cruel stupidity of Nazi anti-Semitism because this fundamental truth was important to them. And because they were willing, in unanimous and concerted action, to stake their lives on this truth. In a word, such action becomes possible where fundamental truths are taken seriously.

THE BLACK REVOLUTION:
Letters to a White Liberal

These "letters" were published in a number of places: Blackfriars,
November 1963; Ramparts, *Christmas 1963;* Motive, *March 1964.
They became a major part of Merton's book* Seeds of Destruction,
published by Farrar Straus and Giroux, Inc., November 16, 1964.

Martin Marty reviewed *Seeds of Destruction* for the *New York
Herald Tribune.* The review was strongly critical of the "Letters
to a White Liberal," in which Merton questioned the sincerity of
the white liberal's commitment to reforms that would actually
benefit black people. In the August 30, 1967 issue of *The National
Catholic Reporter* Marty wrote an open letter in which he apologized to Merton for failure to perceive the prophetic insights in
what Merton had written. "Now it seems to me," he says, "that
you were 'telling it as it is' and maybe 'as it will be.'" For Merton's response to Marty, see *The Hidden Ground of Love,*
454–58.

· · · · ·

Introductory Note

These "Letters to a White Liberal" were written during the early summer of 1963 and revised in the fall of the same year. As they approach
publication in book form, a few remarks are needed to situate them in
the context in which they will quite probably be read.

The developments that have taken place during 1964 have, if anything, substantiated everything these "Letters" attempted to say.

The Civil Rights bill has been passed, after the longest debate in the
history of Congress, after the longest filibuster, after the most sustained and energetic efforts to prevent its becoming law. The new

legislation is, in the main, worthy of praise. But, as the "Letters" point out, it is one thing to have a law on the books and another to get the law enforced when in practice not only the citizenry and "Citizens' Councils" but the police, the state governments and the courts themselves are often in league against the Federal government. To what extent the law will remain a dead letter in the South, to what extent it will simply aggravate pressures and animosities in the North, where such rights are still guaranteed in theory more than in practice, is not quite possible to predict.

One thing is certain: since this law will not be entirely enforced, and since, even if it were perfectly enforced it would still not be able to meet critical problems that are more strictly economic and sociological (jobs, housing, delinquency, irresponsible violence), we are forced to admit that the Civil Rights legislation is not the end of the battle but only *the beginning of a new and more critical phase in the conflict.*

How comforting, how utopian a thought, if we could only convince ourselves that this new law marks the final victory in a patient and courageous struggle of moderate leaders, dedicated to non-violence and to scrupulous respect for social order and ethical principles! It is true of course that Birmingham and the Washington March in 1963 were symbolic of a long non-violent fight for rights. They marked the final stages of the campaign that made the Civil Rights bill an urgent necessity.

At the same time the systematic lawlessness and violence with which the opponents of Civil Rights legislation have set their own "rights" above those guaranteed by the law, have effectively undermined the respect which the Negroes themselves may have had for the legal and administrative agencies that are supposed to keep order and protect rights. Thus the struggle for the bill has also demonstrated that, in order to exercise the rights which the law protects, the Negro (and anyone else whose rights are in fact denied) is going to have to obtain some form of power.

Of course the law specifically removes obstacles to the registration and voting of Negroes, reaffirming that they should have access to the democratic exercise of power by ballot. Obviously, however, it is going to be a long time before Negroes can make full use of this particular form of power. And the use of molotov cocktails and bullets against them when they attempt to vote, unfortunately, encourages them to prefer bullets to ballots themselves.

So it happens that now, after the passage of the bill, a new, tougher Negro leadership promises to emerge, no longer moderate and nonviolent, and much more disposed to make sinister and effective use of the threat of force implied by the great concentration of frustrated, angry and workless Negroes in the ghettos of the North. We can now expect violent, though perhaps disorganized and sporadic, initiatives in force around the edges of the Negro slums. This is already a familiar experience in some cities where, however, the violence has usually been designated under the rubric of "delinquency" rather than that of "revolution." But let us not forget that delinquency itself is simply a spontaneous form of non-political protest and revolt.

When the Civil Rights bill passed, a Southern Senator tragically declared that this would "only add to the hatred." He was of course right in foreseeing that after the bill became law the danger of hatred and violence would be even greater than before. But he was not necessarily right in attributing this to the law as such. He simply knew that the law had not ended the struggle. He knew well enough that the law had left the white South more deeply and grimly entrenched in its refusals. That the Negro, North and South, was more determined to take matters into his own hands, since he was convinced that even the liberal white man was not prepared to give him anything beyond fair promises and a certain abstract good will.

No one can be blind to the possibilities of violence in this situation. Though it is quite true that the vast majority both of whites and Negroes want to solve this problem without force and bloodshed, their "wanting" and their good intentions are no longer enough. It is also obvious that the majority of Americans were shocked and appalled by the senseless murder of President Kennedy. The fact remains that no matter who may have been guilty of actually shooting the President the murder grew out of the soil of hatred and violence that then existed and still exists in the South. It has been said often enough, but not too often, that the President had already been killed a thousand times over by the thoughts and the words, spoken or printed, of the racists. His death was something that John F. Kennedy himself evidently did not understand, or he would have gone into Dallas that day with less confidence and better protection. It is also something that the majority of Americans still do not quite manage to believe. But it must be affirmed: *where minds are full of hatred and where imaginations dwell on cruelty, torment, punishment, revenge and death, then inevitably there will be violence and death.*

Why, in this particular crisis (and this applies to international politics as well as to domestic or economic upheaval), is there so much hatred and so dreadful a need for explosive violence? Because of the impotency and the frustration of a society that sees itself involved in difficulties which, though this may not consciously be admitted, promise to be insuperable. Actually, there is no reason why they *should* be insuperable, but as long as white society persists in clinging to its present condition and to its own image of itself as the only acceptable reality, then the problem will remain without reasonable solution, and there will inevitably be violence.

The problem is this: if the Negro, as he actually is (not the "ideal" and theoretical Negro, or even the educated and cultured Negro of the small minority), enters wholly into white society, then *that society is going to be radically changed.* This of course is what the white South very well knows, and it is what the white Liberal has failed to understand. Not only will there be a radical change which, whatever form it may take, will amount to at least a peaceful revolution, but also there will be enormous difficulties and sacrifices demanded of everyone, especially the whites. Obviously property values will be affected. The tempo of life and its tone will be altered. The face of business and professional life may change. The approach to the coming crucial labor and economic problems will be even more anguished than we have feared. The psychological adjustment alone will be terribly demanding, perhaps even more for Negroes than for whites in many cases.

These are things which the South is able to see. But their reality does not justify the conservative conclusion which clings blindly to the present impossible state of things, and determines to preserve it at any cost, even that of a new civil war. We must dare to pay the dolorous price of change, *to grow into a new society.* Nothing else will suffice!

The only way out of this fantastic impasse is for everyone to face and accept the difficulties and sacrifices involved, in all their seriousness, in all their inexorable demands. This is what our society, based on a philosophy of every man for himself and on the rejection of altruism and sacrifice (except in their most schematic and imaginary forms), is not able to do. Yet it is something which it must learn to do. It cannot begin to learn unless it knows the need to learn. These "Letters" attempt to demonstrate the reality of that need and the urgency of the situation.

· I ·

If I dare to imagine that these letters may have some significance for both of us, it is because I believe that Christianity is concerned with human crises, since Christians are called to manifest the mercy and truth of God in history.

Christianity is the victory of Christ in the world—that is to say, in history. It is the salvation of man in and through history, through temporal decisions made for love of Christ, the Redeemer and Lord of History. The mystery of Christ is at work in all human events, and our comprehension of secular events works itself out and expresses itself in that sacred history, the history of salvation, which the Holy Spirit teaches us to perceive in events that appear to be purely secular. We have to admit that this meaning is often provisional and sometimes beyond our grasp. Yet as Christians we are committed to an attempt to read an ultimate and transcendent meaning in temporal events that flow from human choices. To be specific, we are bound to search "history," that is to say the intelligible actions of men, for some indications of their inner significance and *some relevance to our commitment as Christians.*

"History" then is for us that complex of meanings which we read into the interplay of acts and decisions that make up our civilization. And we are also (this is more urgent still) at a turning point in the history of that European and American society which has been shaped and dominated by Christian concepts, even where it has at times been unfaithful to its basically Christian vocation. We live in a culture which seems to have reached the point of extreme hazard at which it may plunge to its own ruin, unless there is some renewal of life, some new direction, some providential reorganization of its forces for survival.

Pope Paul VI, in opening the second session of Vatican Council II, has clearly spelled out the obligation of the Church to take the lead in this renewal by becoming aware of her own true identity and her vocation in the world of today. He has said without any hesitation or ambiguity that the Church must recognize her duty to manifest Christ to the world, and must therefore strive as far as possible to resemble the hidden Lord of Ages so as to make Him visible in her charity, her love of truth and her love of man. To that end, the Church has the obligation to purify and renew her inner life, because it is "only after this work of internal sanctification has been accomplished that the Church will be able to show herself to the whole world and say: 'Who sees me sees Christ.'" (Opening address of Pope Paul, September 29, 1963) In order to do this the Church herself must "look upon Christ to discern her true likeness."

Now this call to a universal examination of conscience, not only on the part of Catholics but also implicitly of all Christians, came exactly two weeks after a bomb exploded in a Baptist Church in Birmingham, Alabama, killing four Negro girls at Sunday School. On that same day, in the same city, an Eagle scout, of the white race who had been to Sunday School *and* to a racist rally, shot and killed a twelve year old Negro boy for no other reason than that he was a Negro.

These were not the actions of Catholics, but they took place in a region where many Catholics have explicitly and formally identified themselves with racial segregation and therefore with the denial of certain vital civil rights to Negroes. In Louisiana, not long before the Pope's address, Catholics had set fire to a parochial school rather than allow it to be opened to Negro students along with white. In Louisiana also a Catholic priest who had white and Negro children receive their first communion at the same time, though at different ends of the altar rail, was beaten up by his parishioners for this affront to Southern dignity. (In most Catholic Churches of the South, Negro communicants may only approach the altar rail after all the whites have departed.) In light of these events, the following words of Pope Paul have a special seriousness and urgency: "If (the Church) were to discover some shadow, some defect, some stain upon her wedding garment, what should be her instinctive, courageous reaction? There can be no doubt that her primary duty would be to reform, correct, and set herself aright in conformity with her divine Model."

At present, in a worldwide struggle for power which is entirely pragmatic, if not cynically unprincipled, the claims of those who appeal to their Christian antecedents as justification for their struggle to maintain themselves in power are being judged by the events which flow from their supposedly "Christian" choices.

For example, we belong to a nation which prides itself on being free, and which relates this freedom at least implicitly to its source in Christian theology. Our freedom rests on respect for the rights of the human person, and though our society is not officially Christian, this democratic respect for the person can be traced to the Christian concept that every man is to be regarded as Christ, and treated as Christ.

Briefly, then: we justify our policies, whether national or international, by the implicit postulate that we are supremely concerned with the human person and his rights. We do this because our ancestors regarded every man as Christ, wished to treat him as Christ, or at least believed this to be the right way to act, even though they did not always follow this belief.

Now if we advance this claim, and base our decisions and choices upon it, we must not be surprised if the claim itself comes under judgment. If we assert that we are the guardians of peace, freedom, and the rights of the person, we may expect other people to question this, demanding, from time to time, some evidence that we mean what we say. Commonly they will look for that evidence in our actions. And if our actions do not fit our words, they will assume that we are either fools, deceiving ourselves, or liars attempting to deceive others.

Our claims to high-minded love of freedom and our supposed defense of Christian and personalist ideals are going to be judged, we believe, not only by other men, but above all by God. At times we are perhaps rashly inclined to find this distinction reassuring. We say to ourselves: God at least knows our sincerity. He does not suspect us as our enemies do. He sees the *reality* of our good intentions!

I am sure He sees whatever reality is there. But are we absolutely certain that He judges our intentions exactly as we do? Our defense policies and the gigantic arms race which they require are all based on the supposition that we seek peace and freedom, not only for ourselves, but for the whole world. We claim to possess the only effective and basically sincere formula for world peace because we alone are truly honest in our claim to respect the human person. For us, the person and his freedom with his basic rights to life, liberty and the pursuit of happiness, comes absolutely first. Therefore the sincerity and truth of all our asserted aims, at home and abroad, in defense and in civil affairs, is going to be judged by the *reality* of our respect for persons and their rights. The rest of the world knows this very well. We seem not to have realized this as well as they.

We fail to notice that the plans we have devised for defending the human person and his freedom involve the destruction of millions of human persons in a few minutes, not because the great majority of these persons are themselves hostile to us, or a threat to us, but because by destroying them we hope to destroy a *system* which is hostile to us and which in addition, is tyrannizing over them, reducing them to abject servitude, and generally destroying their rights and dignities as human persons. Their oppressors have taken away their rights—but we will compound the injury by also taking away their lives and this in the name of the "person" and of "freedom"!

At the same time, even those who believe that such a war could conceivably be "won," admit that we ourselves, the prospective victors, would necessarily have to live for many years under a military dictatorship while undergoing reconstruction.

Clearly, a defense policy that leads to the out-right destruction of millions of innocent persons and to the severe curtailing of liberties, even of those who have fought for liberty and won, may be accounted a valid defense of a *system,* or an organization, but it is in no sense a defense of persons and personal rights, since it sacrifices these to the supposed interests of the system. In that case, it is not really the person and his rights who come first, but the system. Not flesh and blood, but an abstraction.

Another example: we claim that we are really solicitous for the rights of the Negro, and willing to grant him these rights some time or other. We even insist that the very nature of our society is such that the Negro, as a person, is precisely what we respect the most. Our laws declare that we are not simply a society which tolerates the presence of the Negro as a second class citizen of whom we would prefer to rid ourselves altogether if we only could. They assert that since the Negro is a person, he is in every way equal to every other person, and must enjoy the same rights as every other person. Our religion adds that what we do to him, we do to Christ, since we are a free society, based on respect for the dignity of the human person as taught to the world by Christianity.

How, then, do we treat this other Christ, this person, who happens to be black?

First, if we look to the South which is plentifully supplied not only with Negroes but also with professed Christian believers, we discover that belief in the Negro as a person is accepted only with serious qualifications, while the notion that he is to be treated as Christ has been overlooked. It would not be easy for a Christian to mutilate another man, string him up on a tree and shoot him full of holes if he believed that what he did to that man was done to Christ. On the contrary, he must somehow imagine that he is doing this to the devil— to prevent the devil doing it to him. But in thinking such thoughts, a Christian has spiritually apostatized from Christianity and has implicitly rejected that basic respect for the rights of the person on which a truly Christian and free society depends. From then on anything such a man may say about "Christianity" or "freedom" has lost all claim to rational significance.

Only with the greatest unwillingness have some very earnest Southern Christians, under duress, accepted the painful need to ride in the same part of public conveyances with Negroes, eat at the same lunch counters, use the same public facilities. And there are still not a few of these Christians who absolutely refuse to worship Christ in the same congregations as Negroes. Even some Catholics have refused to receive the Body of Christ together with Negroes in sacramental communion: and they have been astonished to find themselves excommunicated officially for refusing integrated schools, when in point of fact they had already by their own action manifestly excommunicated themselves, acting implicitly as schismatics, rending the unity of the Body of Christ.

Nevertheless, the inner conflicts and contradictions of the South are not to be taken as a justification for the smugness with which the North is doing just as poor a job, if not a worse job, of defending the Negro's rights as a person. The race "problem" is something which the Southerner cannot escape. Almost half the population of the South are Negroes. Though there are greater concentrations of Negroes in Northern slums, yet Northern Negroes can be treated as if they were not there at all. For years, New Yorkers have been able to drive to Westchester and Connecticut without going through Harlem, or even seeing it, except from a distant freeway. The abuses thus tolerated and ignored are sometimes as bad as and worse than anything in the South.

It is clear that our actual decisions and choices, with regard to the Negro, show us that in fact we are not interested in the rights of several million persons, who are members and citizens of our society and are in every way loyal Americans. They pay taxes, fight for the country and do as well as anybody else in meeting their responsibilities. And yet we tolerate shameful injustices which deprive them, by threats and by actual violence, of their right to vote and to participate actively in the affairs of the nation.

Here I can see you will protest. You will point to the Supreme Court decisions that have upheld Negro rights, to education in integrated colleges and schools. It seems to me that our motives are judged by the real fruit of our decisions. What have we done? We have been willing to grant the Negro rights on paper, even in the South. But the laws have been framed in such a way that in every case their execution has depended on the good will of white society, and the white man has not failed, when left to himself, to block, obstruct, or simply forget the necessary action without which the rights of the Negro cannot be enjoyed in fact. Hence, when laws have been passed, then contested, dragged through all the courts, and finally upheld, the Negro is still in no position to benefit by them without, in each case, entering into further interminable lawsuits every time he wants to exercise a right that is guaranteed to him by law.

In effect, we are not really giving the Negro a right to live where he likes, eat where he likes, go to school where he likes or work where he likes, but only *to sue the white man who refuses to let him do these things.* If every time I want an ice cream soda I have to sue the owner of the drugstore, I think I will probably keep going to the same old place in my ghetto. That is what the Negro, until recently, has done. Such laws are without meaning unless they reflect a willingness on the part of white society to implement them.

You will say: "You cannot legislate morality." That phrase may be quite true in its own proper context. But here it is a question not of "morality" but of social order. If we have got to the point where the laws are frequently, if not commonly, framed in such a way that they can be easily evaded by a privileged group, then the very structure of our society comes into question. If you are knowingly responsible for laws that will be systematically violated, then you are partly to blame for the disorders and the confusion resulting from civil disobedience and even revolution.

I think there is possibly some truth in the accusation that we are making laws simply because they look nice on the books. Having them there, we can enjoy the comfort of pointing to them, reassuring our own consciences, convincing ourselves that we are all that we claim to be, and refuting the vicious allegations of critics who question the sincerity of our devotion to freedom.

But at the same time, when our own personal interests and preferences are concerned, we have no intention of respecting the Negro's rights in the concrete: North or South, integration is always going to be not on our street but "somewhere else." That perhaps accounts for the extraordinary zeal with which the North insists upon integration in the South, while treating the Northern Negro as if he were invisible, and flatly refusing to let him take shape in full view, lest he demand the treatment due to a human person and a free citizen of this nation.

That is why the Negro now insists on making himself just as obviously visible as he can. That is why he demonstrates. He has come to realize that the white man is less interested in the rights of the Negro than in the white man's own spiritual and material comfort. If then, by making himself visible, the Negro can finally disturb the white man's precious "peace of soul," then by all means he would be a fool not to do so.

Yet when we are pressed and criticized, and when the Negro's violated rights are brought up before us, we stir ourselves to renewed efforts at legislation, we introduce more bills into Congress, knowing well enough how much chance those bills have of retaining any real significance after they have finally made it (if they make it at all).

The Negro finally gets tired of this treatment and becomes quite rightly convinced that the only way he is ever going to get his rights is by fighting for them himself. But we deplore his demonstrations, we urge him to go slow, we warn him against the consequences of violence (when, at least so far, most of the organized violence has been on our side and not on his). At the same time we secretly desire violence, and even in some cases *provoke* it, in the hope that the whole Negro movement for freedom can be repressed by force.

I do not claim to be a prophet or even a historian. I do not profess to understand all the mysteries of political philosophy, but I question whether our claims to be the only sincere defenders of the human person, of his rights, of his dignity, of his nobility as a creature made in God's image, as a member of the Mystical Body of Christ, can be substantiated by our actions. It seems to me that we have retained little more than a few slogans and concepts that have been emptied of reality.

It seems to me that we have little genuine interest in human liberty and in the human person. What we are interested in, on the contrary, is the unlimited freedom of the corporation. When we call ourselves the "free world" we mean first of all the world in which *business* is free. And the freedom of the person comes only after that, because, in our eyes, the freedom of the person is dependent on money. That is to say, without money, freedom has no meaning. And therefore the most basic freedom of all is the freedom to make money. If you have nothing to buy or sell, freedom is, in your case, irrelevant. In other words, what we are really interested in is not *persons,* but *profits.* Our society is organized first and foremost with a view to business, and wherever we run into a choice between the rights of a human person and the advantage of a profit-making organization, the rights of the person will have difficulty getting a hearing. Profit first, people afterwards.

You ask me, indignantly, to confirm these vicious allegations?

It appears that the one aspect of the Negro demonstrations that is being taken most seriously in the South is that *they hurt business.* As long as there was talk only of "rights," and of "freedom" (concepts which imply *persons*) the Negro movement was taken seriously chiefly by crackpots, idealists, and members of suspicious organizations thought to be under direct control of Moscow, like CORE and the NAACP.

All this talk of Negro rights, especially when accompanied by hymn-singing and religious exhortations, could hardly be taken seriously!

It was only when money became involved that the Negro demonstrations finally impressed themselves upon the American mind as being real.

We claim to judge reality by the touchstone of Christian values, such as freedom, reason, the spirit, faith, personalism, etc. In actual fact we judge them by commercial values: sales, money, price, profits. It is not the life of the spirit that is real to us but the vitality of the *market*. Spiritual values are to us, in actual fact, meaningless unless they can be reduced to terms of buying and selling. But buying and selling are abstract operations. Money has no ontological reality: it is a pure convention. Admittedly it is a very practical one. But it is in itself completely unreal, and the ritual that surrounds money transactions, the whole liturgy of marketing and of profit, is basically void of reality and of meaning. Yet we treat it as the final reality, the absolute meaning, in the light of which everything else is to be judged, weighed, evaluated, and "priced."

Thus we end up by treating persons as objects for sale, and therefore as meaningless unless they have some value on the market. A man is to us nothing more nor less that "what he is worth." He is "known" to us as a reality when he is know to be solvent by bankers. Otherwise he has not yet begun to exist.

Our trouble is that we are alienated from our own personal reality, our true self. We do not believe in anything but money and the power or the enjoyment which come from the possession of money. We do not believe in ourselves, except in so far as we can estimate our own worth, and verify, by our operations in the world of the market, that our subjective price coincides with what society is willing to pay for us.

And the Negro? He has so far been worth little or nothing.

Until quite recently there was no place for him in our calculations, unless perhaps we were landlords—unless we had *real* estate—in Harlem. That of course was another matter, because the Negro was, after all, quite profitable to us. And yet we did not think of profit as coming to us from the beings of flesh and blood, human persons, who were crowded into those rooms. On the contrary it came to us from the only thing that was *real*—our estate. The Negro was so shadowy, so unreal, that he was nothing more than the occasion for a series of very profitable transactions which gave us a good solid reality in our own eyes and in the eyes of our society.

But now, suddenly, we have discovered that there are also some "real" Negroes. For them to be real, they must have the same kind of reality as ourselves. Reality is estimated in terms of (financial) worth.

And so we are delighted to discover that there are a few Negroes who have money.

Why has this rich Negro suddenly earned our benevolent attention? Because he is a person, because he has brains, because of the fantastic talents which alone could enable him to be a professional success against such inhuman odds? None of this. It is now to our interest to recognize him, because we can use him against the others. So now, when the Negro claims he wants to take his full part in American society as a *person*, we retort: you already are playing your part as a person: "Negroes over the years," we now declare, "have had a rapid rise in income." (A nice vague statement, but it satisfies the mind of anyone who believes in money.) "Large numbers of Negroes drive high-priced cars." Another beautiful act of faith! But here we come with "exact figures":

It is estimated that there are now thirty-five Negro millionaires in the United States."

What are these statements supposed to mean? Simply that there is no need for the Negro to make such a fuss, to demonstrate, to fight for recognition as a person. He has *received that recognition already.* "Thirty-five Negroes are millionaires." (Thirty-five out of twenty million!) "Large numbers" drive "high-priced cars." What more do you want? These are indications that the Negro has all he needs, for he has "opportunities," he can make money and thus become real.

What opportunities?

Even though a Negro millionaire may live in a "fine residential neighborhood" he is still living in a ghetto, because when he moves in, the whites move out. The neighborhood is taken over by Negroes, and even if they are millionaires, their presence means that a neighborhood is no longer "fine." For a white man it is no longer even "residential."

So that even when he is worth a million, a Negro cannot buy himself, in the land of the free, the respect that is given to a human person.

Doubtless the mercy and truth of God, the victory of Christ, are being manifested in our current history, but I am not able to see how they are being manifested *by us.*

· II ·

A little time, perhaps only a few more months, and we will realize that we have reached a moment of unparalleled seriousness in American history, indeed in the history of the world. The word "revolution" is getting around. Accepted at first with tolerance, as a pleasantly vivid figure of speech, it is going to be regarded with more and more disapproval, because it comes too near the truth. And why? What is a revolution? What does it mean to say that the Negro's struggle for full civil rights amounts to a revolution?

Much as it might distress Southerners, the fact that a Negro may now sit down next to a white woman at a snack bar and order a sandwich is still somewhat short of revolution. And if by dint of courageous and effective protest the Negroes who have a vote in deep Southern states should actually manage to cast their votes on election day without getting shot: that in itself does not make a revolution, though it may have something radically new about it. The question is, who will they be voting for? Ross Barnett?

Yet I have often thought there is something true, as well as sinister, in the usual conservative claim to "realism." We must admit that the Southern politicians are much more fully aware of the revolutionary nature of the situation than are those Northern liberals who blithely suppose that somehow the Negroes (both North and South) will gradually and quietly "fit in" to white society exactly as it is, with its affluent economy, the mass media, its political machines, and the professional inanity of its middle class suburban folkways.

We seem to think that when the Negroes of the South really begin to *use* their largely hypothetical right to vote, they will be content with the same candidates who were up last year and the year before. If those candidates themselves were under any such illusion, they would have long since done something that would get them the Negro votes.

In point of fact, the Southern politicians realize very well that if the Negroes turn out full force to vote, and thereby establish themselves as a factor to be reckoned with in Southern politics, the political machines of the past are going to collapse in a cloud of dust. To put it succinctly: if the Southern Negro is really granted the rights which are guaranteed to him, *de jure*, by the American Constitution, and if he fully and freely exercises those rights, it is all up with the old South. There are quite enough Negroes in the South to make any really free election catastrophic for the *status quo*. And Negroes, both South and North, are not going to waste time voting for people who sic police dogs on them and drench them with high pressure fire hoses, while occasionally lobbing a bomb onto their front porches for good measure.

So much for the South. But what about the North? Northern Negroes are perhaps able to put a candidate or two of their own into office: but this is only the beginning of what is suddenly becoming a very conscious and concerted drive for real political power.

In the fall of 1963, after the spectacular success of the Washington March (a success which the Negroes themselves regarded as highly ambiguous), steps were taken to form a new political party consisting mostly of Negroes. The "Freedom Now Party" is likely to have a considerable effect on American politics. While in the South we can doubt that Negroes will risk their lives to vote for Southern white politicians, there is every likelihood that they will become more active if they see a chance of getting candidates of their own. And the mere fact of their *attempting* such a thing is likely to throw the South into revolutionary turmoil. In the North, on the other hand, the big cities are now largely populated by Negroes (the whites live in the suburbs) and the Negroes can perhaps without too much difficulty gain control of urban congressional districts.

This drive for political power is going to be more and more accelerated by the problem of jobs. With five million unemployed officially acknowledged in 1963, with no indications other than that this figure *must grow,* and with repeated strikes and protests in which Negroes demand to be hired along with whites, there is going to be violent conflict over the limited number of jobs. With the best will in the world, nobody is going to be able to give jobs to Negroes without taking them away from whites, and there is no indication, at the moment, that the whites intend to retire *en masse* and spend the rest of their lives watching TV so that the Negroes may carry on the work, and collect the paychecks, of the nation.

This represents, whether we like it or not, a radical threat to our present system—a revolutionary situation. And furthermore it accentuates the already clearly defined racial lines dividing the two sides in the conflict. This means that the Negro is going to continue to be what he has decidedly become: aggressively aware of the impact on white society of the mere *threat* of revolutionary violence.

The Negro finds himself in the presence of a social structure which he has reason to consider inherently unjust (since it has seldom done him any real justice except in fair words and promises). He also sees that this society has suddenly become extremely vulnerable. The very agitation and confusion which greet his demands are to him indications of guilt and fear, and he has very little respect for exhortations to "go slow" and "be patient." He feels he has been patient for a very long time and that anyone who cannot see this for himself is not being honest about it. He also feels that there is no hope of any action being taken *unless he takes action* himself, and that the steps taken by the government are mere political maneuvers leading nowhere.

This means that a well-meaning liberal policy of compromises and concessions, striving at the same time to placate the Negro and to calm the seething indignation of the conservative whites, is not going to avert danger. It may, on the contrary, aggravate it. Hence the "realism" again, of the conservatives, who think that the only thing is to stop violence now by the full use of all the repressive agencies—police, national guard, army,—which they themselves still fully control. After all, the traditional line of thought of those who use repressive power to defend the *status quo,* is that they are justified in applying force to prevent a chaotic and explosive outbreak of revolutionary disorder, save many lives, protect property (especially their own, of course) and maintain a semblance of national identity which would otherwise be dissolved in blood. Needless to say, this is identical with the argument which revolutionaries themselves advance for repressing all resistance once they themselves have achieved their aim and have seized full power.

Now, my liberal friend, here is your situation. You, the well-meaning liberal, are right in the middle of all this confusion. You are, in fact, a political catalyst. On the one hand, with your good will and your ideals, your fine hopes and your generous, but vague, love of mankind in the abstract and of rights enthroned on a juridical Olympus, you offer a certain encouragement to the Negro (and you do right, my only complaint being that you are not yet right enough) so that, abetted by you, he is emboldened to demand concessions. Though he knows you will not support all his demands, he is well aware that you will be forced to support some of them in order to maintain your image of yourself as a liberal. He also knows, however, that your material comforts, your security, and your congenial relations with the establishment are much more important to you than your rather volatile idealism, and that when the game gets rough you will be quick to see your own interests menaced by his demands. And you will sell him down the river for the five hundredth time in order to protect yourself. For this reason, as well as to support your own self-esteem, you are very anxious to have a position of leadership and control in the Negro's fight for rights, in order to be able to apply the brakes when you feel it is necessary.

This is probably one of the main reasons why you turned out for the Washington March. Doubtless you were not thinking of any such thing, and I am not questioning your sincerity or your generosity. But there are unconscious motives in political action as well as everywhere else. They must be taken into account. Whatever may have been your conscious motives at Washington, whatever may be the reality of your optimism about the results of the March (and let us admit that it was in many ways admirable), the Negro feels that your principal contribution was to make the whole issue ambiguous and remove its revolutionary sting. He feels that you once again obscured the real issue, which is that American society *has to change* before the race problem can be solved. The atmosphere of congenial fraternity and nobility which marked the great demonstration, and certainly made it edifying from many points of view, seemed once again to indicate that liberal optimism and fair weather principles would be enough, and that the Negro would move into the place that belongs to him in white American society. But to the Negro, that is only a liberal myth. He knows that there is at present *no place for him* whatever in American society, except at the bottom of the totem pole.

Any form of social protest that assumes that the Negro has a place ready and waiting for him, in American society, is simply irrelevant, a mystification, and a fraudulent deception. The Negro has now become very alert to detect such impostures. Indeed he has become obsessively intent upon the slightest indication of fraud, so much so that he overlooks other aspects of the situation, and does not observe, for instance, that though you thought you were in the Washington March because the Negro needed you there, you were really on the march because *you needed to be there.* The health of your soul demanded it, and for that reason I am glad that you were there, and wish that I had been there with you. But the private needs of your liberal conscience are of absolutely no interest to the Negro who has a much more urgent problem to solve. And your presence is not necessarily helping him to solve it.

This is why the Negro has mixed feelings about your support. He does not want you in his way. You are more of a nuisance than anything else. And you, offended at this lack of appreciation, want to reassure the Negro—you are really on his side, and to prove it you will help him to get just a little more. You will be satisfied with the headlines. You will once again feel cozy with your liberal image—for a few days. Thus you make it possible for him, according to the fantasies of conservative thought, to "taste blood." And conservative thought is not always deluded in its choice of metaphors.

On the other hand, when you come face to face at last with *concrete* reality, and take note of some unexpected and unlovely aspects of what you have hitherto considered only in the abstract, you yourself are going to be a very frightened mortal. You are going to see that there are more than ideas and ideals involved in this struggle. It is more than a matter of images and headlines. And you are going to realize that what has begun is not going to be stopped, but that it will lead on into a future for which the past, perhaps, offers little or no precedent. But since it is one of the characteristics of liberals that they prefer their future to be vaguely predictable (just as the conservative prefers only a future that reproduces the past in all its details), when you see that the future is entirely out of your hands and that you are totally unprepared for it, you are going to fall back on the past, and you are going to end up in the arms of the conservatives. Indeed, you will be so much in their arms that you will be in their way, and will not improve the shooting.

These are frank and brutal facts, my good friend. But they are the facts on which you must base your future decisions. You must face it: this upheaval is going to sweep away not only the old style political machines, the quaint relics of a more sanguine era, but also a great deal of the managerial sophistication of our own time. And your liberalism is likely to go out the window along with a number of other entities that have their existence chiefly on paper and in the head.

What are you going to do? Are you going to say that though changes may be desirable in theory, they cannot possibly be paid for by a social upheaval amounting to revolution? Are you going to decide that the Negro movement is already out of hand, and therefore it must be stopped at any cost, even at the cost of ruthless force? In that case, you are retreating from the unknown future and falling back on a known and familiar alternative: namely the alternative in which you, who are after all on top, *remain on top by the use of force*, rather than admit a change in which you will not necessarily be on the bottom, but in which your position as top dog will no longer be guaranteed. You will prefer your own security to everything else, and you will be willing to sacrifice the Negro to preserve yourself.

But it is precisely in this that you are contributing to the inexorable development of a revolution, for revolutions are always the result of situations in which the drive of an underprivileged mass of men can no longer be contained by token concessions, and in which the establishment is too confused, too inert and too frightened to *participate* with the underprivileged in a new and creative solution of what is realized to be *their common problem.*

Is this the case at present in the United States? Instead of seeing the Negro revolution as a manifestation of a deep disorder that is eating away the inner substance of our society, *because it is in ourselves,* do we look at it only as a threat from outside ourselves—as an unjust and deplorable infringement of our rights by an irresponsible minority, goaded on by Red agitators? This would be a totally fanciful view, which removes the crisis from the context of reality into a dream-world of our own in which we proceed to seek a dream-solution. Have we forgotten that the Negro is there *because of us?* His crisis is the result of our acts, and is, in fact *our crisis.* Inability to see this might turn a common political problem into a violent conflict, in which there would be no possibility of real dialogue, and in which the insensate shibboleths of racism would drown out all hope of rational solutions. If this should happen, even those whites and Negroes who would normally be able to work together to find a common solution, will be driven apart, and the white man will become the black man's enemy by the mere fact that he is white.

As Martin Luther King sees so clearly, if the Negro struggle becomes a violent conflict (and this is what would best please the racists whether white or black!) it is bound to fail in its most rational and creative purpose—the real vindication of Negro rights and the definitive asser-tion of the Negro as a person equal in dignity to any other human person.

"I am convinced," says Dr. King, "that if we succumb to the tempta-tion to use violence in our struggle for freedom, unborn generations will be the recipients of a long and desolate night of bitterness; our chief legacy to them will be a never-ending reign of chaos." (*Strength to Love,* Harper, 63)

In one word, there is a serious possibility of an eventual civil war which might wreck the fabric of American society. And although the Negro revolution in America is now unquestionably non-Marxist, and just as unquestionably a completely original and home-grown product of our own, there is no doubt that if it resulted in a violent upheaval of American economic and political life, there might be a danger of Marxist elements "capturing" the revolution and taking it over in the name of Soviet Communism. Remote as it may seem, this fits an al-ready familiar pattern, and furthermore it has to be considered because it already dominates the minds of the segregationist right wing.

My question to you is this: can you think of a better way of conduct-ing yourself?

Does all profoundly significant social change have to be carried out in violence, with murder, destruction, police repression and underground resistance? Is it not possible that the whites might give closer attention to the claims of Negro leaders like Martin Luther King, who assert that they do not want violence, and who give every assurance (backed up by some rather convincing evidence, if you can remember Birmingham) that the Negro is not out to kill anybody, that he is really fighting not only for his own freedom but also, in some strange way, for the freedom of the whites? (This is a new and quixotic concept to us, since we are fully convinced that we are the freest people that ever existed.)

Is it true that even the smallest change of our present social framework is necessarily a disaster so great that any price, however immoral, can legitimately be paid to keep it from coming about? Is it not possible that whites and Negroes might join together in a creative political experiment such as the world has never yet seen, and in which the first condition would be that the whites consented to let the Negroes run their own revolution non-violently, giving them the necessary support and cooperation, and not being alarmed at some of the sacrifices and difficulties that would necessarily be involved?

Is there no alternative but violent repression, in which, reluctantly no doubt, you decide that it is better for the establishment to be maintained by the exercise of the power which is entirely in white hands, and which ought to remain in white hands because they are white (because, of course, Negroes are "not ready" for any kind of power)?

This presupposes a simple view of the situation: a belief that when the chips are down it is going to be either whites or blacks and since whites have proved their capacity to "run the country" and "keep order," it is unthinkable even to permit the possibility of that disorder which, you take it for granted, would follow if Negroes took a leading part in our political life.

Conclusion: revolution must be prevented at all costs; but demonstrations are already revolutionary; *ergo*, fire on the demonstrators; *ergo*. . . . At the end of this chain of thought I visualize you, my liberal friend, goose-stepping down Massachusetts Avenue in the uniform of an American Totalitarian Party in a mass rally where nothing but the most uproarious approval is manifest, except, by implication, on the part of silent and strangely scented clouds of smoke drifting over from the new "camps" where the "Negroes are living in retirement."

· III ·

How is Christianity involved in the Negro struggle? Dr. Martin Luther King has appealed to strictly Christian motives. He has based his nonviolence on his belief that love can unite men, even enemies, in truth. That is to say that he has clearly spelled out the struggle for freedom not as a struggle for the Negro alone, but also for the white man. From the start, the non-violent element in the Negro struggle is oriented toward "healing" the sin of racism and toward unity in reconciliation. An absolutely necessary element in this reconciliation is that the white man should allow himself to learn the mute lesson which is addressed to him in the suffering, the non-violent protest, the loving acceptance of punishment for the violation of unjust laws, which the Negro freely and willingly brings down upon himself in the white man's presence, in the hope that the oppressor may come to see his own injustice.

The purpose of this suffering, freely sought and accepted in the spirit of Christ, is the liberation of the Negro and the redemption of the white man, blinded by his endemic sin of racial injustice. In other words, the struggle for liberty is not merely regarded by this most significant sector of the Negro population, as a fight for political rights. It is this, and it is also much more. It is what Gandhi called *Satyagraha*—a struggle first of all for the *truth*, outside and independent of specific political contingencies.

The mystique of Negro non-violence holds that the victory of truth is inevitable, but that the redemption of individuals is not inevitable. Though the truth will win, since in Christ it has already conquered, not everyone can "come to the light"—for if his works are darkness, he fears to let them be seen.

The Negro children of Birmingham, who walked calmly up to the police dogs that lunged at them with a fury capable of tearing their small bodies to pieces, were not only confronting the truth in an exalted moment of faith, a providential *kairos*. They were also in their simplicity, bearing heroic Christian witness to the truth, for they were exposing their bodies to death in order to show God and man that they believed in the just rights of their people, knew that those rights had been unjustly, shamefully and systematically violated, and realized that the violation called for expiation and redemptive protest, because it was an offense against God and His truth.

They were stating clearly that the time had come where such violations could no longer be tolerated. These Negro followers of Dr. King are convinced that there is more at stake than civil rights. They believe that the survival of America is itself in question. They believe that the sin of white America has reached such a proportion that it may call down a dreadful judgment, perhaps total destruction, on the whole country, unless atonement is made.

These Negroes are not simply judging the white man and rejecting him. On the contrary, they are seeking by Christian love and sacrifice to redeem him, to enlighten him, so as not only to save his soul from perdition, but also to awaken his mind and his conscience, and stir him to initiate the reform and renewal which may still be capable of saving our society. But this renewal must be the work of both the White and the Negro together. It cannot be planned and carried out by the white man alone or even by the Negro under the white man's paternal guidance. It demands some Negro initiative, and the white man cannot collaborate fruitfully until he recognizes the necessity of this initiative. The Negro is not going to be placated with assurances of respect and vague encouragement from our side. He is going to make sure that we are listening and that we have understood him, before he will believe in our attempts to help.

The purpose of non-violent protest, in its deepest and most spiritual dimensions, is then to awaken the conscience of the white man to the awful reality of his injustice and of his sin, so that he will be able to see that the Negro problem is really a *White* problem: that the cancer of injustice and hate which is eating white society and is only partly manifested in racial segregation with all its consequences, *is rooted in the heart of the white man himself.*

Only if the white man sees this will he be able to gradually understand the real nature of the problem and take steps to save himself and his society from complete ruin. As the Negro sees it, the Cold War and its fatal insanities are to a great extent generated within the purblind, guilt ridden, self-deceiving, self-tormenting and self-destructive psyche of the white man.

It is curious that while the Southern whites are surrounding their houses with floodlights, to protect themselves in case Negroes creep up to murder them in the dark, all the violence in the South to date has been on the part of the whites themselves. The tragic September bombings and shootings in Birmingham were a shocking contrast to the peace and dignity of the Washington March of August 28th. This was the white Southern reply to the March! Curious that the ones who repeatedly lecture the Negro on law and order, themselves are in league with murderers and thugs. Such "order" is no order at all, it is only organized injustice and violence. Barbara Deming, a white New England woman who demonstrated with the Negro children in Birmingham, was sent to jail with them. The jail was of course segregated. She was thrown in a cell full of white prostitutes and other delinquents, and found them not only furious and hostile towards her, but terrified lest the Negro children (who were still singing hymns after a sublime display of Christian heroism) might rape and murder them in the jail. Curious that these white Southerners (people to be pitied indeed) from their half-world of violence, petty thievery, vice and addiction, were the ones who felt themselves menaced, and menaced by the clear eyes of children! The truth is that they had very good reason to fear. The action of the children was aimed at them, and aimed directly at them. It was an attack not upon their property, their jobs, their social status, but upon their inmost conscience. And unless that attack could be met and deflected, *these people would not be able to continue as they were.*

In all literal truth, if they "heard" the message of the Negro children, they would cease to be the people they were. They would have to "die" to everything which was familiar and secure. They would have to die to their past, to their society with its prejudices and its inertia, die to its false beliefs, and *go over to the side of the Negroes.* For a Southern white, this would be a real "death."

Here is the radical challenge of Negro non-violence today. Here is why it is a source of uneasiness and fear to all white men who are attached to their security. If they are forced to listen to what the Negro is trying to say, the whites may have to admit that *their prosperity is rooted to some extent in injustice and in sin.* And in consequence, this might lead to a complete re-examination of the political motives behind all our current policies, domestic and foreign, with the possible admission that we are wrong. Such an admission might, in fact, be so disastrous that its effects would dislocate our whole economy and ruin the country. These are not things that are consciously admitted, but they are confusedly present in our minds. They account for the passionate and mindless desperation with which we plunge this way and that, trying to evade the implications of our present crisis.

Certainly some such thoughts as these must underlie the apparent ambiguity in the Southern White's concept of "order." On a certain level, pathological if you like but none the less experientially real, Southern white society feels itself faced with destruction. It is menaced in its inmost being, even though that "inmost being" is in fact only a specter. But we know from experience with other notorious historical forms of fanaticism, that societies which "experience their reality" on this oniric and psychopathic level are precisely those whose members are most convinced of their own rightness, their own integrity, indeed their own complete infallibility. It is this experience of unreality as real, and as something to be defended against objective facts and rights as though against the devil himself, that produces the inferno of racism and race conflict. The South is apparently in a state of perfect ripeness for this disastrous eruption of pathological hatreds and for all the fatal consequences that they bring with them. But the comparative sophistication of the North is no guarantee that the same evil is not present there, though perhaps in a more subtle form.

I have spoken of the ambiguity in the white Southern concept of "order." What is this? When in September of 1963 a cruel and senseless bombing, too carefully planned and executed to have been the work of an ordinary group of criminals, destroyed a Baptist Church in Birmingham and killed four Negro children, Governor Wallace called out the National Guard to "keep order." The Negroes immediately appealed to President Kennedy to send United States troops to protect them against this local Alabama militia. It was evident to all that the white conception of "order" had nothing whatever to do with the protection of the rights of lives of Negroes. In the Southern mind the concept that a Negro might have rights in the same sense and in the same way as a white man simply does not exist. Hence the idea of "order" in the minds of people like Governor Wallace is simply that the whites may be guaranteed safety in doing anything they like to the Negro without fear of retaliation. The function of the National Guard was purely and simply to ensure that the Negroes would not be able to fight back effectively after the bombing. In other words it was to "keep order" in much the same way that the SS kept order under Hitler.

And again, much like their Nazi prototypes, these militia-men are there perhaps also to *provoke* violence in order to have something concrete to "prevent." This is a slightly more subtle phenomenon that at first sight appears, because of the unanimous conviction of Southerners that the Negroes are really thirsting for white blood. This is the form, the only acceptable form, in which the Southern mind can face its own moral hazard. Subconsciously a vestigial Christian sense of guilt proclaims clearly the wrong that is being done and the remedies that are demanded. But this is filtered through into consciousness as a murderous threat to the symbolic "whiteness" which clothes the infantile Southern mind with its fixation on the mythical paradise before the Civil War. In fighting the Negro, the Southerner thinks he is fighting sin, death, the devil, Communism, immorality, lechery, hate, murder, hell itself. But what he is really fighting is the present.

For this reason the "fear of attack" represents in actual fact a very serious and earnest *desire to be attacked*. Not in order to be hurt, or to suffer, far from it: but in order to find the psychopathic myth verified, and all its practical conclusions justified. Therefore when the National Guard is called out to "keep order" it is recognized at least obscurely by all, both blacks and whites, that this act expresses an urgent and almost official need for disorder. It manifests a desire and a need bred by guilt, seeking to turn itself by every possible means into a self-fulfilling prophecy.

The *non-violent* and *religious* protest of the Negro against white racism and injustice is precisely what the Southern White (in his image of himself as upright and Christian) is least prepared to tolerate or to understand. It has to be seen as an obviously sinister cloak for Communist machinations. It has to be unmasked as pure malevolence, so that the appeal it aims at the white conscience may be discredited and ignored.

It has been said that Gandhian non-violence worked because it was aimed against a conscience that was still sensitive to an ethical appeal, and that it would never have worked against the Nazis. Is this a cliche, or is there some serious truth in it? I think that if the Negroes' non-violent campaign continues in the South we will one day know, one way or the other.

There can be no question whatever that the mind of the average Southern White is not only unconsciously but even consciously and willfully tending more and more to identify itself with an explicitly Nazi brand of racism.

Meanwhile, another significant fact must be mentioned. Not only have the local Southern police conspicuously refused to take any serious action in solving nearly fifty bombings that have recently taken place, some with loss of lives, in Southern states. The FBI have also failed to produce any results. The arrival of Federal agents on the scene of violence is prompt and well publicized, but soon the whole affair is simply forgotten. It has been remarked that the FBI shows far greater zeal in exercising its functions when dealing with organizations suspected of affiliation with Communism.

This conspicuous failure of the law to provide adequate protection or redress for Negroes subject to violent attack by whites is having one very serious effect: it is causing Negroes to lose confidence in the efficacy of non-violence as a political tactic, because non-violence presupposes a basic respect for legality, and this is being completely destroyed by the inaction and hesitation of the Federal Government, along with the belligerent contempt of law and justice on the part of some Southern states.

Unfortunately, not all Negroes can appreciate the Christian foundation of non-violent actions as it is practiced by the followers of Dr. King. Many Northern Negro leaders, and especially the organizers of the Black Muslim movement, categorically reject Dr. King's ideas as sentimental. They believe that his non-violence is a masochistic exhibition of defeatism which flatters the whites, plays into their hands, and degrades the Negro still further by forcing him to submit uselessly to violence and humiliation. In some cases, the sharp criticism of Martin Luther King goes so far as to accuse him of deliberately and cynically sacrificing his followers in order to gain power and prestige for himself in white society.

This reaction against what is basically a Christian protest leads to another extreme: a black racism as intransigeant and as fanatical as that of the white racists themselves. It is true that the Black Muslims must not be painted as a corporation of devils. Yet, the Muslim movement is one of absolutely hostile rejection of all that is white, including Christianity, conceived as the "white man's religion." Instead, Islam, regarded as "African religion" and as the worship of a "Black God" or at least of the Black Man's God, is substituted for it. Emphasis is laid on the martial and combative elements in the faith of Islam and the first principle of all race relations is that the white man is never to be trusted. He is incapable of sincere, honest or humane actions. He is worthy only of hatred and contempt. No "dialogue" is possible between white and black, all that can be achieved is a complete separation without violence, in so far as this may be possible: but they will not hesitate to use violence if this becomes necessary. Theoretically, then, the Black Muslims do not have a systematic program of violent attack on the white population, as some seem to imagine. But since the separation of which they dream is, and can be, no more than a dream, the tension between the races in the big cities of the North where the Muslims are concentrated, will most probably erupt in violence sooner or later. It can be said, however, that the fact that the Muslims are disciplined and organized makes them to some extent an asset: they will certainly try to control violence and direct it. This is preferable to completely uncontrolled and in some ways "uncaused" rioting, exploding at the slightest spark and spreading in aimless fury through whole cities until its force is spent. Yet the Muslims, however disciplined they themselves may be, can easily start a general conflagration.

The Black Muslims have so far had no influence in the South, and although the Negro spokesmen in the North are often hostile to Martin

Luther King, he has immense prestige wherever Negroes are to be found in the United States, though Birmingham was not understood by all of them as a "victory" for their race. It seems, however, that all hope of really constructive and positive results from the Civil Rights Movement is to be placed in the Christian and non-violent elements. It is also possible that as the movement gains in power, the reasonableness and the Christian or at least ethical fervor of these elements will recede into the background and the Movement will become more and more an unreasoning and intransigeant mass movement dedicated to the conquest of sheer power, more and more inclined to violence.

If the Christian and non-violent element in Negro protest is finally discredited, it may mean that Christianity itself will become meaningless in Negro eyes. Those Negroes who attack the Christian leaders in the South are usually completely disillusioned with Christianity, if not bitterly hostile to it, because they are convinced that it has no other function than to keep the Negro in passive and helpless submission to his white oppressors. When white Christians express admiration and sympathy for Dr. King, this is immediately interpreted by his Negro critics as evidence of their own negative thesis.

As for the attitude of white Christians toward the Negro freedom movement, Protestants and Catholics alike are at best confused and evasive in their sympathies. One gets the impression that they mean well, and that they recognize the validity of the Negro's protest, but that they are so out of contact with the realities of the time that they have no idea how they can effectively help him. It is true that the American hierarchy has denounced the sin of racism. Here and there a Catholic bishop takes action to integrate his schools or to castigate the worst abuses of discrimination. Here and there Christian leaders get together to make encouraging statements. Yet at the same time, even those white Christians most favorable to the Negro cause, have been quick to react against the protests in Birmingham and Jackson, censuring them and demanding "more patience" on the Negro's part, sincerely believing that the whole problem can be adequately settled only by the administration in Washington. This, to the Negro, is more than naive. He cannot help but interpret it as evasion and bad faith, and consequently he has little or no confidence in *any* white Christian group including the Catholic Church.

Evidently, many white Christians will be grieved and disappointed at this evaluation of their sincere concern over the Negro's struggle for his rights. They will remind the Negro that they *have* taken certain steps in his favor. They will expect him to be more grateful. I think the time has come to say two things about this attitude.

First of all, it shows that these well-meaning critics do not grasp the real dimensions of the problem as the Negro sees it. Like the average liberal, they think that the Negro is simply presenting a few reasonable demands which can be met by legislative action. And, as a corollary to this, they assume that if the Negro were to ask any more than this, he would be unreasonable if not rebellious.

In actual fact the Negro is not simply asking to be "accepted into" the white man's society, and eventually "absorbed by it," so that race relations in the U.S. may finally come to be something like those in Latin America. I think that most Catholics tend, half consciously, to imagine that this would be a reasonable outcome: let the United States imitate those countries that were settled by Catholics in the first place, and where there has never been a very strict color line. Catholic values will triumph and there will be no more racial problems, because the United States will be like Brazil.

As the present events in Brazil make quite clear, this is no solution.

The actions and attitudes of white Christians all, without exception, contain a basic and axiomatic assumption of white superiority, even when the pleas of the Negro for equal rights are hailed with the greatest benevolence. It is simply taken for granted that, since the white man is superior, the *Negro wants to become a white man.* And we, liberals and Christians that we are, advance generously, with open arms, to embrace our little black brother and welcome him into white society.

The Negro is not only not grateful, he is not even impressed. In fact, he shows by his attitude that he is at the same time antagonized and disgusted by our stupidity. This antagonism will be all the stronger in proportion as he has had to struggle heroically to deliver himself from the incubus of inferiority feelings. And here, I think, is where all Christians, including Catholics are, innocently no doubt, doing the gravest harm to Christian truth.

For some unspoken reason, the white man (especially the Southern White) does not seem to realize that he has been rather closely observed, for the last two centuries, by his Negro slaves, servants, sharecroppers, concubines, and bastards. He does not seem to be aware of the fact that they know a great deal about him, and, in fact, understand him in some ways better than he understands himself. This information has never been passed on to the white man, who has never dreamed of asking for it. He has assumed that the ideas of the Negro were more or less worthless in the first place. Do Negroes think? Of course not:

they just sing, dance, make love, and lie in the shade doing nothing, because they are *different*. They haven't got the energy to think!

The Negro knows precisely why the white man imagines that the Negro wants to be a White Man. The White Man is too insecure in his fatuous self-complacency to be able to imagine anything else.

Consequently, when the Catholic Church gives the impression that it regards the South as a vast potential pool of "Negro converts" in which a zealous and ardent white apostolate can transform a few million Uncle Toms into reasonably respectable imitations of white Catholics, this actually does very little to make the Negro respect the truth of Christ, practically nothing to help him understand the mystery of Christ in His Church. Especially when he observes that the converted Negro is still not welcome in every Southern Catholic Church and even where he is admitted at all, he may only receive Communion *after* all the whites.

It is often quite evident that the genuinely warm sympathy which so many Catholics have for the Negro is nevertheless something the Negro himself now accepts only with resignation and disillusionment. What we love in the Negro tends to be, once again, the same old image of the vaudeville darkie, the quaint Black Mammy of plantation days, the Pullman porter with ready wit, the devoted retainer whose whole family has served a white Southern feudal tribe for generations. This is a caricature of the Negro of which the Negro himself has long since grown tired, and its chief function is to flatter the white man's sense of superiority.

One has yet to find very many Catholics, including priests, who are really able to deal with Negroes on an equal footing, that is to say without the specious and fraudulent mediation of this image. Most of us are congenitally unable to think black, and yet that is precisely what we must do before we can even hope to understand the crisis in which we find ourselves. Our best considered and most sympathetic consideration of the Negro's plight is one calculated to antagonize him because it reflects such pitiful inability to *see* him, right before our nose, as a real human being and not as a higher type of domestic animal. Furthermore we do not bother really to listen to what he says, because we assume that when the dialogue really begins, he will already be thinking just like ourselves. And in the meantime we are not too disposed to offend the white racists, either. We still want to please everybody with soft words and pleasant generalizations, which we convince ourselves are necessary for "charity." Is it charity to leave the racists sunk in a sin that cries out to heaven for vengeance?

A genuinely Catholic approach to the Negro would assume not only that the white and the Negro are essentially equal in dignity (and this, I think, we do generally assume) but also that they are brothers in the fullest sense of the word. This means to say that a genuinely Catholic attitude in matters of race is one which concretely accepts and fully recognizes the fact that different races and cultures are *correlative. They mutually complete one another.* The white man needs the Negro, and needs to know that he needs him.

White calls for black just as black calls for white. Our significance as white men is to be seen *entirely* in the fact that all men are not white. Until this fact is grasped, we will never realize our true place in the world, and we will never achieve what we are meant to achieve in it. The white man is *for* the black man: that is why he is white. The black man is for the white man: that is why he is black. But so far, we have managed only to see those relationships in a very unsatisfactory and distorted fashion.

First of all, there was the crude initial concept: the black man was *for* the white man, in the sense that he belonged to him as his slave. But in the relationship of master and slave there is no correlative responsibility. The master is like God, who cannot enter into a relationship with a creature: the creature can only enter into a relationship with Him. So the master could do what he liked with the slave, and perhaps, incidentally, he might find himself, without realizing it, living to some extent *for* the slave whom he had come to trust and love. But though there was a germinating humanity in this "relationship," there was no sense of a real social obligation to slaves as such, who therefore were never really admitted to be human beings. Thus though the South of slavery days was a kind of Eden for the white man (and is still remembered in the collective Southern myth as Eden), it was without human significance because it was empty of basic truth: the truth of *Man* was absent, because here were two different kinds of men who were supposed, in the order of nature, to complete one another as correlatives, and one of them was not admitted to human status.

The Civil War came, and the Negro acquired a human status on the books of law: but only on the books. In actual fact his position gradually became even less human than before.

To assume the superiority of the white race and of European-American culture as axiomatic, and to proceed from there to "integrate" all other races and cultures by a purely one-sided operation is a pure travesty of Catholic unity in truth. In fact, this fake Catholicism, this parody of unity which is no unity at all but a one-sided and arbitrary attempt to reduce others to a condition of identity with ourselves, is one of the most disastrous of misconceptions.

It may be true that a French missionary who brings the truth of the Gospel to a West African pagan is bringing him the truth indeed. But unfortunately, the fatal tendency has too often been to assume that *everything* he was bringing, down to his clothes, his table manners, his Cartesian habits of thought, his Gallic self-esteem and in a word, the infallibility of the *bien pensant* were all pure revelations of God and His Church. In such conditions, missionaries have assumed, with extreme generosity, that their only function was to *give* of their sublime fullness, and that it was never necessary for them to receive, to learn, to accept any kind of a spiritual gift from the native and from his indigenous culture. Material contributions—yes. But nothing else. There has generally been no conception at all that the white man had anything to learn from the Negro. And now, the irony is that the Negro (especially the Christian Negro of the heroic stamp of Dr. King) *is offering the white man a "message of salvation," but the white man is so blinded by his self-sufficiency and self-conceit that he does not recognize the peril in which he puts himself by ignoring the offer.*

Is the white man really in a position to recognize the providential character of this hour? If I say that the Negro offers him an "opportunity," the white man will perhaps scrutinize him afresh in order to find out what he has to sell. And what will he see? Something at once disturbing and unattractive. Processions of discontented black men and women carrying signs. Groups of exalted children singing hymns. Frightened but determined people letting themselves be rolled around the street by the power of firehoses. There is determination there, no doubt; they obviously mean business. But we have determination too, and there is no need at all for us to have the hoses turned on us.

This is not the point. The Negro, in fact, has nothing to sell. He is only offering us the occasion *to enter with him into a providential reciprocity willed for us by God.* He is inviting us to understand him as necessary to our own lives, and as completing them. He is warning us that we cannot do without him, and that if we insist on regarding him as an enemy, an object of contempt, or a rival, we will perhaps sterilize and ruin our own lives. He is telling us that unless we can enter into a vital and Christian relationship with him, there will be hate, violence and civil war indeed: and from this violence perhaps none of us will emerge whole.

It must then be said that this most critical moment in American History is the providential "hour," the *kairos* not merely of the Negro, but of the white man. It is, or at any rate it can be, God's hour. It can be the hour of vocation, the moment in which, hearing and understanding the will of God as expressed in the urgent need of our Negro brother, we can respond to that inscrutable will in a faith that faces the need of reform and creative change, in order that the demands of truth and justice may not go unfulfilled.

It is for this reason that the "prudence" and the (self-styled) wisdom of some white Christian leaders may well prove to be a sign of spiritual blindness, and as such it may be decisive in leading the Negro away from Christian truth and natural reason, to embark on a violent and chaotic fight for power characterized only by brutality and pragmatism. In this struggle the lessons given by the white police and politicians in the South will certainly be turned to good advantage.

What the Negro now seeks and expects (or perhaps what he has entirely given up expecting) from the white Christian is not sermons on patience, but a creative and enlightened understanding of his effort to meet the demands of God in this, his *kairos*. What he expects of us is some indication that we are capable of seeing a little of the vision he has seen, and of sharing his risks and his courage. What he asks us is not the same old string of meaningless platitudes that we have always offered him in lieu of advice. He asks us to listen to him, and to pay some attention to what *he* has to say. He seriously demands that we learn something from him, because he is convinced that we need this, and need it badly.

Negro writers, like James Baldwin, have repeatedly demonstrated that this conviction lends an extraordinary power to his words. There is no question that they have more to say than anybody else writing in America today. Many have read their books and heard their message, but few are prepared to understand it because they simply cannot conceive of a white man learning anything worth while from a Negro. Still less can they imagine that the Negro might quite possibly have a prophetic message from God to the society of our time.

It simple terms, I would say that the message is this: white society has sinned in many ways. It has betrayed Christ by its injustices to races it considered "inferior" and to countries which it colonized. In particular it has sinned against Christ in its lamentable injustices and cruelties to the Negro. The time has come when both white and Negro have been granted, by God, a unique and momentous opportunity to repair this injustice and to reestablish the violated moral and social order on a new plane.

We have this opportunity because the Negro has taken the steps which made it possible. He has refused to accept the iniquity and injustice of white discrimination. He has seen that to acquiesce in this injustice is no virtue, but only collaboration in evil. He has declared that he rejects both the physical evil of segregation and the moral evil of passive acquiescence in the white man's sin. But this is only the beginning. Now the white man must do his share, or the Negro's efforts will have no fruit.

The sin of the white man is to be expiated, through *a genuine response to the redemptive love of the Negro for him*. The Negro is ready to suffer, if necessary to die, if this will make the white man understand his sin, repent of it, and atone for it. But this atonement must consist of two things:

1) A complete reform of the social system which permits and breeds such injustices.

2) This work or reorganization must be carried out under the inspiration of the Negro whose providential time has now arrived, and who has received from God enough light, ardor and spiritual strength to free the white man in freeing himself from the white man.

I state these two conditions as nakedly and unequivocally as I find them in the words of Negro leaders. My only comment is that in making these demands, they are committing themselves very heavily to provide answers, in case we should ever ask the many questions. The Negro is saying that in *effect he has answers*. So far, his action at Birmingham make his claim credible. I, for one, am willing to hear more. But I must admit there is as yet a certain vagueness in the inconclusive remarks so far advanced concerning the future. I am not too sure the Negro knows, any better than anyone else, where this country is actually going.

Yet this is a challenge and a very bold one. The Negro leaders are making some fantastic claims. And they are perhaps all the more fantastic because those who make them have half despaired of ever being heard. Certainly, all the official good will of the Administration is in no sense an acknowledgement that these claims have ever been considered in their depth. That is because Washington is professionally capable only of seeing this as a political issue. Actually, it is a spiritual and religious one, and this element is by far the most important. But it is the element that no one is ready to see.

A white detective in Birmingham, watching the children file by the score into the paddy wagons, gave expression to the mind of the nation when he said: "If this is religion, I don't want any part of it!" If this is really what the mind of white America has concluded, then we stand judged by our own thoughts.

What is demanded of us is not necessarily that we believe that the Negro has mysterious and magic answers in the realm of politics and social control, *but that his spiritual insight into our common crisis is something we must take seriously.*

By and large, in the midst of the clamor of every possible kind of jaded and laughable false prophet, the voice of the American Negro has in it a genuine prophetic ring. Who knows if we will ever get another chance to hear it?

In any case the Negro demands that his conditions be met with full attention and seriousness. The white man may not fully succeed in this—but he must at least try with all the earnestness at his command. Otherwise, the moment of grace will pass without effect. The merciful *kairos* of truth will turn into the dark hour of destruction and hate. The awakened Negro will forget his moment of Christian hope and Christian inspiration. He will deliberately drive out of his heart the merciful love of Christ. He will no longer be the gentle, wide-eyed child singing hymns while police dogs lunge at his throat. There will be no more hymns and no more night prayer vigils. He will become a Samson whose African strength flows ominously back into his arms. He will suddenly pull the pillars of white society crashing down upon himself and his oppressor. And perhaps, somewhere, out of the ruins, a new world (a black world) will one day arise.

This is the "message" which the Negro is trying to give white America. I have spelled it out for myself, subject to correction, in order to see whether a white man is even capable of grasping the words, let alone believing them. For the rest, you have Moses and the Prophets: Martin Luther King, James Baldwin and the others. Read them, and see for yourself what they are saying.

· IV ·

It is related that when Mohammed was seeking the light, he thought of becoming a Christian. He went to some Nestorian Christians in a corner of Arabia, and sought a sign of the truth of Christianity from them. In order to see whether they had faith, he asked them to show him the credibility of the Christian message by walking barefoot on red hot coals. The Nestorians told him that he was mad. Mohammed, saying nothing, departed from them. And soon the conviction that he sought came to him in the burning heat of the Arabian desert. It was a truth of stark and dreadful simplicity—to be proved by the sword.

THE LEGEND
OF TUCKER CALIBAN

Begun as a review of a first novel by a black author, this article was first called: "The Negro Revolt: Review of *A Different Drummer* by William Melvin Kelley and was published in Jublilee in September 1963. The review grew into a larger article that places Kelley's novel in the historical context of black writing. It was this larger article that was published in *Seeds of Destruction*.

· · · · ·

The deep elemental stirrings that lead to social change begin within the hearts of men whose thoughts have hitherto not been articulate or who have never gained a hearing, and whose needs are therefore ignored, suppressed, and treated as if they did not exist. There is no revolution without a voice. The passion of the oppressed must first of all make itself heard at least among themselves, in spite of the insistence of the privileged oppressor that such needs cannot be real, or just, or urgent. The more the cry of the oppressed is ignored, the more it strengthens itself with a mysterious power that is to be gained from myth, symbol and prophecy. There is no revolution without poets who are also seers. There is no revolution without prophetic songs.

The voice of the American Negro began to be heard long ago, even in the days of his enslavement. He sang of the great mysteries of the Old Testament, the *magnalia dei* which are at the heart of the Christian liturgy. In a perfect, unconscious and spontaneous spirit of prayer and prophecy, the Negro spirituals of the last century remain as classic examples of what a living liturgical hymnody ought to be, and how it comes into being: not in the study of the research worker or in the monastery library, still less in the halls of curial offices, but where men suffer oppression, where they are deprived of identity, where their lives are robbed of meaning, and where the desire of freedom and the imperative demand of truth forces them to give it meaning: a religious meaning. Such religion is not the "opium of the people," but a prophetic fire of love and courage, fanned by the breathing of the Spirit of God who speaks to the heart of His children in order to lead them out of bondage. Hence the numinous force of the great and primitive art of the American Negro, a force which makes itself felt precisely where men have lost the habit of looking for "art," for instance in that potent and mysterious jazz which has kept alive the inspiration of the traditional "blues," the contemporary voice of the American Negro. And also in the "Freedom Songs" which he now sings, in the Baptist Churches of the South where he prepares to march out and face the police of states, already frankly Fascist and racist, which arm themselves against him with clubs, fire hoses, police dogs and electric cattle prods, throwing their jails wide-open to receive him. His song continues to resound in prison like the songs of Paul and his companions, in the Acts of the Apostles.

The Negro novelist and essayist has an important part in this creative expression of the present sense of *kairos* which is behind the great drive for "Freedom Now." We remember of course Richard Wright, whose warm voice is now silent, but who speaks still in his followers. We think especially of James Baldwin, who ranks with Martin Luther King as one of the most influential of Negro spokesmen today. *Go Tell It on the Mountain* is at once Baldwin's first novel and his best, as well as the one which has the most to say about the motives and the spirit of the Black Revolution in America. His hard-hitting tract, *The Fire Next Time*, which borrows its title from one of the Negro spirituals and which has an eschatological reference, in a manifesto of the Negro freedom movement which has done more than anything else to shock white readers into recognizing the seriousness and the unfamiliarity of the situation which they have been more or less taking for granted.

The title of the first novel of William Melvin Kelley, *A Different Drummer*, is taken significantly from Henry Thoreau. Thoreau, the hermit and a prophet of non-violence, preached civil disobedience in protest against unjust laws a century ago, before the Civil War. He was an early champion of Negro freedom as well as a notorious nonconformist who seems to have believed that the American revolution had either misfired or had never really taken place. Thoreau said: "If a man does not keep pace with his companions, perhaps it is because he hears a different drummer. Let him step to the music he hears, however measured or far away," It is an admirable title for the most mythical and in some sense the most prophetic of the Negro novels: one which makes quite clear the fact that the Negro hears a drummer with a totally different beat, and one which the white man is not yet capable of understanding. Yet it is imperative for him to pay attention. The trite and nasal hillbilly fiddling to which the white American mind continues its optimistic jig, has long ago ceased to have a meaning, and the "most advanced country in the world" runs the risk of being, in certain crucial matters, precisely the most retarded. Certainly there is great risk for a nation which is still playing cowboys and Indians in its own imagination—but with H-bombs and Polaris submarines at its disposal!

A Different Drummer is more than a brilliant first novel by a young Negro writer. It is a parable which spells out some of the deep spiritual implications of the Negro battle for full civil rights in the United States and for a completely human status in the world today. This is more than a story of Negro protest; it is a myth endowed with extraordinary creative power bringing to light the providential significance of a tragedy in which, whether we know it or not, understand it or not, like it or not, we are all playing a part. Since we are all in the struggle, we might as well try to find out what it really means. The works of Negro writers are there to tell us. Such books cannot be ignored. They must be read with deep attention. They spell out a message of vital importance, which is not to be found anywhere else at the present moment, and on the acceptance of which the survival of American freedom may depend.

The book opens as the loafers on the porch of a general store, in a small town of the deep South, watch a truckload of rock salt pass through on its way to the farm of a Negro called Tucker Caliban. It ends as the same loafers, after watching all the Negroes, mysteriously and without explanation, clear out of the state, lynch the last Negro available to them, a potentate from the North, and founder of a black racist movement.

The heart of the story is the sense of *kairos*, the realization that the Negro's hour of destiny has struck. No one can deny that this is one of the most striking and mysterious characteristics of the Negro freedom movement. It is this sense which awakening everywhere in the Negro masses of the South, especially in the youth, has brought them by the hundreds and thousands out of the ghettos in which they have vegetated for a century of frustrated and despairing expectation. It is this that has moved them to action, not so much because a few inspired leaders like Martin Luther King have called them to action, but because the entire Negro race, and all the vast majority of "Colored races" all over the world, have suddenly and spontaneously become conscious of their real power and, it seems, of a destiny that is all their own.

Hence, inseparable from the sense of *kairos* is a conviction of *vocation*, of a providential role to play in the world of our time. With the awakening of independence in Africa the American Negro has become acutely conscious of his own underprivileged status, and of his yearning not only to become a "part of White Society" (for this is now evidently a doubtful benefit in his eyes) but to play his own creative role in human history. One finds everywhere in American Negro society a more or less explicit anticipation of the end of the white domination of the world and the decline of European-American civilization. The Negro therefore cannot be content merely to be integrated into something he regards as already over and done with. And this is what the myth in Kelley's novel is all about.

Tucker Caliban is the central figure in the myth. He is the New Negro. The completely new Negro: not the Negro organizer from the North, not the Negro who has been to college, but a kind of preternatural figure, the lineal descendant of a giant African chief who came over with his tribe in a slave ship to be bought—and killed—by the first Governor of the mythical Southern state in which the story takes place. The giant "African" is the symbol of the Negro race and of its innate spirit, which the white man has tried first to tame for his own purposes, and then to destroy. Tucker Caliban is not a giant. He is a small, intense, taciturn Negro, aligned with no group, no movement and no cause. The implication is that he sees completely through even the best of movements and of causes. He also understands the problems of white people. He views them completely objectively and without bitterness. He harbors no delusions about them, and he places no hope whatever in the official benevolence of the white man. His is the spirit in which the Negro freedom movement must develop. In him the wisdom and strength of the African ancestor must one day awaken.

Meanwhile, the Calibans have served the family of the Governor for over a century both as slaves and as freemen. Tucker's father is typical of the venerable Negro servant, loyal and entirely devoted to his master, in other words, he is what the Negroes now regard with deepest scorn: he is an "Uncle Tom," or one who has fully accepted an inferior position in white society.

Tucker, without hatred and without rebellion, driven by an inner force which he does not quite understand himself and which baffles everybody who comes in contact with him, first buys a piece of land from the family his family has served so long. Then he leaves their service, and farms his newly acquired land for about a year. Finally, following inscrutable interior messages, he sterilizes his field with rock salt, shoots his mule and his cow, sets fire to his house, and leaves in the night with his pregnant wife. He simply vanishes.

At this, all the Negroes in the state begin to leave. It is not necessary to know where they go. They just go. Out of the state, out of the South. In a few days they are all gone, leaving empty houses which they have not bothered to sell, with the doors wide open, furniture inside.

Their departure is a symbolic statement: it is the final refusal to accept paternalism, tutelage, and all different forms of moral, economic, psychological and social servitude wished on them by the whites. In the last analysis, it is the final rejection of the view of life implied by white culture. It is a definitive "NO" to White America.

The book is about the bewilderment with which this is observed and dimly understood by all the people who see them go: the poor whites, the child of a white sharecropper, the descendants of the first Governor, Southerners educated in the North, and finally the Rev. Bennett Bradshaw, founder of the Black Jesuits, a Northern Negro Leader who is just as mystified as everyone else by the things that are happening. Though he, more than anyone, would have wanted to set all these things in motion, he has never been consulted or even dreamed of. He is not wanted any more than the benevolent white liberal is wanted, because he has no real power to do anything, to start anything, to move anyone. Yet for the Southern whites there has to be some explanation that fits their picture of life, and reassures them that things are what the South has always believed them to be. In a final tragic irony, the loafers at the store follow the irresponsible inspiration of one of their number and blame the Black Jesuits for engineering the hegira. After beating him up they drive him in his own Cadillac to Tucker Caliban's gutted farm and his screams in the Southern night ring down the curtain on this strange morality play about the evil of our time.

Evil is the word. Those who have seen, at first hand, the eerie glow in the eyes of the racist, those who have heard their peculiar silences as they stand together in the shadows waiting for the forces within them to reach some mysterious point where inner confusion and self-hate turn into violent fury—those who have seen this are aware of what it means to see apparently good and harmless men possessed with an evil so total and so complete that they prefer not to understand it, or refer to it, or treat it as if it existed.

Yet this evil is not something purely and simply confined to "white trash" in the South. What is open and expressed in the South may perhaps be hidden and implicit everywhere in the nation that is so fascinated with violence and with the myth of power that it seems to have lost interest in anything else—with the possible exception of sex.

There is no need to intone a litany of cliches in a useless attempt to convey some idea of the power with which this story is told. It is a power without the bitterness and frustration that give such bite to the works of James Baldwin. Kelley, a northern Negro like Baldwin, is much more tranquil and reflective. The force of the myth itself seems to have absorbed and tamed the bitter rage that might have gone into such a story. There is no rage. Resentment is sublimated into irony. This accounts for the book's unforgettable impact. The myth of Tucker Caliban tells the same kind of truth as dreams tell us in our moments of personal crisis, spelling out to us in symbols, ranging from idyll to hallucination and to nightmare, the truths that are struggling for acceptance and for expression in our hearts.

That is the particular value of such a book. It gives us a message which, like all prophetic messages, is mostly in code so that we can both hear and not hear, we can accept just as much of it as we are able. But if we really want to, we can understand completely. What, then, is the message?

The message of this book is very much the same as that which we read in James Baldwin"s *The Fire Next Time* (written and published after *A Different Drummer*). It is the same message which the best American Negro writers are now, with a rather astonishing unanimity and confidence, announcing to the white world as their diagnosis of that world's sickness, with their suggestions for escaping the death which is otherwise inevitable.

First of all, we must seriously face the magnanimity of the statement. It would be all too easy for the Negroes simply to write the whites off as a total loss (as indeed the Black Muslims are doing) and be done with them forever. This solution is appealing not only in its simplicity, but also in its correspondence with the deepest psychological need of the Negro, the need to recover his belief in his own autonomous reality, the need to get the white man, spiritually and psychologically, off his back. But in point of fact, such a solution is not really possible, as the best Negro writers see quite clearly. They have certainly ejected, with all their force, the gross and subtle forms of alienation imposed on them by white society, even where it claims to do most to make them "free." But the thing that so many readers have failed to see in these books is the rather convincing assurance that there is one *kairos* for everybody. The time that has providentially come for the black man is also providential for the white man.

This implies a profoundly Christian understanding of man's freedom in history—a point that must be underscored.

The Negro revolution is a real revolution, and it is definitely not Marxian. It may have some very violent and destructive potentialities in it, but they have nothing to do with Soviet Communism. To identify the Negro freedom movement as a Red-inspired revolt against western democracy is a totally ludicrous evasion, and one which involves complete and incurable ignorance of what is actually happening. This is of course precisely why it is accepted with total satisfaction by the entire South. In Alabama, Mississippi, Georgia, Louisiana, it is an article of faith that "all this trouble with the Negroes" has been fomented by Communist agents.

Though writers like Baldwin and doubtless Kelley lay no claim to be Christians, their view is still deeply Christian and implies a substantially Christian faith in the spiritual dynamism with which man freely creates his own history, not as an autonomous and titanic self-affirmation, but in obedience to the mystery of love and freedom at work under the surface of human events.

In the light of this, then, the hour of freedom is seen also as an hour of salvation. But it is not an hour of salvation for the Negro only. The white man, if he can possibly open the ears of his heart and listen intently enough to hear what the Negro is now hearing, can recognize that he is himself called to freedom and to salvation in the same *kairos* of events which he is now, in so many different ways, opposing or resisting.

These books tell us that it is the Negro who hears, or believes he hears, the true voice of God in history, and interprets it rightly. The white man has lost his power to hear any inner voice other than that of his own demon who urges him to preserve the *status quo* at any price, however desperate, however iniquitous and however cruel. The white man's readiness to destroy the world rather than change it is dictated by this inner demon, which he cannot recognize, but which the Negro clearly identifies.

The tragedy of the present crisis in race relations (say the Negro writers) is therefore essentially the white man's tragedy, and he will destroy himself unless he can understand and undergo the *metanoia* that will bring him into harmony with the awakened forces that are being revealed to him in the struggle of his black brother. The Negro may have much to suffer, and the times ahead may yet prove most terrible: but essentially, for him, the days of tragedy are over. He has awakened and taken his destiny into his own hands.

Tucker Caliban, when he burned his house down and took off into the night, was not a "tragic" hero. On the contrary, the implication of tragedy is all affixed to the comfortable and secure life which his father led as a loyal servant of the white Governor's family. Tragedy is not in freedom but in moral servitude. We are no longer in the world of Aeschylus and Sophocles in which the aspiration to freedom is linked with unbearable guilt and punished by the gods. We are in a Christian world in which man is redeemed, liberated from guilt by the inner truth that makes him free to obey the Lord of History. It is the Lord of History who demands of the Negro a complete break with his past servitudes. And the break must be made by the Negro himself, without any need of the white man's paternalistic approval. It is absolutely necessary for the Negro to dissolve all bonds that hold him, like a navel cord, in passive dependence on the good pleasure of the white man's society.

The real tragedy is that of the white man who does not realize that though he seems to himself to be free, he is actually the victim of the same servitudes which he has imposed on the Negro: passive subjection to the lotus-eating commercial society that he has tried to create for himself, and which is shot through with falsity and unfreedom from top to bottom. He makes a great deal of fuss about "individual freedom" but one may ask if such freedom really exists. Is there really a genuine freedom for the person or only the irresponsibility of the atomized individual members of mass society.

The presence of the Negro in a state of humiliation and dependence may serve, perhaps, to perpetuate the illusion of power and autonomy which the white loafers on the porch of the village store imagine they enjoy. Actually, their own lives are empty, pointless, absurd, totally lacking in freedom. The departure of the Negroes suddenly makes that truth inescapable. Hence the frustrated whites confront the meaninglessness of their world. They know no other way of "facing" such facts than violence.

This, then, according to our Negro writers, is the plight of the white American and indeed of the whole western world. Europe cannot save face by sitting back complacently and viewing with pity the conflicts and confusions of white America. When the house next door is on fire you too are in danger. America does not stand judgment alone. It is the whole white world, including Russia, that stands accused of centuries of injustice, prejudice and racism. All white men together, in spite of their fantasies of innocence, are prisoners of the same illusion, seduced by their own slogans, obsessed by the voice of an inner demon.

They have no better alternatives than the passivities and oral fantasies of the consumer's dream-world and the violent barbarities with which they react, when briefly awakened, to all that threatens to contradict their infantile dream.

In such a situation, it is absurd for the Negro to place any hope either in the white Liberal or in the affluent Negro Leader. Though there may be, in each of these cases, some awareness of the problem, the awareness is not deep enough to mean anything. On the contrary, it only makes matters worse by bringing a new element of delusion into the minds of those concerned. The Liberal and the Negro Leader are, each in his own way, completely committed to the comforts and securities and therefore to the falsities of the *status quo*. Each in his own way has sold out to the establishment. And his defection is all the more vicious because, with his seeming awareness of the problems and his demonstrations of great good will, he only encourages the Negro to continue in hapless submission, to "wait" and to hope for that same magic solution which continues, as always before, to recede further into the future.

To neither of these, says Kelley, can the Negro profitably or even safely listen. The most pitiful character in the book is perhaps the Southern white Liberal who was once a promising young radical writer and crusader in the halcyon days of the thirties, but who allowed himself to be intimidated and silenced, in order to protect his family. His life thereafter is doomed to sterility, impotence, uselessness. He may be prosperous and secure, but he is a total failure. He has betrayed his truth and his vocation, and is therefore miserable.

This comes close to being a standard formula in the new Negro literature. It calls white society before the bar of history and hands down the judgment that it has lamentably failed. Christianity itself is prominently associated in the failure. Without delaying here to make certain distinctions and to defend the basic truth of Christianity we must admit that the judgment is not altogether without foundation. The practical conduct of many Christians, of whole groups and entire "churches," lends it a great deal of support. Christians have perhaps too often been content to delude themselves with vague slogans and abstract formulas about brotherly love. They have too easily become addicted to token gestures of good will and "charity" which they have then taken as a total dispensation from all meaningful action and genuine concern in the crucial problems of our time. As a result they have become unable to listen to the voice of God in the events of the time, and have resisted that voice instead of obeying it.

What is the conclusion? The white man is so far gone that he cannot free the Negro because he cannot even free himself. Hence these books are not in any sense demanding that the whites now finally free the Negroes. On the contrary, the magnificent paradox they utter is that the Negro has a mission to free the white man: and he can begin to do this if he learns to free himself. His first step to freedom must be the clear realization that he cannot depend on the white man or trust him for anything, since the white man is hopelessly impotent, deluded and stupefied by his own alienation.

Such is the "message" of the Negro to White America, delivered by men who, to my mind, are the most impressive and inspired writers in our country today. Is the message "true"?

I must say that messages like this cannot be clearly declared to be either "true" or "false" until time itself lays out all the evidence before us. But that is precisely our difficulty. We cannot wait. We have to decide *now*, before the truth or falsity of the message becomes evident. We have to be willing to make it evident.

The question is, then, not whether the message is true, but whether it is *credible*. And to this I can only give the answer of one man's opinion. Comparing the spiritual earnestness of the message, the creative vitality of the messengers, the fruits of the message, with all the fumbling evasions and inanities of those who disbelieve the message, I can come up with no better choice than to listen very seriously to the Negro, and what he has to say. I for one, am absolutely ready to believe that *we need him to be free, for our sake even more than for his own.*

The school children of Birmingham would have convinced me, if I had not been already convinced. I find the message entirely credible. Doubtless, it may not be infallibly true, but I think there is no hope for us unless we are able to take seriously the obvious elements of truth which it contains.

· 17 ·

A DEVOUT MEDITATION
IN MEMORY OF ADOLF
EICHMANN

This essay was first published in *New Directions in Prose and Poetry* (New Directions Publishing Co.) in the 1964 issue. It was later published in *Ramparts*, October 1966 and, also in 1966, in *Raids on the Unspeakable*. In a letter to Cid Corman of September 5, 1966 (see *CFT*, p. 248), Merton links this essay with his poem "Chants to Be Used in Processions Around a Site with Furnaces," which, he says, "is a sort of mosaic of Eichmann's own double-talk about himself."

* * * * *

One of the most disturbing facts that came out in the Eichmann trial was that a psychiatrist examined him and pronounced him *perfectly sane*. I do not doubt it at all, and this is precisely why I find it disturbing. If all the Nazis had been psychotics, as some of their leaders probably were, their appalling cruelty would have been in some sense easier to understand. It is much worse to consider this calm, "well-balanced," unperturbed official, conscientiously going about his desk work, his administrative job in the great organization: which happened to be the supervision of mass murder. He was thoughtful, orderly, unimaginative. He had a profound respect for system, for law and order. He was obedient, loyal, a faithful officer of a great state. He served his government very well.

He was not bothered much by guilt. I have not heard that he developed any psychosomatic illnesses. Apparently he slept well. He had a good appetite, or so it seems. True, when he visited Auschwitz, the Camp Commandant, Hoess, in a spirit of sly deviltry, tried to tease the big boss and scare him with some of the sights. Eichmann was disturbed, yes. He was disturbed. Even Himmler had been disturbed, and had gone weak at the knees. Perhaps, in the same way, the General Manager of a big steel mill might be disturbed if an accident took place while he happened to be somewhere in the plant. But of course what happened at Auschwitz was not an accident: just the routine unpleasantness of the daily task. One must shoulder the burden of daily monotonous work for the Fatherland. Yes, one must suffer discomfort and even nausea from unpleasant sights and sounds. It all comes under the heading of duty, self-sacrifice, and obedience. Eichmann was devoted to duty, and proud of his job.

The sanity of Eichmann is disturbing. We equate sanity with a sense of justice, with humaneness, with prudence, with the capacity to love and understand other people. We are relying on the sane people of the world to preserve it from barbarism, madness, destruction. And now it begins to dawn on us that it is precisely the *sane* ones who are the most dangerous.

It is the sane ones, the well-adapted ones, who can without qualms and without nausea aim the missiles and press the buttons that will initiate the great festival of destruction that they, *the sane ones*, have prepared. What makes us so sure, after all, that the danger comes from a psychotic getting into a position to fire the first shot in a nuclear war? Psychotics will be suspect. The sane ones will keep them far from the button. No one suspects the sane, and the sane one will have *perfectly good reasons*, logical, well-adapted reasons, for firing the shot. They will be obeying sane orders that have come sanely down the chain of command. And because of their sanity they will have no qualms at all. When the missiles take off, then *it will be no mistake.*

In other words, then, we can no longer assume that because a man is "sane" he is therefore in his "right mind." The whole concept of sanity in a society where spiritual values have lost their meaning, is itself meaningless. A man can be "sane" in the limited sense that he is not impeded by his disordered emotions from acting in a cool, orderly manner, according to the needs and dictates of the social situation in which he finds himself. He can be perfectly "adjusted." God knows, perhaps such people can be perfectly adjusted even in hell itself.

And so I ask myself: what is the meaning of a concept of sanity that excludes love, considers it irrelevant, and destroys our capacity to love other human beings, to respond to their needs and their sufferings, to recognize them also as persons, to apprehend their pain as one's own? Evidently this is not necessary for "sanity" at all. It is a religious notion, a spiritual notion, a Christian notion. What business have we to equate "sanity" with "Christianity"? None at all, obviously. The worst error is to imagine that a Christian must try to be "sane" like everybody else, and that we *belong* in our kind of *society.* That we must be "realistic" about it. We must develop a *sane* Christianity: and there have been plenty of sane Christians in the past. Torture is nothing new, is it? We ought to be able to rationalize a little bit of brainwashing, and genocide, and find a place for nuclear war in our moral theology. Certainly some of us are doing our best along those lines already. There are hopes! Even Christians can shake off their sentimental prejudices about charity, and become sane like Eichmann. They can even cling to a certain set of Christian formulas, and fit them into a Totalist Ideology. Let them talk about justice, charity, love, and the rest. These words have not stopped some sane men from acting very sanely and cleverly in the past. . . .

No, Eichmann was sane. The generals and fighters on both sides, in World War II, the ones who carried out the total destruction of entire cities, these were the sane ones. The ones who have invented and developed atomic bombs, theromonuclear bombs, missiles, who have planned the strategy of the next war; who have evaluated the various possibilities of using bacterial and chemical agents: these are not the crazy people, they are the *sane* people. The ones who coolly estimate how many millions of victims can be considered expendable in a nuclear war, I presume they do all right with the Rorschach ink blots too. On the other hand, you will probably find that the pacifists and the ban-the-bomb people are, quite seriously, just as we read in *Time,* a little crazy.

I am beginning to realize that "sanity" is no longer a value or an end in itself. The "sanity" of modern man is about as useful to him as the huge bulk and muscles of the dinosaur. If he were a little less sane, a little more doubtful, a little more aware of his absurdities and contradictions, perhaps there might be a possibility of his survival. But if he is sane, too sane . . . or perhaps we must say that in a society like ours the worst insanity is to be totally without anxiety, totally "sane."

· 18 ·

GANDHI:
The Gentle Revolutionary

Published in Ramparts, *December 1964*

Merton's interest in Gandhi goes back to his school days at Oakham School (as he mentions in this article). He studied Gandhi's writings and wrote two articles on him. The one became the introduction to a book of selected readings from Gandhi, appearing in the January 1965 issue of *Jubilee* under the title "Gandhi and the One-eyed Giant." The second article is the one that follows, which became part of *Seeds of Destruction* under the title of "A Tribute to Gandhi." Under the different title used here, Merton had sent it in April 1964 to Edward Keating, editor of *Ramparts.* "Does this piece on Gandhi," he asked, "strike you as something that would fit in with the non-violence issue?" He adds quickly, "I have yet to consult the censors about it. It seems to me that this ought to be cleared, though I can never guarantee anything these days."

· · · · ·

In 1931 Gandhi, who had been released from prison a few months before, came to London for a conference. The campaign of civil disobedience which had begun with the Salt March had recently ended. Now there were to be negotiations. He walked through the autumn fogs of London in clothes that were good for the tropics, not for England. He lived in the slums of London, coming from there to more noble buildings in which he conferred with statesmen. The English smiled at his bald head, his naked brown legs, the thin underpinnings of an old man who ate very little, who prayed. This was Asia, wise, disconcerting, in many ways unlovely, but determined upon some inscrutable project and probably very holy. Yet was it practical for statesmen to have conferences with a man reputed to be holy? What was the meaning of the fact that one could be holy, and fast, and pray, and be in jail, and be opposed to England all at the same time?

Gandhi thus confronted the England of the depression as a small, disquieting question mark. Everybody knew him, and many jokes were made about him. He was also respected. But respect implied neither agreement nor comprehension. It indicated nothing except that the man had gained public attention, and this was regarded as an achievement. Then, as now, no one particularly bothered to ask if the achievement signified something.

Yet I remember arguing about Gandhi in my school dormitory: chiefly against the football captain, the head prefect, who had come to turn out the flickering gaslight, and who stood with one hand in his pocket and a frown on his face which was not illuminated with understanding. I insisted that Gandhi was right, that India was, with perfect justice, demanding that the British withdraw peacefully and go home; that the millions of people who lived in India had a perfect right to run their own country. Such sentiments were of course beyond comprehension. How could Gandhi be right when he was *odd*? And how could I be right if I was on the side of someone who had the wrong kind of skin, and left altogether too much of it exposed?

A counterargument was offered but it was not an argument. It was a basic and sweeping assumption that the people of India were political and moral infants, incapable of taking care of themselves, backward people, primitive, uncivilized, benighted pagan, who could not survive without the English to do their thinking and planning for them. The British Raj was, in fact, a purely benevolent, civilizing enterprise for which the Indians were not suitably grateful . . .

Infuriated at the complacent idiocy of this argument, I tried to sleep and failed.

Certain events have taken place since that time. Within a dozen years after Gandhi's visit to London there were more hideous barbarities perpetuated in Europe, with greater violence and more unmitigated fury than all that had ever been attributed by the wildest imaginations to the despots of Asia. The British empire collapsed. India attained self-rule. It did so peacefully and with dignity. Gandhi paid with his life for the ideals in which he believed.

As one looks back over this period of confusion and decline in the West, the cold war, and the chaos and struggle of the world that was once colonial, there is one political figure who stands out from all the rest as an extraordinary leader of men. He is radically different from the others. Not that the others did not on occasion bear witness to the tradition of which they were proud because it was Christian. They were often respectable, sometimes virtuous men, and many of them were sincerely devout. Others were at least genteel. Others, of course, were criminals. Judging by their speeches, their programs, their expressed motives, they were civilized. Yet the best that could be said of them may be that they sometimes combined genuine capability and subjective honesty. But apart from that they seemed to be the powerless victims of a social dynamic that they were able neither to control nor to understand. They never seemed to dominate events, only to rush breathlessly after the parade of cataclysms, explaining why these had happened, and not aware of how they themselves had helped precipitate the worst of disasters. Thus with all their good intentions, they were able at best to rescue themselves after plunging blindly in directions quite other than those in which they claimed to be going. In the name of peace, they wrought enormous violence and destruction. In the name of liberty they exploited and enslaved. In the name of man they engaged in genocide or tolerated it. In the name of truth they systematically falsified and perverted truth.

Gandhi on the other hand was dedicated to peace, and though he was engaged in a bitter struggle for national liberation, he achieved this by peaceful means. He believed in serving the truth *by nonviolence*, and his *nonviolence* was effective insofar as it began first within himself, as obedience to the deepest truth in himself.

It is certainly true that Gandhi is not above all criticism, no man is. But it is evident that he was unlike all the other world leaders of his time in that his life was marked by a wholeness and a wisdom, an integrity and a spiritual consistency that the others lacked, or manifested only in reverse, in consistent fidelity to a dynamism of evil and destruction. There may be limitations in Gandhi's thought, and his work has not borne all the fruit he himself would have hoped. These are factors which he himself sagely took into account, and having reckoned with them all, he continued to pursue the course he had chosen simply because he believed it to be true. His way was no secret: it was simply to follow conscience without regard for the consequences to himself, in the belief that this was demanded of him by God and that the results would be the work of God. Perhaps indeed for a long time these results would remain hidden as God's secret. But in the end the truth would manifest itself.

What has Gandhi to do with Christianity? Everyone knows that the Orient has venerated Christ and distrusted Christians since the first colonizers and missionaries came from the West.

Western Christians often assume without much examination that this oriental respect for Christ is simply a vague, syncretistic and perhaps romantic evasion of the challenge of the Gospel: an attempt to absorb the Christian message into the confusion and inertia which are thought to be characteristic of Asia. The point does not need to be argued here. Gandhi certainly spoke often of Jesus, whom he had learned to know through Tolstoy. And Gandhi knew the New Testament thoroughly. Whether or not Gandhi "believed in" Jesus in the sense that he had genuine faith in the Gospel would be very difficult to demonstrate, and it is not my business to prove it or disprove it. I think that the effort to do so would be irrelevant in any case. What is certainly true is that Gandhi not only understood the ethic of the Gospel, as well as, if not in some ways better, than most Christians, but he is one of the very few men of our time who applied Gospel principles to the problems of a political and social existence in such a way that his approach to these problems was *inseparably* religious and political at the same time.

He did this not because he thought that these principles were novel and interesting, or because they seemed expedient, or because of a compulsive need to feel spiritually secure. The religious basis of Gandhi's political action was not simply a program, in which politics were marshalled into the service of faith, and brought to bear on the charitable objectives of a religious institution. For Gandhi, strange as it may seem to us, political action had to be by its very nature "religious" in the sense that it had to be informed by principles of religious and philosophical wisdom. To separate religion and politics was in Gandhi's eyes "madness" because his politics rested on a thoroughly religious interpretation of reality, of life, and of man's place in the world. Gandhi's whole concept of man's relation to his own inner being and to the world of objects around him was informed by the contemplative heritage of Hinduism, together with the principles of Karma Yoga which blended, in his thought, with the ethic of the Synoptic Gospels and the Sermon on the Mount. In such a view, politics had to be understood in the context of service and worship in the ancient sense of *leitourgia* (liturgy, public work). Man's intervention in the active life of society was at the same time by its very nature *svadharma*, his own personal service (of God and man) and worship, *yajna*. Political action therefore was not a means to acquire security and strength for one's self and one's party, but a means of witnessing to the truth and the reality of the cosmic structure by making one's own proper contribution to the order willed by God. One could thus preserve one's integrity and peace, being detached from results (which are in the hands of God) and being free from the inner violence that comes from division and untruth, the usurpation of someone else's *dharma* in place of one's own *svadharma*. These perspectives lent Gandhi's politics their extraordinary spiritual force and religious realism.

The success with which Gandhi applied this spiritual force to political action makes him uniquely important in our age. More than that, it gives him a very special importance for Christians. Our attitude to politics tends to be abstract, divisive and often highly ambiguous. Political action is by definition secular and unspiritual. It has no really religious significance. We look to the Church to clarify principle and offer guidance, and in addition to that we are grateful if a Christian party of some sort comes to implement the program that has thus been outlined for us. This is all well and good. But Gandhi emphasized the importance of the individual person entering political action with a fully awakened and operative spiritual power in himself, the power of *Satyagraha*, nonviolent dedication to truth, a religious and spiritual force, a wisdom born of fasting and prayer. This is the charismatic and personal force of the saints, and we must admit that we have tended to regard it with mistrust and unbelief, as though it were mere "enthusiasm" and "fanaticism." This is a lamentable mistake, because for one thing it tends to short circuit the power and light of grace, and it suggests that spiritual dedication is and must remain something entirely divorced from political action: something for the *prie dieu*, the sacristy or the study, but not for the marketplace. This in turn has estranged from the Church those whose idealism and generosity might have inspired a dedicated and creative intervention in political life. These have found refuge in groups dominated by a confused pseudo-spirituality, or by totalitarian messianism. Gandhi remains in our time as a sign of the genuine union of spiritual fervor and social action in the midst of a hundred pseudo-spiritual cryptofascist, or communist movements in which the capacity for creative and spontaneous dedication is captured, debased and exploited by the false prophets.

In a time when the unprincipled fabrication of lies and systematic violation of agreement has become a matter of course in power politics, Gandhi made this unconditional devotion to truth the mainspring of his social action. Once again, the radical difference between him and other leaders, even the most sincere and honest of them, becomes evident by the fact that Gandhi is chiefly concerned with truth and with service, *svadharma*, rather than with the possible success of his tactics upon other people, and paradoxically it was his religious conviction that made Gandhi a great politician rather than a mere tactician or operator. Note that *Satyagraha* is matter for a vow, therefore of worship, adoration of the God of truth, so that his whole political structure is built on this and his other vows (*Ahimsa*, etc.) and becomes an entirely religious system. The vow of *Satyagraha* is the vow to die rather than say what one does not mean.

The profound significance of *Satyagraha* becomes apparent when one reflects that "truth" here implies much more than simply conforming one's words to one's inner thought. It is not by words only that we speak. Our aims, our plans of action, our outlook, or attitudes, our habitual response to the problems and challenges of life, "speak" of our inner being and reveal our fidelity or infidelity to God and to ourselves. Our very existence, our life itself contains an implicit pretension to meaning, since all our free acts are implicit commitments, selections of "meanings" which we seem to find confronting us. Our very existence is "speech" interpreting reality. But the crisis of truth in the modern world comes from the bewildering complexity of the almost infinite contradictory propositions and claims to meaning uttered by millions of acts, movements, changes, decisions, attitudes, gestures, events, going on all around us. Most of all a crisis of truth is precipitated when men realize that almost all these claims to meaning and value are in fact without significance, when they are not in great part entirely fraudulent.

The tragedy of modern society lies partly in the fact that it is condemned to utter an infinite proliferation of statements when it has nothing to reveal except its own meaningless, its dishonesty, its moral indigence, its inner divisions, its abject spiritual void, its radical and self-destructive spirit of violence.

Satyagraha for Gandhi meant first of all refusing to say "nonviolence" and "peace" when one meant "violence" and "destruction." However, his wisdom differed from ours in this: he knew that in order to speak truth he must rectify more than his inner *intention*. It was not enough to say "love" and *intend* love thereafter proving the sincerity of one's own intentions by demonstrating the insincerity of one's adversary. "Meaning" is not a mental and subjective adjustment. For Gandhi, a whole lifetime of sacrifice was barely enough to demonstrate the sincerity with which he made a few simple claims: that he was not lying, that he did not intend to use violence or deceit against the English, that he did not think that peace and justice could be attained through violent or selfish means, that he did genuinely believe they could be assured by nonviolence and self-sacrifice.

Gandhi's religio-political action was based on an ancient metaphysics of man, a philosophical wisdom which is common to Hinduism, Buddhism, Islam, Judaism, and Christianity: that "truth is the inner law of our being." Not that man is merely an abstract essence, and that our action must be based on logical fidelity to a certain definition of man. Gandhi's religious action is based on a religious intuition of *being* in man and in the world, and his vow of truth is a vow of fidelity to being in all its accessible dimensions. His wisdom is based on experience more than on logic. Hence the way of peace is the way of truth, of fidelity to wholeness and being, which implies a basic respect for life not as a concept, not as a sentimental figment of the imagination, but its deepest, most secret and most frontal reality. The first and fundamental trust is to be sought in respect for our own inmost being, and this in turn implies the recollectedness and the awareness which attune us to that silence in which a lone Being speaks to us in all its simplicity.

Therefore Gandhi, recognized as no other world leader of our time, has done the necessity to be free from the pressures, the exorbitant and tyrannical demands of a society that is violent because it is essentially greedy, lustful and cruel. Therefore he fasted, observed days of silence, lived frequently in retreat, knew the value of solitude, as well as of the totally generous expenditure of his time and energy in listening to others and communicating with them. He recognized the impossibility of being a peaceful and nonviolent man if one submits passively to the insatiable requirements of a society maddened by overstimulation and obsessed with the demons of noise, voyeurism and speed.

"Jesus died in vain," said Gandhi, "if he did not teach us to regulate the whole life by the eternal law of love." Strange that he should use this expression. It seems to imply at once concern and accusation. As Asians sometimes do, Gandhi did not hesitate to confront Christendom with the principles of Christ. Not that he judged Christianity, but he suggested that the professedly Christian civilization of the West was in fact judging itself by its own acts and its own fruits. There are certain Christian and humanitarian elements in Democracy, and if they are absent, Democracy finds itself on trial, weighed in the balance, and no amount of verbal protestations can prevent it from being found wanting. Events themselves will proceed inexorably to their conclusion. *Pacem in terris* has suggested the same themes to the meditation of modern Europe, America and Russia. "Civilization" must learn to prove its claims by a capacity for the peaceful and honest settlement of disputes, by genuine concern for justice toward people who have been shamelessly exploited and races that have been systematically oppressed, or the historical preeminence of the existing powers will be snatched from them by violence, perhaps in a disaster of cosmic proportions.

Gandhi believed that the central problem of our time was the acceptance or the rejection of a basic law of love and of truth which had been made known to the world in traditional religions and most clearly by Jesus Christ. Gandhi himself expressly and very clearly declared himself an adherent of this one law. His whole life, his political action, finally even his death, were nothing but a witness to his commitment. "IF LOVE IS NOT THE LAW OF OUR BEING THE WHOLE OF MY ARGUMENT FALLS TO PIECES."

What remains to be said? It is true that Gandhi expressly dissociated himself from Christianity in its visible and institutional forms. But it is also true that he built his whole life and all his activity upon what he conceived to be the law of Christ. In fact, he died for this law which was at the heart of his belief. Gandhi was indisputably sincere and right in his moral commitment to the law of love and truth. A Christian can do nothing greater than follow his own conscience with a fidelity comparable to that with which Gandhi obeyed what he believed to be the voice of God. Gandhi is, it seems to me, a model of integrity whom we cannot afford to ignore, and the one basic duty we all owe to the world of our time is to imitate him in "dissociating ourselves from evil in total disregard of the consequences." May God mercifully grant us the grace to be half as sincere and half as generous as was this great leader, one of the noblest men of our century.

· 19 ·

FROM NON-VIOLENCE
TO BLACK POWER

This essay was not written for publication in a journal, as were
most of Merton's articles on social issues; rather it was the introduction to section three of a book called *Faith and Violence*,
published in 1968 by Notre Dame Press. That section dealt with
racial issues and three of its articles, are numbers 20, 27, and 29
in this book.

· · · · ·

"Violence is as American as cherry pie."
(H. Rap Brown)

The non-violent struggle for integration was won on the law books—
and was lost in fact. Integration is more myth than real possibility.
The result has been that non-violence both as tactic and as mystique
has been largely rejected as irrelevant by the American Negro. At the
same time, the struggle for racial recognition has taken on an entirely
new and more aggressive character.

First of all, Frantz Fanon has become the prophet of Black America,
and Malcolm X has become its martyr. Fanon was a black psychoanalyst from the French colony of Martinique. He joined the Algerian
conflict and preached a mystique of violence as necessary for the Third
World to recover its identity and organize for revolutionary self-
liberation. The Black Power movement in America has accepted this
doctrine as simpler, and more effective, and more meaningful than
Christian non-violence.

It must be admitted that for the majority of black Americans, Christian non-violence remained highly ambiguous. The Negro felt himself
imprisoned in the fantasy image of him devised by the white man: an
image of subservient, subhuman, passive tutelage and minority. Part
of this image was the assumption that the Negro was there to be beaten
over the head. Whether he chose to accept his beating with Christian

dignity and heroic, self-sacrificial motives was a matter of supreme indifference to white people like Bull Connor.

It is true that the Montgomery bus strike and the Birmingham demonstrations did communicate to the whole nation an image of Negro dignity, maturity and integrity—an example of restraint and nobility which should not have been lost on a culture with our professed ideals. It was unfortunately soon forgotten when black people in the North began to ask for open housing. Northern liberals might admire black dignity at a distance, but they still did not want all that nobility right next door: it might affect property values. Nobility is one thing and property values quite another.

Second, the Vietnam war has had a great deal to do with the new trend to Black Power. The Negroes have been more keenly aware than anyone else of the war's ambiguities. They have tended to identify themselves with the Vietnamese—indeed with the Vietcong—and have not paid much heed to the official rhetoric of Washington. They have, on the contrary, seen the Vietnam war as another manifestation of whitey's versatility in beating down colored people. They have naturally concluded that white America is not really interested in non-violence at all.

Rap Brown's statement that "violence is as American as cherry pie" is steeped in the pungent ironies which characterize the new language of racial conflict. (One is tempted to explore possible psychoanalytic insights in the droll image used. Orality, mother love, hate of brother . . .) Yes, violence is thoroughly American and Rap Brown is saying that it is in fact the real American language. Perhaps so, perhaps not. But in any event, it is the language the black American has now elected to speak. Oddly enough, he instantly got himself a much better hearing when he did so.

America sat up and began paying a great deal of attention. "Black Power" became an explosive and inexhaustible theme in the white media. It turned out to be a much better money-maker than non-violence (indeed non-violence was found to interest the American public only in so far as it could be seen as an obscure, perverse form of violence— a dishonest and so to speak "inverted" violence—hence the persistent snide allusions attempting to link non-violence with passivity and homosexuality). Black Power was clearly a message that somehow white America *wanted* to hear. Not of course that white America was not scared, it was deliciously afraid. And glad. Because now things were so much simpler. One had perfectly good reasons to call out the cops and the National Guard.

Well, the blacks wanted it that way too. It was also simpler for them. And they turned it into a self-justifying weapon. There is a lot of truth in this arraignment of white America by Rap Brown.

> You sit out there and you pretend violence scares you, but you watch TV every night and you can't turn it on for five minutes without seeing somebody shot to death or karated to death. Violence is part of your culture. There's no doubt about it. You gave us violence and this is the only value that black people can use to their advantage to end oppression . . . Johnson says every day if Vietnam don't come round, Vietnam will burn down. I say that if American don't come around America should be burned down. *It's the same thing.*

My reason for quoting these lines is not necessarily to approve a program of arson, but to make the point that it is quite literally, the same thing and to congratulate Rap Brown on the firm and acute justice of his ironic insight.

An American that destroys Vietnamese non-combatants with napalm has no right to object when blacks at home burn down their slums. Indeed, if there is a difference, it is that the second case is more justifiable than the first: it is a protest against real injustice.

It is perfectly logical that the America of LBJ should be at once the America of the Vietnam war and the Detroit riots. It's the same America, the same violence, the same slice of mother's cherry pie.

The people who have been most shocked by the Black Power movement are the white liberals. And of course they are right, because the whole impact of the movement is directed against *them*. It is a rejection of their tender and ambiguous consciences, their taste for compromise, their desire to eat momma's cherry pie and still have it, their semi-conscious proclivity to use the Negro for their own sentimental, self-justifying ends. The black man has definitely seen through and summarily rejected the white liberal. The overtones of racism in the Black Power program are, in their way, an acknowledgement that the Negro feels the white segregationist to be more honest, in his way, than the liberal. Of course this infuriates the liberal, because it is supposed to do just that. And for that reason it is not to be taken too seriously.

The Black Power movement is not just racism in reverse. This racist suggestion is of course a built-in ambiguity which is at once a strength and a weakness of the movement. For two reasons it has to *appear* racist: to help the black man consolidate his sense of identity, and to rebuff the sentimental and meddling integrationism of the white liberal. There is also a third reason: to get the liberals off the black man's back, and to make it quite clear that the Negro wants to run his own liberation movement from now on, without being told what to do by someone who cannot really understand his situation. If the white liberal wants to help, let him do so indirectly. Let him help poor whites, and let him try to show poor whites that they have much the same problems as the blacks, and that they therefore should not mess with the blacks or oppose them.

Stokely Carmichael has aptly summed up the situation in these words: "Black people often question whether or not they are equal to whites because every time they start to do something, white people are around showing them how to do it" (at Berkeley, November 19, 1966). Hence the Black Power movement means not only that the black people want real and unquestionable political power, but that they want to attain it by their own efforts. It is here that the strategy of Black Power is necessarily most aggressive, most truculent, most anti-white. But there remains a built-in ambiguity because without *some* kind of support from the overwhelmingly large white majority in the United States, Black Power cannot be politically viable at all. This means that whites who support blacks in their struggle for equality in the political and economic fields must be able to adapt to the new situation and understand it correctly. What Black Power asks of them is recognition of the black man's right to fight for his own interests even, if necessary, by revolutionary means. And it also asks a certain acceptance of the new emphasis on black identity—an emphasis which can be called "ethnocentric" rather than "racist"—as a necessary part of the program. As Floyd McKissick defined Black Power (in an admittedly moderate statement) it is ". . . a drive to mobilize the black communities of this country in a monumental effort to remove the basic causes of alienation, frustration, despair, low self-esteem and hopelessness."

But the trouble is that the nature of the revolution is not at all clear, and the future is not guaranteed to conform to the scenario devised by this or that black leader. There is no indication whatever that even the most influential of the new radical leaders have any real control over the course of events in the cities that are always ready to explode into violence.

Obviously, As McKissick points out, Black Power does not and cannot imply the hope of a "black takeover" or of "black supremacy." But it is not crystal clear that McKissick is right in saying that "Black power . . . does not advocate violence and will not start riots." Though the real thrust of the Black Power movement is toward the acquisition of a political power that will ensure real *influence* (which the Negro has never had) and a serious ability to participate in the economic life of the country on equal terms with white people, this perfectly legitimate and just aim gets lost in the anticipation of chaotic and senseless violence aroused both by white fears and by black rhetoric. And in fact the police and military preparations for the summer of 1968 bear witness to a state of polarized conflict in which guns will talk louder than reason.

It is of course to the interests of white society and in particular of the white mass media to confuse and mis-handle the whole Black Power issue. The more it can be treated as an eruption of berserk violence and African blood-lust the better the story will be and the more the white public will be charmed into gooseflesh by it. The frank exploitation of this sensationalist aspect of the race crisis is illustrated by the way *Esquire* got William Worthy to write on Black Power and then, against his will, gave his contribution a highly slanted and misleading publicity campaign (emphasizing "racist" implications). For which Worthy then sued the magazine.

This willful distortion and exploitation make it completely impossible for the average reader to be properly informed about Black Power. He is predisposed to violent and panic reactions, and it can be said that the whole of America is now primed for an explosion of anarchic destructiveness and aimless slaughter. The fault does not lie with Black Power, or not entirely. The Black Power movement is simply elected to act as catalyst, in order that what is deeply hidden in American society may come out into the open. And evidently it will.

The essays that follow cannot pretend to be anything like adequate to the present situation. The first one is by now completely dated: it represents a provisional view of things in 1964. The one on the Summer of 1967 is also provisional, but a few sentences here may serve to retrace the same outlines with firmer and more definite strokes, thanks to better information and to more mature reflection.

The Black Power movement is not really a racist movement, but it is definitely revolutionary. As Rap Brown says, again: "We are not an anti-white movement, we are anti anybody who is anti-black." It is a frankly violent movement. It is an anti-liberal movement, because it takes as axiomatic the belief that liberals are in favor of the established power institutions and of all liberal ideologies which covertly or otherwise aim at preserving these. Black Power claims it wants to destroy white institutions but in this it is perhaps ambiguous. Doubtless there are many in the Black Power movement who are frankly revolutionary, and passionately desire to destroy the American capitalist system. Others, on the other hand, are already moving toward more sophisticated (or more corrupt?) establishment positions, and are accused of careerism, of professional rhetoric, and of complicity with the government-supported intellectuals. In fact they are accused of *becoming* establishment intellectuals. It is not my place here to say whether or not this is true, but it is obviously a familiar development. It is altogether possible that the American establishment will be smart enough to neutralize Black Power by simply sucking the leaders into the government or academic machine, as was done before with the older and less radical Negro organizations. The question then is: how long before Rap Brown becomes another Uncle Tom?

The Black Power movement is explicitly identified with and involved in the world revolutionary ferment in the Third World. "We are members of the Third World." "The liberation of oppressed people across the world depends on the liberation of black people in this country."

Is Black Power a Marxist movement? No. At least not yet. In fact, the danger of the leaders being sucked into a Marxist establishment is just as great as that of their being absorbed by the American establishment. In either case Black Power will become a white movement again—dominated by white ideologies, plugged in to a white tradition. In which case it will be neutralized in a different way.

Black Power thus claims to be relevant not only to American black people but to people of all colors, everywhere, who are held down in tutelage and subservience by the white powers—whether American, European or Russian. It claims to be relevant also to the dissatisfied and disengaged within U.S. society (the hippies). *It is part of a world movement of refusal and rejection of the value system we call western culture.* It is therefore at least implicitly critical of Christianity as a white man's religion and accepts Christianity only as somewhat radically revised: "Christ was (literally and historically) a black man!" (Actually, there is a certain topological point to this, but I cannot discuss it here.)

What is to be said about Black Power? What does it mean to a serious—therefore radical—Christian? I for one do not believe a radical Christian has a moral obligation to manufacture molotov cocktails in the cellar and smuggle them into the ghetto. Nor do I believe he has a moral obligation to convert the Black Power movement back to non-violence (which is unlikely anyhow).

I do believe that the Christian is obligated, by his commitment to Christ, to seek out effective and authentic ways of peace in the midst of violence. But merely to demand support and obedience to an established disorder which is essentially violent through and through will not qualify as "peace-making."

There are no easy and simple solutions to this problem, but in the long run the evil root that has to be dealt with is the root of violence, hatred, poison, cruelty and greed which is part of the system itself. The job of the white Christian is then partly a job of diagnosis and criticism, a prophetic task of finding and identifying the injustice which is the cause of *all* violence, both white and black, which is also the root of war, and of the greed which keeps war going in order that some might make money out of it.

The delicacy and difficulty of the task are due of course to the fact that, in spite of all good intentions, Christians themselves have at times come to identify this evil of greed and power with "Christian order." They have confused it with peace, with right, with justice and with freedom, not distinguishing what really contributes to the good of man and what simply panders to his appetite for wealth and power.

We do not have to go and burn down the slums: but perhaps we might profitably consider whether some of our own venerable religious institutions are not, without realizing it, supporting themselves in part by the exploitation of slum real estate, or capitalizing in some other way on a disastrous and explosive situation.

In any case, we have to make a clear decision. Black Power or no Black Power, I for one remain *for* the Negro, I trust him, I recognize the overwhelming justice of his complaint, I confess I have no right whatever to get in his way, and that as a Christian I owe him support, not in his ranks but in my own, among the whites who refuse to trust him or hear him, and who want to destroy him.

20

RELIGION AND RACE
IN THE UNITED STATES

Published in New Blackfriars, *January 1965*

This article has appeared, in draft and mimeograph, with variant titles. Besides the one used here, it has been called "The Barbarians Are Among Us," and "Christianity and Race in the United States." It first appeared in 1964 in *Frères du Monde* (Bordeaux) under the title "Christianisme et question raciale aux Etats-Unis."

. . . . .

The idea of *kairos*—the time of urgent and providential decision—is something characteristic of Christianity, a religion of decisions in time and in history. Can Christians recognize their *kairos*? Is it possible that when the majority of Christians become aware that "the time has come" for a decisive and urgent commitment, the time has, in fact, already run out?

There can be no question now that the time for a certain kind of crucial Christian decision in America has come and gone. In 1962, and finally in 1963, there were "moments of truth" which have now passed, and the scene is becoming one of darkness, anarchy and moral collapse. These, of course, still call for a Christian response, a Christian decision. But it might seem that the responses and decisions of Christians will necessarily be less clear and more tragic because it is now apparent that there is little left for Christians as such to do to shape the events— or forestall the tragedies—that are to come. At best they can pray, and patiently suffer the consequences of past indecision, blindness and evasion. They cannot lead and guide the nation through this crisis, but they can still help others, if they choose, to understand and accept the sufferings involved in order to make a creative and constructive use of the situation for the future. Are they really likely to do this? Who can say?

In the Negro Christian non-violent movement under Martin Luther King, the *kairos*, the "providential time," met with a courageous and enlightened response. The non-violent-Negro civil rights drive has been one of the most positive and successful expressions of Christian social action that has been seen anywhere in the twentieth century. It is certainly the greatest example of Christian faith in action in the social history of the United States. It has come almost entirely from the Negroes, with a few white Christians and liberals in support. There can be no question that the Christian heroism manifested by the Negroes in the Birmingham demonstrations, or the massive tranquility and order of the March on Washington in August of 1963, had a great deal to do with the passage of the Civil Rights bill. It must also be admitted, as Bayard Rustin, a Negro non-violent leader, has pointed out, that without the Christian intervention of white Protestants and Catholics all over America, the bill would not have been passed. The fact that there is now a Civil Rights Law guaranteeing, at least *de jure*, the freedom of all citizens to enjoy the facilities of the country equally is due to what one might call a Christian as well as a humanitarian and liberal conscience in the United States. However, the Northern Negro is, generally speaking, disillusioned with the Churches and with the Christian preaching of moderation and non-violence. His feeling is that the Churches are part of the establishment (which in fact they are!). They support the power-structure and therefore (he believes) keep the Negro deluded and passive, preventing him from fighting for his rights.

The passage of the Civil Rights Bill has only brought the real problem to a head. The struggle for rights now enters a new and more difficult phase.

Hitherto the well-intentioned and the idealistic have assumed that if the needed legislation were passed, the two races would "integrate" more or less naturally, not without a certain amount of difficulty, of course, but nonetheless effectively in the end. They have also assumed as axiomatic that if something is morally right and good, it will come to pass all by itself as soon as obstacles are removed. Everyone seemed to believe with simple faith that law and order, morality, the "American way of life" and Christianity are all very much the same thing. Now it is becoming quite clear that they are not so at all. Many Christians, who have confused "Americanism" with "Christianity" are in fact contributing to the painful contradictions and even injustices of the racial crisis. For the one thing that has been made most evident by the long and bitter struggle of the South, and now of the North, to prevent civil rights legislation from being passed or enforced or made effective, is that the legislators and the police themselves, along with some ministers and indeed all those whom one can call "the establishment," seem to be the first to defy the law or set it aside when their own interests are threatened. In other words we are living in a society that is not exactly moral, a society which misuses Christian cliches to justify its lawlessness and immorality.

And so there are many who think that non-violence has not proved itself a success. It is considered naive and over-simple and it does not get real results. Certainly non-violence postulates a belief in the fundamental goodness of human nature. But this attitude of optimism can come to be confused with shallow confidence in the morality and intrinsic goodness of a society which is proving itself torn by vicious internal contradictions. Non-violence still continues to be used as a tactic, but the days of its real effectiveness are apparently over. It will probably never again convey the message it conveyed in Montgomery, Birmingham and Selma. Those days are over, and it seems that people who believed in all that was implied by non-violence will look back upon those days with a certain nostalgia. For non-violence apparently presupposed a sense of justice, of humaneness of liberality, of generosity that were not to be found in the white people to whom the Negroes made their stirring appeal. The problem of American racism turned out to be far deeper, far more stubborn, infinitely more complex. It is also part of a much greater problem: one that divides the whole world into what may one day turn into a huge revolutionary interracial war of two camps: the affluent whites and the impoverished non-whites.

One reason why non-violence apparently cannot continue to be a really effective instrument for the vindication of Negro rights is this: it seems that the willingness to take punishment and suffering, which is essential to non-violent resistance, cannot mean the same thing to the Negro minority in the United States as it meant to the Hindus in their vast majority facing English colonialism in India. There, Hindu non-violence bore witness to overwhelming strength. In the Negro ghettos of America it has turned out to mean, Negro inferiority and helplessness. The Negro is always the one who lets his head be bashed in. Whether or not this is what non-violence really means, the confused image of it has now become unacceptable to many activists in the struggle for civil rights, while resentful whites, north and south, are not willing to see its true meaning in any case. The Negroes on the other hand, more and more disillusioned not only with white reactionaries but also with ambiguous liberals, have tended to take a more desperate course. On one hand there has been an increasing trend toward unsystematic and spontaneous violence, and on the other there has been the systematic campaign for "Black Power" which, not properly understood and not always clearly explained, had managed to frighten white people not a little. We will discuss this further on.

In any case there is more and more violent action on both sides, as it becomes increasingly clear that the Civil Rights Law has not really solved the racial problem and that in actual fact the ghetto existence of the Negro has only become better and more inexorably defined by his inability to take advantage of the rights that have been granted him only on paper and too late.

The Negro is integrated by law into a society in which there really is no place for him—not that a place could not be made for him, if the white majority were capable of wanting him as a brother and a fellow-citizen. But even those who have been theoretically in favor of civil rights are turning out to be concretely reluctant to have the Negroes as next-door neighbors. The so-called "white backlash" manifests a change from tolerant indifference to bitter hatred on the part of some Northern whites. It is virulent and passionate and one hears the word "nigger" spat out with a venom which one had thought belonged to the past. And there are reasons, for violence and gratuitous attacks on white people by Negroes are common everywhere in the North. The Negro's clear awareness that he is still despised and rejected, after years of bitter struggle and deception, has destroyed his confidence in legal and peaceful methods. Perhaps he is beginning to want something besides "rights" that are purely Platonic—an opportunity to unburden himself of his bitterness by violent protest, that will disrupt a social "order" that seems to him to have proved itself meaningless and fraudulent.

The problem is much more complex, much more tragic, than people have imagined. To begin with, it is something that extends beyond America. It affects the whole world. The race problem of America has been analyzed (by such writers as William Faulkner, for example) as a problem of deep guilt for the sin of slavery. The guilt of white America toward the Negro is simply another version of the guilt of the European colonizer toward all the other races of the world, whether in Asia, Africa, America or Polynesia. The fact that non-violent resistance did not fully succeed and the fact that its partial failure clearly disclosed the refusal of white America to really integrate the Negro into its social framework has radically altered the Negro's evaluation of himself and of his struggle. Whereas before he might have been willing to believe it possible for him to find a place in white society, he has now largely ceased to find real integration either credible or desirable. True, there are probably countless middle-class Negroes who are able to find life tolerable and who seek only to avoid further trouble and violence. But there are far more numerous Negroes for whom the present situation spells nothing but despair and total rejection from a society which to them has no real meaning. To these Negroes, if any political self-awareness makes sense at all, it is one in which they begin dimly to recognize themselves as identified with the colored races in all parts of the world which are struggling to assert themselves and find their proper place in it. The slogan "Black Power" implies not only the intent to use political means in order to gain what is granted the Negro by law and refused him in fact. It implies a consciousness of revolutionary solidarity with the colored in other parts of the world. This has been brought sharply to attention by the fact, for example, of Negro protest against fighting against "other colored people" in Vietnam, and fighting them for the interests of the white United States. Thus the Vietnam war, ostensibly being fought for "freedom" and "against Communist oppression" is seen to be fraught with its own very unpleasant ambiguities. And this in turn brings into focus all the doubts which radicals, white and Negro alike, are raising about the sincerity of our claim to be the most democratic society on earth.

The civil rights struggle has therefore, in largely abandoning its reliance on non-violence, made a very significant shift in its position. It has changed its basic assumptions. It no longer takes for granted that American society is just, freedom-loving and democratic and that the ways to satisfy the just claims of the Negro are built into our system. On the contrary, it takes for granted that our society is basically racist, that it is inclined toward fascism and violence, and that the rights of Negroes cannot be guaranteed without real political power.

When a nation is torn by contradictions, the problem can be apparently "simplified" and "clarified" if unpleasant choices are excluded and if one falls back on primitive positions—on crude and satisfying myths—for instance the myth that "it was all started by the commies." If the whites insist on attributing to Communism the responsibility for every protest which releases the frustrated energies of the Negro, the Negroes in the end will begin to respect and trust Communism. Up to the present they have been supremely indifferent towards it. Their new international consciousness will dispose them more and more to look with respect toward Red China which claims to lead the colored people of the world in revolution.

In one of the big riots of 1964, the one in Harlem in mid-July, when the streets were filled with people in confusion, running from the police; when bricks and bottles were pelting down from the rooftops and the police were firing into the air (not without killing one man and wounding many others) the police captain tried to disperse the rioters by shouting through a megaphone: "Go home! Go home!"

A voice from the crowd answered: "We are home, baby!" The irony of this statement, and its humor, sum up the American problem. There is no "where" for the Negro to go. He is where he is. White America has put him where he is. The tendency has been to act as if he were not there, or as if he might possibly go somewhere else, and to beat him over the head if he makes his collective presence too manifest. The American Negro himself has tried to return to Africa, but the plan was farcical. The Black Nationalists are even now agitating for a part of the country to be turned over to the Negroes—so they can live by themselves. One of the purposes of the violence which those Negro racists actively foment, is to make white society willing and happy to get rid of them. The fact remains that the Negro is now in the home the white man has given him: the three square miles of broken-down tenements which form the ghetto of Harlem, the biggest Negro city in the world, type of all the Negro ghettos in America, full of crime, misery, squalor, dope addiction, prostitution, gang warfare, hatred and despair. And yet, though Harlem is a problem, it will not become less of a problem if we consider only the negative side. For those who think only of the prostitutes and criminals, Harlem becomes part of the general obsessive national myth of the "bad Negro." The majority of the people in Harlem are good, peaceable, gentle, long-suffering men and women, socially insecure but more sinned against than sinning.

What is to be wondered at is not the occasional mass demonstrations and rioting, not the juvenile delinquency and not the more and more deliberate excursions of small violent groups into other areas of the city to beat up white people and rob them. What is to be wondered at is the persistence of courage, irony, humor, patience and hope in Harlem! In a spiritual crisis of the individual, the truth and authenticity of the person's spiritual identity are called into question. He is placed in confrontation with reality and judged by his ability to bring himself into a valid and living relationship with the demands of his new situation. In the spiritual, social, historic crises of civilizations—and of religious institutions—the same principle applies. Growth, survival and even salvation may depend on the ability to sacrifice what is fictitious and unauthentic in the construction of one's moral, religious or national identity. One must then enter upon a different creative task of reconstruction and renewal. This task can be carried out only in the climate of faith, of hope and of love: these three must be present in some form, even if they amount only to a natural belief in the validity and significance of human choice, a decision to invest human life with some shadow of meaning, a willingness to treat other men as other selves.

Gandhi long ago pointed out that western democracy was on trial. There is no need for me here to show in how many ways the American concepts of democracy and Christianity are here being weighed in the balance.

The problem of American Christianity is the same as the problem of Christianity everywhere else: Christianity is suffering a crisis of identity and authenticity, and is being judged by the ability of Christians themselves to abandon unauthentic, anachronistic images and securities, in order to find a new place in the world by a new evaluation of the world and a new commitment in it.

In the American crisis the Christian faces a typical choice. The choice is not interior and secret, but public, political and social. He is perhaps not used to regarding his crucial choices in the light of politics. He can now either find security and order by falling back on antique and basically feudal (or perhaps fascist) conceptions or go forward into the unknown future, identifying himself with that force that will inevitably create a new society. The choice is between "safety," based on negation of the new and the reaffirmation of the familiar, or the creative risk of love and grace in new and untried solutions, which justice nevertheless demands.

Those who are anxious to discover whether Christianity has had any positive effect on the civil rights struggle seldom ask an equally important question: has the struggle had an effect on Christianity? It has certainly had an effect on the Catholic Church. The case of Father William Du Bay, a young assistant in a Los Angeles Negro parish, is a direct outcome of the racial crisis. His protest was an admitted attempt not only to defend the rights of his Negro parishioners, but also to assert his own right to break through the absolutely ironbound restrictions of clerical submission to canonical authority, not as an act of willful disobedience but as a protest that the priest owes a higher obedience—to the demands of charity and justice—which cannot be shrugged off by simply leaving all responsibility to rest upon superiors. Whatever may have been the rights and wrongs of the case, which was a rude shock to Catholic authority, Father Du Bay was clearly trying to say that he did not believe that the inaction of his bishop entitled him to be passive himself, and that there is such a thing as public opinion in the Church. Not all Catholics have agreed, but all have taken note of this assertion!

The mystique of American Christian rightism, a mystique of violence, of apocalyptic threats, of hatred, and of judgment is perhaps only a more exaggerated and more irrational manifestation of a rather universal attitude common to Christians in many countries. The conviction that the great evil in the world today can be identified with Communism, and that to be a Christian is simply to be an anti-Communist. Communism is the antichrist. Communism is the source of all other problems, all conflicts. All the evils in the world can be traced to the machinations of Communists. The apocalyptic fear of Communism which plays so great a part in the Christianity of some Americans—and some Europeans—resolves itself into a fear of revolution and indeed a fear of any form of social change that would disturb the status quo.

This mentality which we have summarized as "Christian violence" becomes more and more irrational in proportion as it implies both an absolute conviction of one's own rightness and a capacity to approve the use of any means, however violent, however extreme, in order to defend what one feels, subjectively, to be right. This is an axiom. This totalism admits no distinctions, no shades of meaning. "Our side" is totally right, everyone else is diabolically wicked.

Naturally, this synthetic and sweeping "rightness" is compounded of many unconscious doubts and repressed fears. Nor are all the fears repressed. But they take a more or less symbolic form. There is no question that the white racists of the South willingly admit a certain fear of the Negro. The fear is part of their mystique and indeed accounts for a great deal of its emotional power. It is the quasi-mystical obsession with the black demon waiting in the bushes to rape the virginal white daughters of the old South.

The literal truth outdoes all caricature, and it gives us a clue to the mentality and mystique of the "Christian violence" which is coming into being here and there all over the United States, not only among fanatical sects and not only in the South. The intensity of emotion, the sacred and obsessional fear, rising from subliminal levels and reaching consciousness in a panic conviction of spiritual danger, judges all that seems menacing and calls it diabolical. But everything seems menacing and therefore the most innocent of oppositions, the slightest dissenting opinions, calls for the most extreme, the most violent and the most ruthless repressions. At the present time, the Southern pseudo-mystique of sexual and racist obsessions (and of course there have been rapes, and seductions, of whites by Negroes, as well infinitely more rapes and seductions of Negroes by whites) now joins with the deeper and more universal fear of revolution. This combination results in a peculiarly potent climate of aggressive intolerance, suspiciousness, hatred and fear. When we consider that this self-righteous, pseudo-religious faith has its finger terribly close to the button that launches inter-continental ballistic missiles, it gives us food for thought.

The American Negro is well aware of all these obsessions in his regard. He realizes better than the benevolent white liberal to what extent these subliminal fears exist in all white Americans. The tensions created by this dangerous situation are going to increase as the Negro, consciously or otherwise, renounces his hopeful and friendly expectations and begins to test his capacity to shake the foundations of white society by threats of violence.

Well then: what of the *kairos?* Shall we say that it has passed and left the Christian Churches only half awake? It depends upon the sense the Christian gives to his *kairos.* It is certainly possible for us to recognize that we have missed a chance for significant social action. We can edify the world with those subtle and contrite self-examinations which we often substitute for purposeful activity. Or we can do worse, and involve ourselves in the righteous and apocalyptic fury of those whose "Christianity" has emptied itself of serious meaning in order to become a fanatical negation, a refusal of reality, and a ritual hunting of Communist witches.

For those whose Christianity is still a religion of truth and love, not of hate and fear, I think the first thing to do is to admit that our *kairos* is perhaps not always likely to be what we expect. Are we, for example, justified in assuming so complacently that *kairos,* in race crisis, means an opportunity for us as Christians to step in and settle everything with a few wise answers and the adoption of the right attitudes? Are we not called upon to re-evaluate our own notions and see that "right attitudes" are not enough and that it is not sufficient merely to have goodwill, or even to go to jail gloriously for an honest cause? We need a little more depth and a keener sense of the tragedy (or perhaps comedy) of our situation: we are living in a world which is in many ways "post-Christian" and acting as if we were still running things, still in a position to solve all the world's problems and tell everybody what to do next. It might help if we realized that in fact most people have lost interest in our official pronouncements, and while the fanatical type of Christian still thrives on the belief that he is hated, the rest of us are beginning to realize that the wicked world can no longer take the trouble to do even that. It is simply not interested.

This, as a matter of fact, is no disaster. It is really a liberation. We no longer have to take ourselves so abominably seriously as "Christians" with a public and capital "C." We can give a little more thought to the reality of our vocation and bother less with the image which we show to the world.

If there is a *kairos*, and perhaps there still is, it is not a "time" in which once again we will convince the world that we are right, but perhaps rather a time in which the crisis of man will teach us to see a few sobering truths about our now Christian calling and our place in the world—a place no longer exalted and mighty, or perhaps even influential.

In fact we are learning that we are as other men are, that we are not a special kind of privileged being, that our faith does not exempt us from facing the mysterious realities of the world with the same limitations as everybody else, and with the same capacity for human failure. Our Christian calling does not make us superior to other men, does not entitle us to judge everyone and decide everything for everybody. We do not have answers to every social problem, and all conflicts have not been decided beforehand in favor of our side. Our job is to struggle along with everybody else and collaborate with them in the difficult, frustrating task of seeking a solution to common problems, which are entirely new and strange to us all.

The American racial crisis which grows more serious every day offers the American Christian a chance to face a reality about himself and recover his fidelity to Christian truth, not merely in institutional loyalties and doctrinal orthodoxies (in which no one has taken the trouble to accuse him of failing) but in recanting a more basic heresy: the loss of that Christian sense which sees every other man as Christ and treats him as Christ. For, as St. John said: "We know what love is by this: that he laid down his life for us so that we ought to lay down our lives for the brotherhood. But whoever possess this world's goods and notices his brother in need and shuts his heart against him, how can the love of God remain in him? Dear children, let us put our love not into words or into talk but into deeds, and make it real." (I John 3:16–18)

We do indeed have a message for the world, and the Word of God is still as alive and penetrating today "as any two-edge sword." But we have perhaps taken the edge off the sword by our short-sightedness and our complacency. The Christian failure in American racial justice has been all too real, but it is not the fault of the few dedicated and non-violent followers of Christ. It is due much more to the fact that so few Christians have been able to face the fact that non-violence comes very close to the heart of the Gospel ethic, and is perhaps essential to it.

But non-violence is not simply a matter of marching with signs and placards under the eyes of unfriendly policemen. The partial failure of liberal non-violence has brought out the stark reality that our society itself is radically violent and that violence is built into its very structure. We live in a society which, while appealing to Christian ethical ideals, violently negates its Christian pretensions and in so doing drives a radical minority to desperation and violence. The white Christian cannot in such a situation be content merely to march with his black brother at the risk of getting his head broken or of being shot. The problem is to eradicate this basic violence and injustice from white society. Can it be done? How?

21

THE ANSWER OF MINERVA:
Pacifism and Resistance in Simone Weil

A review of *Simone Weil* by Jacques Cabaud (Harvill Press, 1964), this article was first published in *Peace News* (London) in April 1965.

· · · · ·

Like Bernanos and Camus, Simone Weil is one of those brilliant and independent French thinkers who were able to articulate the deepest concerns of France and Europe in the first half of this century. More controversial and perhaps more of a genius than the others, harder to situate, she has been called all kinds of names, both good and bad and often contradictory: Gnostic and Catholic, Jew and Albigensian, medievalist and modernist, Platonist and anarchist, rebel and saint, rationalist and mystic. De Gaulle said he thought she was out of her mind. The doctor in the sanatorium at Ashford, Kent, where she died (August 24, 1943) said, "She had a curious religious outlook and (probably) no religion at all." In any case, whatever is said about her, she can always be treated as "an enigma." Which is simply to say that she is somewhat more difficult to categorize than most people, since in her passion for integrity she absolutely refused to take up any position she had not first thought out in the light of what she believed to be a personal vocation to "absolute intellectual honesty." When she began to examine any accepted position, she easily detected its weaknesses and inconsistencies.

None of the books of Simone Weil (seventeen in French, eight in English) were written as books. They are all collections of notes, essays, articles, journals and letters. Though she has conquered a certain number of fans by the force of her personality, most readers remember her as the author of some fragment or other that they have found in some way both impressive and disconcerting. One cannot help admiring her lucid genius, and yet one can easily disagree with her most fundamental and characteristic ideas. But this is usually because one does not see her thought as a whole. The new biography by Jacques Cabaud (Jacques Cabaud, *Simone Weil* [Harvill Press, 1964, 392 pp. ill.]) not only tells of her active and tormented life, but studies in detail a large number of things (of which a complete bibliography is given), together with the testimony of those who knew her. Cabaud has also avoided treating Simone Weil either as a problem or as a saint. He accepts her as she evidently was. Such a book is obviously indispensable, for without such a comprehensive and detached study it would be impossible to judge her reasonably. In fact, no one who reads this book carefully and dispassionately can treat Simone Weil merely as an enigma or a phenomenon, still less as deluded or irrelevant. Few writers have more significant thoughts on the history of our time and a better understanding of our calamities. On the other hand, probably not even Mr. Cabaud could claim that this book says the last word on Simone Weil or that it fully explains, for instance, her "Christian mysticism" that prompted her of deliberate purpose to remain outside the Church and refuse baptism even on the point of death because she felt that her natural element was with the "immense and unfortunate multitude of unbelievers." This "unbeliever," we note, was one who had been "seized" by Christ in a mystical experience the marks of which are to all appearances quite authentic, though the Catholic theologian has trouble keeping them clearly in a familiar and traditional focus. (Obviously, one of her charisms was that of living and dying as a sign of contradiction for Catholics, and one feels that the climate of Catholic thought in France at the time of Vatican II has been to some extent affected by at least a vague awareness of her experiences at Solesmes and Marseilles.)

Though her spirit was at times explicitly intended to be that of the medieval Cathars and though her description of her mystical life is strongly Gnostic and intellectual, she has had things to say of her experience of suffering and of her understanding of the suffering of Christ which are not only deeply Christian but also speak directly to the anguish and perplexity of modern man. This intuition of the nature and meaning of suffering provides, in Simone Weil, the core of a metaphysic, not to say a theology, of nonviolence. A metaphysic of nonviolence is something that the peace movement needs.

Looking back at Simone Weil's participation in the peace movement of the thirties, Cabaud speaks rather sweepingly of a collapse of pacifism in her thought and political action. It is quite true that the pacifism of the thirties was as naive as it was popular, and that for many people at that time pacifism amounted to nothing more than the disposition to ignore unpleasant realities and to compromise with the threat of force as did Chamberlain at Munich. It is also true that Simone Weil herself underestimated the ruthlessness of Hitler at the time of the Munich crisis though her principles did not allow her to agree with the Munich pact. Cabaud quotes a statement of Simone Weil accusing herself of a "Criminal error committed before 1939 with regard to pacifist groups and their actions." Her tolerance of a passive and inert pacifism was regarded by her as a kind of cooperation with "their disposition towards treason" which, she said, she did not see because she was disabled by illness (Cabaud, p. 197). This reflects her disgust with Vichy and with former pacifists who now submitted to Hitler without protest. But we cannot interpret this statement to mean that after Munich and then the fall of France Simone Weil abandoned all her former principles in order to take up an essentially new position in regard to war and peace. This would mean equating her "pacifism" with the quietism of the uncomprehending and the inert. It would also mean failure to understand that she became deeply committed to nonviolent resistance. Before Munich the emphasis was, however, on nonviolence, and after the fall of France the emphasis was on *resistance*, including the acceptance of resistance by force where nonviolence was ineffective.

It is unfortunate that Cabaud's book does not sufficiently avoid the usual cliche identification of pacifism as such with quietest passivity, and nonresistance. Simone Weil's love of peace was never sentimental and never quietistic; and though her judgment sometimes erred in assessing concrete situations, it was seldom unrealistic. An important article she wrote in 1937 remains one of the classic treatments of the problem of war and peace in our time. Its original title was: "Let us not start the Trojan War all over again." It appears in her *Selected Essays* as "The Power of Words." Cabaud analyzes it in his book (pp. 155–160) where he says that it marks a dividing line in her life. It belongs, in fact, to the same crucial period as her first mystical experiences.

There is nothing mystical about this essay. It develops a theme familiar to Montaigne and Charron—the most terrible thing about war is that, if it is examined closely, it is discovered to have no rationally definable objective. The supposed objectives of war are actually myths and fictions which are all the more capable of enlisting the full force of devotion to duty and hatred of the enemy when they are completely empty of content. Let us briefly resume this article, since it contains the substance of Simone Weil's ideas on peace and is (apart from some of her topical examples) just as relevant to our own time as it was to the late thirties.

The article begins with a statement which is passed over by Cabaud and which is very important for us. Simone Weil remarks that while our technology has given us weapons of immense destructive power, the weapons do not go off by themselves (we hope). Hence it is a primordial mistake to think and act as if the weapons were what constituted our danger, rather than the people who are disposed to fire them off. But more precisely still: the danger lies not so much in this or that group or class but in the climate of thought in which all participate (not excluding pacifists). This is what Simone Weil set herself to understand. The theme of the article is, then, that war must be regarded as a problem to be solved by rational analysis and action, not as a fatality to which we must submit with bravery or desperation. We see immediately that she is anything but passively resigned to the evil of war. The acceptance of war as an unavoidable fatality she clearly saw to be the root of the power political's ruthless and obsessed commitment to violence.

This, she believed, was the "key to our history."

If in fact conflicting statesmen faced one another only with clearly defined objectives that were fully rational, there would be a certain measure and limit which would permit of discussion and negotiation. But where the objectives are actually nothing more than capital-letter slogans without any intelligible content whatever, there is no common measure, therefore no possibility of communication, and hence no possibility of avoiding war except by ambiguous compromises, or by agreements that are not intended to be kept. Such agreements do not really avoid war. And of course they solve no problems.

The typology of the Trojan war, "known to every educated man," illustrates this. The only one, Greek or Trojan, who had any interest in Helen, was Paris. No one, Greek or Trojan, was fighting for Helen, but for the "real issue" which Helen symbolized. Both armies, in this war, which is the type of all wars, were fighting in a moral void, motivated by symbols without content, which in the case of the Homeric heroes took the form of gods and myths. Simone Weil considered that this was relatively fortunate for them since their myths were thus kept within a well-defined area. For us, on the other hand (since we imagine that we have no myths at all), myth actually is without limitation and can easily penetrate the whole realm of political, social and ethical thought. Thus, instead of going to war because the gods have been arguing among themselves, we go because of "secret plots" and sinister combinations, because of political slogans elevated to the dignity of metaphysical absolutes: "Our political universe is peopled with myths and monsters—we know nothing there about absolutes." We shed blood for high-sounding words spelled out in capital letters. We seek to impart content to them by destroying other men who believe in enemy-words, also in capital letters.

But how can men really be brought to kill each other for what is objectively void? The nothingness of national, class or racial myth must receive an apparent substance, not from intelligible content but from the *will to destroy and be destroyed.* (We may observe here that the substance of idolatry is the willingness to give reality to metaphysical nothingness by sacrificing to it. The more totally one destroys present realities and alienates oneself to an object which is really void, the more total is the idolatry, i.e., the commitment to the falsehood that the non-entity is an objective absolute. Note here that in this context the God of the mystics is not "an object" and cannot be described properly as "an entity" among other entities. Hence one of the marks of authentic mysticism is that God as experienced by the mystic can in no way be the object of an idolatrous cult.)

The will to kill and be killed grows out of sacrifices and acts of destruction already performed. As soon as the war has begun, the first dead are there to demand further sacrifice from their companions since they have demonstrated by their example that the objective of the war is such that no price is too high to pay for its attainment. This is the "sledgehammer argument," the argument of Minerva in Homer: "You must fight on, for if you now make peace with the enemy, you will offend the dead."

These are cogent intuitions, but so far they do not add anything beyond their own vivacity to the ideas that prevailed in the thirties. In effect, everyone who remembered the First World War was capable of meditating on the futility of war in 1938. Everyone was still able to take sarcastic advantage of slogans about "making the world safe for democracy." But merely to say that war was totally absurd and totally meaningless, in its very nature, was to run the risk of missing the real point. Mere words without content do not suffice, of themselves, to start a war. Behind the empty symbols and the objectiveless motivation of force, there is a real force, the grimmest of all the social realities of our time: collective power, which Simone Weil, in her more Catharist mood, regarded as the "Great Beast." (How will the soul be saved," she asked her philosophy students in the Lycée, "after the Great Beast has acquired an opinion about everything?")

The void underlying the symbols and the myths of nationalism, of capitalism, Communism, fascism, racism, totalism, is in fact filled entirely by the presence of the Beast. We might say, developing her image, that the void thus becomes an insatiable demand for power, which sucks all life and all being into itself. Power is thus generated by the plunge of real and human values into nothingness, allowing themselves to be destroyed in order that the collectivity may attain to a theoretical and hopeless ideal of perfect and unassailable supremacy: "What is called national security is a chimerical state of things in which one would keep for oneself alone the power to make war while all other countries would be unable to do so . . . War is therefore made *in order to keep or to increase the means of making war.* All international politics revolve in this vicious circle." "But," she adds, "why must one be able to make war? This no one knows any more than the Trojans knew why they had to keep Helen."

Nevertheless, when Germany overran France she herself found a reason for joining the resistance: the affirmation of human liberty against the abuse of power. "All over the world there are human beings *serving as means to the power of others without having consented to it.*" This was a basic evil that had to be resisted. The revision of Simone Weil's opinion on pacifism and nonviolence after Munich does not therefore resolve itself, as Cabaud seems to indicate, with a practical repudiation of both. Munich led her to clarify the distinction between ineffective and effective nonviolence. The former is what Gandhi called the nonviolence of the weak, and it merely submits to evil without resistance. Effective nonviolence ("the nonviolence of the strong") is that which opposes evil with serious and positive resistance, in order to overcome it with good. Simone Weil would apparently have added that if this nonviolence had no hope of success, then evil could be resisted by force. But she hoped for a state of affairs in which human conflict could be resolved nonviolently rather than by force. However, her notion of nonviolent resistance was never fully developed. If she had survived (she would be fifty-six now) she might possibly have written some exciting things on the subject.

Once this is understood, then we can also understand Simone Weil's revulsion at the collapse of that superficial and popular pacifism of Munich, which, since it was passive and also without clear objective, was only another moment in the objectiveless dialectic of brute power. And we can also understand the passion with which she sought to join the French resistance. But she did not change her principles. She did not commit herself to violent action, but she did seek to expose herself to the greatest danger and sacrifice, nonviolently. Though her desire to form a "front line nursing corps" (regarded by De Gaulle as lunacy) was never fulfilled, she nevertheless worked—indeed overworked— until the time of her death, trying to clarify the principles on which a new France could be built. She never gave up the hope that one might "substitute more and more in the world effective nonviolence for violence."

22

AN ENEMY OF THE STATE

This review of Gordon Zahn's book, *In Solitary Witness* (1964), was published in *Pax Bulletin* (London) in May 1965.

· · · · ·

On August 9, 1943, the Austrian peasant Franz Jagerstatter was beheaded by the Germany military authorities as an "enemy of the state" because he had repeatedly refused to take the military oath and serve in what he declared to be an "unjust war." His story has a very special importance at a time when the Catholic Church, in the Second Vatican Council, is confronting the moral problem of nuclear weaponry. This Austrian peasant was not only simultaneously a Catholic and a conscientious objector, but he was a fervent Catholic, so fervent that some who knew him believe him to have been a saint. His lucid and uncompromising refusal to fight for Germany in the Second World War was the direct outcome of his religious conversion. It was the political implementation of his desire to be a perfect Christian.

Franz Jagerstatter surrendered his life rather than take the lives of others in what he believed to be an "unjust war." He clung to this belief in the face of every possible objection not only on the part of the army and the state, but also from his fellow Catholics, the Catholic clergy and of course his own family. He had to meet practically every "Christian argument" that is advanced in favor of war. He was treated as a rebel, disobedient to lawful authority, a traitor to his country. He was accused of being selfish, self-willed, not considering his family, neglecting his duty to his children.

His Austrian Catholic friends understood that he was unwilling to fight for Hitler's Germany, but yet they argued that the war was justified because they hoped it would lead to the destruction of Bolshevism and therefore to the preservation of "European Christianity." He was therefore refusing to defend his faith. He was also told that he was not sufficiently informed to judge whether or not the war was just. That he had an obligation to submit to the "higher wisdom" of the state. The government and the Fuehrer know best. Thousands of Catholics, including many priests, were serving in the armies, and therefore he should not try to be "more Catholic than the Church."

He was even reminded that the bishops had not protested against this war, and in fact not only his pastor but even his bishop tried to persuade him to give up his resistance because it was "futile." One of the priests represented to him that he would have innumerable opportunities to practice Christian virtue and exercise an "apostolate of good example" in the armed forces. All these are very familiar arguments frequently met with in our present situation, and they are still assumed to be so conclusive that few Catholics dare to risk the disapproval they would incur by conscientious objection and dissent.

Jagerstatter's fellow villagers thought his refusal was evidence of fanaticism due to his religious conversion at the time of his marriage in 1936, followed by an "excess of Bible reading." His conscientious objection is still not fully understood in his native village, though on the local war memorial his name has been added to those of the villagers who were killed in action.

The peasant refused to give in to any of these arguments, and replied to them with all simplicity:

> I cannot and may not take an oath in favor of a government that is fighting an unjust war . . . I cannot turn the responsibility for my actions over to the Fuehrer . . . Does anyone really think that this massive blood-letting can save European Christianity or bring it to a new flowering? . . . Is it not more Christian to offer oneself as a victim right away rather than first have to murder others who certainly have a right to live and want to live—just to prolong one's own life a little while?

When reminded that most Catholics had gone to war for Hitler without any such qualms of conscience, he replied that they obviously "had not received the grace" to see things as they were. When told that the bishops themselves expressed no such objections he repeated that "they had not received the grace" either.

Jagerstatter's refusal to fight for Hitler was not based on a personal repugnance to fighting in any form. As a matter of fact Jagerstatter was, by temperament, something of a fighter In his wilder youthful days he had participated rather prominently in the inter-village gang wars. He had also undergone preliminary military training without protest, though his experience at that time had convinced him that army life presented a danger to morals.

Shortly after Hitler took over Austria in 1938, Jagerstatter had a dream in which he saw a splendid and shining express train coming round a mountain, and thousands of people running to get aboard. "No one could prevent them from getting on the train." While he was looking at this he heard a voice saying: "This train is going to hell." When he woke up he spontaneously associated the "train" with Nazism. His objection to military service was, then, the fruit of a particular religious interpretation of contemporary political events. His refusal to fight was not only a private matter of conscience: it also expressed a deep intuition concerning the historical predicament of the Catholic Church in the twentieth century. This intuition was articulated in several long and very impressive meditations or "commentaries" in which he says

> The situation in which we Christians of Germany find ourselves today is much more bewildering than that faced by the Christians of the early centuries at the time of their bloodiest persecution . . . We are not dealing with a small matter, but the great (apocalyptic) life and death struggle has already begun. Yet in the midst of it there are many who still go on living their lives as though nothing had changed . . . That we Catholics must make ourselves tools of the worst and most dangerous anti-Christian power that has ever existed is something that I cannot and never will believe . . . Many actually believe quite simply that things have to be the way they are. If this should happen to mean that they are obliged to commit injustice, then they believe that others are responsible . . . I am convinced that it is still best that I speak the truth even though it costs me my life. For you will not find it written in any of the commandments of God or of the Church that a man is obliged under pain of sin to take an oath committing him to obey whatever might be commanded him by his secular ruler. We need no rifles or pistols for our battle, but instead spiritual weapons—and the foremost of these is prayer.

The witness of this Austrian peasant is in striking contrast to the career of another man who lived and worked for a time in the nearby city of Linz: Adolf Eichmann.

The American sociologist Gordon Zahn, who is also a Catholic and a pacifist, has written an absorbing, objective, fully documented life of Jagerstatter (*In Solitary Witness* [New York: Holt, Rinehart & Winston, 1964]), in which he studies with great care not only the motives and actions of the man himself, but also the reactions and recollections of scores of people who knew him, from his family and neighbors to fellow prisoners and prison chaplains. One of the most striking things about the story is that repeated attempts were made to save the peasant-objector's life not only by his friends, priests, by his attorney but even by his military judges (he was not in the hands of the SS).

Jagerstatter could have escaped execution if he had accepted non-combatant service in the medical corps, but he felt that even this would be a compromise, because his objection was not only to killing other men but to the act of saving his own life by an implicit admission that the Nazis were a legitimate regime carrying on a just war. A few minutes before his execution Jagerstatter still calmly refused to sign a document that would have saved him. The chaplain who was present, and who had tried like everyone else to persuade the prisoner to save himself, declared that Jagerstatter "lived as a saint and died as a hero."

It is important to observe that though the Catholic villagers of his native St. Radegund still tend to regard Jagerstatter as an extremist and a fanatic, or even as slightly touched in the head, the priests who knew him and others who have studied him have begun to admit the seriousness and supernatural impact of his heroic self-sacrifice. There are some who do not hesitate to compare his decision with that of Thomas More.

One of the prison chaplains who knew him said: "Not for an instant did I ever entertain the notion that Jagerstatter was 'fanatic' or even possibly mentally deranged. He did not give the slightest impression of being so." And a French cellmate said of him that he was "one of the heroes of our time, a fighter to the death for faith, peace and justice."

Finally, it is interesting to read the very reserved judgment of the bishop who, when consulted by Jagerstatter about this moral problem, urged him to renounce his "scruples" and let himself be inducted into the army.

> I am aware of the "consistency" of his conclusions and respect them—especially in their intention. At that time I could see that the man thirsted after martyrdom and for the expiation of sin, and I told him that he was permitted to choose that path only if he knew he had been called to it through some

special revelation originating from above and not in himself. He agreed with this. For this reason Jagerstatter represents a completely exceptional case, one much more to be marveled at than copied.

The story of the Austrian peasant as told by Gordon Zahn is plainly that of a martyr, and of a Christian who followed a path of virtue with a dedication that cannot be fully accounted for by human motivation alone. In other words, it would seem that already in this biography one might find plausible evidence of what the Catholic Church regards as sanctity. But the bishop of Linz, in hinting at the possibility of a special calling that might have made Jagerstatter an "exceptional case," does not mean even implicitly to approve the thesis that the man was a saint, still less a model to be imitated. In other words the bishop, while admitting the remote possibility of Catholic heroism in a conscientious objector, is not admitting that such heroism should be regarded as either normal or imitable.

The Second Vatican Council in its *Constitution on the Church in the Modern World* (n. 70) recognized, at least implicitly, the right of a Catholic to refuse on grounds of conscience to bear arms. It did not propose conscientious objection as a sweeping obligation. Nevertheless it clearly declared that no one could escape the obligation to *refuse obedience* to criminal orders issued by the state or the military command. The example of genocide was given. In view of the fact that total war tends more and more in fact to be genocidal, the Council's declaration obviously bears above all on war.

The bishop of Linz, however, did not propose conscientious objection as a rational and Christian option. For him, the true heroes remain "those exemplary young Catholic men, seminarians, priests and heads of families who fought and died in heroic fulfillment of duty and in the firm conviction that they were fulfilling the will of God at their post . . ."

It is still quite possible that even today after the Council and in an era of new war technology and new threats of global destruction, when the most urgent single problem facing modern man is the proliferation of atomic and nuclear weaponry, many Catholic bishops will continue to agree with this one. It is true, they admit that there is such a thing as an erroneous conscience which is to be followed provided it is "invincible." "All respect is due to the innocently erroneous conscience," says the bishop of Linz, "it will have its reward from God."

Of whom is he speaking? Of the Catholic young men, the priests and the seminarians who died in Hitler's armies "in the firm conviction that they were fulfilling the will of God"? No. These, he says, were men (and the word is underlined) acting in the light of "a clear and correct conscience." Jagerstatter was "in error" but also "in good faith."

Certainly the bishop is entitled to his opinion: but the question of whose conscience was erroneous and whose was correct remains one that will ultimately be settled by God, not man. Meanwhile there is another question: the responsibility of those who help men to form their conscience—or fail to do so. And here, too, the possibility of firm convictions that are "innocently erroneous" gives food for some rather apocalyptic thought.

The real question raised by the Jagerstatter story is not merely that of the individual Catholic's right to conscientious objection (admitted in practice even by those who completely disagree with Jagerstatter) but the question of the Church's own mission of protest and prophecy in the gravest spiritual crisis man has ever known.

· 23 ·

ST. MAXIMUS THE CONFESSOR
ON NON-VIOLENCE

Published in The Catholic Worker, *September 1965*

Christians are sometimes so disturbed by the enemies of Christianity that they become convinced that hatred of these enemies is a proof of love for Christ, and that the will to destroy them is a pledge of their own salvation. At such a time it is necessary to go back to the sources and try to recover the true Christian meaning of the first and all-embracing commandment to love all men including our enemies. Failure to understand and observe this commandment brings down the wrath of God on our civilization and means damnation for those Christians who are willfully blind to the clearly expressed teaching of Christ and of the Church from the Apostolic times down to John XXIII and Paul VI. This obligation is not merely a theoretical matter, or something that calls for a rectification of one's inner intentions, without any effect on one's outward conduct. It is on the contrary one of the crucial ways in which we give proof in practice that we are truly disciples of Christ. It is by love and not by hatred that we demonstrate the authenticity of our faith.

Therefore it may be useful to present here a few excerpts from one of the great theologians of the Greek Church, St. Maximus the Confessor (7th Century), on the love of enemies. These quotations are taken from his book on the ascetic life, which is to say that they are part of a context in which he deals with the essentials of Christian holiness.

The theme of the book is our response to the call of Christ who came into the world offering us the gift of salvation, which we will receive if we obey His commandments and become followers of His example. In this book, which is a dialogue between a master and his disciple, the master at one point reminds the disciple of the Christian's obligation to renounce his selfish desires, because "No man can serve two masters" (Matthew 6:24) and if one follows his own desires he will not take seriously the commandments of Christ, but will seek to avoid them. The disciple protests that after all the love of food, comfort, money, possessions, praise, etc. are all good natural desires. If they are good, and if they come from God, why should we renounce them?

It is in replying to this objection that the Master brings up the subject of our relations with our enemies: in fact, it is because we love money, possessions, comfort, etc. more than other men that we enter into conflict with our fellow man, in order to take for ourselves what we do not wish to share with him, even if in order to fulfill our desires we must destroy our enemies.

The Master continues:

> It is true that we can please God by making a good use of the things He has given to us. Nevertheless we are weak, and our spirit is weighed down by matters, so that now we prefer profane and material things to the commandment of love. Because we are attached to these things we fight against other men, whereas we ought to prefer love for our fellow man to every visible thing and even to love for our own body. Such preference as this would be the sign of our authentic love of God, as the Lord said Himself in the Gospel: "He who loves me, keeps my commandments." (John 14:15) And what is this commandment which proves our love for Him? Let us hear Him tell us Himself: "This is my commandment: that you love one another." (John 15:12)
>
> Do you now see that this love for one another is the proof of our love for God, and this is the way to fulfill all the other commandments? It is for this reason that He commands anyone who would like to become His disciple in truth, to renounce all his possessions rather than to become attached to these things.

At this point the disciple protests again: how can he love another man who hates him? This is the usual justification of all enmities: we always claim it is the enemy who hates us. We assert that nothing we can do will make him treat us fairly or kindly. He is indeed confirmed in evil, since he is a kind of diabolical being: how could he otherwise be our enemy? He envies us, he insults us, he is always trying to deceive us. This is of course characteristic of enemies! They are always trying to deceive. We do not reflect that perhaps our enemy sees in us the mirror image of what we see in him. Has he perhaps reason to think that we hate him and wish to destroy him? That we would gladly trick him? That our claim to be ready to come to an agreement with him is itself a trick, because our invitation to negotiate is always offered in terms that we know he cannot possibly accept? Is that why he treats us accordingly?

The Master replies to this allegation that love of enemies is simply impossible. It is after all important to show that it is not impossible, for if the love of enemies is impossible Christ would not have commanded it, and in fact those who today say that we are not seriously obliged to love our enemies are contending that Christ could not have meant what He said when He told us to do this.

The Master's reply:

> Of course it is impossible for snakes and wild beasts, dominated by their instincts, to keep from resisting with all their power anyone who causes them to suffer. But for us, created in the image of God, guided by reason, to whom it has been given to know God, who have received our law from Him, it is indeed possible not to have an aversion for those who cause us pain. It is possible for us to love those who hate us. And so when the Lord says, "love your enemies and do good to those who hate you" (Matthew 5:44) and all that follows, He is not commanding the impossible, but obviously what is possible. Otherwise, He would not punish those who disobey this command.

That it is possible to love our enemies and not retaliate by meeting hatred with hatred, is shown by the example not only of the Lord Himself, but also of His disciples, the saints, the martyrs, and thousands of heroic Christians who have taken His commandment seriously. What was possible for them can, with God's grace, become possible for us. Meanwhile, if it does happen to be impossible for some of us to love our enemies, there must be a reason for it. The reason is that we love money and possessions more than we love our fellow man, and so when he seems to threaten our material interests, we are compelled to hate him.

The Master continues:

> We are held by the love of material things and the attraction of pleasure, and since we prefer these things to the command-

ment of the Lord, we become incapable of loving those who hate us. Rather we find that because of these very things we are often in conflict with those who love us. In this we show that we are even worse than wild animals or snakes. For this reason we are incapable of even understanding the aim He has in view. But knowledge of this aim would give us strength.

Here the Master puts his finger on the center of the trouble. When we are dominated by a selfish and materialistic scale of values, we are not only unable to love our enemies, we even hate our friends when they come between us and our love for possessions and pleasures. And since this is the case, we are completely unable to see any point in the idea of loving our enemies. We cannot really believe it is commanded us because we are not even able to grasp what it is all about in the first place.

The disciple naively objects that he has left the world and abandoned all possessions in order to become a monk, and even then he is not able to love a brother, another monk, if the latter hates him. Why is this, he inquires. Is there some way in which he can learn to love his brother from his heart?

At this the Master returns to the question of *understanding what the Lord has in view when he commands us to love our enemies.*

Even one who thinks he has renounced everything in the world, still remains unable to love those who make him suffer, as long as he has not yet truly understood the Lord's aim in giving us this commandment. But if the grace of God once gives him the capacity to see this aim, and if, having seen it, he conforms his life to it with fervor, then he will become able to love even those who hate and torment him. The Apostles did this once they had received knowledge of the Lord's aim . . .

Here the Master returns to the theme which is central to the whole treatise on the Ascetic life: the Word became Flesh in order to save man. To be precise, Jesus made Himself subject to the Law in order to carry out the injunctions of the Law as man and thus accomplish in Himself what Man had been unable to do since Adam. All the Law and the Prophets are contained in the twofold commandment of Love. "You shall love the Lord your God with your whole heart and your neighbor as yourself." (Matthew 22:37–45)

The demon, says the Master, seeing Jesus keeping the Law of Love, wished to make Him break the Law. Therefore he tempted Him in the desert with those things which men ordinarily, in their weakness, prefer to the Law: food, money and honors. But having failed in this, the demon then sought to tempt Him with hatred by raising up enemies to plot against Him. But instead of hating His enemies, the Lord continued to love them and even laid down His life for them.

> Out of love for His enemies, the Lord fought against the evil instigator of their hatred . . . He was not weary of doing good to those who were stirred up to hate Him, even though they might have refused the temptations of the evil one. He endured blasphemies: He accepted suffering with patience and showed them every kind of love. In this way He fought against the evil one who was the instigator of their actions. He fought by kindness for those who were burning with hatred towards Him. A strange, new kind of warfare! In exchange for hate, He returns only love! By His kindness, He casts out the father of evil. It was for this reason that He endured so much evil from them; or rather to speak more accurately, it was for their sakes that He, as man, fought even to death in order to obey the commandment of Love . . . Hence the Apostle tells us that we "should have in ourselves that same mind which was that of Christ." (Phil. 2:5)
>
> This then was the Lord's aim: to obey His father, as man, even to the point of dying, and to fight against the demon by submitting to those sufferings which the demon inflicted on Him through the men whom he incited to hatred. It is then, in allowing Himself freely to be overcome, that He overcame the evil one who planned to win and who had already wrested the world out of the Lord's grasp.
>
> Thus the Lord was crucified in weakness (2 Cor. 13:4) and by means of this "weakness" He destroyed death . . . and in the same way Paul "gloried in his infirmities in order that the power of Christ might rest on him." (2 Cor 12:9)

After this the Master goes on to quote many New Testament texts on the courageous acceptance of suffering, on the love of enemies, on inflexible patience under persecution. The most important thing is to understand how important all these things are in the Christian life, and to see how they are essential for anyone who wants to attain his aim as a Christian, namely, salvation in imitation of Christ, in participation in the sufferings of Christ, in order to vanquish the enemy of Christ by the power of Christ's love.

Hence the disciple must learn that the love of enemies is not simply a pious luxury, something that he can indulge in if he wants to feel himself to be exceptionally virtuous. It is of the very essence of the Christian life, a proof of one's Christian faith, a sign that one is a follower and an obedient disciple of Christ.

The point the Master is making is this: that a superficial and even illusionary Christianity is one which professes faith in Christ by verbal formulas and external observance, but which in fact denies Christ by refusing to obey His commandment to love. Since no man can serve two masters, and since the Christian life is a bitter struggle to keep the commandments of Christ in spite of everything in order to hold fast to our faith in Him and not deny Him, the enemy of Christ seeks in every way to make us deny the Lord in our lives and in our actions, even though we may remain apparently faithful to Him in our words and in our worship. He does this by leading us to hate others on account of our attachment to money and pleasure or, when we have apparently renounced these, to hate others when they attack us in our own person or in the society to which we belong. But in all these cases we must see that the evil that is done to us, apparently, by others, is a summons to greater faith and to heroic obedience to the word of the Gospel.

The significant thing for us, in this remarkable passage from the Greek saint, is that he portrays non-violent resistance under suffering and persecution as the normal way of the Christian, and shows that the Christian who has recourse to force and hatred in order to protect himself is, in fact, by that very action, denying Christ and showing that he has no real understanding of the Gospel.

Very often people object that non-violence seems to imply passive acceptance of injustice and evil and therefore that it is a kind of cooperation with evil. Not at all. The genuine concept of non-violence implies not only active and effective resistance to evil but in fact a more effective resistance. But Maximus takes pains to make very clear the absolutely uncompromising obligation to resist evil.

But the resistance which is taught in the Gospel is aimed not at the evil-doer but at evil in its source. It combats evil as such by doing good to the evil-doer, by thus overcoming evil with good (Romans 12:21) which is the way our Lord Himself resisted evil.

On the other hand, merely to resist evil with evil, by hating those who hate us and seeking to destroy them, is actually no resistance at all. It is active and purposeful collaboration in evil that brings the Christian into direct and intimate contact with the same source of evil and hatred which inspires the acts of his enemy. It leads in practice to a denial of Christ and to the service of hatred rather than love.

How do we learn to love our enemy? By seeing him as a brother who is tempted as we are, and attacked by the same real enemy which is the spirit of hatred and of "Antichrist." This same enemy seeks to destroy us both by pitting us against one another.

The Master continues:

> If you meditate without ceasing on these truths you will be able to see through all the deceptions of the evil one in this regard, provided that you also understand that your brother is moved by an evil power to hate, just in the same way that you too are tempted. If you understand this you will pardon your brother. If you refuse to fall into the trap, you will be resisting the Tempter who wishes to make you hate your brother who is tempted . . . Resist the devil, and he will fly from you. (James 4:1) Meditating these things you will understand the aim which the Lord and the Apostles had in view, to love means to have compassion for those who fall into sin, and thus by love held in check the malice of the demon.
>
> *But if we are negligent, lazy and blinded in spirit by carnal desires, then we do not make war on the demons but on ourselves and our brothers. Indeed by such things we place ourselves in the service of the demons and in their name we fight against our fellow man.*

The Gospel does, indeed, teach us to make war—but only on our real enemies, lest we serve our enemies and the enemies of Christ by making war on our brothers.

BLESSED ARE THE MEEK:
The Christian Roots of Non-Violence

Published in Fellowship, *May 1967*

On December 7, 1965 Merton received a letter from Hildegard
Goss-Mayr asking him to write an article on "Demut" (Humility)
for the journal *Der Christ in der Welt.* He agreed to do so and
on January 14, 1966 he was able to write her that the article was
completed: "It is the feast of St. Hilary, who said: 'The best way
to solve the problem of rendering to Caesar what is Caesar's is
to have nothing that is Caesar's.' This is a good day then to send
you the essay on 'Demut,' which turned out to be really an essay
on the beatitude of the Meek, as applied to Christian nonviolence." (*The Hidden Ground of Love,* 337) The article, translated
into German, was published in the April-June 1965 issue of *Der
Christ in der Welt.* It was published in English in the May 1967
issue of *Fellowship.* The Catholic Peace Fellowship issued it in
July of that same year as a twelve-page pamphlet with a colorful
cover designed by Sister Mary Corita. The pamphlet was dedicated to Joan Baez.

* * * * *

It would be a serious mistake to regard Christian nonviolence simply
as a novel tactic which is at once efficacious and even edifying, and
which enables the sensitive man to participate in the struggles of the
world without being dirtied with blood. Nonviolence is not simply a
way of proving one's point and getting what one wants without being
involved in behavior that one considers ugly and evil. Nor is it, for
that matter, a means which anyone legitimately can make use of according to his fancy for any purpose whatever. To practice nonviolence
for a purely selfish or arbitrary end would in fact discredit and distort
the truth of nonviolent resistance.

Nonviolence is perhaps the most exacting of all forms of struggle, not only because it demands first of all that one be ready to suffer evil and even face the threat of death without violent retaliation, but because it excludes mere transient self-interest from its considerations. In a very real sense, he who practices nonviolent resistance must commit himself not to the defense of his own interests or even those of a particular group: he must commit himself to the defense of objective truth and right and above all of *man.* His aim is then not simply to "prevail" or to prove that he is right and the adversary wrong, or to make the adversary give in and yield what is demanded of him.

Nor should the nonviolent resister be content to prove *to himself* that *he* is virtuous and right, and that *his* hands and heart are pure even though the adversary's may be evil and defiled. Still less should he seek for himself the psychological gratification of upsetting the adversary's conscience and perhaps driving him to an act of bad faith and refusal of the truth. We know that our unconscious motives may, at times, make our nonviolence a form of moral aggression and even a subtle provocation designed (without awareness) to bring out the evil we hope to find in the adversary, and thus to justify ourselves in our own eyes and in the eyes of "decent people." Wherever there is a high moral ideal there is an attendant risk of pharisaism, and nonviolence is no exception. The basis of pharisaism is division: on one hand this morally or socially privileged self and the elite to which it belongs. On the other hand, the "others," the wicked, the unenlightened, whoever they may be, Communists, capitalists, colonialists, traitors, international Jewry, racists, etc.

Christian nonviolence is not built on a presupposed division, but on the basic unity of man. It is not out for the conversion of the wicked to the ideas of the good, but for the healing and reconciliation of man with himself, man the person and man the human family.

The nonviolent resister is not fighting simply for "his" truth or for "his" pure conscience, or for the right that is on "his side." On the contrary, both his strength and his weakness come from the fact that he is fighting for *the* truth, common to him and to the adversary, *the* right which is objective and universal. He is fighting for *everybody.*

For this very reason, as Gandhi saw, the fully consistent practice of nonviolence demands a solid metaphysical and religious basis both in being and in God. This comes *before* subjective good intentions and sincerity. For the Hindu this metaphysical basis was provided by the Vedantist doctrine of the Atman, the true transcendent Self which alone is absolutely real, and before which the empirical self of the individual must be effaced in the faithful practice of *dharma*. For the Christian, the basis of nonviolence is the Gospel message of salvation for *all men* and of the Kingdom of God to which *all* are summoned. The disciple of Christ, he who has heard the good news, the announcement of the Lord's coming and of His victory, and is aware of the definitive establishment of the Kingdom, proves his faith by the gift of his whole self to the Lord in order that *all* may enter the Kingdom. This Christian discipleship entails a certain way of acting, a *politeia*, a *conservatio*, which is proper to the Kingdom.

The great historical event, the coming of the Kingdom, is made clear and is "realized" in proportion as Christians themselves live the life of the Kingdom in the circumstances of their own place and time. The saving grace of God in the Lord Jesus is proclaimed to man existentially in the love, the openness, the simplicity, the humility and the self-sacrifice of Christians. By their example of a truly Christian under-standing of the world, expressed in a living and active application of the Christian faith to the human problems of their own time, Chris-tians manifest the love of Christ for men (John 13:35, 17:21), and by that fact make him visibly present in the world. The religious basis of Christian nonviolence is then faith in Christ the Redeemer and obedi-ence to his demand to love and manifest himself in us by a certain manner of acting in the world and in relation to other men. This obedience enables us to live as true citizens of the Kingdom, in which the divine mercy, the grace, favor and redeeming love of God are active in our lives. Then the Holy Spirit will indeed "rest upon us" and act in us, not for our own good alone but for God and his Kingdom. And if the Spirit dwells in us and works in us, our lives will be continuous and progressive conversion and transformation in which we also, in some measure, help to transform others and allow ourselves to be transformed by and with others in Christ.

The chief place in which this new mode of life is set forth in detail is the Sermon on the Mount. At the very beginning of this great inaugural discourse, the Lord numbers the beatitudes, which are the theological foundation of Christian nonviolence: Blessed are the poor in spirit . . . blessed are the meek (Matthew 5:3–4).

This does not mean "blessed are they who are endowed with a tran-quil natural temperament, who are not easily moved to anger, who are always quiet and obedient, who do not naturally resist." Still less does it mean "blessed are they who passively submit to unjust oppression." On the contrary, we know that the "poor in spirit" are those of whom the prophets spoke, those who in the last days will be the "humble of the earth," that is to say the oppressed who have no human weapons to rely on and who nevertheless are true to the commandments of Yahweh, and who hear the voice that tells them: "Seek justice, seek humility, perhaps you will find shelter on the day of the Lord's wrath" (Sophonias 2:3). In other words they seek justice in the power of truth and of God, not by the power of man. Note that Christian meekness, which is essential to true nonviolence, has this eschatological quality about it. It refrains from self-assertion and from violent aggression because it sees all things in the light of the great judgment. Hence it does not struggle and fight merely for this or that ephemeral gain. It struggles for the truth and the right which alone will stand in that day when all is to be tried by fire (I Corinthians 3:10–15).

Furthermore, Christian nonviolence and meekness imply a particular understanding of the power of human poverty and powerlessness when they are united with the invisible strength of Christ. The Beatitudes indeed convey a profound existential understanding of the dynamic of the Kingdom of God—a dynamic made clear in the parables of the mustard seed and of the yeast. This is a dynamism of patient and secret growth, in belief that out of the smallest, weakest, and most insignificant seed the greatest tree will come. This is not merely a matter of blind and arbitrary faith. The early history of the Church, the record of the apostles and martyrs remains to testify to this inherent and mysterious dynamism of the ecclesial "event" in the world of history and time. Christian nonviolence is rooted in this consciousness and this faith.

This aspect of Christian nonviolence is extremely important and it gives us the key to a proper understanding of the meekness which accepts being "without strength" (*gewaltlos*) not out of masochism, quietism, defeatism or false passivity, but trusting in the strength of the Lord of truth. Indeed, we repeat, Christian nonviolence is nothing if not first of all a formal profession of faith in the Gospel message that the *Kingdom has been established* and that the Lord of truth is indeed risen and reigning over his Kingdom.

Faith of course tells us that we live in a time of eschatological struggle, facing a fierce combat which marshalls all the forces of evil and darkness against the still-invisible truth, yet this combat is already decided by the victory of Christ over death and over sin. The Christian can renounce the protection of violence and risk being humble, therefore *vulnerable*, not because he trusts in the supposed efficacy of a gentle and persuasive tactic that will disarm hatred and tame cruelty, but because he believes that the hidden power of the Gospel is demanding to be manifested in and through his own poor person. Hence in perfect obedience to the Gospel, he effaces himself and his own interests and even risks his life in order to testify not simply to "the truth" in a sweeping, idealistic and purely platonic sense, but to the truth that is incarnate in a concrete human situation, involving living persons whose rights are denied or whose lives are threatened.

Here it must be remarked that a holy zeal for the cause of humanity in the abstract may sometimes be mere lovelessness and indifference for concrete and living human beings. When we appeal to the highest and most noble ideals, we are most easily tempted to hate and condemn those who, so we believe, are standing in the way of their realization.

Christian nonviolence does not encourage or excuse hatred of a special class, nation or social group. It is not merely *anti*-this or that. In other words, the evangelical realism which is demanded of the Christian should make it impossible for him to generalize about "the wicked" against whom he takes up moral arms in a struggle for righteousness. He will not let himself be persuaded that the adversary is totally wicked and can therefore never be reasonable or well-intentioned, and hence need be listened to. This attitude, which defeats the very purpose of nonviolence—openness, communication, dialogue—often accounts for the fact that some acts of civil disobedience merely antagonize the adversary without making him willing to communicate in any way whatever, except with bullets or missiles. Thomas à Becket, in Eliot's play *Murder in the Cathedral*, debated with himself, fearing that he might be seeking martyrdom merely in order to demonstrate his own righteousness and the King's injustice: "This is the greatest treason, to do the right thing for the wrong reason."

Now all these principles are fine and they accord with our Christian faith. But once we view the principles in the light of current *facts*, a practical difficulty confronts us. If the "gospel is preached to the poor," if the Christian message is essentially a message of hope and redemption for the poor, the oppressed, the underprivileged and those who have no power humanly speaking, how are we to reconcile ourselves to the fact that Christians belong for the most part to the rich and powerful nations of the earth. Seventeen percent of the world's population control eighty percent of the world's wealth, and most of these seventeen percent are supposedly Christian. Admittedly those Christians who are interested in nonviolence are not ordinarily the wealthy ones. Nevertheless, like it or not, they share in the power and privilege of the most wealthy and mighty society the world has ever known. Even with the best subjective intentions in the world, how can they avoid a certain ambiguity in preaching nonviolence? Is this not a mystification?

We must remember Marx's accusation that "the social principles of Christianity encourage dullness, lack of self-respect, submissiveness, self-abasement, in short all the characteristics of the proletariat." We must frankly face the possibility that the nonviolence of the European or American preaching Christian meekness may conceivably be adulterated by bourgeois feelings and by an unconscious desire to preserve the status quo against violent upheaval.

On the other hand, Marx's view of Christianity is obviously tendentious and distorted. A real understanding of Christian nonviolence (backed up by the evidence of history in the Apostolic Age) shows not only that it is a *power*, but that it remains perhaps the only really effective way of transforming man and human society. After nearly fifty years of Communist revolution, we find little evidence that the world is improved by violence. Let us however seriously consider at least the *conditions* for relative honesty in the practice of Christian nonviolence.

1. Nonviolence must be aimed above all at the transformation of the present state of the world, and it must therefore be free from all occult, unconscious connivance with an unjust use of power. This poses enormous problems—for if nonviolence is too political it becomes drawn into the power struggle and identified with one side or another in that struggle, while if it is totally apolitical it runs the risk of being ineffective or at best merely symbolic.

2. The nonviolent resistance of the Christian who belongs to one of the powerful nations and who is himself in some sense a privileged member of world society will have to be clearly not *for himself* but *for others*, that is for the poor and underprivileged. (Obviously in the case of Negroes in the United States, though they may be citizens of a privileged nation, their case is different. They are clearly entitled to wage a nonviolent struggle for their rights, but even for them this struggle should be primarily for *truth itself*—this being the source of their power.)

3. In the case of nonviolent struggle for peace—the threat of nuclear war abolishes all privileges. Under the bomb there is not much distinction between rich and poor. In fact the richest nations are usually the most threatened. Nonviolence must simply avoid the ambiguity of an unclear and *confusing protest* that hardens the warmakers in their self-righteous blindness. This means in fact that *in this case above all non-*

violence must avoid a facile and fanatical self-righteousness, and refrain from being satisfied with dramatic self-justifying gestures.

4. Perhaps the most insidious temptation to be avoided is one which is characteristic of the power structure itself: this fetishism of immediate visible results. Modern society understands "possibilities" and "results" in terms of a superficial and quantitative idea of efficacy. One of the missions of Christian nonviolence is to restore a different standard of practical judgment in social conflicts. This means that the Christian humility of nonviolent action must establish itself in the minds and memories of modern man not only as *conceivable* and *possible,* but as *a desirable alternative* to what he now considers the only realistic possibility: namely political technique backed by force. Here the human dignity of nonviolence must manifest itself clearly in terms of a freedom and a nobility which are able to resist political manipulation and brute force and show them up as arbitrary, barbarous and irrational. This will not be easy. The temptation to get publicity and quick results by spectacular tricks or by forms of protest that are merely odd and provocative but whose human meaning is not clear may defeat this purpose.

The realism of nonviolence must be made evident by humility and self-restraint which clearly show frankness and open-mindedness and invite the adversary to serious and reasonable discussion.

Instead of trying to use the adversary as leverage for one's own effort to realize an ideal, nonviolence seeks only to enter into a dialogue with him in order to attain, together with him, the common good of *man.* Nonviolence must be realistic and concrete. Like ordinary political action, it is no more than the "art of the possible." But precisely the advantage of nonviolence is that it has a *more Christian and more humane notion of what is possible.* Where the powerful believe that only power is efficacious, the nonviolent resister is persuaded of the superior efficacy of love, openness, peaceful negotiation and above all of truth. For power can guarantee the interests of *some men* but it can never foster the good of *man.* Power always protects the good of some at the expense of all the others. Only love can attain and preserve the good of all. Any claim to build the security of *all* on force is a manifest imposture.

It is here that genuine humility is of the greatest importance. Such humility, united with true Christian courage (because it is based on trust in God and not in one's own ingenuity and tenacity), is itself a way of communicating the message that one is interested only in truth and in the genuine rights of others. Conversely, our authentic interest in the common good above all will help us to be humble, and to distrust our own hidden drive to self-assertion.

5. Christian nonviolence, therefore, is convinced that the manner in which the conflict for truth is waged will itself manifest or obscure the truth. To fight for truth by dishonest, violent, inhuman, or unreasonable means would simply betray the truth one is trying to vindicate. The absolute refusal of evil or suspect means is a necessary element in the witness of nonviolence.

As Pope Paul said before the United Nations Assembly in 1965, "Men cannot be brothers if they are not humble. No matter how justified it may appear, pride provokes tensions and struggles for prestige, domination, colonialism and egoism. In a word *pride shatters brotherhood.*" He went on to say that the attempts to establish peace on the basis of violence were in fact a manifestation of human pride. "If you wish to be brothers, let the weapons fall from your hands. You cannot love with offensive weapons in your hands."

6. A test of our sincerity in the practice of nonviolence is this: are we willing to *learn something from the adversary?* If a *new truth* is made known to us by him or through him, will we accept it? Are we willing to admit that he is not totally inhumane, wrong, unreasonable, cruel, etc.? This is important. If he sees that we are completely incapable of listening to him with an open mind, our nonviolence will have nothing to say to him except that we distrust him and seek to outwit him. Our readiness to see some good in him and to agree with some of his ideas (though tactically this might look like a weakness on our part), actually gives us power: the power of sincerity and of truth. On the other hand, if we are obviously unwilling to accept any truth that we have not first discovered and declared ourselves, we show by that very fact that we are interested not in the truth so much as in "being right." Since the adversary is presumably interested in being right also, and in proving himself right by what he considers the superior argument of force, we end up where we started. Nonviolence has great power, provided that it really witnesses to truth and not just to self-righteousness.

The dread of being open to the ideas of others generally comes from our hidden insecurity about our own convictions. We fear that we may be "converted"—or perverted—by a pernicious doctrine. On the other hand, if we are mature and objective in our open-mindedness, we may find that viewing things from a basically different perspective—that of our adversary—we discover our own truth in a new light and are able to understand our own ideal more realistically.

Our willingness to take *an alternative approach* to a problem will perhaps relax the obsessive fixation of the adversary on his view, which he believes is the only reasonable possibility and which he is determined to impose on everyone else by coercion.

It is refusal of alternatives—a compulsive state of mind which one might call the "ultimate complex"—which makes wars in order to force the unconditional acceptance of one oversimplified interpretation of reality. This mission of Christian humility in social life is not merely to edify, but to *keep minds open to many alternatives*. The rigidity of a certain type of Christian thought has seriously impaired this capacity, which nonviolence must recover.

Needless to say, Christian humility must not be confused with a mere desire to win approval and to find reassurance by conciliating others superficially.

7. Christian hope and Christian humility are inseparable. The quality of nonviolence is decided largely by the purity of the Christian hope behind it. In its insistence on certain human values, the Second Vatican Council, following *Pacem in Terris,* displayed a basically optimistic trust *in man himself.* Not that there is not wickedness in the world, but today trust in God cannot be completely divorced from a certain trust in man. The Christian knows that there are radically sound possibilities in every man, and he believes that love and grace always have the power to bring out those possibilities at the most unexpected moments. Therefore if he has hopes that God will grant peace to the world it is because he also trusts that man, God's creature, is not basically evil: that there is in man a potentiality for peace and order which can be realized provided the right conditions are there. The Christian will do his part in creating these conditions by preferring love and trust to hate and suspiciousness. Obviously, once again, this "hope in man" must not be naive. But experience itself has shown, in the last few years, how much an attitude of simplicity and openness can do to break down barriers of suspicion that had divided men for centuries.

It is therefore very important to understand that Christian humility implies not only a certain wise reserve in regard to one's own judgments—a good sense which sees that we are not always necessarily infallible in our ideas—but it also cherishes positive and trustful expectations of others. A supposed "humility" which is simply depressed about itself and about the world is usually a false humility. This negative, self-pitying "humility" may cling desperately to dark and apocalyptic expectations, and refuse to let go of them. It is secretly convinced that only tragedy and evil can possibly come from our present world situation. This secret conviction cannot be kept hidden. It will manifest itself in our attitudes, in our social action and in our protest. It will show that in fact we despair of reasonable dialogue with anyone. It will show that we expect only the worst. Our action seeks only to block or frustrate the adversary in some way. A protest that from the start declares itself to be in despair is hardly likely to have valuable results. At best it provides an outlet for the personal frustrations of the one protesting. It enables him to articulate his despair in public. This is not the function of Christian nonviolence. This pseudo-prophetic desperation has nothing to do with the beatitudes, even the third. No blessedness has been promised to those who are merely sorry for themselves.

In resume, the meekness and humility which Christ extolled in the Sermon on the Mount and which are the basis of true Christian nonviolence are inseparable from an eschatological Christian hope which is completely open to the presence of God in the world and therefore in the presence of our brother who is always seen, no matter who he may be, in the perspectives of the Kingdom. Despair is not permitted to the meek, the humble, the afflicted, the ones famished for justice, the merciful, the clean of heart and the peacemakers. All the beatitudes "hope against hope," "bear everything, believe everything, hope for everything, endure everything" (I Corinthians 13:7). The beatitudes are simply aspects of love. They refuse to despair of the world and abandon it to a supposedly evil fate which it has brought upon itself. Instead, like Christ himself, the Christian takes upon his own shoulders the yoke of the Savior, meek and humble of heart. This yoke is the burden of the world's sin with all its confusions and all its problems. These sins, confusions and problems are our very own. We do not disown them.

Christian nonviolence derives its hope from the promise of Christ: "Fear not, little flock, for the Father has prepared for you a Kingdom." (Luke 12:32)

The hope of the Christian must be, like the hope of a child, pure and full of trust. The child is totally available in the present because he has relatively little to remember, his experience of evil is as yet brief, and his anticipation of the future does not extend far. The Christian, in his humility and faith, must be as totally available to his brother, to his world, in the present, as the child is. But he cannot see the world with childlike innocence and simplicity unless his memory is cleared of past evils by forgiveness, and his anticipation of the future is hopefully free of craft and calculation. For this reason, the humility of Christian nonviolence is at once patient and uncalculating. The chief difference between nonviolence and violence is that the latter depends entirely on its own calculations. The former depends entirely on God and on His word.

At the same time the violent or coercive approach to the solution of human problems considers man in general, in the abstract, and according to various notions about the laws that govern his nature. In other words, it is concerned with man as subject to necessity, and it seeks out the points at which his nature is consistently vulnerable in order to coerce him physically or psychologically. Nonviolence on the other hand is based on that respect for the human person without which there is no deep and genuine Christianity. It is concerned with an appeal to the liberty and intelligence of the person insofar as he is able to transcend nature and natural necessity. Instead of forcing a decision upon him from the outside, it invites him to arrive freely at a decision of his own, in dialogue and cooperation, and in the presence of that truth which Christian nonviolence brings into full view by its sacrificial witness. The key to nonviolence is the willingness of the nonviolent resister to suffer a certain amount of accidental evil in order to bring about a change of mind in the oppressor and awaken him to personal openness and to dialogue. A nonviolent protest that merely seeks to gain publicity and to show up the oppressor for what he is, without opening his eyes to new values, can be said to be in large part a failure. At the same time, a nonviolence which does not rise to the level of the personal, and remains confined to the consideration of nature and natural necessity, may perhaps make a deal but it cannot really make sense.

It is understandable that the Second Vatican Council, which placed such strong emphasis on the dignity of the human person and the freedom of the individual conscience, should also have strongly approved "those who renounce the use of violence in the vindication of their rights and who resort to methods of defense which are otherwise available to weaker parties too." (*Constitution on the Church in the Modern World*, n. 78) In such a confrontation between conflicting parties, on the level of personality, intelligence and freedom, instead of with massive weapons or with trickery and deceit, a fully human solution becomes possible. Conflict will never be abolished but a new way of solving it can become habitual. Man can then act according to the dignity of that adulthood which he is now said to have reached—

and which yet remains, perhaps to be conclusively proved. One of the ways in which it can, without doubt, be proved is precisely this: man's ability to settle conflicts by reason and arbitration instead of by slaughter and destruction.

The distinction suggested here, between two types of thought—one oriented to nature and necessity, the other to persona and freedom—calls for further study at another time. It seems to be helpful. The "nature-oriented" mind treats other human beings as objects to be manipulated in order to control the course of events and make the future for the whole human species conform to certain rather rigidly determined expectations. "Person-oriented" thinking does not lay down these draconian demands, does not seek so much to *control* as to *respond,* and to *awaken response.* It is not set on determining anyone or anything, and does not insistently demand that persons and events correspond to our own abstract ideal. All it seeks is the openness of free exchange in which reason and love have freedom of action. In such a situation the future will take care of itself. This is the truly Christian outlook. Needless to say that many otherwise serious and sincere Christians are unfortunately dominated by this "nature-thinking" which is basically legalistic and technical. They never rise to the level of authentic interpersonal relationships outside their own intimate circle. For them, even today, the idea of building peace on a foundation of war and coercion is not incongruous—it seems perfectly reasonable!

· 25 ·

NHAT HANH IS MY BROTHER

On May 28, 1966 Nhat Hanh, the Vietnamese monk, poet, and peacemaker, visited Merton at Gethsemani in company with John Heidbrink, head of the Fellowship of Reconciliation. Merton was impressed by the visit and wrote the following tribute.

· · · · ·

This is not a political statement. It has no "interested" motive, it seeks to provoke no immediate action "for" or "against" this or that side in the Vietnam war. It is on the contrary a human and personal statement and an anguished plea for the Vietnamese Buddhist monk Thich Nhat Hanh who is my brother. He is more my brother than many who are nearer to me by race and nationality, because he and I see things exactly the same way. He and I deplore the war that is ravaging his country. We deplore it for exactly the same reasons: human reasons, reasons of sanity, justice and love. We deplore the needless destruction, the fantastic and callous ravaging of human life, the rape of the culture and spirit of an exhausted people. It is surely evident that this carnage serves no purpose that can be discerned and indeed contradicts the alleged intentions of the mighty nation that has constituted itself the "defender" of the people it is destroying.

Certainly this statement cannot help being a plea for peace. But it is also a plea for my brother Nhat Hanh. He represents the least "political" of all the movements in Vietnam. He is not directly associated with the Buddhists who are trying to use political manipulation in order to save their country. He is by no means a communist. The Vietcong is deeply hostile to him. He refuses to be identified with the established government which hates and distrusts him. He represents the young, the defenseless, the new ranks of youth who find themselves with every hand turned against them except those of the peasants and the poor, with whom they are working. Nhat Hanh speaks truly for the people of Vietnam, if there can be said to be a "people" left in Vietnam.

Nhat Hanh has left his country and come to us in order to present a picture which is not given us in our newspapers and magazines. He has been well received—and that speaks well for those who have received him. His visit to the United States has shown that we are a people who still desire the truth when we can find it and still decide in favor of *man* against the political machine when we get a fair chance to do so. But when Nhat Hanh goes home, what will happen to him? He is not in favor with the government, which has suppressed his writings. The Vietcong will view with disfavor his American contacts. To have pleaded for an end to the fighting will make him a traitor in the eyes of those who stand to gain personally as long as the war goes on, as long as their countrymen are being killed, as long as they can do business with our military. Nhat Hanh may be returning to imprisonment, torture, even death. We cannot let him go back to Saigon to be destroyed while we sit here, cherishing the warm humanitarian glow of good intentions and worthy sentiments about the ongoing war. We who have met and heard Nhat Hanh, or have read about him, must also raise our voices to demand that his life and freedom be respected when he returns to his country. Furthermore, we demand this not in terms of any conceivable political advantage, but purely in the name of those values of freedom and humanity in favor of which our armed forces declare they are fighting the Vietnam war.

Nhat Hanh is a free man who has acted as a free man in favor of his brothers and moved by the spiritual dynamic of a tradition of religious compassion. He has come among us as many others have, from time to time, bearing witness to the spirit of Zen. More than any other he has shown us that Zen is not an esoteric and world-denying cult of inner illumination, but that it has its rare and unique sense of responsibility in the modern world. Wherever he goes he will walk in the strength of his spirit and in the solitude of the Zen monk who sees beyond life and death. It is for our own honor as much as for his safety that we must raise our voices to demand that his life and personal integrity be fully respected when he returns to his smashed and gutted country, there to continue his work with the students and peasants, hoping for the day when reconstruction can begin.

I have said Nhat Hanh is my brother, and it is true. We are both monks, and we have lived the monastic life about the same number of years. We are both poets, existentialists. I have far more in common with Nhat Hanh than I have with many Americans, and I do not hesitate to say it. It is vitally important that such bonds be admitted. They are the bonds of a new solidarity and a new brotherhood which is beginning to be evident on all the five continents and which cut across all political, religious and cultural lines to unite young men and women in every country in something that is more concrete than an ideal and more alive than a program. This unity of the young is the only hope of the world. In its name I appeal for Nhat Hanh. Do what you can for him. If I mean something to you, then let me put it this way: do for Nhat Hanh whatever you would do for me if I were in his position. In many ways I wish I were.

· 26 ·

ISHI:
A Meditation

Published in the March 1967 issue of The Catholic Worker

This article reviews Theodore Kroeber's book, *A Biography of the Last Wild Indian in North America*. It is one of five essays published in 1976 by Unicorn Press in a book entitled *Ishi Means Man*. The article fits well with Merton's other writings on the struggles between whites and non-whites in American society.

. . . . .

Genocide is a new word. Perhaps the word is new because technology has not got into the game of destroying whole races at once. The destruction of races is not new—just easier. Nor is it a speciality of totalitarian regimes. We have forgotten that a century ago white America was engaged in the destruction of entire tribes and ethnic groups of Indians. The trauma of California gold. And the vigilantes who, in spite of every plea from Washington for restraint and understanding, repeatedly took matters into their own hands and went out slaughtering Indians. Indiscriminate destruction of the "good" along with the "bad"—just so long as they were Indians. Parties of riffraff from the mining camps and saloons suddenly constituted themselves defenders of civilization. They armed and went out to spill blood and gather scalps. They not only combed the woods and canyons—they even went into the bars and ranch houses, to find and destroy the Indian servants and hired people, in spite of the protests of the ranchers who employed them.

The Yana Indians (including the Yahi or Mill Creeks) lived around the foothills of Mount Lassen, east of the Sacramento River. Their country came within a few miles of Vina, where the Trappist monastery in California stands today. These hill tribes were less easy to subdue than their valley neighbors. More courageous and more aloof, they tried to keep clear of the white man altogether. They were not necessarily more ferocious than other Indians, but because they kept to themselves and had a legendary reputation as "fighters," they were more feared. They were understood to be completely "savage." As they were driven further and further back into the hills, and as their traditional hunting grounds gradually narrowed and emptied of game, they had to raid the ranches in order to keep alive. White reprisals were to be expected and they were ruthless. The Indians defended themselves by guerrilla warfare. The whites decided that there could be no peaceful coexistence with such neighbors. The Yahi, or Mill Creek Indians, as they were called, were marked for complete destruction. Hence they were regarded as subhuman. Against them there were no restrictions and no rules. No treaties need be made, for no Indian could be trusted. Where was the point in "negotiation"?

Ishi, the last survivor of the Mill Creek Indians, whose story was published by the University of California at Berkeley three years ago (Theodora Kroeber, *Ishi in Two Worlds: A Biography of the Last Wild Indian in North America*, Berkeley & Los Angeles, U. of California Press, 1961), was born during the war of extermination against his people. The fact that the last Mill Creeks were able to go into hiding and to survive for another fifty years in their woods and canyons is extraordinary enough. But the courage, the resourcefulness, and the sheer nobility of these few stone-age men struggling to preserve their life, their autonomy and their identity as a people rises to the level of tragic myth. Yet there is nothing mythical about it. The story is told with impeccable objectivity—though also with compassion—by the scholars who finally saved Ishi and learned from him his language, his culture and his tribal history.

To read this story thoughtfully, to open one's ear to it, is to receive a most significant message: one that not only moves, but disturbs. You begin to feel the inner stirrings of that pity and dread which Aristotle said were the purifying effect of tragedy. "The history of Ishi and his people," says the author, Theodora Kroeber, "is inexorably part of our own history. We have absorbed their lands into our holdings. Just so must we be the responsible custodians of their tragedy, absorbing it into our tradition and morality." Unfortunately, we learned little or nothing about ourselves from the Indian wars!

"They have separated murder into two parts and fastened the worse on me"—words which William Carlos Williams put on the lips of a Viking exile, Eric the Red. Men are always separating murder into two parts: one which is unholy and unclean: for "the enemy." Another which is a sacred duty: "for our side." He who first makes the separation, in order that he may kill, proves his bad faith. So too in the

Indian wars. Why do we always assume the Indian was the Aggressor? We were in *his* country, we were taking it over for ourselves, and we likewise refused even to share any with him. We were the people of God, always in the right, following a manifest destiny. The Indian could only be a devil. But once we allow ourselves to see all sides of the question, the familiar perspectives of American history undergo a change. The "savages" suddenly become human and the "whites," the "civilized," can seem barbarians. True, the Indians were often cruel and inhumane (some more than others). True, also the humanity, the intelligence, the compassion and understanding which Ishi met with in his friends the scholars, when he came to join our civilization, restore the balance in our favor. But we are left with a deep sense of guilt and shame. The record is there. The Mill Creek Indians, who were once seen as bloodthirsty devils, were peaceful, innocent and deeply wronged human beings. In their use of violence they were, so it seems, generally very fair. It is we who were the wanton murderers, and they who were the innocent victims. The loving kindness lavished on Ishi in the end did nothing to change that fact. His race had been barbarously, pointlessly destroyed.

The impact of the story is all the greater because the events are so deeply charged with a natural symbolism: the structure of these happenings is such that it leaves a haunting imprint on the mind. Out of that imprint come disturbing and potent reflections.

Take, for example, the scene in 1870 when the Mill Creeks were down to their last twenty or thirty survivors. A group had been captured. A delegation from the tiny remnant of the tribe appeared at a ranch to negotiate. In a symbolic gesture, they handed over five bows (five being a sacred number) and stood unarmed waiting for an answer. The gesture was not properly understood, though it was evident that the Indians were trying to recover their captives and promising to abandon all hostilities. In effect, the message was: "Leave us alone, in peace, in our hills, and we will not bother you any more. We are few, you are many, why destroy us? We are no longer any menace to you." No formal answer was given. While the Indians were waiting for some kind of intelligible response, one of the whites slung a rope over the branch of a tree. The Indians quietly withdrew into the woods.

From then on, for the next twelve years, the Yahi disappeared into the hills without a trace. There were perhaps twenty of them left, one of whom was Ishi, together with his mother and sister. In order to preserve their identity as a tribe, they had decided that there was no alternative but to keep completely away from white men, and have nothing whatever to do with them. Since coexistence was impossible, they would try to be as if they did not exist for the white man at all. To be there as if they were not there.

In fact, not a Yahi was seen. No campfire smoke rose over the trees. Not a trace of fire was found. No village was discovered. No track of an Indian was observed. The Yahi remnant (and that phrase takes on haunting biblical resonances) systematically learned to live as invisible and as unknown.

To anyone who has ever felt in himself the stirrings of a monastic or solitary vocation, the notion is stirring. It has implications that are simply beyond speech. There is nothing one can say in the presence of such a happening and of its connotations for what our spiritual books so glibly call "the hidden life." The "hidden life" is surely not irrelevant to our modern world: nor is it a life of spiritual comfort and tranquility which a chosen minority can happily enjoy, at the price of a funny costume and a few prayers. The "hidden life" is the extremely difficult life that is forced upon a remnant that has to stay completely out of sight in order to escape destruction.

This so-called long concealment of the Mill Creek Indians is not romanticized by any means. The account is sober, objective, though it cannot help being an admiring tribute to the extraordinary courage and ingenuity of these lost stone-age people. Let the book speak for itself.

> The long concealment failed in its objective to save a people's life but it would seem to have been brilliantly successful in its psychology and techniques of living. . . . Ishi's group was a master of the difficult art of communal and peaceful coexistence in the presence of alarm and in a tragic and deteriorating prospect. . . . It is a curious circumstance that some of the questions which arise about the concealment, are those for which in a different context psychologists and neurologists are trying to find answers for the submarine and outer space services today. Some of these are: what makes for morale under confining and limiting life-conditions? What are the presumable limits of claustrophobic endurance? . . . . It seems that the Yahi might have qualified for outer space had they lasted into this century.

There is something challenging and awe-inspiring about this thoughtful passage by a scientifically trained mind. And that phrase about "qualifying for outer space" has an eerie ring about it. Does someone pick up the half-heard suggestion that the man who wants to live a normal life span during the next two hundred years of our history must be the kind of person who is "qualified for outer space"? Let us return to Ishi! The following sentences are significant:

> In contrast to the Forty-niners . . . whose morality and morale had crumbled, Ishi and his band remained incorrupt, humane, compassionate, and with their faith intact even unto starvation, pain and death. The questions then are: what makes for stability? For psychic strength? For endurance, courage, faith?

The answers given by the author to these questions are mere suggestions. The Yahi were on their own home ground. This idea is not developed. The reader should reflect a little on the relation of the Indian to the land on which he lived. In this sense, most modern men never know what it means to have a "home ground." Then there is a casual reference to the "American Indian mystique" which could also be developed. William Faulkner's hunting stories, particularly "The Bear," give us some idea of what his "mystique" might involve. The word "mystique" has unfortunate connotations: it suggests an emotional icing on an ideological cake. Actually the Indian lived by a deeply religious wisdom which can be called in a broad sense mystical, and that is certainly much more than "a mystique." The book does not go into religious questions very deeply, but it shows us Ishi as a man sustained by a deep and unassailable spiritual strength which he never discussed.

Later, when he was living "in civilization" and was something of a celebrity as well as an object of charitable concern, Ishi was questioned about religion by a well-meaning lady. Ishi's English was liable to be unpredictable, and the language of his reply was not without its own ironic depths of absurdity:

"Do you believe in God?" the lady inquired.
"Sure, Mike!" he retorted briskly.

There is something dreadfully eloquent about this innocent short-circuit in communication.

One other very important remark is made by the author. The Yahi found strength in the incontrovertible fact that they were in the right.

"Of very great importance to their psychic health was the circumstance that their suffering and curtailments arose from wrongs done in them by others. They were not guilt-ridden."

Contrast this with the spectacle of our own country with its incomparable technological power, its unequaled material strength, and its psychic turmoil, its moral confusion and its profound heritage of guilt which neither the righteous declarations of Cardinals nor the moral indifference of "realists" can do anything to change! Every bomb we drop on a defenseless Asian village, every Asian child we disfigure or destroy with fire only adds to the moral strength of those we wish to destroy for our own profit. It does not make the Vietcong cause just; but by an accumulation of injustice done against innocent people we drive them into the arms of our enemies and make our own ideals look like the most pitiful sham.

Gradually the last members of the Yahi tribe died out. The situation of the survivors became more and more desperate. They could not continue to keep up their perfect invisibility: they had to steal food. Finally the hidden camp where Ishi lived with his sister and sick mother was discovered by surveyors who callously walked off with the few objects they found as souvenirs. The mother and sister died and finally on August 29, 1911, Ishi surrendered to the white race, expecting to be destroyed.

Actually, the news of this "last wild Indian" reached the anthropology department at Berkeley and a professor quickly took charge of things. He came and got the "wild man" out of jail. Ishi spent the rest of his life in San Francisco patiently teaching his hitherto completely unknown (and quite sophisticated) language to experts like Sapir. Curiously enough, Ishi lived in an anthropological museum where he earned his living as a kind of caretaker and also functioned, on occasion, as a live exhibit. He was well treated, and in fact the affection and charm of his relations with his white friends are not the least moving part of his story. He adapted to life in the city without too much trouble and returned once, with his friends, to live several months in his old territory, under his natural conditions, showing them how the Yahi had carried out the fantastic operation of their invisible survival. But he finally succumbed to one of the diseases of civilization. He died of TB in 1916, after four and a half years among the white men.

For the reflective reader who is—as everyone must be today—deeply concerned about man and his fate, this is a moving and significant book, one of those unusually suggestive works that *must* be read, and perhaps more than once. It is a book to think deeply about and take notes on not only because of its extraordinary factual interest but because of its special quality as a kind of parable.

One cannot help thinking today of the Vietnam war in terms of the Indian wars of a hundred years ago. Here again, one meets the same myths and misunderstandings, the same obsession with "completely wiping out" an enemy regarded as diabolical. The language of the vigilantes had overtones of puritanism in it. The backwoods had to be "completely cleaned out," or "purified" of Indians—as if they were vermin. I have read accounts of American GIs taking the same attitude toward the Vietcong. The jungles are thought to be "infested" with Communists, and hence one goes after them as one would go after ants in the kitchen back home. And in this process of "cleaning up" (the language of "cleansing" appeases and pacifies the conscience) one becomes without realizing it a murderer of women and children. But this is an unfortunate accident, what the moralists call "double effect." Something that is just too bad, but which must be accepted in view of something more important that has to be done. And so there is more and more killing of civilians and less and less of the "something more important" which is what we are trying to achieve. In the end, it is the civilians that are killed in the ordinary course of events, and com-batants only get killed by accident. No one worries any more about double effect. War is waged against the innocent to "break enemy morale."

What is most significant is that Vietnam seems to have become an extension of our old Western frontier, complete with enemies of an-other, "inferior" race. This is a real "new frontier" that enables us to continue the cowboys-and-Indians game which seems to be part and parcel of our national identity. What a pity that so many innocent people have to pay with their lives for our obsessive fantasies!

One last thing. Ishi never told anyone his real name. The California Indians apparently never uttered their own names, and were very care-ful about how they spoke the name of others. Ishi would never refer to the dead by name either. "He never revealed his own private Yahi name," says the author. "It was as though it had been consumed in the funeral pyre of the last of his loved ones."

In the end, no one ever found out a single name of the vanished community. Not even Ishi's. For Ishi means simply MAN.

27

THE MEANING OF MALCOLM X

Published in Continuum *in the Summer issue, 1967*

The *Autobiography of Malcolm X* is a book of decisive importance. It is widely read, especially on campuses, and it is certainly helping to crystallize revolutionary thought among students. For one thing, it adds immeasurably to the picture of Malcolm X formed by the mass-media during his life, and gives us some idea of the possibilities that he might have actualized if he had not been brutally eliminated from the political scene. The picture most of us had of him was inadequate, though not altogether untrue. We saw him as a militant, rigid, some-what fanatical agitator, absolutely committed to a naive racist mystique and to a religious organization which was made to sound like a Negro SS. This was partially true of the Malcolm X who came dramatically into view in the early sixties as the most active organizer of the Black Muslims, the right-hand man of their founder, Elijah Muhammad. Malcolm X was then known to be a former thief and hustler who had become a Black Muslim in prison. He received a grudging and fearful respect as one who sought to rehabilitate others like himself by the discipline of an organized religious and paramilitary existence. He and his cohorts explicitly rejected the values of white society along with the white man's image of himself, of the black, and of the world at large.

Even if there were no more to his life than this, his autobiography would not be without interest. But this book shows that there was much more. To begin with, Malcolm X was undoubtedly more gifted, more intelligent, more flexible than he appeared to be when he was deliberately effacing himself behind the ideas and programs of "The Honorable Mr. Elijah Muhammad." Also, his loyalty to the Muslim leader, which seems to have been both simple and genuine, was perhaps too naive. If the Black Muslims had not turned against him and expelled him, Malcolm would possibly have remained content with limitations that seriously restricted his growth. It may be added that the story of his break with the Black Muslims, and even more the story of his death, remain very mysterious. Was he murdered by his former brethren? There is plenty of evidence that he *expected* them to murder him. But he knew himself to be menaced also by others. The epilogue added to this story by the reporter to whom it was narrated does not help us to penetrate the mystery of his assassination. It is certainly strange that Malcolm X should have been gunned down by three men in the front row of the auditorium where he habitually spoke to his own followers, that the men got away even though a special detail of twenty policemen were supposed to have been posted in the hall. Nothing has ever been made public that offers any satisfactory explanation of the murder.

The story of Malcolm X falls into three distinct parts. The son of a Negro preacher, who was also a Black Nationalist and was murdered by whites, Malcolm moved in his teens from a small town in Michigan to Roxbury, the Negro ghetto of Boston. There and in Harlem he got mixed up in every kind of underworld activity: numbers, dope, pandering, burglary. Operating with a small gang of thieves which included two white girls, he was caught and sentenced. In prison, he began to read voraciously. He was converted to the Black Muslims by letters from one of his brothers. Already in prison he became a propagandist for the teachings of Elijah Muhammad, and as soon as he was out of jail he went to meet the Black Muslim leader. In a short time he proved himself to be an unusually effective organizer, and thanks to his efforts the Muslims began to spread all over the country, attracting a great deal of attention in the mass-media by their denunciations of the whites and their absolute segregationism. Like the Black Nationalists of Marcus Garvey, the Muslims declare that they wish to live completely separate from the "white devils," and are looking for separate territory in which to do so.

Can all this be completely dismissed merely as a racism which is by definition a pure myth? Certainly there is a generous element of illusion in the way the idea is elaborated. But is there nevertheless an element of truth in the inexorable refusal to accept *any* profession of sincere friendship, interest, compassion from *any* white man? Malcolm X later recognized that his own earlier refusals were too absolute, that some kind of dialogue between the races had to be possible, some kind of collaboration had to be admitted. Yet he felt that the ordinary white liberal professions of sincerity were not good enough, and he insisted on a tactic of refusal which declared, both implicitly and explicitly, that however honest the white man might feel himself to be subjectively, the

Negro could not objectively accept his protestations of concern at their face value. They were bound to prove deceptive because the white man could not change his essentially distorted view of the relationship between the races. Even when the white man indulged in a veritable cult of the Negro, he betrayed his basic conviction that the Negro was somehow more of an animal, a distinct and exotic species of human being. Observation of whites visiting Harlem in search of certain types of recreation made this supposition rather plausible. Meanwhile, even the most decent, most buttoned-up kind of liberalism still consists in an invitation to Negroes to come and join a superior race—together with concrete refusals to tolerate too close an intimacy when the invitation is accepted.

On the other hand the Black Muslims offer a rather sketchy and not always accurate presentation of the teachings of Islam. On the grounds that Islam is "the original black man's religion," the Black Muslims of America preach a predominantly negative doctrine; anti-Christian and anti-white. In spite of the fact that Malcolm protested against being stereotyped as a preacher of race hatred, there is unquestionably a strong racist element in the Black Muslim code. This is, in fact, a ghetto religion, and the story of Malcolm's relations with Elijah Muhammad suggests that without a ghetto basis for his power, Elijah Muhammad would not last long. The Black Muslims are not without their positive qualities (they do after all help hundreds of Negroes to recover their dignity as human beings who feel that life has a meaning). But they apparently believe a rather unusual amount of naive mythology (including an elaborate account of how the white race was produced by "bleaching" out a certain number of Negroes, over a stretch of many generations, on the island of Patmos—or was it Cyprus?). One might also remark in passing that the idea of Islam as a "black man's religion," contrasted with Christianity as a religion of white slave traders, is a bit over-simplified. After all, the Arab Muslims have always been energetic exploiters of the raw slave material which black Africa presented to them, and they have consistently justified themselves with words like these from the *Koran:* "We have raised some people above others by degrees so they might force one another to compulsory labor" (43:32). In short, both Christians and Muslims have known how to make use of their Scriptures to justify racial injustice when occasion demanded.

Meanwhile, in post-colonial Africa, the relations between Black Africans and Arab Muslims are by no means cordial (witness the bloody conflict in and around the Sudan and Senegal). Nor does this apply merely to rivalry between Muslims and Black Christians. Native Africa is as tragically divided by racial authority as any other part of the world.

The whole second part of the life of Malcolm X, the chapters devoted to his life as a Black Muslim, are rather disconcerting. In order to understand them we have to realize that they are made up of material narrated by Malcolm to his ghost-writer during the time when he was still a loyal follower of Elijah Muhammad, and no changes were made in this material afterwards. Hence the middle section of the book, a faithful portrait of the Black Muslim militant who preached that all whites were devils, measures up to what we were all led to expect by the mass-media. It is an incredible mixture of sincerity, mythology, and militant devotion to what Malcolm believed to be the real cause of the Black Man—the only way to solve his problems. He preaches a foreshortened, impassioned, obsessive racist eschatology which, for all its sweeping ruthlessness, has so far not directly promoted any really significant political action, whether violent or non-violent. But it has certainly contributed much to a particular outlook which, exploited and distorted by the mass-media, has increased tensions, tightened polarities, and doubtless had much to do not only with "hot summer" rioting but even with the death of Malcolm X himself.

The most impressive thing about the *Autobiography of Malcolm X* is, however, the way in which Malcolm outgrew this phase of his development. His expulsion from the Black Muslims was evidently due to jealousies and rivalries within the movement. The peculiar religious temperament of Elijah Muhammad, filled with inner contradictions and inconsistencies not uncommon in certain messiah types, undoubtedly had much to do with it. Malcolm was evidently too big and too smart for the movement, and though he honestly tried to remain an obedient subordinate, this was not possible. He had definitely taken over the center of the stage, and so he had to be driven off it. When he was once again on his own he quickly discovered a whole new dimension of things. He began to get a much deeper, more mature, more sophisticated and more nuanced understanding of the revolutionary situation. He also, at the same time, experienced an unusual deepening of his religious experience of Islam.

The final chapters of the autobiography show us a completely new person. In fact, for the first time we see Malcolm X as a whole person rather than as a character of great energy driven by the symbiotic obsessions of his ghetto milieu. The central fact in this transformation was the religious experience of the *Hajj*, or the pilgrimage to Mecca, which is one of the basic obligations of a Muslim. (I am now using the term Muslim in its complete and "catholic" sense, and no longer in reference to the Black Muslim fore-shortening of Islamism.) Not only was his Islamic faith clarified, not only were many gross misapprehensions corrected, but above all he experienced an extraordinary sense of *community,* of brotherhood with other Muslim pilgrims from all parts of the world, *including many who were white.* After the *Hajj,* which he performed with exemplary devotion and with all the meticulous assent of the convert, Malcolm was no longer thinking in terms of straight racist polarities. Before returning to America, he visited some of the new African nations (where he was a great success) and acquired a new sense of the global revolution of which the Negro revolution in America is only a small part. He saw that it was not a simple question of black angels and white devils in the cities of the United States, but of the formerly colonial, under-developed world, filled with black, white, yellow, red, brown and mestizo populations (in other words the majority of the human race), against a highly developed affluent technological society which cannot really help the others in their struggle for liberation because it needs them to remain in a state of economic and political tutelage.

When Malcolm X returned from his pilgrimage to Mecca, he had changed in two very important ways. First he was an authentic Muslim with a real experience of the meaning of Islam. Second he was no longer a creature of the ghetto. He was ready to become a world citizen. He had begun to experience contemporary realities in a way that remains inaccessible to white travelers in quest of the exotic who see the whole Third World as a potential Acapulco.

Malcolm X returned to America as a revolutionary who could some day have used his African experience and contacts in ways we can barely imagine. Perhaps few people really understood precisely what his new potentialities were, but evidently both white and black enemies of the man sensed that he was, in their terms, highly dangerous.

The meaning of this autobiography comes clear in the final chapters: Malcolm X first outgrew the ghetto underworld of prostitution, dope and crime. He then outgrew the religious underworld, the spiritual power structure that thrives on a ghetto mystique. He was finally attaining to the freedom and fullness of understanding that gives some (still rare) American Negroes the sense of belonging to a world movement that makes them independent, to some extent, of purely American limitations and pressures. Malcolm grew too fast. He was too articulate. He was made to pay for it. The impact of his message to others that may follow him has only been made stronger and more emphatic by his death.

Malcolm X realized that he would not live to read his life story in print. This he prophesied correctly. He also several times announced that after his death he would be despised and discredited as a stereotype of racist-hatred. In this his intuition was less accurate. His autobiography reveals a person whose struggles are understandable, whose errors we can condone. He was a fighter whose sincerity and courage we cannot help admiring, and who might have become a genuine revolutionary leader—with portentous effect in American society!

28

AUSCHWITZ:
A Family Camp

Published in The Catholic Worker, *November 1967*

This essay was a review of *Auschwitz: A Report on the Proceedings against Robert Karl Ludwig Mulka and Others Before the Court of Frankfurt* by Bernd Naumann, translated from the German by Jean Steinberg, with an introduction by Hannah Arendt (London, Pall Mall Press, 1966).

• • • • •

On December 20, 1963, twenty-two former SS men who had played important parts in the "final solution of the Jewish question" at Auschwitz went on trial at Frankfurt. The trial lasted twenty months. Scores of survivors of the camp, together with many other witnesses, testified to the massive torture and butchery accomplished twenty years before, in that curious place "far away, somewhere in Poland." The testimony does not make pleasant reading. It fills a book (*Auschwitz*, by Bernd Naumann), in large format running to nearly 450 pages: and this is only a summary of the most important points. The defendants were convicted and sentenced to prison terms, which they have all appealed. The most curious thing about the trial is that the defendants confidently and consistently denied almost everything. Finally the judge remarked in astonishment that he had "yet to meet anyone who had done anything at Auschwitz"! There was, in other words, a marked contrast between the unanimity of the witnesses saying black and the unanimity of the defendants saying white. Still more curiously, these same defendants had previously admitted much more of the dark side of the picture themselves. But now this has been "forgotten" They have somehow changed their minds. Hannah Arendt, in an important introduction, interprets this to mean that the German public has tacitly come to terms with the grim past. It has now apparently accepted these men, and many others like them.

In spite of the general tone of outrage still noticeable on the level of the court and of the better newspapers, the defendants themselves remained contemptuous and at ease, certain of ultimate freedom and confident that they had the tacit approval of their peers. Keeping this in mind, we now turn to the book. We reflect on the workings of a death factory where some three or four million people were barbarously destroyed. Yet to judge by the testimony of these men who have been sentenced to prison for literally thousands of murders each, the camp was an innocent establishment, a place for "protective custody." It doubtless knew its moments of austerity, but on the whole, it was simply a camp where people went to be "reeducated." At times, it almost sounds like fairyland . . .

Fairyland in Poland

Chief among the defendants was Robert Mulka. In July, 1942, Mulka became deputy of the camp commandant, Hoss. Though second in command for about a year, he claimed to know nothing about the fact that many prisoners seemed to be dying and of course issued no orders that had any connection with these unfortunate occurrences. When questioned about his duties he said he had worried a lot about whether or not the camp could afford some entertainers he wished to bring there. He sometimes encountered death close at hand when he paraded at the honor funeral of one of the SS guards. Gas chambers? Yes, he had heard something about them over the camp grapevine. "Word," he said, "got out in the course of time." Crematory furnaces? He admitted having seen a red glow in the sky and wondered what it was: rumor had supplied details. When pressed to explain why he had not tried to discover the facts himself, he said there was "no one to ask." Not even Commandant Hoss? No, the commandant was an "opaque man." Were there no orders about the "special treatment" of "asocial elements" and the "disinfection" of undesirables? He admitted that "there were probably some general instructions" which of course bypassed his own department, for he was after all only second in command. Confronted with orders signed by himself he offered no explanation. At the end of the trial, when the prosecution was asking that Mulka be given life imprisonment for more than 36,500 murders, Mulka himself simply asked the court to consider "all the circumstances which at the time brought me into my conflict situation."

The other defendants all said the same. Even those who were accused of selecting the prisoners for extermination, of driving them into the gas chambers, naked, with dogs turned loose and tearing their flesh. Of beating them to death on the "Boger swing" in "rigorous interrogations." Of injecting phenol into their hearts and killing them. Of wiping them out in shootings that lasted two or three days. All these people were strangely unaware that Auschwitz had been an extermination camp and that they had been the exterminators. They admitted there were gas chambers "somewhere near the barracks." (And where were the barracks? "Somewhere near the gas chambers!") Yes, sometimes one drove a truck up "near the barracks" and one became aware that "people were busy doing something." It was even observed that "some prisoners were lying around." Resting perhaps? Since resting was not the usual thing at Auschwitz, were they perhaps dead? Altogether hard to say. One had failed to notice.

What about "cap shooting"? Making the prisoners throw their caps away, ordering them to run over to pick up the caps, and then shooting them for "trying to escape"? What about genuine escape attempts (some of which even succeeded)? One of the former SS guards assured the court that there were no attempted escapes. Who would want to escape? Auschwitz, he said, was after all, "a family camp." Another of the defendants, when obligingly describing the camp layout, asked the court if it would like him to point out on the map the place where he had made "a children's playground with sandboxes for the little ones."

Yes, there were even little ones in Auschwitz. They were marked out for play.

"The children were playing ball," says a former prisoner, "and waiting unsuspectingly. . . . A woman guard came, and clapped her hands, and called out: 'All right now, let's stop. Now we take showers.' And then they ran down the steps into the room in which they undressed. And the guard took a little girl on her arm and carried her down. And the child pointed to the eagle emblem on the cap of the SS woman and asked: 'What kind of birdie is that?' And that was the last I saw and heard of the child."

The Installations

No need to describe Auschwitz, the two huge death camps about three miles apart, the guard towers, the high barbwire fences charged with thousands of volts, the barracks, the gas chambers, the furnaces burning day and night. The evil-smelling smoke. The glare in the night sky visible for miles. The ramp where the long freight trains arrived, the "transports" jammed with prisoners, men, women, children, from all parts of Europe. On the ramp, those selected for immediate gassing were told by a gesture to go to the right. Selection depended to some extent on the caprice or mood of the one in charge. But one could be "selected" in the camp itself. If a prisoner became seriously ill or too weak to work. If the barracks were getting too crowded. If conditions became inconvenient, efficiency might demand a housecleaning.

Delousings were not working properly in the women's camp. And a new doctor came along and solved the problem in a businesslike manner. "He simply had an entire block gassed." Having thus disposed of seven hundred and fifty women prisoners, he cleaned out the block, disinfected it, thoroughly deloused another batch of prisoners and moved them in. "He was the first to rid the entire women's camp of lice."

If Auschwitz was one of the main centers for the "final solution of the Jewish question" we must also remember it dealt with other problems too. Polish intellectuals and members of the Polish resistance were sent here for torture and liquidation. Thousands of Russian prisoners of war were exterminated at Auschwitz. According to the written testimony of one of the defendants (a deposition handed to the British at the end of the war) twelve thousand Russian prisoners of war reached Auschwitz early in 1942. In six months, there were only one hundred and fifty of them still alive. "Thousands of prisoners of war were shot in a copse near Birkenau" (wrote the defendant Perry Broad). They were "buried in mass graves . . . the fisheries began to complain that the fish in the ponds in the vicinity of Birkenau were dying. Experts said this was due to the pollution of the ground water through cadaveric poison . . . The summer sun was beating down on Birkenau, the bodies . . . started to swell up and a dark red mass started to seep through the cracks of the earth . . ." This called for a quick and efficient solution, since the camp authorities did not like bad publicity. Twenty or thirty "very reliable SS men" were picked for the job. They had to sign a statement that if they violated their oath of secrecy or even hinted at the nature of their job they would be punished by death. This special detail then rounded up prisoners to do the digging. The prisoners chosen were Jews. The bodies of the Russians were exhumed and burned. "For weeks, thick white smoke continued to rise from that isolated tract of land." There were rumors. Prisoners who refused to do this job were shot. The others did not survive to tell about it. The SS men on this unpleasant detail were rewarded with "special rations from the SS kitchen: 1 quart of milk, sausages, cigarettes and of course liquor." This, it turned out, was standard practice and applied also to those who had the tiresome job of beating prisoners to death, or shooting them at the Black Wall, or putting them into the gas. When things were very busy an SS man, trying to show off his marksmanship, unfortunately shot a colleague. He was, of course, punished. One of the SS men, Klehr, was a male nurse—a "medical orderly." He specialized in injecting his patients in the heart with phenol and thus solving all their problems at once. He was also a notorious drunk, and was sometimes so intoxicated that he could no longer carry on the selections of appropriate candidates for the gas chamber. "Such selections had to be interrupted."

Klehr also had other hobbies. He was in charge of some rabbits: perhaps they were used for scientific experiments like the prisoners. At any rate he was so interested in the rabbits that he often "injected the prisoners two at a time because he wanted to get back to his rabbits." Such was the testimony of a former prisoner who had to hold the patients whom Klehr was injecting. One day the prisoner looked up and recognized the next patient in line. It was his father. Klehr was in a hurry and did not stop to ask why the prisoner was crying. He did so the next day, however. "Why," said Klehr in a burst of arbitrary generosity, "you should have told me. I would have let him live!" Favors were sometimes done at Auschwitz! The prisoner, however, had feared to speak, convinced that if he did so he would have got a shot of phenol in the heart himself.

The Children of Zamosc

Klehr took care of one hundred and twenty Polish children from a village called Zamosc. They were killed in two batches: eighty the first day, the rest on the day after. Their parents were dead and no one quite knew what to do with them. They played in the courtyard of the hospital. "A ball had somehow turned up." Maybe that was when there were sandboxes. Another witness mentioned a balloon. But eventually the children were lined up and filed into the "examination room." Klehr was waiting for them with the syringe and the saucer of phenolic acid. The first ones screamed. After that it was somehow quieter. In the silence of the barrack, one heard the bodies falling off the chair and thumping onto the wooden floor. But Klehr did not do it all. Maybe he got bored and went to his rabbits, handing over the syringe. Scherpe, who took over, broke down under the strain and ran out of the room, refusing to kill any more children. A third SS man had to supply and finish the work begun. Reason for the death of the little boys from Zamosc? As a precaution against "immorality" in the camp. Auschwitz had to be very, very clean!

Other scenes with children: Outside the gas chambers and crematories where mothers with children were sent immediately upon arrival. The mothers sometimes tried to hide the children under the piles of clothing. "Sometimes the voice of a little child who had been forgotten would emerge from beneath a pile of clothing . . . They would put a bullet through its head."

Sometimes, children were not sent at once for "special treatment." They might be kept handy for medical experiments. In the interests of science! Or they might even be assigned to useful work. One witness who entered Auschwitz at fourteen and survived testified that he was on the cart detail that removed ashes from the crematory. "We got ashes from Crematory III and scattered them on the icy roads. When there were no people in the gas chambers, the capo let us warm ourselves there." Another less bucolic scene: an SS man who threw living children into the flames and boiling human fat of the open cremation pyres. And finally this, from a witness: "Early in the morning I saw a little girl standing all by herself in the yard . . . wearing a claret-colored dress and [she had] a little pigtail. She held her hands at her side like a soldier. Once she looked down, wiped the dust off her shoes and again stood very still. Then I saw Boger come into the yard. He took the child by her hand—she went along very obediently—and stood her with her face to the Black Wall. Once she turned around. Boger again turned her head to the wall, walked back, and shot . . ."

Exceptionally gentle for Boger, one of the most brutal professional butchers in the camp. He was sometimes seen to pick up little children by the heels and smash their heads against a brick wall . . . But that was during a moment of stress in the mass liquidation of the Gypsy compound.

The Language of Auschwitz

Language itself has fallen victim to total war, genocide and systematic tyranny in our time. In destroying human beings, and human values, on a mass scale, the Gestapo also subjected the German language to violence and crude perversion.

In Auschwitz secrecy was emphasized. "If you talk about what you can see from here," one prisoner was told, "you'll go through the chimney." Written records were kept cryptic, evasive. Great care was taken to destroy as much paperwork as possible before the Russians arrived. Even mention of corporal punishment was taboo. Any open reference to the realities of life and death in the camp was regarded as treason. Any guard, doctor, prison administrator who let out the truth could be severely punished for "defeatist talk."

This circumlocution was itself highly significant. It admitted the sinister and ironic fact that even knowledge of the truth about Auschwitz could furnish a formidable propaganda weapon to the enemies of the Reich. The very irony of the fact should have raised some urgent questions about the principle behind the camp. But the function of doubletalk and doublethink is to say everything without raising inconvenient questions. Officialese has a talent for discussing reality while denying it and calling truth itself into question. Yet the truth remains. This doubletalk is by its very nature invested with a curious metaphysical leer. The language of Auschwitz is one of the vulnerable spots through which we get a clear view of the demonic.

Gestapo doubletalk encircles reality as a doughnut encircles its hole. "Special treatment," "special housing." We need no more than one lesson, and we gain the intuition which identifies the hole, the void of death, in the heart of the expression. When the circumlocution becomes a little more insistent ("recovery camps for the tired") it brings with it suggestions of awful lassitude, infinite hopelessness, as if meaning had now been abolished forever and we were definitively at the mercy of the absurd.

"Disinfectants," "materials for resettlement of Jews," "ovaltine substitute from Swiss Red Cross"—all references to Zyklon B! When a deadly poison gas is referred to as soothing, restorative, a quasi-medicine to put babies to sleep, one senses behind the phrase a deep hatred of life itself. The key to Auschwitz language is its pathological joy in death. This turns out to be the key to all officialese. All of it is the celebration of boredom, of routine, of deadness, of organized futility. Auschwitz just carried the whole thing to its logical extreme, with a kind of heavy lilt in its mockery, its oafish love of death.

"Work makes free"—the sign over the gate of Auschwitz—tells, with grim satisfaction, the awful literal truth: "Here we work people to death." And behind it the dreadful metaphysical admission "For us there is only one freedom, death."

"To the Bath," said the sign pointing to the gas chambers. (You will be purified of that dirty thing, your life!) And as a matter of fact the gas chambers and crematories were kept spotlessly clean. "Nothing was left of them [the victims] not even a speck of dust on the armatures."

"Assigned to harvest duty"—this, in the record of an SS man, meant he had been posted to Auschwitz. The double meaning of "harvest" was doubtless not random. It has an apocalyptic ring.

Yet the Gestapo people had an acute sense of the importance of words. One of them became quite excited in court, over the distinction between "transferred" and "assigned."

Those who tortured excapees or resisters (and resistance could be expressed even by an expressionless face) praised the "Boger Swing" as their most effective language machine. The victim was hung from a horizontal pole, upside down, by wrists and ankles. He was whipped so vigorously that he often spun clean around on the pole. "You'll learn to talk, we have language for you," said the Gestapo men. "My talking machine will make you talk," said Boger, who was proud of his invention. In fact he has earned himself a place in history on account of it. Not an enviable place.

One of the results of the Frankfurt trial is that it makes an end of the pure Auschwitz myth: the myth of demented monsters who were twice our size, with six eyes and four rows of teeth, not of the same world as ourselves. The demonic sickness of Auschwitz emanated from ordinary people, stimulated by an extraordinary regime. The trial brought out their variety, their ordinariness, their shades of character, and even their capacity of change. In strict justice to Klehr, it must be said that he was profoundly affected by a visit from his wife in 1944, "a good kind woman . . . her two children were decent and well brought up." She did not suspect that her husband was involved in murder, but she knew that everything was not well at the camp. A witness overheard her saying to him, "I heard that terrible things happen here. I hope you're not involved." Klehr replied that he "cured people." But after his wife's visit, he began to treat prisoners more decently and to react against the camp methods. He even volunteered for front line duty, and when his request was refused, he denounced a brutal camp officer and had him transferred, thus improving conditions.

It is nevertheless eerie to read the testimony of a witness who had been a neighbor of the defendant Dr. Capesius in Bucharest, and met him on the ramp where he sent her sisters, brothers and father to the gas chamber. "I still knew Dr. Capesius from Bucharest . . . We lived in the same building. He was a representative of Bayer. Sometimes I spoke to him and his wife . . ." The witness had even had coffee with

Capesius and his wife in a park. That was the last time she saw him until 1944, at Auschwitz. "I recognized him right away . . . I was happy to see him. When I stood in front of him all he said was, 'How old are you?' and sent me to the right." However, it may be noted that in sending her to the right he had saved her life. Not even Boger can be regarded without qualification as a pure monster. Auschwitz becomes a little more horrible when we have to admit that Boger too is a human being.

Boger and his colleagues were all more or less the products of a society at least as respectable and as civilized as that of New York or London. They had all received an education, some of them higher education. They had been brought up, it is said, in "Christian homes," or at least in middle-class homes—not quite the same, but Christianity has been willing to overlook the possible differences. Before Hitler, they lived and moved among "respectable people" and since Hitler they have done the same. How is it that for twelve years in between they could beat and bash and torment and shoot and whip and murder thousands of their fellow human beings, *including even their former neighbors and friends*, and think nothing of it?

In the first place it would be wrong to say that they all thought nothing of it. One among the defendants who comes close to being tragic is Dr. Lucas. We sense in him a complex, lonely, tormented character who knew he was involved in a wrong that he could not entirely escape. Perhaps he might have escaped it. No one will ever be able to say with finality. But in any event he elected to go along with the system, to participate in the "selections," while at the same time practicing the ambivalent quasi-unconscious resistance technique of the "good soldier Schweik." Witness after witness spoke out in favor of Dr. Lucas. He was different from the others. Yes, he sent people to their death, but many witnesses recognized that he had saved their lives. Still he remained identified with the machinery of organized murder, and recognized that in so doing he had ruined his own life. Another who admitted that Auschwitz had been a doubtful quality in his life was Stark. He had gone to the camp as an SS guard when still in his teens. He had not yet finished school. Shooting, beating and killing were, for him, normal facts of life. He accepted them without question. He had practically grown up under Hitler and did not learn the difference until later. "I regret the mistakes of my past," he said, "but I cannot undo them."

What about Boger? Though he consistently denied everything said by witnesses, in the end his defense was content to ask for leniency rather than life imprisonment, on the grounds that Boger had merely done his duty as a good policeman.

This seems to sum up Boger's rather aggrieved view of his own case. Boger defended his "swing" right to the end. How could one refuse a conscientious police official the right to use "rigorous methods of interrogation"? Boger bluntly addressed the court on the virtues and necessity of these methods. They were highly practical. His defense lawyer expostulated with the jury: "The swing was not intended as torture: it was the only effective means of physical suasion."

The shocking thing about the views of both Boger and his lawyer is that they are evidently quite sincere. Not only that, they are views with which, it is assumed, other people will sympathize without difficulty.

In his final statement to the court, Boger made a distinction between the genocidal extermination of the Jews, which he admitted was perhaps a bit rough, and what he himself thought most important at the time: *"the fight against the Polish resistance movement and Bolshevism."*

Boger's case has now become an open appeal to the "good Germans" who, he assumes, agree with him; they will easily approve the rigors of his interrogation methods since they were justified by anti-Communism.

At this point, there swims into view a picture taken at another investigation, (hardly a trial) in the state of Mississippi. We see the smiling, contemptuous, brutal faces of the police deputies and their colleagues who are allegedly the murderers of three civil rights workers in the summer of 1964. Whatever may have been the facts in the case, one feels that in Mississippi and Auschwitz the basic assumptions are not very different. Instead of seeing the Bogers and Klehrs of Auschwitz as fabulous, myth-sized and inhuman monsters, we come to recognize that people like them are in fact all around us. All they need is the right kind of crisis, and they will blossom out.

Salutary Reflections

Such is the first conclusion. We have learned to associate the incredible brutality and inhumanity of Auschwitz with ordinary respectable people, in an extraordinary situation.

Second: Auschwitz worked because these people wanted it to work. Instead of resisting it, rebelling against it, they put the best of their energies into making genocide a success. This was true not only of one or two psychopaths but of an entire bureaucratic officialdom, including not only the secret police and Nazi party members but also managers and employees of the industries which knowingly made use of the slave labor provided in such abundance by the camp.

Third: although it was usual to argue that "they had no choice" and that they were "forced" to comply with orders, the trial showed a more complex and less excusable picture of the defendants. Almost all of them committed gratuitous acts of arbitrary cruelty and violence which were forbidden even by the Gestapo's own rules. Some were even punished by the SS for these violations. Was there no choice? There are on record refusals of men who simply would not take part in murder and got themselves transferred. Why was not this done more often? Let us clearly spell out two of the circumstances. Auschwitz was safe. One was not at the front, and there was practically no danger from bombing planes. And there were privileges: the work was no doubt disagreeable to some, but there were extra rations, smokes, drinks. Finally, there can be little doubt that many of these men tortured and killed because they thoroughly enjoyed it.

Fourth: what does all this add up to? Given the right situation and another Hitler, places like Auschwitz can be set up, put into action, kept running smoothly, with thousands of people systematically starved, beaten, gassed, and whole crematories going full blast. Such camps can be set up tomorrow anywhere and made to work with the greatest efficiency, because there is no dearth of people who would be glad to do the job, provided it is sanctioned by authority. They will be glad because they will instinctively welcome and submit to an ideology which enables them to be violent and destructive without guilt. They are happy with a belief which turns them loose against their fellow man to destroy him cruelly and without compunction, as long as he belongs to a different race, or believes in a different set of semi-meaningless political slogans.

It is enough to affirm one basic principle: ANYONE BELONGING TO CLASS X OR NATION Y OR RACE Z IS TO BE REGARDED AS SUBHUMAN AND WORTHLESS, AND CONSEQUENTLY HAS NO RIGHT TO EXIST. All the rest will follow without difficulty.

As long as this principle is easily available, as long as it is taken for granted, as long as it can be spread out on the front pages at a moment's notice and accepted by all, we have no need of monsters: ordinary policemen and good citizens will take care of everything.

· 29 ·

THE HOT SUMMER
OF SIXTY-SEVEN

Published in Winter 1967–68 issue of Katallagete

The following pages are presented without apology for their inadequacy. Who can pretend to give a satisfactory explanation of the events in Newark, Detroit, and so many other Northern and Eastern cities of nineteen sixty-seven? These are my own hasty and personal reactions. They were not originally intended for publication at all. I simply wanted to share a few ideas with my friends, and particularly with readers of an essay I had previously written—"Letters to a White Liberal"—during the "Birmingham Summer" of 1963. This essay was published in the book *Seeds of Destruction*. Many readers thought that my views were too pessimistic. Recently, however, I was gratified by the way in which one of my reviewers—Martin Marty, who condemned the book—took back his judgment and admitted that the events of this summer put things in a different light (*National Catholic Reporter*, Aug. 30, 1967).

In the "Letters to a White Liberal" I was interpreting the efforts of Dr. Martin Luther King to solve the race problem by Christian nonviolence. I said at that time that this was the *last chance* to really do something by a peaceful revolution and that it was perhaps already too late. I maintained then, as I do now, that the only possible solution was for Negroes and whites to pool their resources and work together for a radical and creative change in our social structures. The only hope of peace and order would be, I think, the creation of a truly new and truly "Great Society" in which the two races could share the same advantages not only on paper but in fact. I held (and still hold) that only a deep Christian renewal of conscience and consciousness on the part of black and white could make this possible. In other words political change, however momentous, would be useless without reconciliation. I felt that in 1963 there was still a chance of this taking place, but that time was just about running out. I added that if this failed, the only prospect was violence. In fact, the murder of the three civil rights workers in Mississippi the following year, the Liuzzo and Daniels murders, then Watts, were all steps in the direction of hopelessness.

It also seems to me that the gradual, irreversible escalation in Vietnam has had a lot to do with the violence at home. There is such a thing as mental contamination. Bad ideas can be very contagious. In Vietnam, the U.S. has officially adopted the policy that the best way to get across an idea is by fire and dynamite. Is it surprising that the Negro has caught on, and decided that he will try a little bit of the same? Note also that Vietnam seems to teach another perilous lesson: we know how to escalate, but we apparently don't know how to reverse the process and de-escalate. There is only one way: up. Make it hotter. Make it worse. This does not make the prospects for the future in our cities very pleasant. The Negroes are very likely to escalate too, without knowing how to put the thing in reverse. In my opinion, this is practically certain. And obviously white society is not going to stand around idly and let it happen without a reply in kind, indeed without anticipating it perhaps with "preventive first strikes." We'll see.

The Black Power movement has now, in any case, replaced Christian non-violence. Dr. King no longer retains his position of preeminent moral authority as the greatest Negro leader. But though the Black Power movement is trying to channel the exploding energies of the Negro ghettos in a political direction, we can see that the violence of today is, and the violence to come will probably be, more and more aimless, nihilistic, arbitrary, destructive and non-amenable to reasonable control.

Already it is evident that those whites who reviled Dr. King as a "Communist" and rabble rouser will have reason to regret that the guidance of the Negro struggle for rights has slipped from his hands into the hands of those who hold rifles.

Indeed, this is no longer a Negro struggle for legal rights but a more elemental, nihilistic revolution which these notes will attempt to consider.

I would like to emphasize two points: 1. The situation is now really serious. Violence will *certainly* continue. 2. This demands great realism and foresight on the part of everyone. We must learn to deal with this and all our other critical problems with as few delusions as possible, whether they be optimistic or fatalistic and destructive. The point is this: we are on the edge of revolution, perhaps even a limited civil war. Certainly a kind of civil cold war. But can we keep this violence from becoming purely catastrophic? The problem of racial conflict is part and parcel of the whole problem of human violence anyway, all the way up from the suppressed inarticulate hate feelings of interpersonal family and job conflicts to the question of the H-bomb and mass extermination. The problem is in ourselves. It is only *one* symptom.

In order to understand the racial violence that confronts us we need first of all to interpret what it is trying to say. When we see pictures of Detroit looking like a city that has just undergone an air raid we realize that this is no longer a political struggle to obtain rights guaranteed by law in the existing order of things. What we have, on the contrary, is a massive attack on the order itself. What is being attacked is not just regional prejudice, not just "police brutality," but the system we live in. This is not a campaign for civil rights, it is in effect a kind of declaration of war. The Negroes are saying, on various different levels, that white American society is so unjust, so corrupt, so hopeless, so tied up in its own inner contradictions that it deserves to be attacked and even, if possible, destroyed. The end justifies the means. No means are to be considered foul. Every form of trickery and violence has been used against them and they intend to return the compliment.

Why are the Negroes, themselves American citizens, saying such a drastic thing? (And of course here we have to qualify: to what extent is this what they are "all" saying? To what extent is this still only the contention of a rabid minority? To what extent can we still avoid driving all the moderate Negroes to this same extreme position? I am concerned here only with spelling out the message of the current riots.)

There is one snap answer: Communists. This is a knee-jerk reaction that is so tired, so automatic, so futile that it is fatal. It cannot give a true understanding of what we are contending with. It makes us hunt imaginary enemies instead of trying to confront the complexities of a human problem that is terribly near. It puts the root of the evil thousands of miles away, it exonerates our own system from all defect and all guilt, and makes us forget to look for the solution where we have to find it: in our own backyard. In fact, in our own heart.

It is true that the Negro revolution in our country is in fact part of a world revolution. And the Communists are trying to exploit that world revolution for their own ends. But this is something much deeper and more elemental than a political revolution, and if it is not understood in depth it can lead to fatal mistakes. The Negroes of America have become conscious of the worldwide nature of the violent conflict which they interpret in terms of color. Whether this interpretation is naive, false, stupid and so on is beside the point. It is an interpretation which, for better or for worse, is gradually coming to have an ever greater influence everywhere. I fully admit that it may be absurd to look at things that way, it may even be suicidal: but nevertheless we live in a world which for practical purposes is now a racist world. God knows it should not be!

The Negroes of America have—at least the most militant elements have—adopted a fundamentally racist position. They wish now not to become integrated but to assert their own identity in the most forceful possible manner and, if possible, even to separate from the whites. Obviously, apart from the dreams of fanatics, such a separation is completely impossible. Racism which attempts to evade the problem simply intensifies it. Meanwhile the Negroes interpret the war in Asia as a color-war, in which they are asked to support white power in an attempt to subjugate Asian colored people. Once again, this is a sweeping over-simplification: but it is what people are thinking, and it is a basis for their decisions. Drastic decisions to bomb and burn at home.

Now this same pattern is reproducing itself all over the world. Everywhere, in Africa, Asia, Melanesia, you find movements that are something more than political. They are messianic, quasi-political, eschatological movements which all have certain factors in common: they are violently hostile to white European-American civilization, and they are anti-Christian because they identify Christ as a "white God." Yet at the same time they tend to incorporate a kind of Christian eschatology with elements of pagan religion. The result: dedicated, sometimes fanatical, sometimes crazy messianic movements which all believe themselves called to resist, reject and if possible destroy white civilization and to put in its place a new culture which takes on the aspect of a religious messianic Kingdom and a new creation, a totally new kind of existence.

Whatever may be the value of these cultic movements, they are not only very influential but they are symptoms that have the highest significance. They represent an entirely new consciousness, an awakening of an awareness and of an intent that white people can barely grasp, let alone understand dispassionately. Yet it is of the greatest importance for us to *understand* this new consciousness if we can. The place where this new consciousness comes closest to us is in the Negro ghettos of our own country. The new highly destructive riots are manifestations of this new mythical interpretation of present-day reality: a sense that white society has been judged and found wanting, that it has been consistently cruel, hypocritical, unjust, inhuman. That the day of retribution has come. It is the time of judgment and of blood. All these movements start with a violent repudiation of white culture and of everything that it stands for: i.e. everything that implies its superiority, everything that justifies the subjection of non-white peoples and cultures.

So there is first of all a spasm of rejection. This rejection is most effectively preached by some prophetic figure who is primarily a liberator, also mythologized as a prophet-messiah, and usually (by courtesy of an obliging opposition) elevated in due course to the rank of martyr. Lumumba is a case in point. And in America we have also had Malcolm X, an uncompromising black separatist, who was "martyred" and has now become a symbol of the black man who found his identity by a kind of moral liberation: he was imprisoned in the underworld by the corrupt society of whitey. He fought his way free, became a fearless and lucid black man who realized that no white man could be trusted, et cetera. This is becoming a standard pattern all over the world.

The colored peoples form the vast majority of the world's population and also are the have-nots in a world where sixty percent of the wealth is in the hands of a tiny minority of Americans and others. These colored people have, they think, a mission first of all to liberate themselves from the whites, and second, perhaps even to destroy white civilization if this becomes necessary.

Obviously, white civilization is not about to let itself be passively destroyed.

Note that I am simply spelling out the message: I am not saying whether the message is nuts, or whether it may have something to it: I am saying that it has to be taken seriously insofar as it is an expression of impassioned convictions which will gradually take clearer shape in the minds of millions of people in the next ten years or so.

That being the case, we have to readjust our own thinking at least on a few points like the following.

1. Our own well-meant efforts to help solve economic and political problems, at home or abroad, whether by peaceful aid (Alliance for Progress, Peace Corps) or by business or military support and intervention, are going to be interpreted, rightly or wrongly, as strategy to gain or to maintain control over others. This also goes for the desperate and belated efforts to improve life in the ghettos at home: playgrounds, schools, and so on. No one is about to accept these as valid solutions of anything.

2. The American ideology of freedom and democracy is now largely discredited everywhere, even among a significant proportion of Americans. The fervent celebration of American ideals by Congressmen and publicists is useful mainly for bolstering up their own morale. In others, even in those who want to agree, this incantation raises more and more serious doubts. Can we possibly be sincere about these grandiose concepts? Do we believe that they are likely to be used in really constructive ways to solve our problems? Or are they going to become fanatical shibboleths to justify an armed and violent reaction on the part of white society against the attacks leveled against it? In other words, is "freedom" simply going to become the copyrighted trademark of the States Rights types, the KKK, the CIA or the Pentagon? In other words will "freedom" simply mean armed repression? What I am saying is this: our American ideals and principles can retain their credibility only insofar as they are capable of *radical adaptation* to this crisis, and *creative response* to a turbulent time that is heavy with unimagined possibilities both for growth and for pathological decay. Slogans are not enough. And slogans backed up with machine guns and napalm are not inspiring much real belief! They only consolidate hatred and determined opposition. "Freedom" cannot retain its meaning if it continues to be only freedom for some based on the violent repression of others.

3. Instead of merely reacting emotionally to the threat of violence and destruction, we need to understand the spiritual and psychological implications of the present crisis, first of all in the Negro in America and then in the colored races everywhere. The nonviolent movement in America worked (and doubtless continues to work) only for a few dedicated and trained specialists who really understood it and practiced it rightly. For the majority both of Negroes and of whites, its message has never been really clear. For the American Negro, in an intense identity crisis, feeling himself a morally mutilated non-person reduced to playing a role determined entirely for him by someone else, nonviolence was not yet practicable. Only for exceptionally mature and spiritually gifted people (of whom there are perhaps still many) was it really meaningful. For the penniless and hopeless Negro who stood aside and viewed it from afar, nonviolence simply reinforced the feelings of hopeless passivity and despair which were his. On the other hand, an appeal to violence, an assurance that he could burn houses and loot stores with relative impunity, proved an outlet to explosive suppressed hate—more satisfying to him than just being beaten over

the head for the ten thousandth time by a Southern cop, without recourse to anyone on this earth.

It is pointless to say that the laws guarantee the Negro all the same rights as white people. We know that the laws are not enforced and the Negro is often denied his obvious rights; but also economically speaking the Negro remains in the same position as he was before, perhaps worse. He is convinced that there is no real place for him in our established society except the very secondary place which we will give him. It is a psychological impossibility for most white Americans really to accept a Negro as an equal, in every respect, and the violent struggle against open housing has proved it. This incidentally is one of the reasons why Negroes have finally resorted to a war on white property which may eventually attain very serious proportions (sabotage of central power plants or of water supply). In short: the Negro considers that it is impossible for him really to acquire a place as an equal in this society of ours. Such being the case he will do the best he can to louse things up and make them unpleasant for whitey. It is perhaps not a rational or virtuous decision in terms of our own very nice ethic, but he is no longer interested in our own very nice ethic. We must not be too surprised if he fails to respond to our exhortations in this regard—especially when they emanate from the Chief of Police.

4. The real problem as I see it is this: the limited and distorted view which almost inevitably dictates a white reaction of violence. Now that the Negro in America has clearly and articulately declared war on white property and white power—if not already on the white man as such—the reaction of the whites is easily predictable. I already pointed to it four years ago. A violent clamp-down, ruthless retaliation both organized and non-organized, official and unofficial. An all-out indiscriminate effort to put down the Negro at any cost. Let us be quite clear about it: the Negro himself seems to be provoking this kind of reaction. He seems to *want* this kind of reaction. The seriousness of this possibility of violence arises not from a logical sequence of political and economic causes, but from pathological involvement in violence on both sides, white and Negro.

The problem as I see it is no longer merely political or economic or legal or what have you (it was never merely that). It is a spiritual and psychological problem of a society which has developed too fast and too far for the psychic capacities of its members, who can no longer cope with their inner hostilities and destructiveness. They can no longer really manage their lives in a fully reasonable and human way—

only by resort to extreme and possibly destructive maneuvers. A nuclear arms race. A race to get on the moon. A stupid war in Asia that cannot be won by either side. An affluent economy depending on built-in obsolescence and the ever increasing consumption of more goodies than anyone can comfortably consume. A bored, ambivalent over-stimulation of violence and sex. We are living in a society which for all its unquestionable advantages and all its fantastic ingenuity just does not seem to be able to provide people with lives that are fully human and fully real.

There are wonderful people in it, and it is a marvel we are not ten times crazier than we already are, but we have to face the fact that we live in a pretty sick culture. Now if in this sick society, where there are a lot of very scared, very upset, very unrealistic people who feel themselves more and more violently threatened, everyone starts buying guns and preparing to shoot each other up (remember the fuss about the gun in the fallout shelter in 1962), we are going to have an unparalleled mess. The result may eventually be that people will decide that the only way to maintain some semblance of order will be the creation of a semifascist state with storm troopers and, yes, concentration camps. And many will be quite ready to accept it if the Negroes continue to make them ready.

To sum it up: the problem as I see it is this: The Negro has in some sense abandoned the struggle for Civil Rights. He has given up Christian nonviolence as futile idealism. He has decided that whitey only understands one kind of language: violence. The Negro has concluded that if whitey wants to terrorize Vietnamese with napalm and other cozy instruments of war, he should have a little taste of what fire and terror feel like at home. So in effect the Negro is declaring guerrilla war on white society. "The Negro" I say, meaning those who have decided to take upon themselves the mandate to represent black men by acting in their name. Obviously, the majority of Negroes would still prefer to go on as best they can and at least have relatively peaceful, relatively livable lives. These moderate Negroes will perhaps have the worst time of all, caught in between two violent groups of extremists and becoming the victims of everybody. They will be tempted to become extremists themselves. Their choice is limited. They cannot join the KKK.

Now the Negro knows, or should know, that he cannot really win this kind of civil war. But he can become so provocative as to dislocate this highly organized technological system of ours. If President Johnson continues trying to pull the country together by getting it more and more involved in fighting an outside enemy (Asians) and if the country gets mixed up in a war with China, and if the Negro then decides it is a good time to shake the foundations here at home . . . I need not elaborate on the picture. It could be catastrophic. But in any event, there is nothing in sight but the violence of desperation *unless* it turns out that the SNCC people are smart enough to really gain some kind of political power for the Negro and get him really implicated in the affairs of the nation. Maybe. I would not gamble on it myself. The forces involved are too unpredictable, and far too explosive.

A victorious Negro revolution is out of the question unless the country is crippled by some disaster (such as nuclear war or catastrophic collapse of the economy). The most likely thing is that extreme provocation by irrational violence may create such disorder and such panic in the country that a new order based on force (a police state) may have to be established. In that event, the possibility of extremists on the white side taking over and ruling by irrational and arbitrary violence is very likely. Even "prison camps" for Negroes and then for other unacceptables are not beyond the bounds of possibility. At times one feels that the Negroes are unconsciously willing to provoke this.

Much as we may all sympathize with the frustrations of the Negro, and much as we may tolerantly understand his drive for a new sense of identity by means of aggressive and separatist assertion, we cannot get around the fact that this is simply another form of the same racist delusion that keeps cropping up everywhere in different forms. The trouble with delusionary thinking is that, starting perhaps from a basis of reality (or even from no real basis whatever!), it proceeds to exempt emotion and violence from all reasonable control. It creates a sense of transcendent justification, of absolute validity, a seemingly plausible claim to be beyond good and evil, in an area where anything goes. The result is an explosion of emotion, an orgiastic climax of hate which carries everything before it until its power is spent. We have seen this at work in Nazism—its extreme manifestation, backed by all the instruments of political and military power. We have seen it in Russian anti-semitism, in French hatred of Algerians, in Arab hatred of Jews, in conflict between Hindu and Moslem, between Sudanese Moslems and Black Africans. We see it in South African apartheid and in American segregationism.

The new segregationism now preached by the Black Power movement is unfortunately no improvement. It is little more than desperation, which substitutes the emotional orgy for a hopeless and frustrated effort to achieve anything by ordinary political means. The only thing that can be said for it at the moment is that it is probably not yet as general as it seems. It is taken with full seriousness by a minority of Negro extremists. It is still taken, I think, with a grain of salt by the majority of American Negroes who know it won't work but who are perhaps secretly hopeful that it will stir things up enough to influence the whites more forcefully than anything that has so far happened. In my opinion, the real aim of the Black Power people is still probably to use the noise about separation as a threat rather than as a serious political policy. On the other hand, we are in a climate of dangerous mental contagion in which there is no guarantee that anyone will continue to act reasonably once an emotional chain reaction gets going. In a situation like this, the delusions on both sides reinforce and aggravate each other, and there is enough emotional violence packed into America today to blow the whole place sky high, no matter how reasonable some of us may still hope to be.

One of our own tasks (and perhaps now it is too late to tackle it effectively) is the serious examination of the delusions behind our own thinking. For instance: what about the contradiction implied in our willingness to preserve the Union by a resort to violence that will inevitably destroy it? Or, alternately: what about the internal contradiction in our apparent willingness to preserve "freedom" by instituting a police state? This simply ties in with so many other contradictions: our determination to "liberate" South East Asians from Communism by burning them, if necessary, to death. Of course we'd much rather do it by giving them candy bars but, when the chips are down. . . . The big question to which all these others add up is: have our formulas about democracy finally become just that, empty formulas, and masks for delusionary thinking? If that is the case, then we had better get to grips with reality. The Negroes are trying to point to a redefinition of reality: they are saying that they find themselves in a society in which theoretically everything is fine for them and where in fact they have no hope of being fully accepted in every way as human beings on an equal basis with others. The affirmation of this has now become so strident and so harsh that, whether you agree or not, you are bound to listen. This does not make all the conclusions automatically right. On the contrary, the stridency and hate may simply be attempts to *enforce* impossible conclusions.

On the other hand, we have to recognize that a climate of irrationality and panic is just what the extremists of both sides thrive on. If everyone is kept in a state of fear and uncertainty, if tensions are maintained at a high pitch, then explosions and reprisals can be managed by those who think they will profit by them. The policy of the Black Power movement is twofold: to use this threat of revolutionary terror in order to give the Negro himself more confidence, and in order to get some kind of leverage with which to work on whitey. In other words, it is an attempt to consolidate all American Negroes into a bloc with unequivocal bargaining power. But this bid for power rests on the exploitation of free-floating and radically uncontrollable violence which may at any time get out of hand. If and when the violence becomes so widespread as to disrupt American society, there may be a real civil war, and the Black Power program takes this as a realistic, acceptable option.

Much as I hate to see such a situation arise, I still feel it is one to which the Negroes have been driven by us. I believe we still have to take this into account in our attempts to respond. I do not think any form of white extremism will be an adequate answer. And I do hope that we will keep our heads enough to prevent a complete polarization, a split which makes all reasonable communication between the races impossible. We must continue to treat our Negro friends as persons and as friends, not as members of a hostile and incomprehensible species, and it is to be hoped that they will do us the same honor. Above all, the Negro has a right to self-respect in his identity as a person of his race and we must continue to do all that we can to help him in this—as well as doing all we can to see that his human and civil rights are guaranteed him, even when he may seem to be acting in such a way as to forfeit them in the eyes of a truculent and critical white society.

As Christians, we must remember that in Christ there is no meaning to racial divisions. There is no white and black in Christ: but if Christianity is being discredited in the eyes of Negroes, that does not dispense us from our duty to be authentic Christians toward the Negro whether he likes us or not. It is not our job to convince him that Christianity is "true" or "genuine," but to live up to what we ourselves profess to believe, so that we may not be judged by God for a mere lip-service that has (as we now begin to realize too late) reached the proportions of worldwide scandal.

Appendix: The Question of Guilt

A number of readers of "Letters to a White Liberal" [See above #15] object to the idea that the racial conflict and its consequences are largely the "fault" of the white race, and that it is necessary to admit "guilt" in a certain sense, in order to deal with the problem. Of course the word "guilt" may be ambiguous here. At the same time, it is possible that these readers have an exclusively individualistic notion of responsibility. They do not feel they are "at fault" or responsible for a wrong except when they have made a deliberate personal choice of something they know to be out of line, and feel shame for having done so. They do not believe that they have made any such choice in regard to Negroes, and do not see how any responsibility attaches to them. They think they are not "unjust" to the Negro and that they owe him nothing. They are in fact free to sit back and condemn everything he does. The Negro is the one who is "wrong."

There is, however, such a thing as collective responsibility, and collective guilt. This is not quite the same as personal responsibility and personal guilt, because it does not usually follow from a direct fully conscious act of choice. Few of us have actively and consciously *chosen* to oppress and mistreat the Negro. But nevertheless we have all more or less acquiesced in and consented to a state of affairs in which the Negro is treated unjustly, and in which his unjust treatment is directly or indirectly to the advantage of people like ourselves, people with whom we agree and collaborate, people with whom we are in fact identified. So that even if in theory the white may believe himself to be well disposed toward the Negro—and never gets into a bind in which he proves himself to be otherwise—we all collectively contribute to a situation in which the Negro has to live and act as your inferior. I am personally convinced that most white people who think themselves very "fair" to the Negro show, by the way they imagine themselves "fair," that they consider the Negro an inferior type of human being, a sort of "minor," and their "fairness" consists in giving him certain benefits provided he "keeps in his place," the place they have allocated to him as an inferior. I would like to say that this state of mind is itself an act of inhumanity and injustice against the Negro and is in fact at the root of the trouble with the Negro, so that anyone who holds such opinions, even in the best of faith, is contributing actively to the violence of the present situation whether he realizes it or not. One of the reasons why the Negro has finally in desperation become so hostile and truculent toward whites is that he wants to bring this fact out into the open. He wants to push things to the point where no one can any longer pretend that by treating the Negro as a minor and a semi-savage he is being "just" and "fair." On the contrary, this kind of treatment is part of a whole subtle system of moral and psychological oppression which is essentially *violent*. Anyone who has such an attitude is then partly responsible for what is going on, and in that sense "guilty."

In the case of collective guilt like this, as also in other such cases (favoring an unjust war, participating in the economic oppression of colonials, and so forth), it is necessary for a man who wants to be in good faith to cease identifying himself with actions that are causing the evil in question, and to disclaim any intention of further participating in these acts, while also doing whatever he can to restore the balance of justice and of violated rights. The problem is of course that in deep and complex problems of this nature, the responsibility goes far into the area of the unconscious attitudes and prejudices we all have, and in that area we cannot control all our reactions at will. That is what makes the whole thing so terribly hard. But we must at least desire to have a lucid, honest and non-mythical view of the hard realities, in order to try to deal with them.

· 30 ·

WAR AND THE
CRISIS OF LANGUAGE

The draft of this article was written by Merton in 1968. It was
not published till after his death: in 1969 as an essay in *The
Critique of War: Contemporary Philosophical Explorations*, edited
by Robert Ginsberg (Chicago, Henry Regnery Company).

• • • • •

The Romans, to speak generally, rely on
force in all their enterprises and think it
incumbent upon them to carry out their projects
in spite of all, and that nothing is
impossible when they have once decided upon it.
Polybius

· I ·

Long before George Steiner pointed out that the German language
was one of the casualties of Naziism and World War II, Brice Parain
in France had studied the "word sickness" of 1940, the mortal illness
of journalese and political prose that accompanied the collapse of
France. In proportion as the country itself accepted the denatured
prose of Vichy—in which peace meant aggression and liberty meant
oppression—it lost its identity and its capacity for valid action. It
succumbed to "a full armed language without practical application."
This, Parain reflected, had already happened before, in World War I,
when words meant one thing in the trenches and another behind the
lines. (See Sartre's essay on Parain in *Situations I* [Paris, 1947], p. 192.)

The reflections that follow are random and spontaneous insights—
less of a philosopher than of a poet. For poets are perhaps the ones
who, at the present moment, are most sensitive to the sickness of
language—a sickness that, infecting all literature with nausea, prompts
us not so much to declare war on conventional language as simply to
pick up and examine intently a few chosen pieces of linguistic garbage.

But of course, one does not have to be endowed with a peculiar poetic sensibility, still less with political genius, to recognize that official statements made in Washington, about the Vietnam war, for instance, are symptoms of a national—indeed worldwide—illness. Nor is it very hard to see that race riots and assassinations are also symptoms of the same illness, while they are also (and this is more important) a kind of universal language. Perhaps one might better call them an anti-language, a concrete expression of something that is uttered in fire and bullets rather than in words. And this in itself expresses an acute awareness of the gap between words and actions that is characteristic of modern war, because it is also characteristic of political life in general.

The malaise is universal. There is no need to quote a Swedish poet to prove it. But these lines from Gunnar Ekelof may serve as an aperitif for what is to follow. He begins his poem "Sonata For Denatured Prose" in these words:

> crush the alphabet between your teeth yawn
> vowels, the fire is burning in hell vomit and
> spit now or never I and dizziness you or never
> dizziness now or never.
>
> crush the alphabet between your teeth yawn
> vowels, the fire is burning in hell vomit and
> spit now or never I and dizziness you or never
> dizziness now or never.
>
> we will begin over.
>
> crush the alphabet macadam and your teeth
> yawn vowels, the sweat runs in hell I am dying
> in the convolutions of my brain vomit now or
> never dizziness I and you . . .

(Gunnar Ekelof: *Late Arrival on Earth*, selected Poems, trans. Robert Bly & Christine Paulston [London: 1967],p. 63)

There is no need to complete the poem. It is an angry protest against contemporary, denatured language. Ironically, it declares that ordinary modes of communication have broken down into banality and deception. It suggests that violence has gradually come to take the place of other, more polite, communications. Where there is such a flood of words that all words are unsure, it becomes necessary to make one's meaning clear with blows; or at least one explores this as a valid possibility.

· II ·

Meanwhile, it is interesting to observe that religion too has reacted to the same spastic upheaval of language. I do not here refer to the phenomenon of a radical "God is Dead" theology—which in effect is our effort to reshape the language of religion in a last-minute attempt to save it from a plague of abstractness and formalism. This phenomenon is of course important. And so much has been said about it already—perhaps a great deal more than the subject deserves. I merely want to point out, in passing, that the fifties and sixties of our century have witnessed a curious revival of glossolalia—"speaking in tongues." Without attempting to evaluate this as charisma, I will at least say that it is significant in a context of religious and linguistic spasm. It is in its own way an expression of a curious kind of radicalism, a reaction to a religious language that is (perhaps obscurely) felt to be inadequate. But it is also, it seems to me, a reaction to something else. Glossolalia has flowered most abundantly in the United States, in fundamentalist and Pentecostal sects of white Protestants, and perhaps most often in the South about the time of the Freedom Rides and nonviolent civil rights demonstrations. (I do not have much information on what has taken place most recently.) This was also the time when the cold war was finally building up to the Cuba Crisis and the U.S. intervention in Vietnam was about to begin. Surely there is something interesting about this. At a time when the churches were at last becoming easily aware of a grave responsibility to *say something* about civil rights and nuclear war, the ones who could be least expected to be articulate on such subjects (and who often had solid dogmatic prejudices that foreclosed all discussion) began to cry out in unknown tongues.

At precisely the same moment, the Roman Catholic Church was abandoning its ancient liturgical language, the medieval Latin that was unknown to most of its members, and speaking out in a vernacular that many critics found disconcertingly banal and effete. If I refer to these things, it is not in scorn or in criticism. They are simply further expressions of a universal uneasiness about *language*—a sense of anxiety lest speech become entirely deceptive and unreal.

Can this apply to glossolalia? Of course. Fundamentalist religion assumes that the "unknown language" spoken "in the Spirit" is (though unintelligible) *more real* than the ordinary tired everyday language that everybody knows too well. Whether or not one believes that simple Texas housewives can burst out in the dialects of New Guinea head-hunters, under direct inspiration from God, there is here a significant implication that ordinary language is not good enough, and that there is something else which is at once more *real* and less comprehensible. Has ordinary language somehow failed?

I do not wish to hazard all sorts of incompetent guesses about something I have not studied and do not intend to study. But one thing is quite evident about this phenomenon. He who speaks in an unknown tongue can safely speak without fear of contradiction. His utterance is *definitive* in the sense that it forecloses all dialogue. As St. Paul complained, if you utter a blessing in a strange language the congregation cannot answer "Amen" because it does not know it has been blessed. Such utterance is so final that nothing whatever can be done about it (see I Corinthians 14). I wish to stress this unconscious aspiration to *definitive* utterance, to which there can be no rejoinder.

· III ·

Now let us turn elsewhere, to the language of advertisement, which at times approaches the mystic and charismatic heights of glossolalia. Here too, utterance is final. No doubt there are insinuations of dialogue, but really there is no dialogue with an advertisement, just as there was no dialogue between the sirens and the crews they lured to disaster on their rocks. There is nothing to do but be hypnotized and drown, unless you have somehow acquired a fortunate case of deafness. But who can guarantee that he is deaf enough? Meanwhile, it is the vocation of the poet—or anti-poet—*not* to be deaf to such things but to apply his ear intently to their corrupt charms. An example: a perfume advertisement from *The New Yorker* (September 17, 1966).

I present the poem as it appears on a full page, with a picture of a lady swooning with delight at her own smell—the smell of *Arpege*. (Note that the word properly signifies a sound—*arpeggio*. Aware that we are now smelling music, let us be on our guard!)

> For the love of Arpege . . .
> There's a new hair spray!
>   The world's most adored fragrance
> now in a hair spray. But not hair spray
> as you know it.

A delicate-as-air-spray
Your hair takes on a shimmer and sheen
that's wonderfully young.
You seem to spray new life and bounce
right into it. And a coif of Arpege has
one more thing no other hair spray has.
It has Arpege.

One look at this masterpiece and the anti-poet recognizes himself beaten hands down. This is beyond parody. It must stand inviolate in its own victorious rejection of meaning. We must avoid the temptation to dwell on details: interior rhyme, suggestions of an esoteric cult (the use of our product, besides making you young again, is also a kind of gnostic imitation), of magic (our product gives you a hat of smell—a "coif"—it clothes you in an aura of music-radiance perfume). What I want to point out is the logical *structure* of this sonata: it is a foolproof tautology, locked tight upon itself, impenetrable, unbreakable, irrefutable. It is endowed with a finality so inviolable that it is beyond debate and beyond reason. Faced with the declaration that "Arpege has Arpege," reason is reduced to silence (I almost said despair). Here again we have an example of speech that is at once totally trivial and totally definitive. It has nothing to do with anything real (although of course the sale of the product is a matter of considerable importance to the manufacturer), but what it says, it says with utter finality.

The unknown poet might protest that he (or she) was not concerned with truth alone but also with beauty—indeed with love. And obviously this too enters into the structure and substance (so to speak) of the text. Just as the argument takes the form of a completely self-enclosed tautological cliche, so the content, the "experience," is one of self-enclosed narcissism woven of misty confusion. It begins with the claim that a new hair spray exists solely for love of itself and yet also exists for love of *you*, baby, because you are somehow subtly identified with Arpege. This perfume is so magic that it not only makes you smell good, it "coifs" you with a new and unassailable identity: it is you who are unassailable because it is you who have somehow become a tautology. And indeed we are reminded that just as Arpege is—or has—Arpege, so, in the popular psychology of women's magazines, "you are eminently lovable because you are just *you*." When we reflect that the ultimate conceptions of theology and metaphysics have surfaced in such a context—hair spray—we no longer wonder that theologians are tearing their hair and crying that God is dead. After all, when every smell, every taste, every hissing breakfast food is endowed with the transcendental properties of being . . . But let us turn from art, religion, and love to something more serious and more central to the concerns of our time: war.

· IV ·

A classic example of the contamination of reason and speech by the inherent ambiguity of war is that of the U.S. major who, on February 7, 1968 shelled the South Vietnamese town of Bentre "regardless of civilian casualties . . . to rout the Vietcong." As he calmly explained, "It became necessary to destroy the town in order to save it." Here we see, again, an insatiable appetite for the tautological, the definitive, the *final*. It is the same kind of language and logic that Hitler used for his notorious "final solution." The symbol of this perfect finality is the circle. An argument turns upon itself, and the beginning and end get lost: it just goes round and round its own circumference. A message comes in that someone thinks there might be some Vietcong in a certain village. Planes are sent, the village is destroyed, many of the people are killed. The destruction of the village and the killing of the people earn for them a final and official identity. The burned huts become "enemy structures"; the dead men, women, and children become "Vietcong," thus adding to a "kill ratio" that can be interpreted as "favorable." They were thought to be Vietcong and were therefore destroyed. By being destroyed they became Vietcong for keeps; they entered "history," definitively as our enemies, because we wanted to be on the "safe side," and "save American lives"—as well as Vietnam.

The logic of "Red or dead" has long since urged us to identify destruction with rescue—to be "dead" is to be saved from being "Red." In the language of melodrama, our grandparents became accustomed to the idea of a "fate worse than death." A schematic morality concluded that if such and such is a fate worse than death, then to prefer it to death would surely be a heinous sin. The logic of war-makers has extended this not only to the preservation of one's own moral integrity but to the fate of others, even of people on the other side of the earth, whom we do not always bother to consult personally on the subject. We weigh the arguments that they are not able to understand (perhaps they have not even heard that arguments exist!) And we decide, in their place, that it is better for them to be dead—killed by us—than Red, living under our enemies.

The Asian whose future we are about to decide is either a bad guy or a good guy. If he is a bad guy, he obviously has to be killed. If he is a good guy, he is on our side and he ought to be ready to die for freedom. We will provide an opportunity for him to do so: we will kill him to prevent him falling under the tyranny of a demonic enemy. Thus we not only defend his interests together with our own, but we protect his virtue along with our own. Think what might happen if he fell under Communist rule *and liked it!*

The advantages of this kind of logic are no exclusive possession of the United States. This is purely and simply the logic shared by all war-makers. It is the logic of *power*. Possibly American generals are naive enough to push this logic, without realizing, to absurd conclusions. But all who love power tend to think in some such way. Remember Hitler weeping over the ruins of Warsaw after it had been demolished by the Luftwaffe: "How wicked these people must have been," he sobbed, "to make me do this to them!"

Words like "pacification" and "liberation" have acquired sinister connotations as war has succeeded war. Vietnam has done much to refine and perfect these notions. A "free zone" is now one in which anything that moves is assumed to be "enemy" and can be shot. In order to create a "free zone" that can live up effectively to its name, one must level everything, buildings, vegetation, everything so that one can clearly see anything that moves, and shoot it. This has very interesting semantic consequences.

> An American Captain accounts for the leveling of a new "free zone" in the following terms: "We want to prevent them from moving freely in this area . . . From now on anything that moves around here is going to be automatically considered V.C. and bombed or fired on. The whole triangle is going to become a Free Zone. These villagers here are all considered hostile civilians."
>
> How did the Captain solve the semantic problem of distinguishing the hostile civilian from the refugee? "In a V.C. area like this there are three categories. First there are the straight V.C. . . . Then there are the V.C. sympathizers. Then there's the . . . There's a third category . . . I can't think of the third just now but . . . there's no middle road in this war." (See Jonathan Schell in *The New Yorker* [July 15, 1967], p. 59.)

"Pacification" or "winning the hearts" of the undecided is thus very much simplified. "Soon" says a news report, (*The New York Times,*

January 11, 1967) "the government will have no need to win the hearts and minds of Bensuc. There will be no Bensuc." But there are further simplifications. A high-ranking U.S. Field commander is quoted as saying: "If the people are to the guerrillas as oceans are to the fish . . . we are going to dry up that ocean." (Quoted in the *New Statesman* [March 11, 1966]). Merely by existing, a civilian in this context becomes a "hostile civilian." But at the same time and by the same token he is our friend and our ally. What simpler way out of the dilemma than to destroy him to "save American lives"?

· V ·

So much for the practical language of the battlefield. Let us now attend to the much more pompous and sinister jargon of the war mandarins in government offices and military think-tanks. Here we have a whole community of intellectuals, scholars who spend their time playing out "scenarios" and considering "acceptable levels" in megadeaths. Their language and their thought are as esoteric, as self-enclosed, as tautologous as the advertisement we have just discussed. But instead of being "coiffed" in a sweet smell, they are scientifically antiseptic, businesslike, uncontaminated with sentimental concern for life—other than their own. It is the same basic narcissism, but in a masculine, that is managerial, mode. One proves one's realism along with one's virility by toughness in playing statistically with global death. It is this playing with death, however, that brings into the players' language itself the corruption of death: not physical but mental and moral extinction. And the corruption spreads from their talk, their thinking, to the words and minds of everybody. What happens then is that the political and moral values they claim to be defending are destroyed by the *contempt* that is more and more evident in the language in which they talk about such things. Technological strategy becomes an end in itself and leads the fascinated players into a maze where finally the very purpose strategy was supposed to serve is itself destroyed. The ambiguity of official war talk has one purpose above all: to mask this ultimate unreason and permit the game to go on.

Of special importance is the *style* of these nuclear mandarins. The technological puckishness of Herman Kahn is perhaps the classic of this genre. He excels in the sly understatement of the inhuman, the apocalyptic, enormity. His style is esoteric, allusive, yet confidential. The reader has the sense of being a privileged eavesdropper in the councils of the mighty. He knows enough to realize that things are going to happen about which he can do nothing, though perhaps he can save his skin in a properly equipped shelter where he may consider at leisure the rationality of survival in an unlivable world. Meanwhile, the cool tone of the author and the reassuring solemnity of his jargon seem to suggest that those in power, those who turn loose these instruments of destruction, have no intention of perishing themselves, that consequently survival must have a point. The point is not revealed, except that nuclear war is somehow implied to be good business. Nor are H-bombs necessarily a sign of cruel intentions. They enable one to enter into communication with the high priests in the enemy camp. They permit the decision-makers on both sides to engage in a ritual "test of nerves." In any case, the language of escalation is the language of naked power, a language that is all the more persuasive because it is proud of being ethically illiterate and because it accepts, as realistic, the basic irrationality of its own tactics. The language of escalation, in its superb mixture of banality and apocalypse, science and unreason, is the expression of a massive death wish. We can only hope that this death wish is only that of a decaying Western civilization, and that it is not common to the entire race. Yet the language itself is given universal currency by the mass media. It can quickly contaminate the thinking of everybody.

· VI ·

Sartre speaks of the peculiar, expert negligence of the language used by European mandarins (bankers, politicians, prelates), the "indolent and consummate art" they have of communicating with one another in double-talk that leaves them always able to escape while their subordinates are firmly caught. (Op. cit., p. 202.) On others, ambiguous directives are imposed with full authority. For others, these are final and inescapable. The purpose of the language game is then to maintain a certain balance of ambiguity and of authority so that the subject is caught and the official is not. Thus the subject can always be proved wrong and the official is always right. The official is enabled to lie in such a way that if the lie is discovered, a subordinate takes the blame. So much for European democracy. The same has been true in America in a somewhat different context—that of wheeler-dealing and political corruption rather than the framework of authoritarian and official privilege. But power in America, we find, can become mean, belligerent, temperamental. American power, while paying due respect to the demands of plain egalitarian folksiness, has its moments of arbitrary bad humor. But lest this bad humor become too evident, and lest repression begin to seem too forceful, language is at hand as an instrument of manipulation. Once again, the use of language to extol freedom, democracy, and equal rights, while at the same time denying them, causes words to turn sour and to rot in the minds of those who use them. In such a context, the effort of someone such as Lenny Bruce to restore to language some of its authentic impact was a service despairingly offered to a public that could not fully appreciate it. One might argue that the language of this disconcerting and perhaps prophetic comedian was often less obscene than the "decent" but horrifying platitudes of those who persecuted him.

· VII ·

Michel Foucault has described the evolution of the dialogue between medicine and madness in the Age of Reason. (Michel Foucault, *Madness and Civilization* [New York: 1967], p. 188.) Therapeutic experiments with manic-depressives in the eighteenth century assumed a certain inner consistency in the delirium of the mad and, working within the suppressed framework of this consistency, sought to suggest to the madman an alternative to his madness—or, rather, to push the "logic" of his madness to a paroxysm and crisis in which it would be confronted with itself and "forced to argue against the demands of its own truth." Thus, for instance, in cases of religious mania and despair, patients who believed themselves damned were shown a theatrical tableau in which the avenging angel appeared, punished, and then gave assurance that guilt was now taken away. Patients who were dying of starvation because, believing themselves dead, they would not eat, were shown representations of dead persons eating and were thus brought face to face with an unexpected syllogism: you claim you are dead and cannot eat, but dead men can eat . . . The beauty of Foucault's book is that we become fascinated by the way in which the "reason" of the Age of Enlightenment unconsciously shared so much of the madness with which it was in dialogue.

Reading of this dialogue between reason and madness, one is reminded of the language of power and war. In the deliberate, realistic madness of the new language we find an implicit admission that words, ordinary discourse, won't do—not exactly that language itself has broken down, is no longer valid as such. But the enemy is at once so perverse and so irrational—such a psychopathic liar in fact—that he has to be cleverly treated as a beast or as a manic. We all know that it is customary for one who resorts to violence to do so on the ground that the adversary "does not understand anything else." The "language of escalation" is a more sophisticated application of this principle, but on a massive scale implemented by the threat of a nuclear strike. It seems, indeed, that since the adversary understands nothing but force, and since force means everything up to and including the use of H-bombs, we will eventually get beyond the mere threat of a nuclear strike: one of us will actually strike. This will demonstrate that if you face an enemy with the conviction that he understands nothing but force, you will yourself necessarily behave as if you understood nothing but force. And in fact it is highly probably that if you say he understands nothing but force, it is because you yourself are already in the same plight.

In any case, it is quite obvious that the military on whatever side must be quite convinced of the superior efficacy of force, or they would not be military. If they worry about this at all, they can always reason that force is necessary because we are faced by various bunches of madmen who understand nothing else. The dialogue then proceeds in a way that reminds us of Foucault:

1. Rational discourse with the enemy is useless. He does not understand rational discourse and makes negotiation an opportunity for lying and pathological trickery. He *has* to cheat.

2. Therefore he has to be dealt with solely in the framework of his madness and wickedness, his propensity to lie and cheat. One does not bargain with such a one, because bargaining implies the acceptance, on both sides, of conditions. He must be pushed to the point where his surrender is unconditional in terms of his own madness. To grant him reasonable conditions would be to treat a madman as a rational being, which would be the worst possible kind of mistake and indeed (if you believe in sin) a sin.

3. His madness has roots in guilt, because he is, after all, wicked. He understands *punishment*. But the punishment must be shown to him in terms of his own madness. He must see that his own destructive violence will lead inexorably to one consequence: his own annihilation. But to translate this into words would lead to confusion. The message must be got to him in the unmistakable language of force itself. Of course, verbal formulas have to be restored too, in order to define what force is all about, to set conditions, etc. But the verbal formulas must be kept deliberately ambiguous, unclear. The clear and unmistakable message is not that of the *terms offered* but of the escalation itself.

In other words there is an *appearance* of dialogue on the verbal and political level. But the real dialogue is with weapons and may be a complete contradiction of what appears to be said in the prose of politics.

The effect of this, of course, is a vicious circle: it begins with a tacit admission that negotiation is meaningless, and it does in fact render the language of negotiation meaningless. War-makers in the twentieth century have gone far toward creating a political language so obscure, so apt for treachery, so ambiguous, that it can no longer serve as an instrument for peace: it is good only for war. But why? Because the language of the war-maker is *self-enclosed in finality.* It does not invite reasonable dialogue, it uses language to silence dialogue, to block communication, so that instead of words the two sides may trade divisions, positions, villages, air bases, cities—and of course the lives of the people in them. The daily toll of the killed (or the "kill ratio") is perfunctorily scrutinized and decoded And the totals are expertly managed by "ministers of truth" so that the newspaper reader may get the right message.

Our side is always ahead. He who is winning must be the one who is right. But we are right, therefore we must be winning. Once again we have the beautiful, narcissistic tautology of war—or of advertising. Once again, "Arpege has Arpege." There is no communicating with anyone else, because anyone who does not agree, who is outside the charmed circle, is wrong, is evil, is already in hell.

· VIII ·

It is a dictum of Marxism that a word is true if it can be verified by being carried out in action. But this idea is not a monopoly of the Communists. It is now universal. It is everybody's property. Modern politics is a matter of defining how you think things ought to be and then making them come out that way by cunning or by force. If you aren't strong enough or smart enough to verify your ideas by putting them into effect, then you have no business saying how things should be in the first place: follow somebody else who has the necessary power! The strange thing is that this idea is not so modern after all. In fact it is quite ancient. Another word for it is magic, or witchcraft.

Of course, the shaman and the medicine man in primitive society did not possess the advantages of a technological skill that would enable them to say that white was black and then prove the point by turning white into black. Yet even unlimited power does not always succeed in making one's own words come true—as the Vietnam war has conclusively shown.

One of the most curious things about the war in Vietnam is that it is being *fought to vindicate the assumptions upon which it is being fought.* Now it turns out that these American assumptions are quite wrong: the White House and the Pentagon have consistently interpreted the war as a military invasion of South Vietnam by the North. In other words it is the Korean War over again, a "conventional limited war" in which the problems are above all military and can be handled in terms of bombing, sending in more troops, wiping out ares in which the enemy tends to concentrate, cutting supply lines, etc. By the escalation of the war and the bombing of North Vietnam (after the "Tonkin Bay Incident," which has now been shown to have been exaggerated if not actually faked) the United States did actually turn the war into the kind of war it was supposed to be in America—apart from the fact that the aggression was the other way around. But this did nothing to alter the fact that the war in the South remained essentially a revolutionary guerrilla struggle that could not be adequately handled by conventional military operations.

Alastair Buchan, analyzing this curious fact in *Encounter* (January–February, 1968), wonders how it was possible for such a policy to be accepted when the U.S. government relies on "a wide range of research institutes and universities to give greater depth and accuracy to its own operational and political analysis." He hazards a guess that the unassailable self-confidence of science somehow contributed to the error: "Probably technology (helicopters, new small arms, infra-red sensors and all the rest) with the element that corrupted judgment, making it seem possible that the Americans could do what the natives (i.e. the French) could not." In other words, there is a certain hubris built into technological thinking that encloses it within itself and its own suppositions and makes it fatal to ignore decisive realities that do not fit those suppositions.

However, in such a situation, power can still vindicate itself by *declaring* that its estimate was the correct one and that it is still winning. Since statistics can be made to prove anything, it adduces statistics to show that its words are in fact coming true. Unfortunately, the Tet offensive of the Vietcong in 1968 made it finally clear that no amount of juggling with words or figures could make this "politics of inadvertence" (the words of Arthur Schlesinger's) come out level with reality.

Lyndon Johnson is certainly well versed in all the appropriate skills, and yet in this instance he turned out to be a singularly failed witch.

What needs to be noted is that the massive effort of the United States to gain acceptance for its own version of the Vietnam war by doing all in its power to turn that version into accomplished fact has had profoundly significant effects. And these effects are not what was intended. Confidence in the Washington government, in the American political system, in the credibility of American officials, even in the basic human integrity and sincerity of the American Establishment is now seriously undermined at home and abroad. The *political language* of the United States, which was suspect before, has now been fatally denatured. It has probably lost all its value as intellectual currency. The crisis of the dollar is intimately connected with the crisis of human communication that has resulted from the sinister double-talk of the American Establishment about itself, about the war, about the race situation, about the urgent domestic problems that are being ignored or set aside while the government puts more and more money and manpower into the war. The tragedy is not so much that America has come out of its pristine isolationism but that it has decided to rule the world without paying serious attention to anybody else's view of what the world is all about. Language has been distorted and denatured in defense of this solipsistic, this basically isolationist and sometimes even paranoid, attitude.

· IX ·

What next? The illness of political language—which is almost universal and is a symptom of a Plague of Power that is common to China and America, Russia and Western Europe—is characterized everywhere by the same sort of double-talk, tautology, ambiguous cliche, self-righteous and doctrinaire pomposity, and pseudoscientific jargon that mask a total callousness and moral insensitivity, indeed a basic contempt for man. The self-enclosed finality that bars all open dialogue and pretends to impose absolute conditions of one's own choosing upon everybody else ultimately becomes the language of totalist dictatorship, if it is not so already. Revolt against this is taking the form of another, more elemental and anarchistic, kind of violence, together with a different semantic code. Space does not permit us to study this other language, but it must be acknowledged as immensely popular and influential all over the world. It is the language of Che Guevara, of Regis Debray, of Frantz Fanon: the violent language and the apocalyptic myth of the guerrilla warrior, the isolated individual and the small group, enabled by revolutionary charisma to defy all the technological might of the biggest powers in the world. In spite of the failure of Che in Bolivia—a failure that only resulted in his canonization as a martyr of the post-colonial revolution—the Vietnam war has had the result of awakening revolutionary hopes all over the world, from Harlem to Angola. Che Guevara called for Vietnams everywhere, and the Black Power movement, introducing the language of Fanon into American political life, is set on making the inner cities of the United States "other Vietnams." At the moment, when the full tragedy has not yet manifested itself, this might to some seem an inspiring revolt against the inhuman pride of technological white power. But all the hopes of Fanon—which may have some basis in the jungles of Africa—are couched in the same terms of magic and witchcraft that assert something and then proceed to make it so in fact, thereby vindicating their own prophecy. If this went wrong for U.S. power in Vietnam, it may also go wrong in the American ghettos, where, unfortunately, the Negro does not have miles of swamp and jungle to maneuver in but is enclosed in a small and highly vulnerable area in which he can easily be destroyed or arrested and taken off to concentration camps.

However that may be, the revolutionary tactic that tends to harass and immobilize the Goliath of technological military power and bring it down largely by its own elephantine weight has at the same time created a new language that mocks the ponderous and self-important utterances of the Establishment. This new language, racy, insolent, direct, profane, iconoclastic, and earthy, may have its own magic incantation myth. It may be involved in its own elaborate set of illusions. But at least it represents a healthier and more concrete style of thought. It does not reduce everything to abstractions, and though it is fully as intransigent as the language of the Establishment, it still seems to be more in contact with relevant experience: the hard realities of poverty, brutality, vice, and resistance.

Yet, flexible though it might be in some respects, it remains another language of power, therefore of self-enclosed finality, which rejects dialogue and negotiation on the axiomatic supposition that the adversary is a devil with whom no dialogue is possible.

· 31 ·

THE VIETNAM WAR:
An Overwhelming Atrocity

Published in The Catholic Worker, *March 1968*

"No country may unjustly oppress others or unduly
meddle in their affairs."
(Pacem in Terris, n. 120)

"As men in their private enterprises cannot pursue
their own interests to the detriment of others,
so too states cannot lawfully seek the development
of their own resources which brings harm to other
states and unjustly oppresses them."
(Pacem in Terris, n. 92)

In 1967 several young members of the International Volunteer Service
in Vietnam resigned and returned to America, in protest against the
way the war was, in their opinion, needlessly and hopelessly ravaging
the country.

The International Volunteer Service is a nonprofit organization
meant to help American youth to contribute to international goodwill
by person-to-person contacts and service programs in other countries.
Ambassador Lodge had called it "one of the success stories of American assistance," and obviously the men serving in Vietnam were in
very close touch with the people, knew the language, and were perhaps
better able to judge the state of affairs than most other Americans. As
they said, they "dealt with people, not statistics," and they were in a
position to know that the story of the Vietnam war is a very different
one when it is learned from women and children whose flesh has been
burned by napalm than it is when those same women and children
appear in statistics as "enemy" casualties.

At this point, in case the reader is not fully aware of what napalm is, we might quote from a report of four American physicians on "Medical Problems of South Vietnam":

Napalm is a highly sticky inflammable jelly which clings to anything it touches and burns with such heat that all oxygen in the area is exhausted within moments. Death is either by roasting or suffocation. Napalm wounds are often fatal (estimates are 90%). Those who survive face a living death. The victims are frequently children.

Another American physician wrote (Dr. R. E. Perry, *Redbook*, January 1967):

I have been an orthopedic surgeon for a good number of years with rather a wide range of medical experience. But nothing could have prepared me for my encounters with Vietnamese women and children burned by napalm. It was shocking and sickening even for a physician to see and smell the blackened and burned flesh.

By their resignation and by the statement they issued in an open letter to President Johnson, these men attempted to get through to the American public with a true idea of what the war really means to the Vietnamese—our allies, the ones we are supposedly "saving" from Communism. The attitude and feelings of the Vietnamese *people* (as distinct from the government) are too little known in the United States. They have been systematically ignored. Pictures of GI's bestowing candy bars upon half-naked "native" children are supposed to give us all the information we need in this regard. These are happy people who love our boys because we are saving them from the Reds and teaching them "democracy." It is of course important, psychologically and politically, for the public to believe this because otherwise the war itself would be questioned, and as a matter of fact it is questioned. Never was there a war in American history that was so much questioned! The official claim that such questioning is "betrayal" is a transparently gross and authoritarian attack on democratic liberty.

According to these Americans in the International Volunteer Service, men who cannot be considered leftists, still less as traitors, the American policy of victory at any price is simply destroying Vietnam. It is quite possible that the United States may eventually "win," but the price may be so high that there will be few left around to enjoy the fruits of victory and democracy in a country which we will, of course, obligingly reconstruct according to ideas of our own.

The people of South Vietnam have already had some experience of this kind of resettlement and reconstruction. Having seen their own homes burned or bulldozed out of existence, their fields and crops blasted with defoliants and herbicides, their livelihood and culture destroyed, they have been forcibly transplanted into places where they cannot live as they would like or as they know how, and forced into a society where, to adapt and be "at home" one has to be a hustler, a prostitute, or some kind of operator who knows how to get where the dollars are.

The people we are "liberating" in Vietnam are caught between two different kinds of terrorism, and the future presents them with nothing but a more and more bleak and hopeless prospect of unnatural and alienated existence. From their point of view, it doesn't matter much who wins. Either way it is going to be awful: but at least if the war can stop before everything is destroyed, and if they can somehow manage their own destiny, they will settle for that.

This, however, does not fit in with our ideas. We intend to go on bombing, burning, killing, bulldozing and moving people around while the numbers of plague victims begin to mount sharply and while the "civilization" we have brought becomes more and more rotten. The people of South Vietnam believe that we are supporting a government of wealthy parasites they do not and cannot trust. They believe that the 1967 election was rigged, and they know that the two newspapers which protested about it were immediately silenced and closed down by the "democratic" government which we are supporting at such cost.

To put it plainly, according to the men who resigned from the International Volunteer Service, the people of South Vietnam are hardly grateful for "democracy" on such terms, and while they are quite willing to accept our dollars when they have a chance, they do not respect us or trust us. In point of fact, they have begun to hate us.

Far from weakening Communism in Asia by our war policy, we are only strengthening it. The Vietnamese are no lovers of China, but by the ruthlessness of our war for "total victory" we are driving them into the arms of the Red Chinese. "The war as it is now being waged," say the Volunteers, "is self-defeating." They support their contentions by quoting people they have known in Vietnam.

A youth leader: "When the Americans learn to respect the true aspirations in Vietnam, true nationalism will come to power. Only true nationalists can bring peace to the South, talk to the North and bring unification."

While a Catholic bishop in the United States was soothing President Johnson with the assurance the war in Vietnam is "a sad and heavy obligation imposed by the mandate of love," a Buddhist nun said in Vietnam: "You Americans come to help the Vietnamese people, but have brought only death and destruction. Most of us Vietnamese hate from the bottom of our hearts the Americans who have brought the suffering of this war . . ." After which she burned herself to death. That, too, was a drastic act of violence. Whether or not we may agree with it, we must admit that it lends a certain air of seriousness to her denunciation! Unfortunately, such seriousness does not seem to get through to those Americans who most need to hear and understand it.

Meanwhile Billy Graham declared that the war in Vietnam was a "spiritual war between good and evil." A plausible statement, certainly, but not in the way in which he meant it. At the same time a Saigon Catholic leader gave another view of the picture: "We are caught in struggle between two power blocs . . . Many people told me you cannot trust Americans, but I never accepted it. Now I am beginning to believe it. You come to help my people, but they will hate you for it."

The tragic thing about Vietnam is that, after all, the "realism" of our program there is so unrealistic, so rooted in myth, so completely out of touch with the needs of the people whom we know only as statistics and to whom we never manage to listen, except where they fit in with our psychopathic delusions. Our external violence in Vietnam is rooted in an inner violence which simply ignores the human reality of those we claim to be helping. The result of this at home has been an ever-mounting desperation on the part of those who see the uselessness and inhumanity of the war, together with an increasing stubbornness and truculence on the part of those who insist they want to win, regardless of what victory may mean.

What will the situation be when this book appears in print? Will the 1968 presidential election force the issue one way or another? Will the candidates *have* to make sense out of this in spite of everything? We are getting to the point where American "victory" in Vietnam is becoming a word without any possible human meaning. What matters is the ability and willingness to arrive at some kind of workable solution that will save the identity of the nation that still wants to survive in spite of us, in spite of Communism, in spite of the international balance of power. This cannot be arrived at unless the United States is willing to deescalate, stop bombing the North, stop destroying crops, and recognize the NLF as among those with whom we have to deal if we want to make peace. Obviously a perfect solution is impossible but some solution can be realized and lives can be saved.

It is still possible to learn something from Vietnam: and above all we should recognize that the United States has received from no one the mission to police every country in the world or to decide for them how they are to live. No single nation has the right to try to run the world according to its own ideas. One thing is certain, the Vietnam war is a tragic error and, in the words of the resigned volunteers, "an overwhelming atrocity."

How do we explain such atrocities? Obviously, they are well-meant and the Americans who support the war are, for the most part, convinced that it is an inescapable moral necessity. Why? For one thing, as the more sophisticated reader is well aware, the picture of the war given by the mass media and the official version of what is happening are both extremely one-sided and oversimplified, to say the least. Some claim that the public has been deliberately misinformed. In any case, Americans do not seem to realize what effect the war is really having. The hatred of America which it is causing everywhere (analogous to the hatred of Russia after the violent suppression of the Hungarian revolt in 1956) is not just the result of Red propaganda. On the contrary, the Communists could never do such a fine job of blackening us as we are doing all by ourselves.

There is another, deeper source of delusion in the popular mythology of our time. One example of this popular mythology is examined in the first chapter of this section. It is the myth that all biological species in their struggle for survival must follow a law of aggression in which the stronger earns the right to exist by violently exterminating all his competitors. This pseudoscientific myth is simply another version of the cliche that "might makes right" and of course it was explicitly used and developed by the ideologists of Nazism. This canonization of violence by pseudoscience has come to be so much taken for granted, that when Konrad Lorenz in his carefully thought out study *On Aggression* sought to qualify it in very important ways, his book has simply been lumped with others, like Mr. Ardrey's, as one more rationalization of the aggression theory. Thus in *The New York Times Book Review* (Christmas issue, 67) the paperback edition of *On Aggression* is summarized with approval in this one line: "Like all other animals man is instinctively aggressive." True, of course, up to a point. But this contains the same implicit false conclusion ("therefore he *has* to beat up and destroy members of his own kind") and explicitly ignores the real point of Lorenz's book. The point is that man is the *only species*, besides the rat, who wantonly and cruelly turns on his own kind in *unprovoked* and murderous hostility. Man is the only one who deliberately seeks to *destroy* his own kind (as opposed to merely resisting encroachment).

To quote a prominent Dutch psychoanalyst who, among other things, has studied the mentality of Nazi war criminals:

> What we usually call hatred or hostility is different from normal self-assertive aggression. The former are hypercharged fantasy products, mixed with reactions to frustrations. They form an aura of intense anticipation of revenge and greater discharge in the future . . . This finds its most paradoxical action in the hatred of those who want to break out into history. They destroy because they want to be remembered. NO OTHER ANIMAL AVAILS HIMSELF OF PLANS FOR MOBILIZATION AND FUTURE ATTACK. However, man gets caught in his own trap, and what he once dreamed up in a fatal hour takes possession of him so that he is finally compelled to act it out.

(I am grateful to my friend Dr. Joost A. M. Meerloo for permission to quote from his unpublished manuscript of the English version of *Homo Militans.*)

Now this develops the point made by Lorenz in *On Aggression.* Lorenz *distinguishes* the destructive hostility of men and of rats from the natural self-assertive aggression common to all species, and indicates that far from pointing to the "survival of the fittest" this drive toward intraspecific aggression may perhaps lead to the self-destruction of the human race. That is the thesis developed in detail by Dr. Meerloo. Mr. Ardrey's book, like so much other popular mythology on the subject, serves to contribute to those "hypercharged fantasies" by which modern man at once excuses and foments his inner hostilities until he is compelled to discharge them, as we are now doing, with immense cost for innocent and harmless people on the other side of the globe.

(I have examined elsewhere the psychological connection between the Indian wars of extermination in the last century, and the Vietnam war. See: "Ishi: A Meditation," in the *Catholic Worker,* March 1967.)

It is because of these obsessions and fantasies that we continue to draft our young men into the army when in fact a professional army of enlisted men would suffice, along with our fabulous nuclear arsenal, to meet any conceivable need for national defense. The Vietnam war has called the legality and justice of the draft law into question, and rightly. Our young men feel that they are simply being imposed upon and that their lives are being stupidly sacrificed, not to defend the country but to act out the manias of politicians and manufacturers who think they have a mission to police the world and run the affairs of smaller countries in the interests of American business. The draft law ought to be abolished. That would somewhat lessen the temptation to get involved in any more "overwhelming atrocities" like the one in Vietnam.

· 32 ·

NOTE FOR *AVE MARIA*

| This "Note," published in *Ave Maria* magazine in the issue of September 7, 1968, bore the original title: "Non-Violence Does Not . . . Cannot . . . Mean Passivity."

· · · · ·

There seems to be a general impression that nonviolence in America has been tried and found wanting. The tragic death of Martin Luther King is supposed to have marked the end of an era in which nonviolence could have any possible significance, and the Poor People's March has been described as a sort of post mortem on nonviolence. From now on, we hear, it's violence only. Why? Because nonviolence not only does not get results, but it is not even effective as communication.

I might as well say clearly that I do not believe this at all. And in spite of the fact that the Montgomery bus boycott, for instance, was a great example of the effective use of nonviolence both as tactic and as communication, in spite of the freedom rides, Birmingham, Selma, etc., I don't think America has yet begun to look at nonviolence or to really understand it. It is not my business to tell the SNCC people how to manage their political affairs. If they feel that they can no longer make good use of nonviolence, let them look to it. There are certainly reasons for thinking that a seemingly passive resistance may not be what the Black people of America can profitably use. Nor do I think, incidentally, that "Black Power" means nothing but mindless and anarchic violence. It is more sophisticated than that.

But we are considering the Peace Movement.

The napalming of draft records by the Baltimore nine is a special and significant case because it seems to indicate a borderline situation: as if the Peace Movement too were standing at the very edge of violence. As if this were a sort of "last chance" at straight nonviolence and a first step toward violent resistance. Well, we live in a world of escalation in which no one seems to know how to deescalate, and it does pose a problem. The Peace Movement may be escalating beyond peaceful protest. In which case it may also be escalating into self-contradiction. But let me make it clear that I do not think the Baltimore nine have done this.

What were the Berrigans and the others trying to do?

It seems to me this was an attempt at prophetic nonviolent provocation. It bordered on violence and was violent to the extent that it meant pushing some good ladies around and destroying some government property. The nine realized that this was a criminal act and knew that they could go to jail for it. They accepted this in the classic nonviolent fashion. The standard doctrine of nonviolence says that you can disobey a law you consider unjust but you have to accept the punishment. In this way you are distinguished from the mere revolutionary. You protest the purity of your witness. You undergo redemptive suffering for religious—or anyway ethical—motives. You are "doing penance" for the sin and injustice against which you have protested. And in the case of the Berrigans, I would say there is present a sort of "jail mystique," as a way of saying dumbly to the rest of the country that in our society nobody is really free anyway. That we are all prisoners of a machinery that takes us inevitably where we don't want to go. Presumably *everyone* in the country wants peace in one way or other. But most Americans have prior commitments—or attachments—to other things which make peace impossible. Most people would rather have war and profits than peace and problems. Or so it seems. In such a situation, we speak peace with our lips but the answer in the heart is war, and war only. And there is certain indecency involved when Christians, even prelates, canonize this unpleasant fact by saying that the war in Vietnam is an act of Christian love. Small wonder that certain more sensitive and more questioning people are driven to extremities.

The evident desperation of the Baltimore nine has, however, frightened more than it has edified. The country is in a very edgy psychological state. Americans feel terribly threatened, on grounds which are partly rational, partly irrational, but in any case very real. The rites of assassination recur at more and more frequent intervals, and there is less and less of a catharsis each time. The shocking thing about the murder of another Kennedy is that we seem to have such a terrible propensity to destroy the things and people we admire, the very ones we identify with. (I say, "we" insofar as we all have a real stake in the society which makes such things not only possible but easy.) There is, then, a real fear, a deep ambivalence, about our very existence and the order on which we think it depends. In such a case, the use of nonviolence has to be extremely careful and clear. People are not in a mood for clear thinking: their fears and premonitions have long ago run away with their minds before anyone can get to them with a cool nonviolent statement. And it has long ago become automatic to interpret nonviolence as violence merely because it is resistance.

The classic (Gandhian) doctrine of nonviolence, even in a much less tense and explosive situation, always emphasized respect for the just laws in order to highlight clearly and unambiguously the injustice of the unjust law. In this way, nonviolence did not pose a sort of free-floating psychological threat, but was clearly pinpointed, directed to what even the adversary had to admit was wrong. Ideally, that is what nonviolence is supposed to do. But if nonviolence merely says in a very loud voice *"I don't like this damn law,"* it does not do much to make the adversary admit that the law is wrong. On the contrary, what he sees is an apparently arbitrary attack on law and order, dictated by emotion or caprice—or fanaticism of some sort. His reply is obviously going to be: "Well, if you don't like law and order you can go to jail where you belong." And he will send you to jail with a firm and righteous conviction that the law is just. He will not even for a moment have occasion to question its justice. He will be too busy responding to what he feels to be aggressive and indignant in your near-violent protest.

It seems to me that the protest and resistance against the Selective Service Law is all oriented to the affirmation of the rightness, the determination and the conviction of the protesters, and not to the injustice of the law itself. In other words, people who are protesting against the draft seem to be communicating, before everything else, their own intense conviction that the law is wrong, rather than pointing out where and how the law is wrong. It boils down to saying, "We don't like this law and feel strongly that it is bad." To which the opposition is content to reply: "The real reason why you don't like the draft is that you are a coward."

What is to be done? First, on a short-term and emergency basis, the whole Vietnam problem has to be solved even if it demands a certain political compromise. It is idiotic to hold out for negotiations in which the position of the other side is completely ignored. Senator McCarthy seems to me to be the only presidential candidate who has the remotest idea of how to end the war, and he is the only one for whom I personally, in conscience, can vote. The war being ended, I think it is necessary that we realize the draft law is unjust, useless and an occasion of further interference in the affairs of small countries we cannot understand. It should be abolished. It has no relation to the real defense needs of the country. On a long-term basis, I think the Peace Movement needs to really study, practice and use nonviolence in its classic form, with all that this implies of religious and ethical grounds. The current facile rejection of nonviolence is too pragmatic. You point to one or two cases where it does not seem to have got results and you say it has completely failed.

But nonviolence is useless if it is merely pragmatic. The whole point of nonviolence is that it rises above pragmatism and does not consider whether or not it pays off officially. *Ahimsa* is defense of and witness to *truth*, not efficacy. I admit that may sound odd. Someone once said, did he not, "What is truth?" And the One to who he said it also mentioned, somewhere: "The truth shall make you free." It seems to me that this is what really matters.

APPENDIX
Merton's Prayer for Peace

This prayer, written by Thomas Merton, was read in the House of Representatives by Congressman Frank Kowalski (D, Connecticut) on April 12, 1962, the Wednesday in Holy Week.

· · · · ·

Almighty and merciful God, Father of all men, Creator and Ruler of the Universe, Lord of History, whose designs are inscrutable, whose glory is without blemish, whose compassion for the errors of men is inexhaustible, in your will is our peace.

Mercifully hear this prayer which rises to you from the tumult and desperation of a world in which you are forgotten, in which your name is not invoked, your laws are derided and your presence is ignored. Because we do not know you, we have no peace.

From the heart of an eternal silence, you have watched the rise of empires, and seen the smoke of their downfall.

You have seen Egypt, Assyria, Babylon, Greece and Rome, once powerful, carried away like sand in the wind.

You have witnessed the impious fury of ten thousand fratricidal wars, in which great powers have torn whole continents to shreds in the name of peace and justice.

And now our nation itself stands in imminent danger of a war the like of which has never been seen!

This nation dedicated to freedom, not to power,

Has obtained, through freedom, a power it did not desire.

And seeking by that power to defend its freedom, it is enslaved by the processes and policies of power.

Must we wage a war we do not desire, a war that can do us no good,

And which our very hatred of war forces us to prepare?

A day of ominous decision has now dawned on this free nation.

Armed with a titanic weapon, and convinced of our own right,

We face a powerful adversary, armed with the same weapon, equally convinced that he is right.

In this moment of destiny, this moment we never foresaw, we cannot afford to fail.

Our choice of peace or war may decide our judgment and publish it in an eternal record.

In this fatal moment of choice in which we might begin the patient architecture of peace

We may also take the last step across the rim of chaos.

Save us then from our obsessions! Open our eyes, dissipate confusions, teach us to understand ourselves and our adversary!

Let us never forget that sins against the law of love are punished by loss of faith,

And those without faith stop at no crime to achieve their ends!

Help us to be masters of the weapons that threaten to master us.

Help us to use our science for peace and plenty, not for war and destruction.

Show us how to use atomic power to bless our children's children, not to blight them.

Save us from the compulsion to follow our adversaries in all that we most hate, confirming them in their hatred and suspicion of us.

Resolve our inner contradictions, which now grow beyond belief and beyond bearing.

They are at once a torment and a blessing: for if you had not left us the light of conscience, we would not have to endure them.

Teach us to be long-suffering in anguish and insecurity.

Teach us to wait and trust.

Grant light, grant strength and patience to all who work for peace,

To this Congress, our President, our military forces, and our adversaries.

Grant us prudence in proportion to our power,

Wisdom in proportion to our science,

Humaneness in proportion to our wealth and might.

And bless our earnest will to help all races and peoples to travel, in friendship with us,

Along the road to justice, liberty and lasting peace:

But grant us above all to see that our ways are not necessarily your ways,

That we cannot fully penetrate the mystery of your designs

And that the very storm of power now raging on this earth

Reveals your hidden will and your inscrutable decision.

Grant us to see your face in the lightning of this cosmic storm,
O God of holiness, merciful to men:
Grant us to seek peace where it is truly found!
In your will, O God, is our peace!
Amen

INDEX